ARCHAEOLOGICAL EXAMINATION OF CULTURAL INTERACTIONS IN THE UPPER NILE CATCHMENT AREAS: 6000-1500 BP

Kyazike Elizabeth

E&D Vision Publishing
Dar es Salaam

Reviewed by Prof. Felix Chami
And supported by
African Archaeology Network
University of Dar es Salaam
P.O.BOX 35050
Email: fchami@udsm.ac.tz

Published by E&D Vision Publishing Limited
P.O.BOX 4460
Dar es Salaam
Email: info@edvisionpublishing.co.tz
Web: www.edvisionpublishing.co.tz

Archaeological Examination of Cultural Interactions in the Upper Nile Catchment Areas: 6000-1500 BP

© Elizabeth Kyazike, 2013

Published PhD Thesis of 2013 – University of Dar es Salaam

ISBN:9987735363

This book is a copyright material protected under the Berne convention, the Copyright Act, 1999, and other international and national enactments, in that behalf, on intellectual property. It may NOT be reproduced by any means, in full or in part, except for short extracts in fair dealings, for research or private study, critical scholarly review or discourse with acknowledgement, without the written permission of the author and E&D Vision Publishing Limited.

LIST OF FIGURES

Figure 2.1:	Study Sites in Uganda (Southern Upper Nile Catchment Areas)	21
Figure 2.2:	Archaeological sites in the Nsongezi Area	27
Figure 4.1:	Kansyore Island Site Map	58
Figure 4.2:	The Island of Deserters Site Map	59
Figure 4.3:	The Ancient World According to Herodotus	64
Figure 5.1:	Frequency of Pottery Traditions from Surface Collections	74
Figure 5.2:	(1) Western Wall and (2) Northern Wall Profiles of Nsongezi STP 1	78
Figure 5.3:	The Stratigraphy of Kansyore STP2	81
Figure 5.4:	The Plan of Trenches in Kansyore Trench 1	82
Figure 5.5:	The Western Wall of Kansyore Island Trench 1	86
Figure 5.6:	The Stratigraphy of Kansyore Trench 1B Facing East	90
Figure 5.7:	Plan of Kansyore Trench 2 Showing its Divisions	91
Figure 5.8:	Southern Wall Profile of Trench 2 Kansyore Island	95
Figure 5.9:	Western Wall Profile of Trench 2A Kansyore Island	100
Figure 5.10:	Stratigraphy of Trench 2A Facing East	103
Figure 5.11:	Southern Wall Profile of Trench 2B	107
Figure 5.12:	Stratigraphy of the Western Wall of Trench 2B	108
Figure 5.13:	Frequency of Cultural Materials in Kansyore Trenches	108
Figure 5.14:	Stratigraphy of the Western Wall of Trench 3 at Kansyore Island	111
Figure 5.15:	Southern Wall Profile of Trench 1 at Island of Deserters	115
Figure 5.16:	Distribution of Cultural Materials in Trench 2 per Level	116
Figure 5.17:	Stratigraphy of Trench 2 Island of Deserters	119
Figure 5.18:	Eastern Wall Profile of Trench 3 at the Island of Deserters	122

Figure 5.24: Stratigraphy of the Eastern Wall of Trench 4 Island of Deserters...126

Figure 5.20: Stratigraphy of the Western Wall of Trench 5, Island of Deserters...130

Figure 5.21: Eastern Wall Profile of Trench 5A at the Island of Deserters..133

Figure 5.22: Northern Wall Profile of Trench 5 and 5A Island of Deserters..134

Figure 6.1: Frequency of Lithic Artefacts per Provenience and Site........145

Figure 6.2: Scrapers..148

Figure 6.3: Scrapers, Utilised Flakes, Points and a Burin......................149

Figure 6.4: Geometrics per site from both surface collections and excavation...164

Figure 6.5: Geometrics..168

Figure 6.6: Pick Axe..173

Figure 6.7: Non-Flaked Stones and Preforms.......................................174

Figure 6.8: Lithic Flakes, Core Scrapers, and Discoid...........................180

Figure 6.9: Cores...183

Figure 6.10: Periphery worked Cores...187

Figure 6.11: Frequency of Lithic Raw Material Utilisation.....................193

Figure 6.12: Diagnostic Pottery..200

Figure 6.13: Kansyore Pottery Decoration Elements..............................204

Figure 6.14: Kansyore Rim Profiles...213

Figure 6.15: Rim profiles for Pots (j, k, l) and Bowls (m,n)....................214

LIST OF TABLES

Table 5.1: Material Inventory of Surface Collections 72

Table 5.2: Material Inventory for Nsongezi STP1 and Kansyore STP2 79

Table 5.3: Material Inventory of Kansyore Island Trench 1 and IA 84

Table 5.4: Material Inventory of Kansyore Trenches 1B, 1BI and 1B2..... 88

Table 5.5: Material Inventory of Trench 2 Kansyore Island 93

Table 5.6: Material Inventory of Kansyore Island Trenches 2A and 2Ai 97

Table 5.7: Material Inventory of Trench 2Aii Kansyore Island 101

Table 5.8: Material Inventory of Trench 2B Kansyore Island.................. 105

Table 5.9: Material Inventory of Trench 3 at Kansyore Island 109

Table 5.10: Material Inventory of Trench 1 Island of Deserters 113

Table 5.11: Trench 2 Island of Deserters Material Inventory 117

Table 5.12: Material Inventory per level for Trench 3 Island of Deserters 121

Table 5.13: Material Inventory per level from Trench 4 Island of Deserters...124

Table 5.14: Material Inventory per Level for Trench 5 Island of Deserters... 128

Table 5.15: Material Inventory per Level for Trench 5A Island of Deserters ... 131

Table 5.16: Carbon 14 Dates... 136

Table 5.17: List of Informants 139

Table 6.1: Inventory of Analysed Artefacts 142

Table 6.2: Analysed Lithic Artefacts... 144

Table 6.3: Lithic Tool Types per site 146

Table 6.4: Scrapers other than Core Scrapers per site and provenience .. 154

Table 6.5: Frequency of Geometrics at the different Sites 163

Table 6.6: Blade/Flake Types 176

Table 6.7: Broad and Specific Core Types 182

Table 6.8: Total Debitage Collected from all Sites 191

Table 6.9:   Weight of Debitage in Grams 192
Table 6.10: Frequency of Lithic Raw Material Types 193
Table 6.11: Pottery Inventory 195
Table 6.12: Frequency of Decoration Elements 206
Table 6.13: Colours of Kansyore Ceramics 210
Table 6.14: Frequency of Surface Finishing 212
Table 6.15: Faunal Remains 217
Table 6.16: Frequency of Bones per Trench 221
Table 7.1:   Ancient Pottery Sequence for Eastern, Central, Southern Africa and Middle Nile 253
Table 7.2:   Carbon 14 Results 256

LIST OF PLATES

Plate 2.1: A landscape with synclines and anticlines on the way to Nsongezi...24

Plate 2.2: Nsongezi Rock Shelter..30

Plate 2.3: The Second Rock Shelter discovered during Survey in Nsongezi...30

Plate 2.4: The Pyramidal Structure...32

Plate 2.5: Kalamba Slag Site..34

Plate 4.1: Survey and Surface Collection...57

Plate 4.2: Participant Observation with a Pot maker.....................................62

Plate 5.1: Artifacts from Surface Collections..75

Plate 5.2: Stone Mortar at Kansyore Island...75

Plate 5.3: The Floor of the Aquatic Layer in Trench 1A...............................85

Plate 5.4: Trench 2 Kansyore Island Divisions and Extensions....................91

Plate 5.5: (a) Neolithic Roulette..99

Plate 5.6: Trench 3 Kansyore Island at Bedrock..110

Plate 5.7: Trench 1 divisions into 1A and 1B at the Island of Deserters....112

Plate 6.1: A Grinding Stone from the Island of Deserters...........................176

Plate 6.2: Foreign Pottery...215

Plate 6.3: Ethreria Shells..218

Plate 6.4: Limicolaria Shells..219

Plate 6.5: Edouardia Shells..219

Plate 6.6: Bone Tools from Kansyore Island...222

Plate 6.7: (a) Fish Vertebrae (b) Elephant Tusk Fragments........................223

Plate 6.8: Some of the Metal Objects..225

Plate 7.1: Kansyore Banded Motifs..242

Plate 7.2: Kansyore Banded Motifs..243

Plate 7.3: Kansyore Dotted lines..244

Plate 7.4: Rows of Horizontal Dotted and Impressed Lines.......................244

Plate 7.5: Dotted Zig Zag Lines...245

ACKNOWLEDGEMENTS

A study of this nature would not have been possible without the assistance, guidance, and kind words of many people. I am especially grateful to the invaluable support of the following:

My supervisors Professors I. N. Kimambo, Felix Chami, and F .T Masao from the University of Dar es Salaam, who guided me throughout the course, supervised, advised, and patiently withstood all my shortcomings. Without their combined effort, the formulation, and completion of this research would have been difficult. However special mention goes to Professor I.N. Kimambo: Thank you so much and may God reward you richly for despite your physical weaknesses you were always there for me. Thank you for encouraging me to make the best of this fulfilling assignment of my life. Special thanks go to other members of the Archaeology Unit, University of Dar es Salaam especially Prof Mapunda, Dr. E. Kessy, Prof. A. X. Z Mabulla, Dr Sanane, Dr. Bushozi, and Dr. Biginagwa T. Thank you all for nurturing me and for all your support in all ways and providing a conducive and friendly academic environment.

I am greatly indebted to the African Archaeology Network for their sponsorship especially the general coordinator Professor Felix Chami, Tibesaasa Ruth (AAN Uganda contact), Gido Laswaai, and Upendo Semu the administrators. My special thanks go to my employer Kyambogo University for the study leave without which this study and the subsequent formulation of this thesis would not have been possible, and to the African Humanities Programme. I am also indebted to members of Makerere University Department of History, especially Dr. Asiimwe G., Dr. Odoi Tanga, Dr Charlotte Karungi, Mr Mwambtsya Ndebesa, Dr. Deo Katono, Mr Muwonge Herman, and Ms Sanyu Josephine.

I am also very grateful to the M.A Archaeology class of UDSM 2009-2011 with whom I audited the archaeology courses that grounded me with the basics of archaeology especially Mrs Nakaweesa Esther Wasswa. My gratitude goes to Mr Coster Mahuwi, the chief Cartographer University of Dar es Salaam for the illustrations, and Mr Shirikisho for the computer applications.

At another special level, I am forever indebted to my family for the academic, material, and moral support they gave me to make this course bear fruit. I am indebted to my husband Mr James Kiwanuka who stood by my side at all trying moments during this course, thank you for your love and encouragement. I thank my brothers Robert Ssemulende, Richard Kikayira and sister Jesca Namutebi; nephews and nieces: Joyce Nvuma, Joel Luyombya, Josiah Luyima and Sam Nswagiro Junior, my father Mzee Sam Nswagiro, my in-laws especially Ms Donah Nakamya, Maama Nalongo Tomusange, Maama 'Smart' Kikayira, Musawo Justine and my aunties Robina Nalugya, Nankonge Agnes and Nakatudde Mary. I appreciate the phone calls of encouragement; packing for me eats as your baby and medicine thank you for standing with me. Richard thank you so much for the air tickets and sending Joy to give me company, Robert you always loaded my phone with airtime, may God bless you richly.

Many thanks go to my research assistants that were: Wamutu Godfrey, Chikoni Abel, Lilian Onyango, Fatumah Mirembe, Herman Muwonge, Nsubuga Nathan, Ssemulende Robert; the drivers Henry Semwogerere and Tibesaaasa Milton and the Kansyore team including: Byaruhanga Peter, Gumoshabe, and Kafureka. I appreciate the assistance of the Mobile Police Patrol Unit of Nsongezi and the Local council chairpersons in all the research areas. I would like to thank the Uganda Museum especially Madam Rose Nkaaale and Ms Nyaracyiza Jackie.

Finally yet importantly, I thank the Almighty God who made everything possible for me to carry out this task. The lord provided me with the wisdom and understanding which gave me the strength to carry on despite the trying moments in the entire course. I withstood all trying moments by referring to the word of God. In this regard, I appreciate the Tanzania Assemblies of God (TAG) Changanyikenyi especially Pastor Muro, Mrs. Hosiana Muro, and the entire TAG church who persistently prayed for God's will to be accomplished through this work. I give all glory and honour to God for this achievement as this work is a living testimony of Mark 10:27.

Despite the contribution of all the people and institutions mentioned above, I am entirely responsible for all the outcomes of this work.

DEDICATION

This thesis is dedicated to my parents Mr Sam Nswagiro and the late Ms Joyce Nakagulire. Thank you so much Mzee Sam for the endless sacrifice, love, and tender care. Special dedications go to my late mum whose untimely departure on 28th May 1980 did not allow her to raise us but God took care of us with a lot of support from Taata Nswagiro. May the Lord rest your soul in eternal peace Amen and may He reward Taata abundantly.

TABLE OF CONTENTS

List of Figures..iii
ACKNOWLEDGEMENTS...ix
DEDICATION..xi
LIST OF ABBREVIATIONS AND ACRONYMS......................................xviii

CHAPTER ONE..1
INTRODUCTION..1
1.1. General Introduction..3
1.2. The Geographical Focus...6
1.3. Statement of the Problem...7
1.4. Objectives of the study..8
    1.4.1 General Objective..8
    1.4.2 Specific Objectives..8
1.5. Research Questions...8
1.6. Significance of the Study..8
1.7. Definition of Key Terms...9
1.8. Theoretical Considerations..11
1.9. Chapter Summary..17

CHAPTER 2..19
THE SITES AND THEIR BIO-GEOGRAPHY..19
2.1. Introduction...19
2.2. Bio-geography of Kansyore Island and the Island of Deserters............21
    2.2.1 Topography..22
    2.2.2 Flora...24
    2.2.3 Soils...25
    2.2.4 Fauna..25
    2.2.5 Population and Economic Activities...26
    2.2.6 Rainfall and Temperature..26

2.3. The Sites..27
    2.3.1   Mobile Police Patrol Unit (MPPU) Detach Gardens................28
    2.3.2   Kagera Basin Road Site...28
    2.3.3   Nsongezi Quarry Site and the Island of Deserters....................28
    2.3.4   Nsongezi Rock Shelters...29
    2.3.5   MPPU Prison Garden.. 31
    2.3.6   Pyramidal Monument Site.. 31
    2.3.7   Nsongezi Landing Site..32
    2.3.8   Kansyore/Nsongezi Island Site...33
    2.3.9   Kalamba Slag Site.. 33
2.4. Chapter Summary..33

CHAPTER THREE..36
LITERATURE REVIEW..36
3.1. Introduction..36
3.2. Literature Arguing for the Existence of Interactions............................36
3.3. Literature Negating Interactions..43
3.4. Literature on Archaeological Work Done in Uganda..........................44

CHAPTER FOUR... 53
RESEARCH METHODOLOGY...53
4.1. Introduction..53
4.2. Research Design...53
4.3. Sampling Procedures..54
4.4. Sample Size..54
4.5. Pre-Field Preparations..55
4.6. Field Data Collection Methods..55
    4.6.1   Archaeological Survey..55
    4.6.2   Mapping..58
    4.6.3   Shovel Test Pit Excavations..60
    4.6.4   Intensive Excavation...60
    4.6.5   Ethnographic Inquiries..61

4.6.6 Examination of Ancient Historical Records..............................63

4.6.7 Data Processing and Analysis Procedure...............................70

CHAPTER FIVE..72
FIELD WORK RESULTS...72
5.1 Introduction..72
5.2 Survey Findings..72
    5.2.1 Surface Collections..73
5.3 Shovel Test Pits (STPs)..76
    5.3.1 Nsongezi Shovel Test Pit 1...76
    5.3.2 Material Finds From Nsongezi Shovel Test Pit......................76
    5.3.3 Stratigraphy of Shovel Test Pit 1 Nsongezi............................77
    5.3.4 Kansyore Shovel Test Pit 2..78
    5.3.5 Material Finds From Kansyore Island Shovel Test Pit 2.........78
    5.3.6 The statigraphy of Kansyore Shovel Test Pit 2......................80
5.4. Excavation Finds..81
    5.4.1 Kansyore Island Excavation...81
    5.4.2 Kansyore Trench 1...81
    5.4.3 Kansyore Island Trench 1 Division...82
    5.4.4 Material Finds for Kansyore Trench 1....................................83
    5.4.5 Stratigraphy of Kansyore Trench 1..85
    5.4.6 Kansyore Island Trench 1B..87
    5.4.7 Stratigraphy of Trench 1B..88
    5.4.8 Trench 2 Kansyore Island..90
    5.4.9 Trench 2 Kansyore Findings..91
    5.4.10 The Stratigraphy of Trench 2 Kansyore Islands...................94
    5.4.11 Trench 2A Kansyore Island..96
    5.4.12 Trench 2Ai Kansyore Island...96
    5.4.13 Trench 2A and 2Ai Finding...96
    5.4.14 Stratigraphy of Trench 2A and 2Ai.......................................98
    5.4.15 Trench 2Aii Kansyore Island...100
    5.4.16 The Findings of Kansyore Trench 2Aii...............................100
    5.4.17 Stratigraphy of Kansyore Trench 2Aii................................102

		5.4.18 Trench 2B Kansyore Island..103
		5.4.19 Trench 2B Findings..104
		5.4.20 Stratigraphy of Trench 2B...106
		5.4.21 Trench 3 Kansyore Island..106
		5.4.22 Findings from Trench 3 Kansyore Island....................109
5.5	Island of Deserters..111	
	5.5.1	Trench 1 Island of Deserters.......................................111
	5.5.2	The Findings of Trench 1 Island of Deserters..............112
	5.5.3	The Stratigraphy of Trench 1 at the Island of Deserters....114
	5.5.4	Trench 2 Island of Deserters.......................................115
	5.5.5	Trench 2 Island of Deserters Findings........................115
	5.5.6	Trench 2 Island of Deserters Stratigraphy..................118
	5.5.7	Trench 3 Island of Deserters.......................................119
	5.5.8	Trench 3 Island of Deserters Findings........................120
	5.5.9	Trench 3 Island of Deserters Stratigraphy..................121
	5.5.10	Trench 4 Island of Deserters......................................123
	5.5.11	Trench 4 Island of Deserters Findings........................123
	5.5.12	Trench 4 Island of Deserters Stratigraphy..................125
	5.5.13	Island of Deserters Trench 5......................................125
	5.5.14	Island of Deserters Trench 5 Findings........................127
	5.5.15	Island of Deserters Trench 5 Stratigraphy..................129
	5.5.16	Trench 5A Island of Deserters...................................130
	5.5.17	Trench 5A Findings..131
	5.5.18	Stratigraphy of Trench 5A 132
5.6	Dating Results..134	
5.7	Data From Ethnographic Inquiries...135	
5.8	Chapter Summary..136	

CHAPTER SIX..138
ANALYSIS OF RESEARCH FINDINGS....................................138
6.1	Introduction...138
6.2	Lithic Analysis.. 139

6.2.1	The Typology	143
6.2.2	Shaped tools	144
6.2.3	Scrapers	146
6.2.4	Core Scrapers	150
6.2.5	Types of Core Scrapers	150
6.2.6	Flake Scrapers	153
6.2.7	End Scrapers	153
6.2.8	Side Scrapers	157
6.2.9	Thumbnail Scrapers	160
6.2.10	Denticulates	160
6.2.11	Points/ Percoirs	161
6.2.12	Becs	162
6.2.13	Geometrics	162
6.2.14	Crescents	164
6.2.15	Curve Backed Pieces	165
6.2.16	Straight Backed Pieces	165
6.2.17	Triangles	166
6.2.18	Trapezes	166
6.2.19	Angle Backed Pieces	167
6.2.20	Diverse Backed Pieces	167
6.2.21	Backed Drills	167
6.2.22	Oblique Truncated and Orthogonal Truncated Pieces	168
6.2.23	Burins	169
6.2.24	Composite Tools	170
6.2.25	Outils' Escailles	170
6.2.26	Heavy Duty Tools	170
6.2.27	Discoid	170
6.2.28	Hand Axes	171
6.2.29	Pick Axes	172

6.2.30 Core Axes………………………………...………………..…… 173

6.2.31 Preforms……………………………………….……....………..174

6.2.32 Pestle Rubber……………………….…………..……..…….….. 174

6.2.33 Hammer Stones……………….………………………..….…….175

6.2.34 Grinding Stones………………….…………………..……....…..176

6.2.35 Flakes/ Blades…………………………………...……..……..… 176

6.2.36 Whole Blades…………….……………….……....…………..… 177

6.2.37 Utilized Blades…………………………………..…...………….177

6.2.38 Whole Flake…………………………………….…..…………...177

6.2.39 Utilized Flake……………………………………..……..……… 178

6.2.40 Levallois Flakes………………………………….……..…...…..178

6.2.41 Core Rejuvenated Flakes………..……...………………..……...179

6.2.42 Cores……………………………………………………..….…..181

6.2.43 Platform Cores…………………………………….…….....……184

6.2.44 Single Platform Cores………………………………..……..….. 184

6.2.45 Double Platform Cores……………………….…….......……….185

6.2.46 Multiplatform Cores…………………………………………..…185

6.2.47 Periphery Worked Cores…………………………….…..…..…..186

6.2.48 Intermediate Cores……………………………………...………. 188

6.2.49 Bipolar Cores………………………………………..….....……..189

6.2.50 Amorphous Cores………………………………………...….…..190

6.2.51 Debitage……………………………………………..……..…….190

6.2.52 Raw Material………………………………….…....……...….… 192

6.2.53 Pottery Analysis…………………………………..………...…… 194

6.2.54 Local Pottery…………………………….……………….……... 196

6.2.55 Kansyore Pottery………………………….…….……..…….…...200

6.2.56 Decoration………………………………………….…….……... 201

6.2.57 Decoration Elements…………………………..……......………. 202

6.2.58 Kansyore Ceramic Decoration Technques……………….…….. 207

      6.2.59 Kansyore Ceramic Decoration Placement……..……….....207

      6.2.60 Technological Attribute Analysis……………….....……... 208

      6.2.61 Kansyore Ceramic Paste and Temper ………………….…208

      6.2.63 Wall thickness……………………………………….……... 210

      6.2.64 Kansyore Ceramic Surface Finishing…………….....…….. 211

      6.2.65 Kansyore Ceramic Rim Profile………………….………212

      6.2.66 Foreign Pottery……………………………………….…...215

      6.2.67 Faunal Remains…………………………………....……...215

      6.2.68 Shells……………………………………………....……...216

      6.2.69 Etheriaelliptica ……………………………….…………… 218

        6.3.1. Limicolaria……………………….……....…………..218

        6.3.2   Edourdia…………………………………...…..………219

        6.3.3   Bones……………………………………………….…220

6.4   Metallurgical Materials………………………………….………223

      6.4.1 Iron Slag…………………………………………….….....223

      6.4.2 Metal Object……………………………….....…..….…..224

6.5   House Daubs………………………………………….…..……...225

      6.6   Red Ochre…………………………………………….…226

      6.7   Clay Mace and Smoking Pipes………………….……. ………226

      6.8   Data from Ethnographic Inquiries…………………….………226

      6.9   Chapter Summary………………………………….…………227

CHAPTER SEVEN …………………………………..........……………..231

COMPARATIVE DISCUSSION………………………….………………..231

7.1   Introduction………………………………………………..……..231

7.2   Lithics…………………………………………….………………231

7.3   Pottery……………………………………………………………239

7.4   Faunal Remains…………………………………………….…….248

7.5   Chronology………………………………………………….……251

7.6	Stratigraphy	252
7.7	Aquatic Civilization	257
7.8	Red Ochre	259
7.9	Chapter Summary	260

CHAPTER 8 .... **261**

DISCUSSION 261

| 8.1 | Introduction | 261 |
| 8.2 | Cultural Affinity and Correlations | 269 |

Conclusion 269

References 270

ABBREVIATIONS AND ACRONYMS

BP: Before Present (i.e. 1950)
DTLM: Down the Line Trade Model
EIA: Early Iron Age
ESA: Early Stone Age
ITCZ: Inter-Tropical Convergence Zone
Km: Kilometres
LIA: Late Iron Age
LSA: Late Stone Age
M: Metres
MNFP: Murchison Falls National Park (Kabalega National park)
MSA: Middle Stone Age
Mya: Million Years Ago
STP: Shovel Test pit
UWA: Uganda Wild Life Authority
Ya: Years Ago

Section 1
INTRODUCTION

CHAPTER ONE

INTRODUCTION

1.1. General Introduction

This book is the outcome of a PhD Thesis that made an archaeological examination of cultural interactions in the Upper Nile catchment areas in the period 6000-1500 BP. Specifically it made a comparative study of the Ugandan Kansyore sites (Kansyore Island and Island of Deserters) and Khartoum Neolithic sites in central and southern Sudan such as Lokabulo, Itohom, Jebel Kathangor, Shaqadud and Esh- Shaheinab. The study examined the credibility of diffusion and migration theories as previously used to explain how cultures of Africa were formed and developed with the assistance of ecological theories to examine the state of cultural connections and affinity in the Upper Nile catchment areas. This involved examination of cultural materials like pottery decoration, vessel shapes, and fabric; lithic typology, and faunal remains. The aim of the study was to examine cultural connections and affinity in the Upper Nile catchment areas.

In this investigation, the study employed the basic archaeological field methods, which were survey and excavations but also utilised written records especially the ancient historical records and ethnographic inquiries. The findings included; lithics, ceramics, faunal remains, metallurgical remains, red ochre, daub pieces, and charcoal samples. The results from the study showed that affinity existed as traced from pottery, lithic artefacts, and the faunal remains but not in dates in the Upper Nile catchment areas. The absence of domesticates in Kansyore sites did not necessarily imply these were not Neolithic sites as indirect evidence could be obtained from the presence of grinding stones and pottery abrasion hence we could talk about the Neolithic outside the rift valley.

The discovery of roulette pottery dated 2710±44 BP implied that rouletting started in the Neolithic period. Chronometric dating suggested that Kansyore sites are younger compared to the Khartoum Neolithic sites. The study also identified wavy line pottery which showed affrinity with the Khartoum Mesolithic. The study concluded that cultural affinity existed in the upper Nile catchment areas and hence the Nile was not a cul de sac. Though movement existed in the past, at times people were not merely migrants, for example the Egyptian deserters who moved for war purposes. It was also established that diffusion is not a one-way colonial relationship from north to south as the aqualithic culture suggested diffusion from the south to the north.

Arkell (1949a, 1953) pioneered research in the Nile Valley that identified two distinct model ceramic components each characterized by a decorative motif: the Khartoum Mesolithic associated with the 'wavy line' and the Khartoum Neolithic associated with 'dotted wavy line' (Mohammed-Ali and Khabir, 2003:28). He therefore proposed an evolutionary sequence of cultural development from the Mesolithic to a Neolithic stage with its origin in Khartoum (Hays, 1974: 27). Khartoum was then regarded as the core area for the spread of what Hugot (1963) termed as the 'Neolithic of Sudanese Tradition'. This extended from Khartoum along the Nile to the Fayum in Egypt and as far West into the Sahara to Meniet (Algeria) before 3400 B.C.

The Mesolithic wavy line and Neolithic dotted wavy-line pottery have a very wide spatial-temporal distribution (Haaland, 1992:47). The sites stretch from as far as the Khartoum area in the Nile valley dated 9300BP to north-eastern Niger dated 9500BP and Libya (Ti-n-Torha) dated 9300BP, to East Africa located around Lake Turkana which is later than that from the Nile valley and the Sahara (Halaand, 1992:47). Phillipson (1977) suggests a date of 10,000-8000 years ago for the northern extension of the Sahara for the Early Khartoum Neolithic while Shaqadud in the Nile valley was dated 8000-6000 years ago (Marks and Mohammed-Ali, 1991). In East Africa, Lowasera was dated 9000 years ago while Ishango close to Lake Edward / Rutanzige on the border between Uganda and Congo was considerably older as much as 18,000-16,000 years (Phillipson, 2005).

The spatial distribution of the dotted wavy line has been the centre of investigation for scholars who have battled with the task of examining the variability of this Sudanese culture in time and space. For instance, Hugot (1968:185) basing on decorative techniques and motifs suggested that the Neolithic Sudan tradition extended along the Nile from Khartoum to the Fayum in Egypt and as far west into the Sahara as Meniet by 3400 BC. Robertshaw (1982) identified the Lokabulo tradition (Khartoum Neolithic) in south-east Sudan as having similarities with the Kansyore tradition and yet Chapman (1967) had earlier on noted similarity between the Kansyore pottery and Sudanese pottery. Several theories have been advanced to account for the spatial distribution of the Khartoum culture. For instance Haaland (1992: 47), suggested migration and diffusion as she commented that; "I don't think the same type of pottery was independently invented in these different areas. I suggest that it was invented in the Nile Valley and carried to the Sahara/savanna region and East Africa by gradual expansion of people". Sutton (1974, 1977) coined the term 'aquatic civilization' to account for the large scale geographical distribution of the pre-Neolithic culture and to him they reflected cultural-historical connections.

Most publicity and publications on the spread and similarity of the Khartoum Neolithic mainly focused on Sudan especially Northern Sudan's relations with Egypt, the Sahara areas, West Africa and at times parts of East Africa like the Turkana area. Therefore, areas to the south especially the Upper Nile catchment areas where the Nile starts its course and parts of central and southern Sudan had not been adequately addressed in terms of investigating cultural connections and affinity with the Khartoum Neolithic. This work addresses the neglected geographical gap because there has been limited archaeological evidence beyond the middle Nile, as suggested by O'Connor and Reid (2003). Furthermore, generally there has been very little archaeological work done in Uganda and the little there is, is concentrated on western and northeastern Uganda (Kiyaga-Mulindwa, 2004).

Chapman (1967) identified the similarity between the Lake Victoria Kansyore and Sudan pottery which was attributed to the use of similar decoration techniques rather than genetic developments. This was however rejected by Collet and Robertshaw (1980) who made a comparison between Kansyore ceramics and 'dotted wavy line' pottery from Sudan based on their work at Gogo Falls. This is because though the use of similar decoration techniques may reflect similar adaptations; the absence of shared decoration concepts (modes) did not reflect similarity in socio-economic adaptations (Collet and Robertshaw, 1980).

They referred to the published Khartoum Neolithic material of Arkell (1949, 1953) in which none of the Kansyore types occurred in the assemblages in their view. This could partly be due to emphasis on tracing cultural interactions being placed on pottery decoration without consideration of the total artifact inventories, technical traditions, ecological settings, and settlement patterns

(Hays, 1974:85). However, Sutton (1974) suggested that the similarity could probably be due to similar adaptive strategies which he referred to as the aquatic civilization.

The Kansyore is a ceramic tradition spanning six millennia (c.6000 BC – AD 500) in an expanse spanning from south-eastern Sudan through a core area surrounding Lake Victoria to northern Tanzania (Prendergast, 2010:1-2). Robertshaw (1991) and Dale and Ashley (2010) on the other hand argued that time and geography may explain the range of ceramic types. The decorative similarities between Kansyore and northeastern African pottery might also have come as a result of the gradual migration of ceramic producing communities from the north into the Great Lakes region (Dale, 2007: 42).

It was against such a background that this study made an examination of the cultural and economic correlations of the cultural materials in the upper Nile catchment areas. This involved use of a comparative approach in examining cultural interactions in the Upper Nile catchment areas which made a contribution on the causes of cultural and economic correlations through examining cultural materials retrieved like ceramics, lithics and faunal remains while giving due respect to diffusion, migration, trade and ecological considerations. The scope of the study was 6000 to 1500 BP. The year 6000 was significant because it was identified for the Khartoum Neolithic (Mohammed-Ali, 1982) and at the same time for the Kansyore pottery tradition (Prendergast, 2008, 2010). The scope was limited to 1500BP to cater for the dates from Kansyore Island obtained by this study.

1.2. The Geographical Focus

The Upper Nile catchment in the current research was regarded as an area encompassing areas drained by the Nile from its source in present day Uganda in the south to the 6th cataract in Sudan. This encompassed parts of central and southern Sudan and parts along and in the Kagera River (Kansyore Island, Island of Deserters and Nsongezi) a principal source of the Nile (Figure 1). This area is significant because in the Later Iron Age times this was the route used by Nilotic-speaking people notably the Luo. It was also of importance in the EIA expansion of Bantu speakers (Phillipson, 1976a) and yet in earlier times the affinities of the LSA harpoon-fishers of the Lake Rudolf basin were clearly with the Sudanese Nile valley (Sutton, 1974; Phillipson, 1977). Therefore, the Nile River was considered as a probable channel for cultural interaction and movement of people from one area to another. The fact that the area below the 6th cataract is where the Blue and White Nile meet at Khartoum to form the Nile proper the area was envisaged to give a better picture of cultural interaction in the Upper Nile catchment areas.

1.3. Statement of the Problem

The existence of cultural affinity in the Upper Nile catchment has been explained differently. Previous authors used a small portion of the total number of similar artefacts to suggest homogeneity among African sites by explaining the relationship basing on the existence of particular pottery designs. While a number of scholars realized the existence of interaction as evidenced through material culture like (Robertshaw, 1982, 1991; Sutton, 1971, 1974; Chapman, 1967; Kiyaga-Mulindwa, 2004, 2006; Chami, 2006) the nature and cause of this interaction was not ventured into. Chapman (1967) for instance considered the distance between Kansyore Island and Sudan and the existence of the water mass as limitations to cultural interaction. While evidence had been gathered to relate the Khartoum culture and the Nilo-Saharan areas as far west as Algeria limited effort had been made to trace the same south wards as far as Uganda. The limited effort at the same time laid emphasis on either tracing similarity of pottery decoration motifs while neglecting other aspects of material culture or comparing Sudan Neolithic with cultural material from Egypt, West Africa, sites in the Sahara or the Turkana area in East Africa.

The approach used to answer this question was always the use of the diffusion unidirectional model that looks at innovations as emanating from the north to the south. Sanders (1969), MacGaffey (1970) and Smith (1923, 1928, 1971) viewed cultural affinity in terms of migration and diffusion or the spread of culture by a supposedly superior group of people. However, these theories overlook the contribution of interaction and its multi-directional nature. Hence, the research examined cultural and economic interaction in the Upper Nile catchment by not only examining pottery but beefing it up with evidence from the lithics, faunal remains and ancient historical records in order to examine whether the Nile was a corridor or an end to interaction and the nature of cultural contact and affinity in the Upper Nile catchment areas. This was done by examining cultural and economic interactions in the Upper Nile catchment areas from 6000-1500 BP.

1.4. Objectives of the study

The study had one general and three specific objectives. These are:

1.4.1 General objective

The general objective of this research was to examine cultural connections and affinity and trace cultural-economic correlations within the upper Nile catchment from 6000 to 1500 BP.

1.4.2 Specific objectives

The specific objectives of this research were:

1. To examine the form of cultural and economic interactions that existed in the Upper Nile catchment area using lithic, ceramic and faunal attributes that portrayed affinity in the upper Nile catchment areas from 6000 to 1500 BP.
2. To assess whether the Nile River was a facilitator or a barrier (*cul de-sac*) for cultural interaction.
3. To examine theories that account for cultural similarities and interaction.

1.5. Research questions

The study was guided by the following research questions:

1. What form of cultural similarities and differences existed in the upper Nile catchment from 6000 to 1500 BP in time and space?
2. To what extent did the river Nile question facilitate interaction in the upper Nile catchment areas?
3. What contributed to cultural and economic spread? Was it adaptation, migration, diffusion or trade?

1.6. Significance of the study

This research is significant because it was largely the Nile that put Uganda on the map both literally and metaphorically (Dixon, 1971: 123-125). Thus, the research provides the multi factors that contributed to the emergence of complex societies in the region studied. The research also contributed towards the debate concerning the unity of Africa pioneered by Diop (1981a, 1981b) and later on by Chami (2006) and the Nile catchment's contribution in world civilization. The research is significant as it focuses on the spatial distribution of the civilizations of the Nile known to have affected the ancient world basing mainly on cultural materials such as ceramic and lithic technology and faunal remains to shed light on the relationship between past cultures of the Nile catchment areas. This further highlights the theme of interaction and cultural economic affinity that has hitherto been attributed to migration and diffusion.

1.7. Definition of Key Terms

Aquatic Civilization

Aquatic civilization refers to the late Paleolithic assemblages. Other terms of the same period are Mesolithic, Neolithic of Capsian Tradition (NCT), Neolithic of Sudanese Tradition (NST) and Saharo Sudanese Neolithic (NSS), aqualithic and (ceramic) Late Stone Age (LSA) (Holl, 2005). This was a term coined by Sutton (1974, 1977) referring to early civilizations whose subsistence depended on water resources especially fish and shell fish.

Interaction

This refers to the action or influence of things and people on each other. That is the mutual human action variously described as the connection, communication or collaboration, whereby two or more people act reciprocally on and between each other (Skeates, 2009:557).

Adaptation

The development of specified cultural responses designed to cope with the natural and social environments of a given people in a given place and time (Staeck, 2002:36). Therefore to the archaeologists adaptation is a product of selection (Mabulla, 1996).

Neolithic

Neolithic was a term first used by Sir John Lubbock to mean the 'New Stone Age' characterized by ground and polished stone tools and pottery. This was modified to incorporate domestication of plants/animals as the prime criterion. However evidence of all these need not to be found together (cultural package). Therefore presence of some can qualify a site to be Neolithic; the position taken in this study is in line with the resolution of the 1965 Wenner-Gren African symposium which suggested applying the term Neolithic to isolated pieces or to groups of artefacts possessing one or more characters of Neolithic industrial complexes (Hays, 1971). The current study compares the Khartoum Neolithic with the Kansyore tradition.

The terms 'Khartoum Neolithic' or 'Sudanese Neolithic' are used to refer to sites characterized by the presence of dotted wavy-line pottery, characteristic lithic artifacts and fishing gear. Evidence for either plant cultivation or herding may or may not be present at these sites. Sites with a pottery type referred to as 'wavy line' and with no evidence of food production are referred to either as 'Khartoum Mesolithic' or 'Early Khartoum' (Hassan, 1986:84).

Kansyore Pottery Tradition

Kansyore/ Kantsyore means "let me return" (Chapman, 1967). It is a place name of an Island situated on the Kagera River, one of the sites where the current research was undertaken. Kansyore pottery then refers to the 'coarse' pottery reported by Leakey but formerly identified by Chapman (1967) as Kansyore ware that is named after the type site (Kansyore Island) (Dale, 2007). Since then this pottery has been identified in a number of sites in East Africa (Uganda, Kenya, and Tanzania) and south eastern Sudan (Lokabulo).

Kansyore is a ceramic tradition that spanned some six millennia (c.6000 BC-AD 500) in an expanse stretching from south eastern Sudan, through a core area surrounding Lake Victoria, to northern Tanzania (Prendergast, 2010:2). The sites are identified on the basis of highly decorated ceramics, wild fauna, and non-uniform lithics and to a lesser degree on location (Dale, 2007). Due to the wide variety of decoration, environmental contexts, and range of dates, Robertshaw suggested that there may be different facies of Kansyore and suggested the name Oltome for the Lake Victoria facies of the Kansyore archaeological culture but the name was not generally adopted and the term Kansyore ware has continued in use.

Urewe (EIA) Tradition

This is also referred to as dimple based or Urewe ware/ Early Iron Age (EIA) pottery. Urewe pottery tradition is a variant of EIA pottery just like Lelesu and Kwale are in other parts of East Africa. The Iron Age pottery in East Africa has been divided into three and these are: EIA (typical Urewe), contact Urewe and Late Iron Age pottery or roulette (Ashley, 2010). Typical Urewe was also referred to as the Early Iron Age pottery dated c. 500-A.D 800 (Ashley, 2010) while Posnansky *eta'l* (2005) dated Urewe in the Great Lakes region to have span from 500BC to AD 800.

Bourdine Tradition/Chobe Ware

The bourdine tradition was a name given by Hiernaux following his findings in Rwanda/Burundi, which is the same as Soper's (1971b) Chobe ware. Bourdine refers to the finger marked ware distinguished by one or more irregular horizontal ridges or finger pinching or channelling with no other decoration apart from occasional rows of finger- nail impressions (Soper, 1971b: 56) and exposed coils on the vessel body that were not smoothed properly. This could be close to what Ashley (2010) regards as contact Urewe, which is an emulation of typical Urewe but lacking its details. No emphasis was placed on quality and surface finishing for this pottery tradition. Bourdine pottery is heavily tempered with irregular inclusions implying that they were used between agriculturalists and hunter-gatherers (Ashley, 2010).

Roulette (LIA) Tradition

Roulette is a pottery-decorating tool that can be either rolled or impressed on to a wet surface of a clay vessel (Haour et al, 2010: 193). Roulette is also regarded as a Late Iron Age (LIA) pottery tradition for ceramics at the EIA/LIA juncture (c. A.D 800-1100) identified from the 11th century. Posnansky (1968b, 1973, and 2005) regarded it as transitional Urewe (19th-13th century) or devolved Urewe and it is the same type of Hieranaux and Maquet in Rwanda also regarded as Middle Iron Age ceramics of Nyanza (Posnansky *et al*, 2005, Lane *et al*, 2007 and Robertshaw, 1991). Roulette had forms of decoration such as twisted string roulette, knotted grass roulette, and curved wooden roulette.

1.8. Theoretical Considerations

The study employed diffusion, migration, and ecological theories to examine cultural interactions, affinity and connections in the Upper Nile catchment areas. Successive generations of archaeologists have approached interaction in terms of theory and method by using three broad schools of thought (Skeates, 2009). The first is the traditional or culture-historical archaeology, the second is the New or processual archaeology and the third is the post processual, interpretative or anthropological archaeology. The traditional or culture–history archaeologists, whose founding father is Childe, look at interaction as well as cultural change in terms of diffusion and migration of dominant and progressive ideas between advanced and less developed areas. Culture-historical archaeology has been criticized for its descriptive and narrative style of writing history. This style accords little respect to cultural processes.

The second criticism of the culture-historical archaeologists rotates on its concerns with ancient origins and movements of ethnic groups which have led to frequent manipulation in support of nationalistic and colonial interpretations of the past. This gave birth to the Hamitic theory (Sanders, 1969). This caused cultural change and development to be attributed to diffusion and migration. This means that cultural change and interconnectedness were viewed as a product of population diffusion from outside Africa arriving in waves (Trigger, 1989: Macgaffety, 1970). Unfortunately, diffusion in that original form was embedded with racism that robbed Africans of their achievements.

Diffusion is a theory that views the growth of culture in terms of the growth of " cultural similarities", "mutual contact", "cultural cradle" and, "cultural area", "*kulturkreise*" (or culture circle or culture district) (Makhana,1983). Therefore a cultural trait develops only at once at one location of the world and later on diffuses to the rest. Migrating people may at times exercise the diffusion of ideas. This then explains cultural parallels or similarities. Diffusion is a 19th century theory that implied that man is uninventive and therefore cultural inventions occurred at once in a place and spread to other regions. There are three types of diffusion theorists. These include classical diffusionists of British scholars pioneered by G.E. Smith with his followers W.H.R, Rivers, and W.J. Perry Rivers; the German school termed as *Kulturkreise* or culture circle that was found by Ratzel with key followers as Graebner, Frobenius and Wilhelm Schmidt; while the American "culture area" theory of diffusion was found by Franz Boaz whose followers were Clark Wissler and Kroeber (Harris, 1968).

The British or Egyptologist diffusionist school of Elliot Smith regarded Egypt as a culture centre from which culture spread to the rest of the world from about 4000 BC. The basic assumptions of this school were that man is uninventive, culture rises at exceptionally favorable circumstances that only existed in Egypt, and as culture spreads, it is diluted. To the German diffusion school, development of culture takes place not only at a particular place like Egypt or Sudan but occurs at different places at several times which were regarded as culture circles. The German school questioned the psychic unity and inventive capacities of man. However, their major explanatory device was migration rather than diffusion (Makhan, 1983:62).

The German school considered the environment to have played a key adaptive role. However, Ratzel warned that not every similarity is proof of historical connection because material objects in order to have any utility at all must possess certain features. Frobenius noted that not only similarities but also even significant differences related to ecological adaptation could become indicators of historical connections (Makhan, 1983: 68). Therefore to both the German and British schools history never repeats itself. The American culture area school propounded the view that inside a culture centre was a culture core where all traits emanated from and traits diminished with increase in distance from the centre. When such traits increased with time, they would create another cultural centre.

The diffusion theory has been used to explain cultural similarities and differences among Africans south of the Sahara. In line with diffusion was the Hamitic myth through which pastoralism and all its attributes became endowed with the aura of superiority of culture (Sanders, 1969:530). The pastoralist Hamites were regarded as of Caucasian heritage by the Europeans and were credited with all aspects of early civilization in African societies (Chami, 1994:19; Kusimba 1999:48-9; Sinclair *et al,* 1993:10). On the other hand, the Negroes were taken as agriculturalists and subordinates of the pastoralists. Diffusion should not be viewed as where contact between people is often a result of complicated and repeated migration and trade patterns (Darvill, 2008:131) but rather where cultural adaptive change occurs.

However, diffusion of material culture does not necessarily have to show the same patterns as human migration or movement (Brown, 1968:29). The diffusion theory was embedded with racial discrimination (Chami, 2007). Thus, the African was stripped off any intellectual or artistic genius and any ability that would allow him to be the master of his life and country and even incapable of civilization. This led to the emergence of two divergent views, whereby, while scholars like Cole (1964) and Zayed (1981) contest diffusion others such as Chami (2006) and Whicker (1990) accepted existence of interactions. On the other hand, Smith (1928) used diffusion to show how civilizations emerged and spread to the rest of the world. Harris (1968) defended other people's capacity to invent and innovate. While, Johnson (2010) viewed the easiest way as, always attributing cultural changes to foreign influence in the form of diffusion and migration. The study examined the credibility of diffusion and migration theories as previously used to explain how cultures of Africa were formed and developed with the assistance of trade and ecological theories to examine the state of cultural connections and affinity in the upper Nile catchment areas.

The migration theory is difficult to separate from diffusion. Migration is, the gradual movement of people spreading from one geographical area to another (Darvill, 2002). There are four forms of migrating (Manning, 2006). These are: home community migration, cross-community migration, whole community migration and colonization. Africanists who reject the migration theory base on the notion that migration seems to support the colonial ideology that bounded pre historic cultures to technologies and ethnicity (Chami, 2009). Yet it is no longer accepted to simply equate for instance ceramics with ethnicity (Ashley, 2010:158). That is attributing Kansyore pottery to the Sahelians, Iron Age pottery to Bantu speakers and roulette to the Luo speakers.

Migration could have been due to population growth and social stress in the nucleus area that caused a one-time dispersal termed as "cataclysmic discontinuous spread (Huffman, 1989; Collet, 1982). Soper (1971) by means of archaeology and Ehret (1998, 2001, & 2002) using linguistics viewed the migration model as a "wave of advance" due to population growth. Oliver (1966) employed historical linguistics to support migration. Using lexicostatistics Ehret (1998, 2002a; Vansina, 1994-95; Ehret and Posnansky, 1982) dropped the original concept of massive Bantu expansion or waves of migration in Sub-Saharan Africa. However, scholars like Chami (2001) see Bantu speakers as dynamic as all other people of the earth who should not be taken as, "migratory locusts" but also as settled people doing various enterprises. Mass migrations, cultural exchanges, contacts and large-scale diffusion of individual cultural components have existed in one form or the other, throughout the history of the world (Serghei, 1978:94) in two ways that were; either innovation could be introduced in any culture that is known as independent invention or through cultural borrowing from an existing culture.

The migration theory in East Africa has been used in relation to the Bantu migration. The Bantu have been taken as a group that replaced the Khoisan hunter-gatherers who also, are assumed to have done all the rock paintings. Like in the modern times people migrated in the past too, for instance, the gods of Egypt are known to have migrated from the upper Nile catchment to the lower Nile catchment areas. However, cultural change does not have to be entirely due to migration. The research employed the concept of migration to examine how cultures could have been affected by movement of ideas. Migration, like the diffusion theory denied Africans settled life, for instance, Coon (1965:51) stated that, "in Africa peoples and cultures do not replace one another they simply move aside". Reid (2002:89) states that, "the picture of tentative introduction of agriculture, metallurgy and fundamental changes in food exploitation patterns occurring subsequently contrasts with the conventional one of Bantu speakers boldly emerging from the forests, subduing all before them, and immediately instituting a stable farming economy. Binford and Binford (1968) pointed out that cultural similarity has been attributed to either the linear transmission of diffusion between cultural units or independent development.

From the on-going discussion it is evident that cultural interactions were viewed as a one-way colonial relationship from north to south. Hence, cultural change and development were attributed to diffusion and migration. This means cultural change was viewed as a product of population diffusion from outside Africa arriving in waves (Trigger, 1989; Macgaffety, 1970). This is just like any traces and/or signs of what is usually termed 'civilized' in Africa have been attributed to aliens using the Hamitic theory (Sanders, 1969). For instance, African developments like those in Egypt and Zimbabwe were attributed to Hamitic pastoralists.

A number of scholars have employed diffusion and migration among other theories in explaining cultural affinity with the Sudanese Neolithic. For instance, Arkell (1949, 1953) suggested an evolutionary model to explain the sequence of cultural development from the Mesolithic to the Neolithic stage with its origin in Khartoum. Khartoum was regarded as the core area for the origin of the Khartoum culture. From the Khartoum core this culture had evidence established which extended from Khartoum along the Nile to the Fayum in Egypt and stretching westwards into the Sahara to Meniet (Algeria) before 3400 B.C (Hays, 1974). However, defining African cultural attainment should not be measured in European terms along a unilinear, evolutionist continuum that explains its past in a manner that pays scarce attention to the actions or histories of non-Egyptian Africans (Stahl, 1999a; Appiah, 1997) cited in (Mitchell, 2005: 5).

On the other hand, Clark (1965:158) proposed diffusion or migration as responsible for similarities with the Khartoum culture. Kroeber (1939) instead suggested ecological factors by proposing that sites containing cultural similarity with Sudan are expected to show strong similarities in adaptive patterns and material artefacts related to the environment. That is, if ecological conditions were similar then communication should not have been difficult. Hays (1971, 1974) concurs with Arkell (1949, 1953) that the common elements shared like the use of a common decorative style (comb and pivoting impression) and instrument (fish spine) should be attributed to diffusion and migration with the hypothesis that: if sites contained similar pottery then they were homogeneous and this was due to migration. However, if sites were not homogeneous then they were cultural areas and the similarity was due to diffusion. In Hay's (1974) view, the 'Khartoum Horizon Style' through diffusion and not migration, explains the use of a common decorative instrument. A Horizon style is a specialized cultural continuum represented by widespread distribution of a recognizable art style where the horizon style occupies a great deal of space but very little time which means that a new idea spreads over a wide geographical area.

Outside Sudan, Bishop and Posnansky (1960:59) suggested that, the lithic tool typology especially at Nsongezi indicated evidence of cultural diffusion in the Paleolithic around the Great Lakes from the Saharan fringe of the Sudan. Therefore the revival of evolutionary thinking and the introduction of a general systems model in archaeology are systematically related; and these in turn, are related to the development of environmental concerns into ecological ones (Willey and Sabloff, 1974:189).

Smith (1923) argued that, savages are totally without the initiative, desire or capacity for inventing a device, a myth or an institution and hence all major inventions were made once by some chosen people. This means that diffusion stripped off racism is a potential theory to understand how cultures exchanged cultural aspects (Chami, 2007). This theory has been utilized in this study to examine interactions that existed in the upper Nile catchment areas in the period 6000-1500 BP.

Since, "we know very little about the interactions between the groups that occupied Neolithic East Africa" (Karega-Munene, 1996:253), there was need for a new model to explain cultural and economic interactions. It was in line with this plea that the research was undertaken. The research examined the ecological model in view of the importance of migration and diffusion to scrutinize explanations for periodic changes related to contemporaneous cultural developments in the upper Nile catchment areas in order to check the racist sentiments previously expressed.

Though Chapman's (1967) research at Kansyore Island considered the ecological factors as an obstacle to interaction this work used ecological adaptations as one of the theories that could account for cultural interactions in the Upper Nile catchment areas. Adaptation in this research is viewed as where subsistence has the evident archaeological consequence for adaptive strategies and tactics measured using artifact assemblages where adaptation is viewed as a product of selection (Mabulla, 1996). Similarly Sutton (1971) had earlier suggested that cultural similarities and social change were due to similar adaptive strategies. Therefore, ecological adaptability in this research was tested to see how it explained cultural affinity between the Khartoum Neolithic and the Ugandan Upper Nile catchment. This called for an examination of man's response to environmental changes.

1.9. Chapter Summary

Early archaeological works (Arkell, 1949, 1953; Chapman, 1967; Hays, 1974; Robertshaw, 1991) in the Nile Valley made statements illuminating the possibility of cultural and economic connections. Emphasis was put on pottery decoration and the connections were attributed to evolution, migration and diffusion theories. This warranted a detailed study in the upper Nile catchment areas to examine the credibility of migration and diffusion theories in explaining the spatial distribution of the Khartoum Neolithic 'dotted wavy-line pottery' that was first identified by Arkell (1953) at Shaheinab. This pottery was later identified at other sites in Sudan like Shaqadud (Marks and Mohammed-Ali, 1991a) and has long been recognized as a significant innovation in Sub-Saharan Africa (Mohammed-Ali and Khabir, 2003). Though first recognized in the Nile valley it was thought to represent an expansion westward into the desert (Hays, 1974) but its evidence has been identified southwards as far as the Turkana area in Kenya (Barthelme, 1977).

However recent evidence demonstrates that some of their occurrences into the Sahara are older than those of the Nile valley or that of the Mediterranean coastal regions of Africa where the local Saharan pottery invention has been dated 9500 years ago. This is supported by an independent development of a settled life style settlement which made it possible for the adoption of heavy fragile receptacles that were ill suited for the mobile life styles of earlier times (Phillipson, 2005). Therefore the research set out to investigate the nature of this similar culture in time and space in the Upper Nile catchment areas by comparing cultural material attributes from sites in Uganda (Chobe, Kikubamitwe, Kansyore Island, Island of Deserters and Nsongezi) that constituted the southern part of the Upper Nile catchment with Khartoum Neolithic sites below the 6th Cataract such as Lokabulo, Itohom, Jebel Kathangor in Southern Sudan; Shaqadud, Sorourab, Kadero and Esh-Shaheinab in Central Sudan representing the north for purposes of this research that were examined from 6000-1500 BP.

CHAPTER 2

THE SITES AND THEIR BIO-GEOGRAPHY

2.1. Introduction

This chapter discusses the sites where the research was undertaken in the Upper Nile catchment (Figure 1) and their bio-geography. The chapter undertakes a discussion of the climate, topography, vegetation and animal population of the focus areas. The study was conducted in the geographical area termed as the upper Nile catchment area. This is the part drained by the Nile partly located in Uganda and parts of central and southern Sudan to the 6th cataract. This chapter will only discuss the bio-geography of the two sites of the Island of Deserters and Kansyore Island in the south that are in present day Uganda where survey and excavations were conducted and that had Kansyore cultural material. This means issues concerning the other two sites investigated that did not have the Kansyore cultural materials that is Chobe and Kikubamitwe will be reported in other subsequent publications.

The fresh water lakes that are Lakes Edward, Albert (Mobutu) and Victoria (Nyanza) form part of the basin of the upper Nile. These lakes are in the western arm of the East African Rift Valley system (Langlands, 1993: 895). Uganda is a landlocked country that ranges from lush and fertile green landscapes around the northern shores of Lake Victoria (the source of the Nile) to the snow covered Ruwenzori Mountains in the West and to the arid semi deserts in the north. Although crossed by the equator, the altitude of over 3500 feet moderates the tropical heat. Rainfall ranges between 40 and 60 inches while temperature ranges from 62°F to 83° F. The Nile runs between latitude 4° South and 3° North. Geologically the great proportion of Uganda contains pre-Cambrian material dated between 3000-600 mya (Uganda Lands and survey department: 1962:8) largely of gneiss and schist into which granites intruded. In the western part of Uganda, distinct series of metamorphosed rocks occur largely of phyllites and shales and in which mineralized zones contain small quantities of tin (in Kikagati close to Nsongezi and Kansyore Island.

The Nile catchment covers an area of 2.9 million square kilometers. River Nile has a length of 6,695 km; however, the total length with its tributaries is 37,205 square kilometers. The Nile gets water from three catchments that are the plateau of equatorial lakes, Bahr el Ghazal and the Ethiopian highlands.

Lakes Victoria and Kyoga feed the Victoria Nile while Lakes Edward and George join the Semliki River; Lake Albert forms the Albert Nile flowing down to Nimule thereafter becoming the Bahr el Jebel. In the same catchment is the Kagera River the principal source of the Nile. The Bahr el Ghazal catchment area is located in Southwestern Sudan whose waters all flow in the Sudd area and into the White Nile through Lake No. Finally is the Ethiopian highland catchment that has its source of water as the Ethiopian highlands before running into the White Nile through three rivers that are the Sobat River originating from Ethiopia through the two tributaries of Baro and Pipor with Bara River crossing the Macha marshes (Klerruu, 1962).

River Nile begins from the Ruwenzori Mountains in the Kagera River's tributary Ruvironza in Burundi and joins Lake Victoria (Victoria Nyanza) locally called *Nalubaale*. Throughout the course of its journey, the Nile passes through contrasting environments, some of which are among the driest in Africa, if not indeed the whole world. It is because the river flows through so much arid country that, for much of its length, the river and its narrow valley have played an important role in human history. The lower and middle Nile has cataracts and a series of rocky swift rapids with rocky outcrops and narrow canyons.

In the south was Nubia that received a little seasonal rain (Langlands, 1993). A well-defined wet season therefore characterizes the climate of the Upper Nile valley. The Nile valley was characterized by winds that blow from north to south and it is in this direction where currents facilitated downstream navigation. Due to this climate, vegetation varies from total desert to acacia desert scrub and thick vegetation. Though this study was undertaken in Chobe, Kansyore Island, Nsongezi and Kikubamitwe that constituted the southern part of the upper Nile catchment (Figure 1) the discussion in this work will be restricted to Kansyore and the Island of deserters that had data that addressed the problem of the research. The data from Chobe and Kikubamitwe is left out and will be published in form of journal articles. Kansyore Island and Nsongezi areas lay in the same bio-geography and within each several sites were located

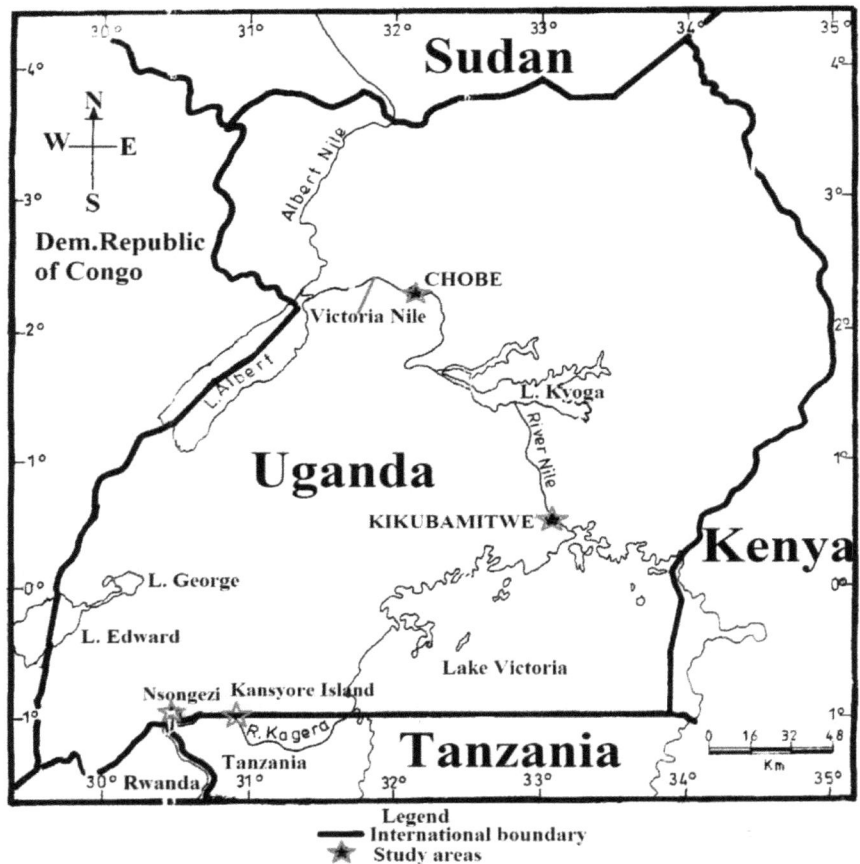

Figure 2.1: Study Sites in Uganda (Southern Upper Nile Catchment Areas)

2.2. Bio-geography of Kansyore Island and the Island of Deserters

This area incorporates sites in Nsongezi village, Kansyore Island and the Island of Deserters that are situated in southwestern Uganda. These were banded together because they share the same biogeography. Nsongezi area was popularized by the Nsongezi Rock Shelter where the first dimple-based pottery in Uganda and Stone Age material was obtained. Close to the Nsongezi rock shelter is a site termed *"the Island of Deserters"* by this study. The Island of Deserters is a large site with cultural materials stretching from the MSA period to the Late Iron Age. The area was referred to as the Island of Deserters in this study a term derived from Herodotus' map that indicates a point of deserters where the Nile turns west. Since through its course the Nile only turns west where it is joined by the Kagera the area was named the Island of Deserters which was a probable island for the Egyptian deserters.

Other than the historical considerations, the place had evidence of an ancient meandering river that was also confirmed by the oral traditions while the swampy marshes were an indicator of a river channel. The Island of Deserters is likely to have been the result of the rift valley disturbances that changed the course of the Kagera River. Since it had past settlement signatures, the name Island of Deserters was coined for the area by this research. The Nsongezi village and the River Kagera in the north and south respectively border the Island of deserters.

Kansyore Island lies in River Kagera at the point where the river forms two channels. The eastern channel borders Tanzania's Kagera region while the western side is bordered by Uganda. The Kagera was initially flowing west towards the Atlantic but due to the up-tilt of shoulders along the Western Rift of the East African Rift valley system the Kagera river flow was tilted from east to west in the reverse direction. Henceforth the Kagera became incorporated into the Nile system and became one of the major sources of water that feeds Lake Victoria and the Nile (Hamilton, 1982; Willoughby, 2007 and Bushozi, 2011). This reversal of the Kagera has been dated to the pre-Pleistocene days or even probably the Pliocene (O'Brien, 1952:4) or Middle Pleistocene (Willoughby, 2007). While to Bishop and Posnansky (1960) this was prior to the crustal warping due to the rift valley back-tilt in the Middle Pleistocene.

The Kagera Valley therefore was due to the tilting and possible warping that applied to the whole of western Uganda during the Pleistocene that produced a total uplift since it is important to note the effects of volcanicity on environments (Howell and Bourliere, 1964:632). The Kagera lies between 30° 30- and 31° 30- close to the volcanic Kasirimbi in the western arm of the Great Rift Valley formed 50 mya due to the sinking and tearing of the earth's crust. The first implements (hand axes) from a stratigraphic sequence in Uganda came from the lacustrine deposits of the Kagera river valley (Bishop and Posnansky, 1960:53).

2.2.1 Topography

The general landscape of western Uganda as part of the wider Western rift region owes some of its most characteristic features to the processes associated with rift valleys and their associated highlands and the geological time scales (Baker, 1958:1-2). The relief according to Ojany (1968: 24-5) is plateau-like characterized by a landscape of rolling and undulating plateau which is 5000 to 6000 feet (Langlands, 1964:3). Therefore, the area is also characterized by anticlines and synclines (Plate 2.1). The anticlines and synclines are probably due to folding or volcanic actions and specifically due the East African Rift Valley system that forced some areas to go up while others went down. Within the pre-Cambrian rocks that constitute the main geological formation of the plateau landscapes are the arenas that were first described in Uganda by Wayland. The granite-floored arenas owe the foundation of their character to the events in the pre-Cambrian era (Baker, 1958). The arena is an area of granite–floored country surrounded by steep inward facing slopes as the Ankole–Karagwe phyllites that weathered into fluted escarpments.

Laterisation is wide spread and remnants of laterite are of Miocene age or older, cap many hills in this Karagwe-Ankole system (Uganda lands and survey department, 1962). The lower Kagera Valley is an earlier Pleistocene drainage located at 1° 0' S, 30° E across the Uganda Plateau in the western Rift Valley. The drainage was interrupted during the Middle Pleistocene hence; the down-warped Victoria extended its waters westward as far as the Nsongezi area. Kansyore Island slopes towards the river but the middle part of the Island is flat. The middle flat part forms the oldest earth deposits or the first terrace.

Closer to the riverbanks on any part of the island the landscape slants towards the river. The sloping part on the northern side of the island generally contains the initial cliff evidenced by hard-concretized rocks formed due to river deposition made of cobbles of various sizes and sandstones. The sloping edge forms the second earth formation or terrace. Below the second terrace as one descends to the river banks is the third terrace which is low lying and the greatest part of it being marshy. This is the latest earth formation on the island. River Kagera at the point of Kansyore Island lies between huge anticlines and synclines, with low lands and gentle slopes.

Kansyore Island is mainly composed of phyllite ridge covered in some places by indurate gravel composed chiefly of pebbles and small cobbles. Above this, there is commonly 30-75 cm of unconsolidated sediments capped by a well-developed soil horizon. These sediments have been disturbed by the tree fall, cultivation, the interment of burials, animal footfall when muddy and burrowing animals (Nelson, 1973). Generally in the Nsongezi/ Kansyore area sandstone and quartzite are important although thin and persistent over wide regions.

Plate 2.1: A landscape with synclines and anticlines on the way to Nsongezi

2.2.2 Flora

Generally, Uganda's vegetation is characterized by wooded grasslands (Morgan, 1973: 48). Ojany (1968: 36) describes the vegetation of this area as woodland savannah mosaic that consists of scattered tree grasslands of low tree and high grass. This vegetation type of wooded savannah complex is dominated by moist acacia savannah or *combretum* savannah. The area falls within the Karagwe-Ankole system where the grassland was wooded, with *acacia gerardii* standing in *themeda triandra* or *cymbopogon afronardus*, although can be replaced by *combretum spp*. The vegetation of this area is dry acacia savanna with *hyparrhennia* associated with *themeda* (Lands and survey department, 1962). On the higher grounds from Mbarara are the stands of pure grasslands that continue into Karagwe (Morgan, 1973: 254). The vegetation specifically at Kansyore Island for instance was characterized by grassland dotted by few trees especially *acacia erthrina*. The island had limited vegetation cover composed of scatters of wild palm (*borassas* palm) locally known as *mitooma* and a few occurrences of artificially planted eucalyptus especially on the upper terrace. The palms are interspersed with aquatic grasslands and herb swamps (Nelson, 1973). The biggest portion of the island was subjected to cultivation of mainly food crops and cereals like sorghum, millet, maize, cassava, sweet potatoes, yams, and sugar cane. The later were mainly along the banks in the swampy marshy part close to the papyrus.

The banks of the island are marshy and dominated by papyrus and occasional trees. At the edge of the island was a wetland with characteristic wetland species, marshy with papyrus and *palmae*. The vegetation was generally poor due to the thin soil layers caused by the underground basement rock that also explains the growing of drought-resistant species on the island. Therefore, the vegetation was brownish in colour (personal observation). Nelson (1973) identified three ecological zones in this area and these are the plain zone covered with dry acacia savanna associated with *Themeda*. The second zone is composed of the mountainous ridges and valleys in the north and east. At the lower elevations are mosaic of dry acacia savanna associated with *Themeda* and euphorbia vegetation approaching a shrub and a succulent steppe thicket. This vegetation gives way to a mosaic of grass savanna associated with *Themeda* and a moist *Albizia-markhamia* semi-deciduous forest. The third ecological zone is the Kagera valley that contains a complex gallery of vegetation.

2.2.3 Soils

Soil formation is intimately related to climate, geological formations, topography, living organisms and to the time factor but climate is the most important because it influences the rate of weathering and leaching and the rate at which living organisms break up the soil (Ojany, 1968: 37-38). The soils by nature have a thin dark loam layer. The alluvial soil was stony and rocky mixed with lots of river cobbles. In some areas, especially at the terraces, the soils are loose sandy soils and clayish which supports the growth of yams. The soils are rocky towards the riverbanks and sandy on the flat top. The deeper the soils the rockier it becomes, therefore, the soils are slightly lateritised sandy loams, clay in aggraded valleys while sand and gravels dominated the river terraces.

2.2.4 Fauna

The area is predominantly a pastoral region with cows, goats and sheep. The system of rearing is nomadic pastoralism that is carried out on hilltops and in the synclines. River Kagera is the major source of water for people and animals. The river provides plentiful supply of fish especially the Ripon Falls barbell and a wide variety of edible mollusks that include the *etheria, caelatura* and *mutela* (Nelson, 1973:46). The thick vegetation in many parts of the Kagera valley acts as a habitat for hippos, crocodiles and monkeys. Though no wild animal was seen at the time of research this area seems to have had a variety of wild animals in the past as evidenced by the rich faunal remains obtained for wild terrestrial species like elephant and buffalo at Kansyore Island and in the Nsongezi area. The ecological zones in this area support a wide variety of game including the common duiker, topi, impala, oribi, eland, buffalo, zebra and elephant. This ecological zone and its ecotones with river and plains support animals like: bush pigs, klipspringer, situtunga and antelopes.

2.2.5 Population and Economic Activities

The area is currently inhabited by the Banyankole-Bakiga Bantu speakers. The Tanzanian side at this spot has mainly the Banyambo who interact regularly with the people on the Ugandan side. The Banyankole pastoralists (Bahima) were regarded as dominant using the Hamitic myth as opposed to the agricultural Bairu. Thus, the major economic activities in this area are pastoralism, agriculture and fishing. Other ethnic groups in the area were the Baganda, Banyambo and Rwandese.

2.2.6 Rainfall and Temperature

The western parts of Uganda get some rain from the Atlantic Ocean or Congo south-westerly air-streams during the northern summer, and Lake Victoria that is intensive enough to generate its own maritime climate. This area lies within the InterTropical Convergence Zone (ITCZ) and therefore rainfall depends on the movement of the sun that creates distinct rainfall seasons (Ojany, 1968:31). The rainfall is marked by a double peak with April and October as the wettest months. The average rainfall in these months falls between 40-60 inches.

The area receives 30-35 inches of rainfall per annum but at higher elevations rainfall increases to more than 40 inches per annum unlike the plains that receive 30-35 inches of rainfall per annum (Nelson, 1973). Therefore, there is a clear correspondence of high rainfall with high relief; and the InterTropical Convergence Zone plays part in producing this bi-seasonal rainfall. Another factor that influences rainfall in this area is the moist air from the Congo Basin and perhaps from the South Atlantic Ocean (Baker, 1958:2-3). A convergence zone between westerly air-streams and south-easterly or northerly streams lies normally over the eastern part of Congo Basin accompanied by a belt of rainfall, this frontal zone moves fairly frequently over western Uganda. The diurnal range of temperature is 20° to 25°F, maximum day temperature being 75°F increasing at times to 95° (Colonial report, 1949) but the mean annual temperature is 69° F (Baker, 1958:3).

2.3 The Sites

Nsongezi is among the few areas outside the western Rift where Acheulean evidence was found (Bishop and Posnansky, 1957: 48). Wayland excavated Nsongezi in 1953 and 1954. The Nsongezi area is situated in Ishingiro District, Ishingiro South Constituency, Kikagate Sub-county, Ruyanga Village. The area is situated along the banks of River Kagera (Figure 2.2).

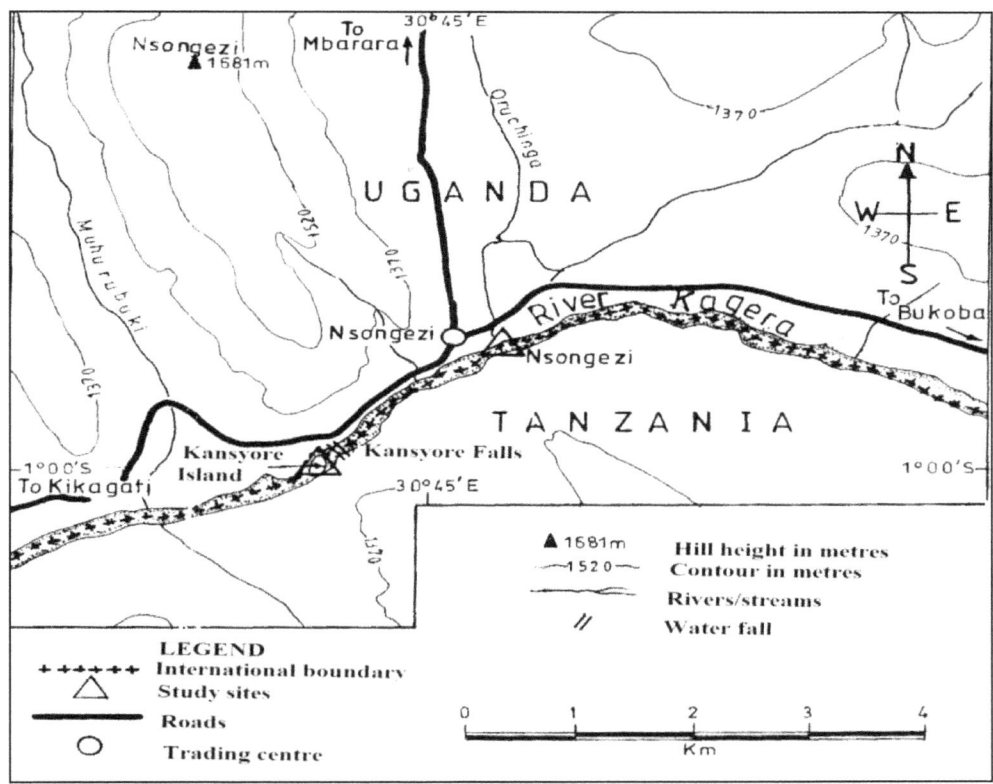

Figure 2.2: Archaeological sites in the Nsongezi Area

Nine archaeological sites were identified in the Nsongezi/Kansyore and Island of Deserters area. These are the three Nsongezi rock shelters, Mobile Police

Patrol Unit detach gardens, Mobile Police Patrol Unit prison gardens, the Kagera basin road site, Nsongezi quarry and Island of Deserters, pyramidal monument, Nsongezi landing site, Kalamba slag site and Kansyore Island.

2.3.1 Mobile Police Patrol Unit (MPPU) Detach Gardens

The first site in the Nsongezi area was in a garden behind the Nsongezi MPPU detach house. This site is at the former Ministry of Works' camp (Nelson, 1973). The site was located at 00° 59' 28.8"S and 030° 45' 03.9"E with a surface elevation of 1248 metres above sea level. At this site, lithics and LIA pottery lay in the ditch. At the T-junction of Mbarara, Kikagati/Rwanda and Kagera basin/ Tanzania (Kyaka border) close to the MPPU were faunal remains observed in the road cut in-situ. This is a Late Stone Age site comprising of microliths that were exposed in cultivated land. The MPPU detach site extended with the slope towards the road heading to the Kagera Basin. The major threats to the site include farming as the site lies in the farmland of the policemen at the MPPU detach and construction for example at the time of research was a latrine that had been constructed in the midst of the site.

2.3.2 Kagera Basin Road Site

Another site in the Nsongezi area was located just after crossing the road leading to the Kagera basin. The site was covered by a banana plantation. The site had a high concentration of lithic artefacts and pottery that showed that it was inhabited till the EIA period. The site was bordered by the road to Kagera Basin in the east, the Nsongezi Rock Shelter in the west and the Island of Deserters and quarry sites in the south.

2.3.3 Nsongezi Quarry Site and the Island of Deserters

The name Island of Deserters that was used in this research was derived from the ancient writings that showed an Island of Egyptian deserters which on Herodotus' ancient map was located where the Nile turns west (Chami, 2006) (Refer to Figure 5 for details). Since in the course of its journey the Nile is only linked from a west direction by the Kagera River, this led to the proposition of this place to be called the Island of Deserters. Besides, there was the physical evidence at the site and oral information that confirmed the island nature. Such evidence included the place being littered with river cobbles of various sizes. The Island of Deserters also had marshy channels that served as evidence of an old water channel surrounding it. The fertility as detected from the crops due to the alluvial soils that are so commonly formed due to water deposition and the depression on the eastern side which is currently River Kagera were another indicator. The assumption was that the river channel had continually moved east since ancient times because the land slopes eastward on the Ugandan side and westward on the Tanzanian side living a valley in between that forms the Kagera River. The Island of Deserters is an enormous island located on the western bank of River Kagera covering about 400 metres.

This site stretches from the quarry area encompassing the Island of Deserters. This site is located at 00° 59′ 22.8″S and 030 ° 45′ 20.2″E and 1221 metres above sea level. The quarry part is an area where murram had been extracted for road construction close to the stretch of River Kagera where canoes cross from Uganda to Tanzania and vice versa. A commercial route used to ferry trade goods from Tanzania for sale in Uganda linking the Kagera basin road before joining the Kikagati-Mbarara road bisects the site. The current transactions made the area viable for this study on cultural connections to examine if even in the past it was used as a commercial route. This was a multi-component site with lithic artefacts for as far as the Middle Stone Age, pottery of all traditions in the region and a few faunal remains.

2.3.4 Nsongezi Rock Shelters

This is an extensive site with three rock shelters. The first rock shelter is located along the road to Kikagati on the northern margins of the modern flood plain of the Kagera River consisting of a shallow notch at the base of a low cliff cut by the river in lateritic conglomerate (Nelson, 1973). This is immediately above the left bank of the Kagera where the river emerges from the Kikagati-Nsongezi gorge at Nsongezi 100 yards from the Kagera River (Lowe, 1952:99). That is at GPS reading 00° 30′ 07.2″ N and 033° 07′56.8″ E and 1260 metres above sea level on the northern banks of the Kagera River. This renowned site has been subjected to archaeological research by several scholars such as: Wayland (1932); Lowe (1952); O'Brien (1939); Pearce and Posnansky (1963) and Nelson and Posnansky, (1970). The well-known Nsongezi Rock Shelter (Plate 2.3) is one of the most famous Stone Age sites in Uganda. However, Wandibba (1990) noted that the only potsherd from Nsongezi Rock shelter described as Kansyore by (Pearce and Posnansky, 1963) belongs to the Early Iron Age period. The Nsongezi famous rock shelter site is threatened by both human and natural activities. Humans use the site as a shelter from rain; they use it as a fireplace for cooking, roasting maize and bush-burning which have stained the walls (Plate 2.2). The natural threats are detected from the collapse of part of the shelter. The first step could probably be having a signpost to direct tourists and researchers. Despite the lack of a signpost one could easily be directed as the site is well-known to the inhabitants as a place for Stone Age research. The two other rock shelters are situated southward from the well-known Nsongezi Rock Shelter 10 metres away from each other on the northern edges of River Kagera. The two other shelters were discovered during a survey by the researcher (Plate 2.3).

Plate 2.2: Nsongezi Rock Shelter

(a) The author at Nsongezi Rock Shelter during preliminary survey

(b) The author and a research assistant at the Nsongezi Rock Shelter during intensive survey

Plate 2.3: The second rock shelter discovered during a survey in Nsongezi

2.3.5 MPPU Prison Garden

Moving across the road heading first west and then south of the MPPU detach is a small incarceration cell for the MPPU unit. The cell is surrounded by a piece of land referred to as the MPPU prison garden by this study. This was a LIA site depicted from dominance of twisted cord roulette with a herringbone pattern resulting from a change in the direction of the knotting midway down the roulette (Haour, 2010). A similar sherd was recovered from the surface of Ntusi 1 by Andrew Reid dated ca. AD 1400 and at Chobe by this research. This suggests inter-site cultural interactions in the Iron Age. The site stretches from the prison gardens and encompasses a steep slope adjacent to the pyramidal site close to the road to Kikagate in south western Uganda.

2.3.6 Pyramidal Monument Site

The pyramidal monument is south of the MPPU police post. It is referred to as a pyramidal site due to the existence of a pyramidal structure (Plates 2.4a and 2.4b). This pyramid is on top of the hill with no close inhabitants. The oral information suggested that the pyramid was a monument that was used as a burial place for a white man who drowned in River Kagera while he was fishing. However this monument had been partially demolished at the part where the arrow points in Plate 2.4. The destruction occurred during (former President Idi) Amin's regime (1971-1979) on suspicion that it contained mercury.

The pyramidal monument is situated northeast of Kansyore Island and River Kagera. It was initially built of mud while later on cement and coarse sand were used as the binding materials. This could probably be a cultural tomb. This site has archaeological potential if excavated. While pyramids were common in Sudan to Egypt it was not the same case in Uganda. It should be noted that Egyptians never buried their rulers since they believed they were living yet the pyramid is said to have been used for burial. Locally the pyramid is called *akanaala*. The term '*kanaala*' could even mean a mast, probably it was used for defensive purposes to see afar and to monitor the security of the place because at this site one has a clear view over the border into Tanzania, Uganda especially Kansyore Island and the Island of Deserters and the Kagera River. The fact that it overlooks the *andachi* (these are underground pits dug during the Kagera Salient War between Uganda and Tanzania in the 1970's) may make it even near-modern but also confirming its security role. A similar structure exists in Kyeirumba covered with iron sheets which to the locals was documented by Sir Samuel Baker one of the explorers who came to Uganda. This means the second pyramid discussed could be dating to the historical period. Sir Samuel Baker served as the Governor-General of the Equatorial Nile Basin, an area encompassing present-day Southern Sudan and northern Uganda, from 1869-1873. He is also remembered for 'discovering' Lake Albert in the western arm of the East African rift valley system.

Plate 2.4: The Pyramidal Structure

2.3.7 Nsongezi Landing Site

The Nsongezi landing site was just opposite Kansyore Island the two places being separated by River Kagera. This was the place used by canoes going to and from Kansyore Island commencing with this project hence the name Kyazike landing site. From the site crossing to Kansyore island takes 10 minutes in a canoe ride. At the time of survey the area had been recently dug which permitted clear visibility.

A remarkable percentage of lithics and pottery were littered all over the garden. The soil at the site was dark loam in texture and black (2.5/1 HUE 5YR) in colour just like the pottery. Basing on the surface concentration of artefacts a 1×1 m^2 test pit was sunk at this site. The lithics at the site showed that it was more of a factory of LSA lithic material due to the huge amounts of debris. In addition were faunal remains and pottery.

2.3.8 Kansyore/Nsongezi Island Site

Kansyore Island also known as Nsongezi Island is a very rich LSA site with pottery of all traditions in the region scattered all over. The pottery traditions that Chapman (1967) identified included Kansyore pottery characterized with dotted lines; Urewe or E I A pottery that is finely decorated and characterized with a dimple base; bevels and flutes on the thickened rims and decorated with fine incisions, grooves, punctates and stabs among the many; roulette pottery (LIA) especially knotted strip roulette; bourdine/Chobe ware characterized by finger impressions and stepped up ridges; and channel ware (looped and scrolled grooves) taken as a transition/channel ware in this research. Though the channel pottery had elements of mainly Urewe, at times these occurred with Kansyore pottery decorative elements. Despite that the predominant elements are the channels/grooves.

Besides pottery are the microliths, faunal remains, metallurgical remains, red ochre and daub. This is a type site for the Kansyore pottery tradition of ceramic using fisher-hunter-gatherers in East Africa (Dale and Ashley, 2010). Agricultural activities and politicians who claim they bought it and plan to develop it soon threaten the site.

2.3.9 Kalamba Slag Site

This is a site with mounds of slag (Plate 2.5) along the road to the Kagera basin. The site is in the farm land of Mr. Kalamba. Despite reports by earlier scholars suggesting absence of slag in the Nsongezi area this site offers a unique opportunity for the study of iron working on the Uganda side close to Buhaya (Tanzania).

This could enrich the archaeology of western Uganda where emphasis has hitherto been on lithics and ceramics at the expense of metallurgical studies. This site therefore suggests similarity in subsistence strategies in the Kagera region in the past in both present day Uganda and Tanzania. However, close to the Kalamba site was ESA evidence.

Plate 2.5: Kalamba Slag Site

2.3. Chapter Summary

Generally, the upper Nile catchment is characterised by undulating plateau, savannah grassland with dry thickets. The climate is mainly conditioned by ITCZ. It had a rich fauna though part of it is becoming extinct. The sites identified range from the Stone Age to the historical period and most of them are greatly threatened by human activities and in a few cases nature as in the case of Nsongezi rock shelter. The biogeography and the sites have highlights that illuminate cultural connections in prehistory. The vegetation of Chobe is wooded savannah combretum associated with hyparrhenia, in Kikubamitwe it is forest savannah mosaic with forest remnants of hyparrehenia while the Nsongezi/Kansyore area had dry acacia savannah with hyparrhenia associated with themeda.

This implies that all sites were located in an area whose vegetation was savannah and this could partially explain cultural and economic affinities observed. Geologically all sites like the rest of Uganda are characterised by Precambrian rocks. In Chobe were quartzite, slates, phyllites, schists, amphibolites and gneiss; Kikubamitwe possessed Cainozoic Pleistocene to recent sediments while the Nsongezi/Kansyore area had quartzite, phyllites and schists. The rainfall is heaviest in the Kikubamitwe area with 60 -70 inches, followed by Chobe with 40-50 inches and the Nsongezi Kansyore area receives 30-35 inches on average. It was in this kind of geography that sites were located that spanned from the ESA to near modern.

CHAPTER THREE

LITERATURE REVIEW

3.1. Introduction

This chapter examines the available literature that is related to cultural and economic interactions in the Upper Nile catchment areas from 6000-1500 BP. The literature is divided into sub-sections focusing on supporters of interaction, literature that negates interactions and literature on East Africa in general and Uganda in particular. The speculations that emphasize the passive receipt of external influences were closely linked to European colonial conceptualizations of Africa as a dark and timeless continent where little changed except through contact from the outside (Mitchell, 2005). Such ideas have affected Africanist scholarship and cast a shadow to today (Hall, 2002). Archaeologically, the evidence of contact is slighter and more ambiguous than that provided by the oral traditions (Posnansky, 1975:220). A review of related literature therefore shows that whereas some scholars support cultural interactions, others negate it.

3.2. Literature Arguing for the Existence of Interactions

Cultural connections in Africa have mainly been addressed by either looking at Africa in connection with Egypt, or Egyptian connections with West Africa or the East African coast. This could be due to Diop's (1997) assertion that, the history of Africa cannot be written correctly until African historians connect it with the history of Egypt. A number of scholars tackled Egyptian connections with West Africa including; Lucas (1942) who examined Yoruba religion and identified similarities between the Yoruba traditional religion and Egyptian religion. Meyerowitz (1960) examined Akan religion and identified its correlations with Egypt while Pageard (1963) examined court rituals and the culture of the Mossi of the Volta republic that were related to Egyptian systems. In all these works, it is shown clearly that Egyptian influence diffused to West Africa. This implied the existence of cultural unity in Africa (Diop, 1981a, 1981b; Chami, 2006). This made it more worthwhile to study Egypt's relations with the rest of Africa in detail than hitherto (Amodou-Mokhtar, 1981).

Outside West Africa, using Greco-Roman evidence Hurst (1952:201), advocated for the existence of Egyptian influence to the south in an area the Bible termed as the land of Kush and concluded that, "there must have been trade between the coast and the interior". This could probably have been due to the thinking that the Land of Punt or the land of the gods that traded with Egypt since 2500 BC or even before was the most interesting part of Egyptian knowledge about sub-Saharan Africa (Chami, 2006). This Land of Punt was located as far as East Africa (Kitchen, 2004) whose relations with Egypt were tackled by O'Connor and Reid (2003). However, contact was in both directions since whereas Egypt influenced its neighbors it was also influenced (Aldred, 1961).

Cultural connections in the Nile valley can be traced from the several theories advanced for the spread of iron-working. These include diffusion of iron-working from Meroe in present-day Sudan southwards (Posnansky, 1961; Arkell, 1961 and Leclant, 1981; Schmidt, 1975). This was challenged by Roland Oliver's expedition in southern Sudan (1977-1981) that suggested that no Early Iron Age pottery of the Urewe tradition had been found anywhere to the north of the banks of the Somerset Nile. However, Noten (1979:77) cited Leakey *et al* (1948) who was of the view that Urewe pottery could be compared to pottery from two ruined towns in the Sudan. Noten (1979:80), though an advocate of the diffusion of iron technology was of the view that the various decoration patterns present on the pottery of the western sites support the hypothesis that the interlacustrine region might be considered a nuclear area back to which may be traced several EIA pottery traditions found east and south of the region considered here. This implied that while the former supported diffusion from the north to the south, the latter supported diffusion from the south elsewhere. This supports the view that diffusion is not unilinear but multi-directional. However, Mapunda (1995) and Schmidt (2006) advocated for the independent development of iron working. This implied that local inventions were also responsible for some of the similar cultural aspects.

Shinnie (1971) outlined the legacy of Egypt to Africa but decried the neglect of Africa's legacy to Egypt. However, much as Egyptian contributions could be traced in many fields, it had been impossible to determine how they were passed on to subsequent cultures and the cultural milieu in which inventions first appeared (Zayed, 1981; El-Nadoury, 1981). This led to the suggestion of several theories as responsible for cultural similarities. For instance in the examination of the Later Stone Age period that was characterized by specialization, Sutton (1981:453) suggested that features that developed in one region would be carried to another either by migration or by cultural contact. Unfortunately, Sutton did not elaborate on the form of cultural contact.

There are several evidences besides the theories that suggest contacts in the Upper Nile catchment areas. Among these was the earlier search for the source of the Nile for instance expeditions sent by Emperor Nero in the mid-1st Century A.D. These suggested the existence of a Nile route to East Africa (Shinnie, 1967). The 'Egyptian Legacy in sub-Saharan Africa' identified by Sutton (1971) showed that there was unity and there were common features, though hard to analyze or define one could speak of an African culture. Interaction in the Great Lakes region also existed in the form of a trade route along the Nile where people traded in slaves and ivory though the connection was very tenuous and stopped at an early date (Dixon, 1971:124).

A Dutch work, *Beschrijvinge van't koninckrijck van Congo* published in Amsterdam in 1658 stated that, "The Nile traverses a great lake south of the equator. On this Lake are people who stay with great boats, have books, money, weights and build stone houses". This was the time of trying to locate the source of the Nile and the statement by the Dutch suggested the existence of contact. However, the nature of trade goods mentioned by Dixon (1971) like ivory and slaves and the people having books may imply that this was a recent period when writing had begun.

Bernal (1987, 1991) controversially emphasized a range of supposed cultural borrowings from Pharaonic Egypt in the Classical and Bronze Ages. This concurs with the view that "one of the characteristics of African societies was never to have lived in isolation" (Bathily and Meillassoux, 1988:734). The contact between Egypt and the Nubians of the Nile valley south of Aswan is also among such indicators of contact (Groove, 1989). The contact between the north and the south was eminent to the extent that Egyptians considered their gods or ancestors as having originated from the lands in Eastern and Southern Africa (Whicker, 1990). For instance the first pharaoh was considered to have originated from a region in the south (Casson, 1960). Other indicators of the North/South connection can be identified from records of the last millennium BC that showed that the most powerful Egyptian god and goddess Osiris and Isis were blacks originating from countries in the south of Africa (Kendall, 1997; Waterfield, 1967). Despite such studies there was limited archaeological evidence beyond the Middle Nile for contact (O'Connor and Reid, 2003b). This was an analysis made as a result of the twelve probing essays addressing the question of, "To what extent can ancient Egyptian civilization be characterized as 'African'?" by the latter. However the examination of how Africa interacted with other continents showed that Africans were not merely consumers but were equal and active partners in the exchange of goods, ideas and people (Mitchell, 2005).

For instance, in East Africa there were possible interior trade links between the coast of East Africa and the Nile valley (Miller, 1969). Though contacts existed between the interlacustrine region and the East African coast they extended as far as Sudan (Posnansky, 1975). These contacts were in form of trade links between the East African coast and the Nile valley suggestive of the unity of Africa (Chami and Kwekason, 2003; Chami 2004a, 2004b, 2006, 2007, 2008). This is because there were cultural links in the ancient world (Chami, 2008).

This however, does not mean that nothing has been done in this geographical region of the current research illuminating cultural connections. For instance the drum chimes of Buganda had some affinities with the drum ensembles from Ethiopia and possibly India (Watchsman, 1965). At Bigo and Kibengo earthwork sites, musical instruments and smoking pipes similar to the type introduced by the Portuguese or the Dutch and beads that were too undiagnostic for dating were identified by Lanning (1960, 1966). In Chobe, Fagan and Lofgren (1966:203,206) obtained a single cowrie shell which to them suggested evidence of long distance trade while the decoration of pottery from the two unusually fine pieces was foreign. At Bweyorere in 1959 a turquoise blue bead and small pearly white spherical glass beads were identified. The turquoise blue beads were similar to those at the East African coast whose origin could be traced as far as Venice or India. Though the beads could attest to trade, their limited nature might mean that the trade was probably through tribal contact intermediacy (Posnansky, 1968b). The smoking pipes however, were a further indication of a break in the isolation of western Uganda in the 18th century. Using cattle as another case study, possible contact routes between the Mountains of the Moon and Egypt were traced (Whicker, 1990) between the South and the North. Another indicator of early interaction between the mainland and the islands in the Lake Victoria region was the Urewe pottery from Bugala Island that Reid (2002) recovered.

Finally, a relationship between the interlacustrine region and Egypt was established using the Hutu-Tutsi identity issue though with emphasis on how it portrays the Hamitic myth (Reid, 2003).

The oral traditions from the Kikubamitwe fieldwork indicated strong links between the Jinja area (Nile banks) communities and the Buvuma Islands, especially through trade in pots up to the last century (Kiyaga-Mulindwa, 2004). Archaeological research in Mutunda (close to Chobe) pointed out a number of indicators for the area just below the Nile being an important gate way both to the north and south of River Nile (Kiyaga-Mulindwa, 2006). This was through a number of indicators for cultural connections that included: examining roulette and pinching or thumb nail impression decorations that indicated an import from neighbouring communities and therefore a pointer to cultural interaction in the region. A place called Wankwa/ Fajoor (Kampala) was identified that is remembered in historical traditions through which the southern bank of the Nile at this crossing had a famous market where grain and cattle from the north of the river were bartered for trade items from the south especially iron implements from Bunyoro. Wangcoro (Wankwa) located between Bedmont and Okwece was said to have rock engravings in the form of *Coro* (African chess) which in Palwo history are related to a meeting place of Palwo chiefs and those from across the river (Nile) (Kiyaga-Mulindwa, 2006). This suggests the existence of cultural contacts and connections as this was a meeting place of people from different areas.

Other than that, cultural connections have been traced using mainly ceramics. Some of the decoration motifs of Kansyore pottery were thought to be similar to those of earlier fisher-gatherers from the northern part of the Upper Nile valley by Chapman (1967), Sutton (1971, 1974), Robertshaw (1982) and Ambrose (1990). For instance, similarity was identified between Kansyore ware and the Early Sudan pottery, especially the internal decoration on the rim (Chapman, 1967:177). The likeness was partly attributed to the use of the same tools in decoration, in particular the *Etheria elliptica* shells, though this did not explain the similar rims and base. The comparisons were quite precise in Chapman's (1967) view that it would be extremely unwise to make any conclusions because of the distance involved and the differences in the estimated dates between Kansyore ware (1000 A.D) and Sudan ware (3300B.C) (Chapman, 1967). Dale (2007:69) who employed the Caneva (1988) ceramic analysis scheme to analyse Kansyore pottery from East

Africa suggested that similarities in ecological adaptations and comparable ceramic decoration between some early North and East African sites led some researchers like; Arkell (1949a), Chapman (1967), Clark (1980, 1989), Leakey (1936), Phillipson (1977) and Sutton (1974, 1977) to posit a cultural link between the regions.

In a related development Robertshaw (1982:92) was of the view that a far better case can be made linking Lokabulo tradition in Sudan with the Kansyore tradition around Lake Victoria. The Lokabulo tradition in southeastern Sudan and Kansyore tradition shared pottery decorations, decoration techniques, stone artifact types and subsistence (Robertshaw, 1982). The decoration modes shared included alternating vertical and horizontal impressions and circular motifs and decoration techniques of rocked zigzag and walked punctates (Collet and Robertshaw, 1980). Internal decoration was another shared attribute for both Kansyore ware and Lokabulo ware at Itohom in southern Sudan (Robertshaw, 1982). Though they shared stone tool types, especially baked pieces and some scraper types, hunting and gathering subsistence means the dates were not compatible. This is because while Lokabulo was dated 2000-1000 AD (Robertshaw, 1982), Kansyore has been dated c. 6000 BC- AD 500 (Prendergast, 2010). However, David in press cited by Robertshaw (1982) considered the Lokabulo tradition as a variant of the aquatic civilization of Middle Africa (Sutton, 1974) or aqualithic (Sutton, 1977). However, Lokabulo tradition lacked bone harpoons just as the Shaqadud Neolithic levels despite huge faunal remains they had no evidence of fishing (Robertshaw, 1982). Despite that, wavy line pottery and bone harpoons are widely distributed in this part of Africa that has been attributed to a horizon style by Hays (1974). Though Robertshaw (1982) suggested that the Lokabulo LSA should be disassociated with the aqualithic, Kryzaniak (1978) suggested that the assemblages of Early Khartoum tradition can be regarded as a local manifestation of the Middle African socio-economic development defined as the aquatic. Therefore the Kansyore sites are a late manifestation of the aqualithic (Prendergast, 2008). This implies that the Lokabulo like the Kansyore tradition cannot be disassociated from the aqualithic.

Cultural connections have also been drawn between the dotted wavy line tradition and ceramics in both Lake Turkana and Lake Victoria sites (Prendergast, 2008) since Kansyore pottery was in the same line as dotted wavy line pottery of Khartoum (Dale and Ashley, 2010). The Holocene

Mollusca and fish fauna of Lake Turkana show very close Nilotic affinities with no endemism. This suggests that during the quaternary there had been links with the Nile system. Robertshaw (1980) excavated the Jebel Kathangor ash mound in Southern Sudan whose finds include incised lined pottery that had affinities with the Turkwell tradition of the Turkana basin approximately dated 1500BP (Harvey and Grove, 1982:334-5). Oliver (1982) extended the similarity of Early Khartoum pottery to North Western Tanzania. These implied that rivers and large water bodies were not and have never been physical barriers to movement, contact, and trade and the Nile was not a *cul-de-sac* (Kiyaga-Mulindwa, 2004). On the contrary, despite the similarity of archaeological materials from near Khartoum with those from the Turkana sites, it was unlikely that the swampy overflow would have been an attractive site for occupation or movement and this would have acted as a barrier to cultural and ecological mobility in the early Holocene pluvial. (Sutton, 1974) However, the movement of lithic raw materials between the rift valley and Nyanza at the beginning of the Neolithic suggested a series of contacts among the communities (Seitsonen, 2010). This therefore called for an investigation into the apparent similarities in material culture and economic patterns between parts of the Nile valley and the Lake Victoria Basin (Dale and Ashley, 2010; Prendergast, 2010).

It should be noted that similarities were also identified between the Sahara and Sudanese archaeological cultures dated 9000-6000 BP (Arkell, 1949). Arkell argued for cultural connections between widely dispersed fishing and hunting cultures of the Holocene wet phase based on similarities in pottery decoration and other kinds of material especially bone harpoons (Arkell, 1949:112). This was in relation to sites such as Tamaya Mellet and Taferjit, the former dated 9350± 170 (Close, 1995). The proposal was not strange in the diffusionist era (Dale, 2007). However, connections with sites outside North Africa especially a 'somewhat similar' lithic industry associated with the Upper Kenya Capsian (Eburran) from Gamble cave and the differences in the lithic industry were only due to differences in raw material types. It is following this that Sutton, (1974) proposed the aquatic beginning in the 9th millennium that stretched from the far-west through the southern Sahara to the Middle Nile and then upriver to the East African rift valley system that was tied to climatic changes though again another diffusionist explanation for the wide spread similar cultures. The weakness of the latter view was its reliance on general survey of literature rather than research on the ceramic assemblages to explain cultural change (Dale, 2007).

A look at the literature advocating for cultural and economic interactions shows that these scholars do not go further than their statements to pursue the issue of cultural interactions that is the gist of the current study. Besides examining pottery as suggested by Robertshaw (1982:95) was the need to study other aspects of material culture such as the lithics and faunal remains to obtain more evidence for cultural and economic interactions as some indicators of contact appeared outside the realm of material culture. However, unlike the above literature the current study does not concentrate on either West Africa or the East African coast or Africa's relations with Egypt but rather on the Upper Nile catchment below the 6th cataract from 6000-1500 BP.

Smith (1928, 1971) suggested that differences and similarities in material culture are reflections of the dynamic relationships that existed between the people responsible for its production and consumption. However, the current research found it important to look at geographical and regional proximity in terms of connections instead of comparing the upper Nile directly to Egypt without understanding the region in proximity. This is because local and regional networks of interaction were essential and still attract disproportionate interest (Mitchell, 2005). Scholars like Chami (2004a) employed evidence of Graeco-Romans like *Periplus*, *Diogenes,* and *Theophilus* to put across the trade theory as responsible for contacts between the East African coast and the Great Lakes region. Interaction between cultures north and south of the Sahara was attributed to interregional trade, the coming of Islam, and the introduction of camel transport, focusing on connections of the Muslim world and West Africa (Bathily and Meillassoux, 1988:734). Interaction was viewed in terms of the spread of mining and metallurgy, agriculture; crafts; trading techniques and techniques of war. My research examined cultural interactions within the upper Nile catchment by examining the credibility of diffusion, migration and trade theories in view of the importance of ecological adaptability to examine cultural interactions in the Upper Nile catchment areas from 6000-1500 BP.

3.3. Literature Negating Interactions

Despite recognition of similarities between the ceramics and economics of Early Khartoum sites, resistance came in right from the local level from scholars such as Close (1995), Robertshaw *et al* (1983); Robertshaw (1991) due to anti-diffusionist attitudes (Dale, 2007). Therefore contrary to the literature presented in section 3.2, some scholars contest the possibility of ancient interactions in prehistory. For instance, Lane (1963:315) in the discussion of the manners and customs of Egyptians stated that while its manufacturers attracted the admiration of surrounding nations, its inhabitants were in no need of foreign commerce to increase its wealth or their comforts. At the time Egyptian influence seems to have been slight within the African continent, since Egyptians were self-sufficient and had no desire to diffuse their civilization among barbaric neighbors (Cole, 1964).

The theories for the spread of iron technology further highlight the denial of the existence of cultural interaction. For instance an examination of the spread of iron from Meroe showed that the Nile catchment connection with the rest of East Africa did not exist (Trigger, 1969). However, this diffusionist explanation for the spread of iron was rejected by Schmidt (1996, 1997) who instead suggested a West African route or independent invention (Schmidt, 2006). Another level of evidence to negate interaction was through the examination of ceramics. Collet and Robertshaw (1980) suggested that Khartoum Neolithic material showed none of the pottery types, defined based on vessel form and decoration recognized in the Kansyore tradition assemblages from the Lake Victoria basin. This could probably be due to archaeological research not revealing decisive evidence of contact between Egypt and Africa south of Meroe (Zayed, 1981). However, cultures of humankind are not environmental fixations (Chami, 2006). The fact that there is limited evidence negating interaction implies that cultural and economic interaction existed in prehistory.

3.4. Literature on Archaeological Work Done in Uganda

Prior to the 1960's, the staff of the Uganda Geological Survey Department especially under Wayland primarily carried out archaeological research in Uganda (Kiyaga-Mulindwa, 2004). The initial research was basically survey and in the process a lot of archaeological material was recovered and several sites were located. A team led by Wayland in 1919 and in the 1930's carried out the earliest formal research in the country (Posnansky, 1967). Wayland and his colleagues of the Uganda Geological Survey initiated investigations in the Kagera area in the 1920's and between 1930 and 1939 more detailed work including extensive pits, trenches and opening up of paddocks was carried out (Wayland, 1934; O'Brien 1939; Solomon, 1939). The pioneering work in the Nsongezi area was undertaken by Wayland (1934) and Solomon (1939) while the stratigraphy was examined by O'Brien (1939) and Lowe

(1952) who described the typology and the artifact level which was referred to as the M-N horizon. Wayland's work in 1924 reported Stone Age cultures (Kessy 2005:24); established chronology, culture history and explained culture change (Robertshaw 1990). In 1926, Wayland excavated the Still Bay site at Magosi in Karamoja (Wayland, 1934 and Leakey 1936). Wayland also surveyed the Lake Victoria basin and found stone artefacts at Sango Bay in 1920 that he named Sangoan (O'Brien, 1939; McBrearty, 1988). Typical Sangoan artefacts include; core axes, picks and core scrapers that have affinities to the Acheulian and MSA (Mercader, 2002). Other areas researched by Wayland included Napak in 1920, Tanda Pits in 1921, Luzira Hill (Luzira head) in 1930, Entebbe Aerodrome in 1934 and Ntusi in 1954-56. Wayland carried out more excavations in the Nsongezi area from 1953 to 1954 though the results remained unpublished. Bishop and Posnansky (1960) made five trips to the Kagera area from 1956-1959 during which extensive leveling was carried out and the stratigraphy of many of the earlier pits and trenches was recorded.

O'Brien (1939) redefined the Sangoan and re-interpreted the Still Bay Magosian Wilton sequence earlier on done by Wayland. As a result three terminologies for LSA industries in Uganda namely Kageran, Wilton A, and Wilton B were developed (Kessy 2005:31). The Sangoan "Tumbian" was renamed and subdivided by focusing on surface collections recovered from erosion gullies in the Orichinga Valley. However, it was not clear whether all tool types occur in primary association with one another (Nelson, 1973). Lowe (1952) like O'Brien (1939) worked at Nsongezi rock shelter in an effort to outline the Neolithic sequence but eventually focused on the Wilton–Neolithic. This is a microlithic culture best represented in caves and rock shelters such as the Nsongezi shelter (O'Brien, 1939). These employed traditional methods which were based on the classification and description of artefacts (Chami, 1994:19). The cultural materials got by O'Brien (1939) and Lowe (1952) were used to deduce that the more sophisticated pottery in the area was of dimple-based variety. This is associated with the introduction of iron working during the first millennium AD.

Van Riet Lowe (1952) published an appraisal of much of the prehistoric material recovered through the activities of the Uganda Geological Survey department and results of the investigations by O'Brien (1939) during his eighteen month stay in Uganda in the mid 1930s. In 1957, L.P Shinnie excavated at Bigo in a research that threw some light on the historical problems connected with the legends concerning the earthworks. This revealed that the material culture of the builders of the earthworks was locally attributed to Bachwezi but was also attributed to the Portuguese, Abyssinians or Romans. This was not strange as hitherto many African developments were attributed to foreigners using migration and diffusion paradigms to explain cultural change. The conclusion based on the findings however suggested that Africans constructed the earthworks (Shinnie 1960).

In the 1960's Brachi (1960) excavated Hippo Bay Rock Shelter in Entebbe where findings like Later Iron Age (LIA) pottery (Entebbe ware), water jar sherds, polished black ware sherds, lithics, floral and a few iron objects were obtained that showed that the shelter was occupied for a short time (Cole, 1964:327). The same research at Hippo bay identified a single potsherd that was attributed to the Kansyore tradition. More work was done in the 1960s at seven sites, where two were Kansyore Island and Nsongezi while five were connected to Lake Victoria that included Lolui Island, Mwiri, Jinja, Luzira, and Waiya Bay at Entebbe (Posnansky, 1961). These studies cited discrepancies in the report of Chapman (1967). Chapman (1967) conducted archaeological work at Kansyore Island and identified different types of pottery including: Kansyore pottery with six types (variants), dimple-based (Urewe), bourdine and roulette.

Following this study, Chapman suggested that Kansyore pottery had some resemblance with the Khartoum Neolithic pottery but due to the distance involved such a connection could not be concluded. This was probably due to the existence of the Nile that might have been regarded as an impediment to communication yet water bodies were not a cul-de-sac. Fagan and Lofgren (1966) examined archaeological sites on the Nile-Chobi confluence where abundant MSA, LSA and IA material in a geologically stratified sequence were identified but no cultural connections were suggested. In 1961, Nelson and Posnansky (1970) re-excavated the Nsongezi rock shelter to clarify the sequence at the site where O'Brien had described the first dimple-based pottery in Uganda in 1939. This study challenged some of the conclusions of Pearce and Posnansky (1963).

Pearce and Posnansky (1963:93) while excavating at Nsongezi rock shelter, found a piece of Kansyore ware below the dimple-based layer lying over the Late Wilton layer, though the use of the term 'Wilton' was discontinued (Karega-Munene, 2003; Posnansky, 1970). Pearce and Posnansky (1963:93) therefore concluded that the earliest material at Nsongezi was the late Wilton dated 925±150BP, which was recent according to Nelson and Posnansky (1970). The latter further noted that the one fragment of Kansyore overlying dimple-based pottery belonged to the same time within the second millennium (Cole, 1964:247).

Further research was undertaken by Glen H. Cole, in collaboration with the Uganda Museum, who looked at the cultural changes manifested between the Later Acheulian and the Sangoan industries from 1962-1967 (Clark and Howell, 1964: 488-491). Jean Hiernaux and Emma Maquet in 1957 attempted to construct a pottery sequence of Kibiro based on limited excavation. In 1959, Hiernaux excavated a 12-foot mound and discovered wide flat dishes used for evaporation in salt working. Half of the sequence was graphite ware of the Bunyoro type that must have been traded extensively mainly for royal use (Cole, 1964:326).

In 1968, Soper (1971b) excavated the Chobi sector in Murchison falls National Park in a study aimed at establishing whether Urewe was present far north and if it was contemporary with the more recent Iron Age remains. This followed collections made by G. Jackson in 1963, a visit by Dr. Fagan in 1965 and collections of Mrs. Jane Hartley in 1968. These collections were identified by Posnansky (1967:630) as Urewe. Soper's (1971b) work established three pottery types that are; Urewe associated with the Early Iron Age dated 3rd century A.D, Chobi ware contemporary or partly later than Urewe, and roulette-decorated pottery of recent type.

Soper (1971:7) noted that, "while the Early Iron Age never seems to have penetrated the 'East African Neolithic' area to any extent, to the west it does seem to have superseded pre-existing pottery-using people represented by the "Kansyore Ware". To Soper the distribution of this kind of pottery overlaps the Neolithic. According to Kessy (2005:iv) such thinking calls into question earlier assumptions, generally applied to sub-Saharan Africa, that LSA peoples were replaced or absorbed by Iron Age agro-pastoralists. Although it is now possible to identify several traditions in what has been called Kansyore, no scholar has yet accepted the possibility that the people of Kansyore are the same people as those who adopted EIA cultural traditions (Chami, 2006:95). This implied that the chronology and associations of Kansyore ware required further investigations (Phillipson, 1977:81). This would examine views like "the makers of Kansyore ware were hunters and fishermen but it's not clear whether they were agriculturalists or pastoralists" (Sutton, 1968).

Chronological variation within Urewe ware (Posnansky, 1967:630-632) in Nsongezi and Lolui respectively was doubtable (Soper, 1971). Much as, "I am not trying to suggest that there were no chronological differences within Urewe ware, I have doubt if such variation will in due course be found to exist if suitable collections from adjacent sites are available for analysis" (Soper, 1971). Following work done in Uganda from 1987 to 1991, Andrew Reid (1994-95) examined the settlements and social organization of the Urewe society. The results showed that, "the picture of tentative introduction of agriculture, metallurgy and fundamental changes in food exploitation patterns occurring subsequently contrasts with the conventional one of Bantu speakers boldly emerging from the forests, subduing all before them, and immediately instituting a stable farming economy.

Connah (1996) further noted that in the lower Victoria Nile (Chobi), there was frequency of iron in surface collections that to him suggests that iron smelting and forging were important activities in the area and concludes that iron was a trade commodity that underpinned the former state of Bunyoro. This view is an indicator of cultural connections in this area which enriched the current research. Connah (1996), between 1989 and 1994 carried out research in the western rift valley of Uganda and came up with what he termed as a tentative chronological framework along the north-eastern shores of Lake Albert and along the Victoria Nile below the Murchison falls as a follow-up on his work in Kibiro whose pottery showed affinity more with the northeast than the southwest. Connah (1996:533) remarked, that, "nothing was known of the archaeology of the region between Kibiro and Chobi". Connah (1997) tried to establish to what extent the Kibiro pottery sequence could be used as a key to understanding its cultural and chronological context. Connah's work suggested a widespread cultural homogeneity from Lake Albert to the Victoria Nile. Kibiro pottery was viewed as having had more affinity with pottery to the North-East than that to the South-West.

The 1970s till 1980 were years of political turmoil in Uganda hence the limited work done in these years. Reid (2002:89) asserted that, 'our research suggests a long-term and widespread tradition of agriculture throughout the Buganda region extending farming traditions that include the recovery of Urewe'. Despite all the research done however, in the Great Lakes region they were not able to establish a complete sequence covering the last 5000 years (Chami and Kwekason, 2003). This is because past excavations were from disturbed contexts (Chapman, 1967; Soper and Golden, 1969; Noten, 1979; Collett and Robertshaw, 1980; Schmidt, 1997; Reid, 2002 and Kiyaga-Mulindwa, 2004).

Reid (2003) examined the archaeology of Buganda with emphasis on iron smelting and bananas. However, Reid (2005) took a regional approach by focusing on the Great Lakes Region that is Karagwe, Nkore and Buhaya while examining the growth of cattle. Kiyaga-Mulindwa (2006:224) carried out research in the Mutunda/Karuma area in northern Uganda exploiting historical, ethnographic and archaeological data that evaluated the history of the Palwo and their pottery traditions. This Victoria Nile research attempted to further investigate Soper's observations in Chobi that pointed to this area as the border-line between EIA (urewe) and late iron age communities. Kiyaga (2006) noted that further archaeological research might also help to explain the velocity with which the LIA (Roulette) ceramic traditions appear to have swept through the interlacustrine region in the Late Iron Age and in a sense, submerged or absorbed the EIA/Urewe and its related traditions that were most predominant in the region for a millennia before. Reid and Ashley (2007) re-examined the Luzira head while Reid (2002) centred on the Kasubi tombs with emphasis on the role of the local communities and the management of the tombs.

Tibesaasa (2008) carried out excavation aimed at establishing a cultural sequence on Bussi Island in Lake Victoria at Nkuba site and identified Neolithic pottery the Akira ware. This was related to Nakaweesa (2011) whose study at Nyero rock shelter to examine the relationship between LSA and IA resulted in a sequence showing continuous occupation of Nyero from LSA through Neolithic and finally to IA and identified Kansyore pottery in eastern Uganda. Finally, Muwonge (2009) in central Uganda identified the LSA occurrences from open-air sites since hitherto it was taken that in East Africa it was only the rift valley and highlands that were settled by stone-using herders (Phillipson 2005).

3.5 Chapter Summary

The review of the related literature shows that none of the authors came out specifically to address the issue of cultural interactions in the Upper Nile catchment areas. Studies on cultural contacts were restricted to Egyptian contacts with the rest of Sub-Saharan Africa, West Africa and Egypt and south as far as Sudan. The few that identified aspects of cultural connections as far as East Africa mainly employed migration and diffusion theories as the key answers to material correlations in the various areas of study. This shows that the literature highlights the gap that is addressed by the current research. Therefore the question of the nature of contrasts between ceramic using lacustrine and riverine Holocene hunter-gatherers of North and East Africa is dependent on the quality of empirical research and on proposed similarities and dissimilarities that also depend on archaeological sequences and broad comparative studies dependent on comparison of methods/ typology used (Dale, 2007).

A critical analysis of the above literature shows that archaeological work in Uganda had been centered on cultural sequences, culture history, heritage practices and general archaeology of Uganda. Outside Uganda scholars have addressed the issue of contact and link between Egypt and the rest of Africa with emphasis on West Africa, the East African coast and the Sahel while others have examined cultural and economic interactions between Uganda and the Nile Valley. The literature further indicates that there is a knowledge gap in Uganda's prehistory as compared to the rest of the East African countries. Kiyaga-Mulindwa (2006) noted that, while most of the archaeological research in Uganda has been confined to the west of the country and more recently in the central districts, it is only Soper's (1971b) and Connah's (1966) work which monumentally stood in the area to the north and north west, through which the river Nile winds its way out of Uganda to Sudan and beyond. It is evident that rigorous work was done from the colonial period to the early years of independence (1960's). But research at this time was largely descriptive championed by the Uganda Geological survey Department then headed by Wayland. They tended to describe phases and areas of cultural change that is; this culture followed another culture by employing the traditional approach (Johnson, 2010). This meant that they did not venture into why there were changes. Wayland focused on establishing pluvial sequences than the reconstruction and analysis of cultural material. In the 1960's emphasis was also laid on rock shelters and caves and little or no attempt was made to study open-air sites. Some of the above literature was marked by an outright prejudice against sub-Saharan Africa as distinct from the north. Limited attention was paid to North-South relations and where it was done, it was viewed as unidirectional. Thereafter to date there is still a gap concerning cultural and economic interactions. The current study therefore contributed towards the existing body of literature through examining the nature of interactions in the Upper Nile catchment areas from 6000 -1500 BP.

Section 2
FIELD WORK & FINDINGS

CHAPTER FOUR

RESEARCH METHODOLOGY

4.1. Introduction

This chapter presents the strategies employed in the course of archaeological field research in the Upper Nile catchment areas. The current study employed diverse methods as presented in this chapter to tackle the research problem. These included consultation of ancient historical records, documented and oral sources, archaeological survey and excavation. The objective of undertaking this investigation was addressed in Chapter One.

4.2. Research Design

This study used a deliberate cluster sampling strategy which entailed purposefully choosing a representative sample of sites along the Nile banks or those in the riverine areas linked to the Nile. In this respect, Kikubamitwe close to the source of the Nile where the Nile starts its journey and Chobe along the Victoria Nile where the Nile winds up its course from Uganda were chosen. On the other hand, Nsongezi and the Island of Deserters along the banks of River Kagera and Kansyore in River Kagera also formed a cluster. This is because the Kagera is the longest river flowing into Lake Victoria which is considered as the source of the Nile. It should be noted that though Lake Victoria is mainly considered as the source of the Nile, the Nile can be traced further to the headwaters of the Kagera. The research design therefore determined the way the collection, measurement and analysis of data was undertaken as recommended by (Kothari, 2004: 31).

These are the decisions concerning the what, where, when, how much and by what means the research was undertaken that are part of the research design. In order to examine the nature of cultural and economic interactions in the Upper Nile catchment areas the research used both qualitative and quantitative approaches yet at the same time collecting both primary and secondary data. Data was primarily obtained from archaeological surveys and excavations, while secondary data was obtained from oral and documentary sources. This entailed observing cultural materials collected from a stratified context as a primary tool.

4.3. Sampling Procedures

The study employed a multi-stage sampling procedure. This was because it assures geographical representation of the whole site, helps to minimize costs and the problems of selective bias while it increases sampling efficiency. The Upper Nile catchment area constituted the population Universe. The population universe was stratified by ecological zones basing on geographical location and each zone was divided into clusters. That is the low-lying zone at the source of the Nile (Kikubamitwe), the riverine zone where the Nile heads out of the country (Chobe), the Island zone (Kansyore Island) in the Kagera River and the fourth was along the headwaters of the Nile, the Kagera River, which was partly a riverine and mountainous zone (Island of Deserters).

Each stratum had an average of eight sites forming clusters out of which one was sampled using a purposive deliberate sampling procedure and that became the excavation universe that was further subdivided into elements that were the trenches and Shovel Test Pits (STPs). Only three ecological zones were excavated that were at Kansyore Island, Nsongezi and the Island of Deserters. In this case, each cluster constituted a group of elements like artefacts, features and ecofacts.

4.4. Sample Size

The units of excavation were selected using deliberate sampling based on the occurrence of archaeological materials. The sample size was composed of the assemblage of the four clusters. This study relied on archaeological materials that were recovered from surveys and excavations and written and oral data from texts and interviews respectively. The sample size was intentionally selected in line with the research objectives. Since the study aimed at examining the economic and cultural interactions in the Upper Nile catchment all subsurface materials such as ceramics, lithics, faunal remains, metallurgical remains, house daubs and red ochre were collected and documented. Surface collections were also administered in the same manner as the subsurface cultural materials; though efforts were made to eliminate un-diagnostic artefacts, a few were still collected. All cultural materials recovered from surveys and excavations were subjected to detailed analysis. Following the analysis a decision was taken to use only the data from Nsongezi, Kansyore Island and the Island of Deserters for the discussion and conclusions made since the data from Kikubamitwe and Chobe was not adequately answering the research problem.

4.5. Pre-Field Preparations

The initial stage involved acquisition of an introductory letter from the University of Dar es Salaam Research Office. Following that, permission was secured from the Uganda Museum that gave the researcher leeway to secure a research permit from the Uganda National Council for Science and Technology (UNCST) and the Uganda Wildlife Authority (UWA). The UWA permission was a pre-requisite for working in Murchison Falls National Park where Chobe is situated and permission was granted. The UNCST gave the researcher a research permit and introductory letters for the Resident District Commissioners (RDCs) for the different districts where the research was to be undertaken. The letters to the RDC's were used by the researcher to secure permission from the local council leaders in the areas of study and finally permission was secured from the respective land-owners who owned the land where the study sites were located especially owners of land where test trenches and trenches were established. The research was undertaken and thereafter permission sought from the Uganda Museum for the transfer of materials from Uganda to Dar es Salaam that were loaned to the researcher for two years and during the loan period they were housed at the African Archaeology Network (AAN) laboratory in Mbezi (Dar es Salaam).

4.6. Field Data Collection Methods

The study collected data in two major phases. The first phase was the desk or literature review. Literature review was conducted at the libraries in Dar es Salaam and Uganda and this was the principal source of data on the northern part of the Upper Nile catchment (Sudan). Literature was gathered from textbooks, articles in journals, ancient historical records and all forms of written documents. The second phase of data collection was archaeological survey and excavation and this was restricted to the southern part of the Upper Nile catchment areas (Uganda) due to the limitation of funds. The study also utilized oral sources especially interviews and participant observation for the interpretation of material recovered from survey, excavation and features encountered.

4.7. Archaeological Survey

Survey was intended to locate, identify and record the distribution of archaeological materials and determine where data would be collected. This was undertaken in two phases that were reconnaissance survey and intensive survey. The former entailed only surface collection while the later entailed surface collection and establishment of STPs. Reconnaissance survey was undertaken at Entebbe rock shelter, Chobe sector, Nsongezi area and Kikubamitwe. Following reconnaissance survey no further research was undertaken at Entebbe rock shelter since the study had more interest in the Nile catchment areas but not those just close to Lake Victoria as Entebbe rock shelter. The aim of reconnaissance survey was to locate sites that lie within the Upper Nile catchment and to establish the possibilities for further excavation and intensive survey. The latter was carried out in Chobe, Kikubamitwe, Nsongezi, and on Kansyore Island. At all the sites surface collections were carried out. In addition to that, STPs were excavated that varied in number from site to site. For instance, Chobe had two STPs; Kikubamitwe with three STPs whereby Cluster 1 had two while Cluster 2 had one STP; Nsongezi had one STP while Kansyore Island also had one STP. All STPs were $1 \times 1m^2$ in size.

At Kansyore Island, survey concentrated on the areas outside the three-in-one structure (former hotel foundation) and areas close to the riverbanks. The house foundation at the site was reported by Chapman (1967) to be for a former hotel and a house of Mrs. Nuti that was confirmed by the oral information gathered by this research as well. Survey in Chobe started at Chobe Lodge and the airfield which were littered with potsherds and lithics. Survey concentrated on the eroded side of the airfield following erosion gullies, animal tracks, park roads and poacher's routes. This was because the thick vegetation, forest cover and wild animals limited systematic survey in addition to the objectives of the study. Surveying Chobe area entailed visiting the actual Murchison Falls site where crossing from Paraa to Murchison Falls necessitated use of a ferry.

In Kikubamitwe the survey exercise was entirely unsystematic following footpaths and erosion gulleys in this area. The survey was conducted in Kikubamitwe and the neighbouring villages such as; Bujagali, Nankwanga, Malindi, Kasambya and Kalagala. Undertaking survey in the neighbouring villages was meant to examine if there were cultural material correlations that could aid in tracing cultural interaction at the local level. The sites identified in Kikubamitwe were mainly Iron Age sites.

Survey was unsystematic because of the need to acquire data that would ably address the research question without the restrictions posed by systematic survey and also due to the need to properly address the research objectives. Areas with clear visibility were surveyed using foot walks where walkers moved a distance of 50 metres from each other (Plate 4.1). In each area, the walker recorded all artefacts but collected only the movable diagnostic artefacts they came across, recorded, bagged and kept them for further analysis. The unmovable artefacts like the mortar stone at Kansyore (Plate 5.1 chapter 5) were photographed and recorded. Surface collection also involved counting and recording artefacts in each walker's area. The diagnostic artefacts for the case of pottery were all vessel parts that were decorated and undecorated rims, bases, necks and shoulders. Survey in areas without clear visibility followed footpaths and erosion gullies as was the case in Chobe, Nsongezi, and Kikubamitwe.

The second phase of survey entailed intensive pedestrian walks carrying out surface collections and STPs. Surveyors in both categories of survey recorded densities of material artefacts, presence of archaeological sites, and detailed physiographic and environmental data on standardized survey forms for each site. Archaeological sites within each survey unit were photographed, and documented by completion of comprehensive archaeological site survey forms. The recording of longitude/latitude coordinates was done using a global positioning system (GPS) device. Other survey equipment included digital cameras, trowels, notebooks, pens, pencils, plastic bags, a sieve, shovels, and a machete. Site boundaries and features were defined and mapped, and each recorded site was assessed for its potential for archaeological excavation, threats from developers and potential for future preservation.

Plate 4.1: Survey and Surface Collection at Kansyore Island

4.6.2 Mapping

Topographic and contour mapping of the four major study clusters documented during survey was done. Mapping of all sites was done at the site while plotting the maps took place at the camps. The datum points were set at relatively elevated areas to allow clear visibility of all the features to be mapped. For example mapping of Kansyore Island was done by setting up two datum points, one at the upper terrace and the other at the lower terrace, each high enough to map all places close to the landing site. The second datum point was obtained by extending the eastward line using a line level and a tape measure. The purpose of this was to ensure that areas in the lower terrace are also included on the map where Trench 2 and 3 were positioned. The Island of Deserters was also mapped using two datum points (Figure 4.3). In the process of mapping, two topographic maps were generated for Kansyore Island and the Island of Deserters (Figures 4.2 and 4.3).

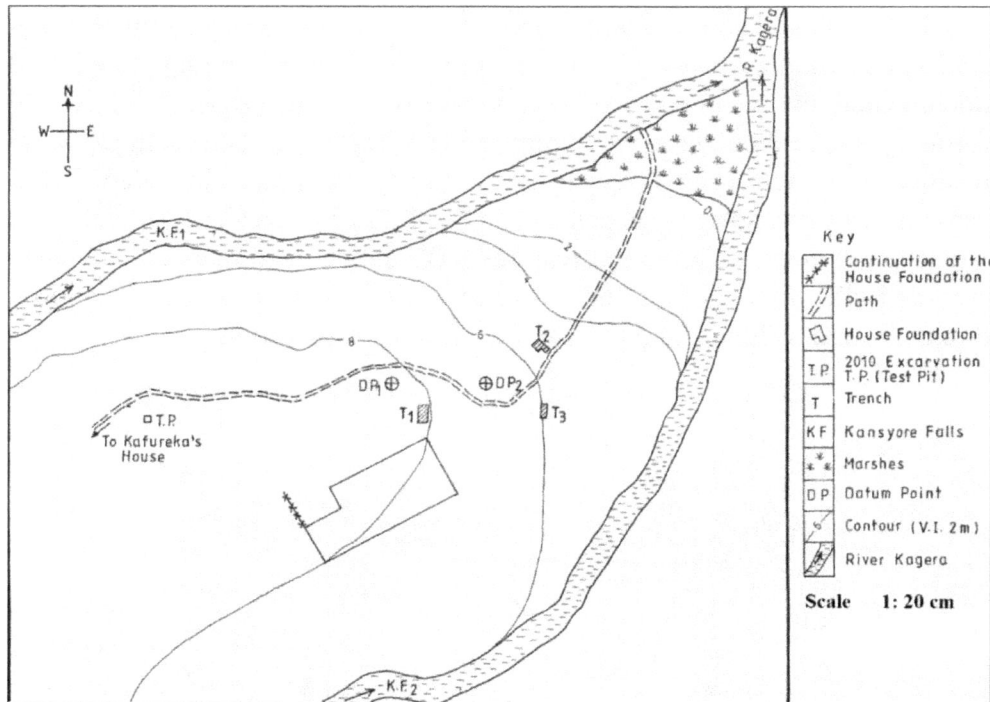

Figure 4.2: Kansyore Island Site Map

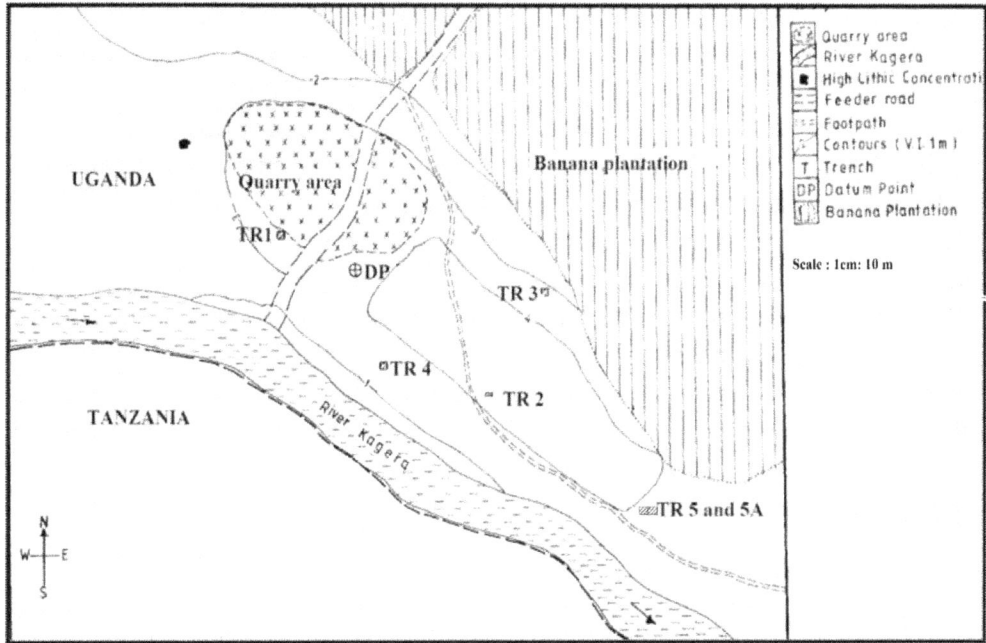

Figure 4.3: The Island of Deserters Site Map

Dating Techniques

The study used both relative and absolute dating methods to reconstruct the history of the Upper Nile catchment areas. Since relative chronology is considered the foundation of archaeological research, observation of the stratigraphy or placing artefacts in chronological order was undertaken as suggested by Fagan and Decorse (2005: 188) and Kwekason (2010:208). Absolute chronology was also used in this work to determine the exact age of the artifacts obtained on seven samples. These were sent to Uppsala (Sweden) and Waikato (New Zealand). The first batch sent to Uppsala had four charcoal samples with Kikubamitwe and Chobe having two samples each.

Sample 1 from Chobe Trench 1 at 80-90 cm below surface dated microliths associated with pottery that had zigzag decorative elements above and below the layer. Sample 2 from Chobe Trench 1 was obtained at 70-75 cm targeting zigzag pottery. Sample 3 was obtained from Kikubamitwe Trench 1 Cluster 1 at a depth of 70-80 cm aimed at dating roulette. Sample 4 was at a depth of 40-50 cm in the same trench as Sample 3 and aimed at dating pottery with channel (grooves) decorative elements.

The second batch of datable materials was taken from Kansyore Island comprising of three samples taken to the University of Waikato Laboratory in New Zealand. In this batch Sample 1 was from Trench 2Ai at a depth of 60-65 cm below surface. This was a bone sample meant to date pottery with cross-hatching that had flat/squared rims. Unfortunately the sample was abandoned in the Waikato laboratory because the Carbon 13 stable isotope value (delta 13C) measured on prepared graphite using the AMS spectrometer, the radio date 13C was corrected to isotopic fractionation but the AMS measured delta 13C value can differ from the delta 13C of the original material, was not shown and the sample was abandoned. The second sample from Kansyore Island was also a bone from Kansyore Island Trench 2B at 50-55 cm. The intention was to date wavy line pottery. The third sample was a herbivore tooth from Trench 2Ai at 65-70 cm for dating roulette pottery that was in association with lithics.

4.6.3 Shovel Test Pit Excavations

'Shovel test pit' (STP) excavations were undertaken at the major survey clusters of Chobe, Kikubamitwe, Nsongezi, and Kansyore Island. The STPs were all 1× 1m² in size and were excavated using arbitrary 10 cm spit levels and materials sieved through a 5 mm wire mesh. In Chobe, two STPs were established, Kikubamitwe had three of which two STPs were in Cluster 1 and one in Cluster 2, Nsongezi area encompassing Kansyore Island had two STPs one each at the Nsongezi landing site and Kansyore Island (Chapter 5). All in all the aim of the STPs was to crosscheck if the material evidence on the surface was replicated in the subsurface, to examine the stratigraphy and material concentration of the surveyed areas and to determine the areas which were viable for eventual excavation.

4.6.4 Intensive Excavation

Having surveyed the sites in the upper Nile catchment areas of Uganda the research embarked on excavation. Twelve major trenches were established where some had extensions while others were divided. Bigger trenches were preferred due to the shallow stratigraphy and limited cultural material concentration in some areas; therefore, size was thought to compensate for the depth. In Chobe, two trenches were established at the Chobe airstrip while in Kikubamitwe two trenches were established with one in each cluster (Kikubamitwe had two clusters). At Kansyore Island three trenches were sunk yet the Island of Deserters had five trenches. The trench sizes ranged from 1× 2m² to 2× 4m². The excavated materials were sieved in a 5 mm wire-mesh.

In Chobe where the clay soils were compacted by animal trampling, water was poured before proceeding with excavation. Since in the Kikubamitwe Test Pit 3 the soil in the lower levels was water logged clay, both wet and dry sieving were utilised. To record artefact distribution among others for each excavation level excavation forms were filled. At the bottom of each excavation level photographs were taken while wall profiles were recorded basing on soil colour and arbitrary levels. Initial bagging and labelling of all the recovered cultural materials was done at the sites. Then cleaning and re-bagging was done at the camps and back filling of the excavated trenches was done at the end of the excavation of each trench. Excavation was conducted in areas which had a high concentration of archaeological surface signatures. This was done systematically using arbitrary 5 cm or 10 cm spit levels. The purpose of employing these criteria was due to the need to have a better control of material recovery, monitor the sequence, and be able to use the archaeological materials to examine intra-site cultural and economic interactions in the upper Nile catchment areas.

4.6.5 Ethnographic Inquiries

Ethnographic inquiries were specifically carried out for the analysis of excavated materials or for seeking explanations of the encountered structures and features. This was because the areas where the research was undertaken were known and so did not necessitate oral data to locate them. Oral inquiries entailed oral interviews and participant observation. The oral interviews were executed by exploiting the snowball method where key informants with whom contact had been established were used to lead the researcher to other informants. Therefore in Chobe the game rangers were used to refer the researcher to knowledgeable informants. In this case, Mr. Guma Scot who was then the community conservation ranger at Murchison Falls National Park in charge of liaising with the community around the park played a key role. In the Kansyore-Nsongezi area the defense secretary and Mr. Peter Byaruhanga and his father were used to identify informants who could avail the researcher with information concerning the house foundation at Kansyore Island.

These directed the researcher to a former worker at Kansyore Island who was interviewed. Interviews in this area also focused at the pyramidal structure on top of the hill adjacent to the Nsongezi rock shelter. Interviews were also carried out with the elders to seek ideas about how the Nile and the Kagera rivers have been utilized to interact in the respective areas of study. Lastly, interviews entailed establishing the decorative instruments and the persistent coil breakage of pottery obtained. With the purpose of examining how the theory of migration emerged from different accounts and the political and social context of the information, interviews were held in the Chobe areas. The first question addressed the meaning of Chobe followed by one that concerned the peopling of the area. The question of the interaction in the Nile catchment was another area investigated through ethnographic inquiries in the Chobe area. The study employed discourse analysis of oral data.

Participant observation was also utilized by observing the pottery making process at the home of Ms. Elema Grace (Plate 4.6). In Plate 4.6 the pot maker who acquired the skill from her parents just like her sisters and brothers demonstrates pot making. Plate 4.6a, is a stage of making coils while in 4.6b coils are joined starting with the base of the pot. Plate 4.6c is smoothing the coils using a piece of plastic from a plastic jerrycan. This is followed by decoration as shown in Plate 4.6d using a twisted string while in Plate 4.6e and is a complete pot the arrow points to. The end product is a short necked pot with a twisted string roulette decoration below the neck.

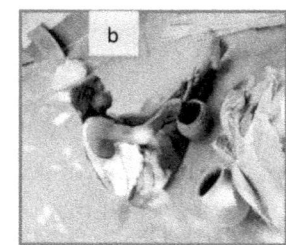
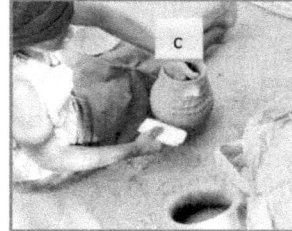
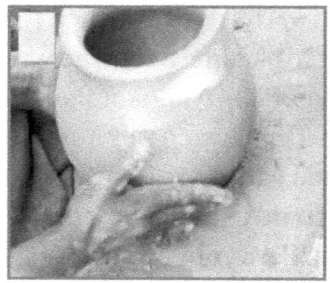

Plate 4.6: Participant Observation with a Pot maker

(a) Making the coil (b) coil building to form a pot (c) smoothing the surface to bind the coils (d) roulette decoration (e) plastic twisted cord instrument for rouletting and (f) the finished pot

4.6.6 Examination of Ancient Historical Records

In an attempt to examine if the Nile was an end to interaction or not, historical records were examined. Historical connections can be traced since Herodotus who came to Egypt in 457 B.C. and used rectangular maps that showed the end of Africa where the location of the Sahara is. The fact that Africa was assumed to end at the southern tip of the Sahara suggests that they had no concept of Africa from about Ethiopia southwards. Despite that there are a number of indicators from the ancient historical records that prehistoric interactions existed in Africa and especially in the Nile valley.

Some historical records like the literature reviewed earlier on also emphasized Egyptian links with several parts of Africa as far as East Africa. The World Encyclopaedia (1978:92) mentioned Egypt at the height of its power influencing the Nile valley as far as the 4th cataract in Nubia, parts of ancient Ethiopia as far north-east as the Euphrates River in Western Asia in 1450 BC. In addition, as early as 1900 BC the Egyptians are said to have dug a canal to link the eastern part of the Nile Delta with the Red Sea and being the first to use the dangerous route as far as the Cape of Good Hope not mentioning the several expeditions to Nubia and attempts to locate the source of the Nile.

Historical connections between the north and the south existed with the land of Punt and with Queen Hatshepsut in about 1460 BC (Davidson, 1959). Herodotus mentions 400 years before Julius that a team of English adventurers vowed to cross the Sahara from North to South despite Davidson suggesting that it was a barrier at that time. However, the contact with the people of the south and south-west of the Nile valley was frequent though not continuous (Davidson, 1959:41). Egypt carried out expeditions of conquest to the south. There was also contact with the people of Libya (Fezzan) as evidenced from the rock paintings and pictures of Nile boats that echo an Egyptian model in the Tassili Mountains that is west of the Nile valley. The contacts with the west unlike those with the south reveal conquests and not settlements. In the same rock pictures of horses, two-wheeled chariots exist across the desert from Fezzan in the north to a hill in the south-west leading down to Niger with a flying gallop pictured in ancient Crete around 1200 BC (Davidson, 1959).

There is evidence to suggest that Egyptian expeditions went far south up the Nile and along the southern coasts of the Red Sea. This is identified from traders and soldiers who are said to have reached the land of Punt, the land of

Kush-Ethiopian, Somaliland, and the Sudan (Davidson, 1959: 43). Perhaps they went further up to the shores of Lake Chad and the forests of Congo and the uplands of Uganda. Though no signs of this contact were left the transmitters of the Egyptian civilization were Ethiopians (blacks) (Diop, 1981). Userkaf founder of the 5th dynasty inscribed his conquering name on the rocks of the 1st cataract at Assuan 400m south of the delta. Sahure who followed him sent a fleet of ships down to the land of Punt and made the first direct record of communication with the distant lands although the son of Cheops had already owned a Puntite slave. Another 5th expedition was commanded by Burded, "treasurer(?)" of the pharaoh, and among other things he came back with a dwarf probably the ancestor of the pygmies of central Africa. Pharaohs of the 6th dynasty (c.2423-2242 BC) like Pepi I controlled Nubia where Nubians were incorporated in the army to work in the north. The reliefs on the rocks of the 1st Cataract show the last king of the 6th dynasty Mernere leaning on his staff while Nubians bow down in homage. Harkhuf was the lord of the 1st Cataract who reached the Upper Nile or even Darfur and took a dwarf to Egypt and the pharaoh's letter of thanks for the dwarf is preserved almost intact on the face of the tomb that Harkhuf had prepared for himself that was later completed in the old Kingdom. Traffic with Punt increased in the reign of Amenemhat II or the 20th dynasty and continued under Sesostris II to Wadi Halfa. As Davidson (1959:45-46) noted there was no reason why Egypt should not have pushed its power much further south.

The Hyksos invasion of 1700 BC was a temporary setback but the 3rd Pharaoh Tutmosis extended the influence to Dongola that is evidenced from his inscriptions at Tumbus near the northern end of the Dongola reach. His influence went as far as Kurgus that was less than 400m from Khartoum or less than 300m from Meroe. This was followed by dramatic inscriptions that dealt with the Egyptian prowess to the south as the story of Queen Hatshepsut's expedition to the land of Punt where they were greeted by the chief of Punt Perehu and his wife who were remarkable for their dark skin. Trading with Punt and the power over Kush continued until Rameses II (c. 1292-1225 BC) who was the strongest of all the 19th century pharaohs. With the civilization of Kush-Napata and Meroe, contacts were established further south and west related with the drying up of the Sahara.

The period of Egyptian decadence starting in 950 BC saw three civilizations that influenced Africa south of the Sahara and these were the land of Kush, Carthage and the southern tip of Arabia. However, the available evidence suggests that contact was via the sea though it is also possible that there were land routes. Kashata, the 1st "great king" of Kush, embarked on the conquest of Egypt itself which his son Piankhy completed in about 725 BC ruling from the Mediterranean to the borders of modern Ethiopia and for all we know of Uganda too (Davidson, 1959: 55). This brief historical contact dwells much on evidence of contact between Egypt and as far south as Uganda which suggests that the water bodies were not barriers to interaction. This therefore required beefing up the historical evidence with archaeological evidence making the current research paramount.

Another level of evidence deduced from the ancient records concerned the 'Island of Deserters'. Cary and Warmington, (1963) suggested the existence of an island and actually *Periplus* and *Ptolemy's Geographia* mentioned only one Island though the map given by Lacroix (1998) suggested several Islands (Chami, 2006). It was through this Island that ships bound for Egypt passed to trade with Punt. The report of Iambulus revolves around one Island (Chami, 2006:151). The acknowledgement of other Islands in the same waters basing on modern experience, to Chami, (2006:152) the island was probably Zanzibar as the modern tendency has been to refer to it as an island despite the fact that it contains several islands, therefore Punt was located in East Africa. However, since this was the time of the spread of the Khartoum/Kansyore pottery traditions, the only area south of Egypt with large lakes is the area around the Great Lakes and the rift valley and this is possibly where the Island of Deserters was located that encompassed Uganda's Nile catchment hence the term Island of Deserters used in this text.

From Herodotus' map of the world, the island of Egyptian deserters was an area where Egyptian soldiers were left behind in an expedition (Chami, 2006). This was beyond Meroe and where the Nile begins in East Africa. The deserting followed the Persian conquest of Egypt under Cambyses II in 525 B.C who was not content with Egypt alone and sent his troops to other parts of Africa to conquer all lands linked to Egypt and sent the troops to the land of the long-lived Ethiopians that was Nubia / Upper Nile (Cary and Warmington, 1963:206). Cambyses II then took counsel and planned three expeditions; the third was against the long-lived Ethiopians who dwelt in that part of Libya which borders the Southern Sea (Rawlinson, 1964: 218). Since Nubia does not border any Southern Sea then this was the Indian Ocean (according to Herodotus) or *Oceanus* (according to Hecataeus) which was known as the

Southern Sea (Chami, 2006:154-5), this showed as indicated on Herodotus's map (Figure 4.5) that the Island of Deserters was where the Nile begins.

Writers such as Eratosthenes, Strabo, and Pliny tried to correct some of the earlier distortions carried forward at the times of Herodotus though they also made some distortions as well. However, what is clear from all this is the fact that Punt and Herodotus' land of long-lived Ethiopians were in eastern and southern Africa, as shown in his interpretation of the Egyptian records that the Nile originated from the Mountains of the Moon, and the last record mentioning Punt is 715-664 BC (Kitchen, 1993:602). Egyptian records suggest that the Nile floods were caused by rainfall upon the mountain of Punt, and this was in the general area where the Egyptian deserters were located in the mountains reported to be snow-capped. It is only East Africa that has snow-capped mountains like Kilimanjaro, Ruwenzori, and Kenya. According to Johnson (1903), since the snow-capped mountains were also referred to as ranges, this implied that these were the Ruwenzori Mountains since they are the only ranges that are snow-capped.

The whole record concerning the deserters can be linked with the thinking that the source of the Nile hails from the west. The deserters are shown to have stayed at a place where the river turns or emerges from the west (Figure 4.5). This means that at this point in time there was awareness that the Nile had its source from the west. In the course of the Nile, there is nowhere the River turns west apart from the side of Kagera that is considered as a source of the Nile emerging from the west. It is on this basis that the Island near the Kagera River is referred to as the Island of Deserters in this text.

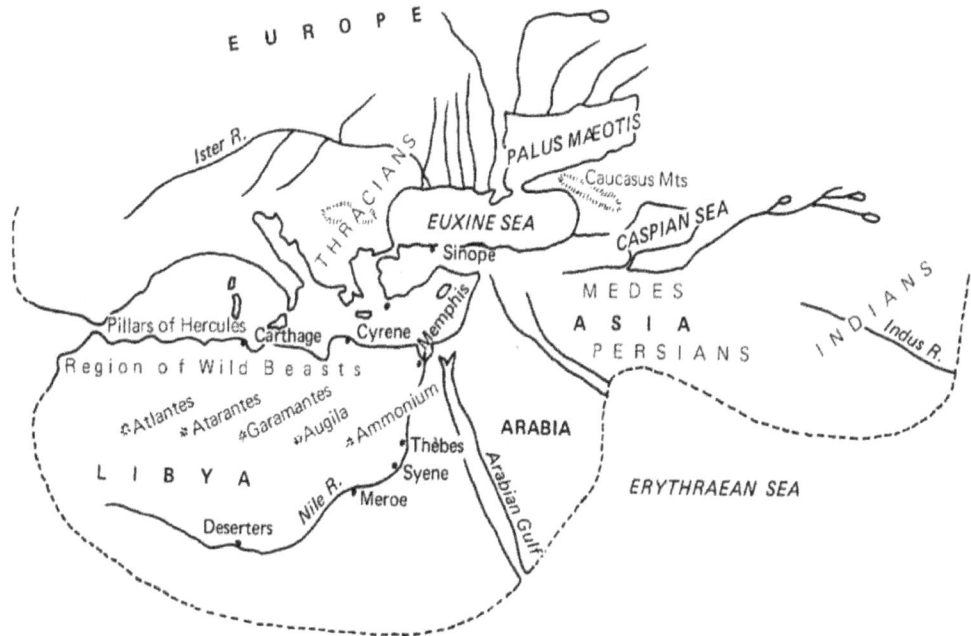

Figure 4.5: The Ancient World According to Herodotus

Adapted from Chami (2006: 156)

Strabo's (63 BC-AD 21) writings after the middle of the 1st century BC suggested that before Roman rule it was not safe to travel and trade abroad (Chami, 2006:166). Strabo gave a detailed account of the interior of East Africa that lay on the equator. Strabo's other contribution can be seen in examining the importance of red ochre. He mentions people in the far south of Meroe who smeared themselves with red ochre and others feeding on locusts. Some of these traditions have continued where archaeological evidence suggests the use of red ochre for many purposes including burial and painting as it is shown for Olduvai Neolithic sites (Leakey and Leakey, 1950; Chaplin, 1974). Besides people in the southern Upper Nile catchment area, still take the *ensenene* (grasshoppers) as a delicacy probably reported as locusts.

The Nile was not a *cul de sac* due to the existence of an overland route to the Land of Punt (Somaliland) (Johnson, 1903). This was either through Abyssinia or to the west where unclosed traffic always existed. That at the end of the Pleistocene or beginning of the Quaternary Epoch there was a land connection over the south as well as over the north end of the Red Sea joining Arabia to Ethiopia, Egypt and the area then represented by the Congo pygmies and the South African bushmen (Johnson, 1903). The significance of these historical connections is that they show that there was interaction and communication in the Nile catchment areas.

Nero (AD 37-68) in the Roman times sent an expedition to explore the Nile valley at the time of writing of the Pliny and *Periplus* accounts. The target was the Great Lakes region and specifically the source of the Nile. It is suggested that the King of Meroe who had been in contact with the Great Lakes region wrote a letter of introduction for the Roman explorers (Chami, 2006:181-182). Though it is noted that the Roman explorers were led to a mysterious source of the Nile to discourage them from going on with the expedition this is evidence of contact in the Nile valley. The letter introducing them to the Great Lakes people implied that there was some mutual relationship that existed to the extent that such a kind of recommendation would be welcome.

In the course of the movements, definitely even cultures might have diffused from one area to another. This therefore backs up the evidence from the material cultures to explain the similarities depicted which were also acquired through such expeditions. However since most of the material cultures obtained were relatively older than the times of the expedition this gives room to other possible causes of interaction like adapting to a similar environment and possibly trade. It could also have been economic strain rather than normal distance decay fall-off that explains the frequency of similar traits (Hodder, 1979).

Cultural interaction from ancient historical records can still be traced from the history of mapping the source of the Nile. The mapping of the Nile suggested that man had been thinking about the source of the Nile for almost two and half millennia before Speke made his 'discovery' (Langlands, 1962). The genesis was the explanation for the Nile floods that gave a clue to earlier contacts in the ancient records. Thales in the 6th century, like St. Isidore in the 7th century, attempted a scientific explanation that attributed the floods to annual formation of sandbanks off the mouth of the Nile by the blowing of the Etesian winds and the consequent damming of the river. This was later disproved by other Greek thinkers like Oenipides, Diogenes of Apollonia, and Ephorus who instead suggested that the Nile had underground stretches that generated the floods. The importance, without dwelling so much on the history of searching for the source of the Nile, shows that the explanation of the floods was in terms of events taking place in the south. This was especially expressed in the mid-fifth century B.C that the Nile originated from the snows of mountains, as advanced by Anaxagoras, who initially regarded them as the Ethiopian mountains. Greek and Roman thinkers followed this as did writers like Strabo, Pliny, and Sir George Bacon.

Though doubted by Herodotus on the basis that how snow could occur in latitudes in which the sun was strong enough to blacken the people? The snow source near the equator was later to be proved close to the source of the Nile.

The importance of this early thinking about the cause of the floods was in as much as the thinking was directing the cause of the Nile floods to the south. This implied that there was conceptualisation of the relationship and interaction in the Nile catchment areas.

Lastly, inquiry into the cause of the floods generated interest in the actual source of the Nile. The fact that the causes of the floods were associated with the twin lakes and mountains, the search for the source too was associated with the south (Langlands, 1962:2). Despite earlier mythical thinking about the cause of the floods such as being the tears of the goddess Isis for her husband, in the 6th century BC the search for the origin of the river began under Hecateus who believed that the Nile made a circumfluent stream of the ocean through southern Libya. Like accounts of Juba and Pliny that talk of a disappearing western Nile, Mela in about 42 AD suggested a disappearing southern Nile and showed that, the Nile emerged from a southern Sea. This theory still maintained a surrounding ocean and incorporated a new line of thinking that the river was blocked by a desert to move further south claiming the source to be in Ethiopia just like Ptolemy. This means they were only referring to the Blue Nile. Another view that regarded the Nile to hail from India was propounded by people like Alexander the Great.

On the other hand were those who attributed the Nile to connections with the Mediterranean Sea and the Red Sea as per Behaim's globe of 1492. Though common for the medieval Christian writers to place the source of the Nile near the Red Sea for the Moslem geographers it was near the East African coast/ Indian Ocean. Beginning with Al Massoudy in the 10th century who claimed that the river derived from the mountains of Zenj and flowed through the Negro land (Sudan) with a branch flowing to the black man's sea (Indian

Ocean). Abdul Fida in the 14th century stated that the Nile rose from the Comr Mountains which word has been equated by Crawford (1949:8) as Arabic *Kamar* or moon hence later interpreted by Ptolomey as the Mountains of the Moon. The significance of the view that the Nile comes from the East African coast is still important as it shows the southern connection and contacts with the north (Langlands, 1962).

Another prominent view that dominated the 5th and 9th centuries (Roman and early Christian times) was that the Nile emanated from the west, where it was mistaken with the Niger. Later on the idea of a dual source - the south and west - was adopted in the 19th century but this was still reduced to only the south source in about 350 AD, a thinking pioneered by Aristotle and eventually in 1859 the mystery of the source of the Nile was resolved by John Speke (Langlands, 1962).

4.6.7 Data Processing and Analysis Procedure

Preliminary analysis of cultural materials was done in the field. This involved washing, sorting and cataloguing according to material type. Further analysis that involved secondary sorting was carried out at the Uganda Museum and Kyambogo University History department. Detailed analysis was undertaken at the African Archaeology Network laboratory in Mbezi and the Archaeology Unit laboratory at the University of Dar es salaam. This entailed morphological analysis of the artefacts. Data analysis was both quantitative and qualitative.

Quantitative analysis entailed statistical analysis using codes and tables and these were interpreted by employing the qualitative data generated from ethnographic inquiries. Data for each individual artifact analyzed was first recorded in a book and then later transferred to a spreadsheet using the Microsoft excel program using a laptop computer. Pottery decoration elements, placements, techniques and temper, surface finishing, rim profiles and vessel shapes were analyzed using a scheme generated by this study (Appendix). Lithic typology, raw materials and metric attributes were analyzed based on Mehlman (1989) and Nelson (1973)'s typological schemes with limited reference to Kessy (2005) and Masao (1979a) analysis procedures. All faunal remains were given to experts that were Professor Bukenya from the Makerere University Veterinary Department; Mr. Mambusho and Ms. Upendo Ulaya M.A Archaeology (Osteology), both graduates from Gotland University of Sweden, and Dr. T. Biginagwa and Dr. Charles Sanane (Archaeology Unit,

University of Dar es salaam) analyzed the bones; while the shells were analyzed by Ms. Sarah Musaalizi (Paleontologist) from the Uganda Museum. The metallurgical remains (metal objects and iron slag) were analysed using a scheme that followed Mapunda's scheme.

CHAPTER FIVE

FIELD WORK RESULTS

5.1. Introduction

This chapter presents results of raw data from the three phases of fieldwork. These are archaeological survey, archaeological excavation and ethnographic inquiries. The data from survey is from both surface collections and STPs while data from excavation is from trench excavations. Data presented from ethnographic inquiries was generated using oral interviews that followed survey and excavations. All these forms of data presented were from the sites of Nsongezi, Kansyore Island and Island of the Deserters. As stated earlier the data from Chobe and Kikubamitwe is excluded because it did not contribute towards answering the research problem, but it will be considered for future publications.

5.2. Survey Finds

Survey finds as noted included finds from surface collection (Table 5.1) and from the STPs. The finds presented in Table 5.1 are finds from surface collections that were subjected to analysis. The plain ware presented in Table 5.1 was not an independent tradition like that from the East African coast but it refers to the plain diagnostic potsherds that were analysed.

Artefacts		Sites			Total	% age
		Nsongezi	Island of Deserters	Kansyore Island		
Pottery	Roulette	41	35	87	163	18.3
	Urewe		51	212	263	29.5
	Boudine	7	1	17	25	2.8
	Kansyore	7	5	49	61	6.8
	Channel			40	40	4.5
	Plain		13	31	44	4.9

Lithics	Geometrics	3	3	1	7	0.8
	Other tools	4	1	1	6	0.7
	Scrapers	16	5	5	26	2.9
	Cores	57	14	9	80	9.0
	Non-flaked		2	1	3	0.3
	Flake/blades	71	30	25	126	14.1
Faunal remains	Shells		13	27	40	4.5
	Bones	2		2	4	0.4
Metallurgical objects	Metal objects			1	1	0.1
	Tuyere		1		1	0.1
Other artefacts	Smoking pipe			1	1	0.1
	Clay mace			1	1	0.1
Total		208	174	511	893	100.0
% age		23.3	19.5	57.2	100	

Table 5.1: Material Inventory of Surface Collections

5.2.1 Surface Collections

A total of 893 artefacts were obtained from surface collections at Nsongezi, 208 (23.3%); Kansyore Island, 511 (57.2%) and the Island of Deserters 174 (19.5%). Pottery (596) constituted the majority followed by lithics (248), faunal remains (44) out of which were shells (40) and bones (4), a metal object (1) and tuyere (1), a smoking pipe fragment (1) and a clay mace (1) (Table 5.1). The pottery from surface collections showed a chronology from Kansyore ware to roulette basing on pottery decorations.

Therefore, the pottery traditions identified from the surface collections were Kansyore (61), Urewe (263), bourdine (25), channel (40) and roulette (163) (Figure 5.1). Kansyore pottery was obtained mainly from Kansyore Island (49) with a few sherds from Nsongezi (7) and the Island of Deserters (5). Urewe was the dominant tradition (44.1%) in the pottery assemblage from surface collection (Figure 5.1). Urewe was characterized by mainly crosshatching, bevels, flutes and dimple bases from the decoration. Roulette pottery (27.3%) was composed of either twisted cord or knotted strip roulette. Bourdine/Chobe ware (4.2 %) was characterized by finger impressions and poorly smoothed coils exposed on the body. The channel ware (6.7%) was characterized by scrolls and grooves which Chapman (1967) classified under Urewe however the current study suggests this to be an independent tradition which is a transitional ware probably between Kansyore and Urewe. This is because this ware combined elements of typical Urewe and Kansyore pottery decorative elements.

All the pottery collected showed evidence of the chronology from the LSA (Kansyore ware, 10.2%) to the LIA (roulette). From the surface were plain but diagnostic sherds (7.4%). The lithics from surface collection were dominated by flake/blades (126), followed by cores (80), scrapers (26), backed pieces (7), other shaped tools (6) and non-flaked stones (3). The lithics from Kansyore Island and MPPU sites characterized by backed pieces (geometrics), blades and flakes showed these were LSA sites. Kansyore Island had a unique find of a stone mortar (Plate 5.2).

The faunal remains were composed of bones (4) and shells (40). The latter were for wild terrestrial fauna and the former were the limicolaria shells (Chapter 6). This implies the interaction between fishers and hunters. A smoking pipe fragment (Plate 5.1a) from the neighboring island that is 100m from Kansyore Island, a stone mortar and a clay mace (Plate 5.1b) obtained from Kansyore Island were also part of surface collections. The smoking pipe may be dated to the Early Iron Age from the decoration characterized by a herringbone band and though it was associated with twisted cord rouletted pottery. The practice of smoking continues to date in this area and is done by both men and women implying cultural continuity.

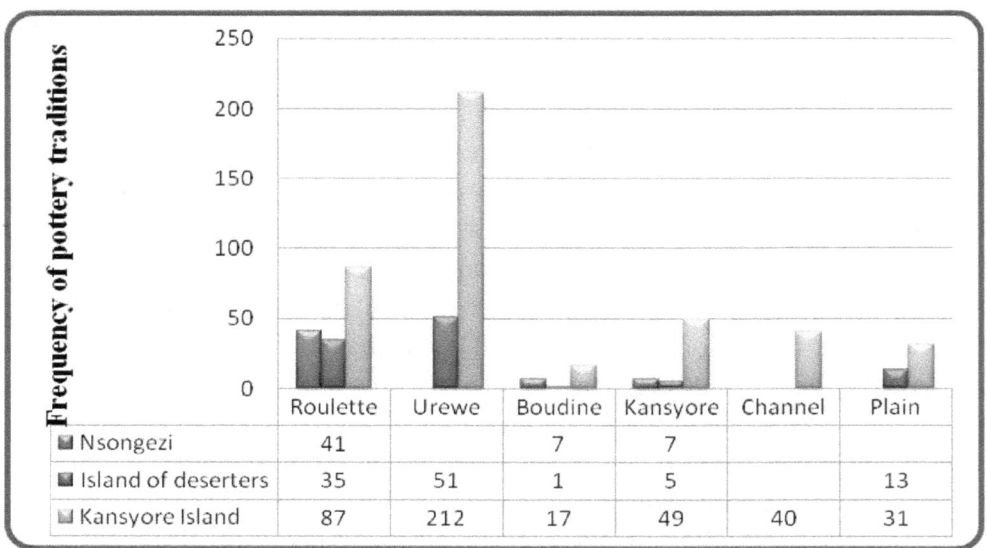

Figure 5.1: Frequency of Pottery Traditions from Surface Collections

Plate 5.1: Artifacts from Surface Collections
(a) Smoking pipe fragments (b)   clay mace

Plate 5.2: Stone Mortar at Kansyore Island

The finds from the Island of Deserters indicated that it is a multi-component site of MSA, LSA, EIW and LIA. This was determined from the lithics and pottery finds. The lithics consisted of a core axe, grinding stone, scrapers, backed pieces, burins and flakes/blades. The pottery included roulette pottery with knotted grass and twisted string roulette decorative elements for LIA (16) and incisions, hatches and punctates typical of EIW (15) and dotted lines for Kansyore wares (4) were collected. The tuyere (1) collected confirmed further the Iron Age occurrences but the frequency was not sufficient to establish the possibility of iron smelting. The surface collections reflect cultural interconnectedness among the Nsongezi, Kansyore and the Island of Deserters' sites and therefore in the Nile catchment from the Stone Age to the Iron Age.

5.3. Shovel Test Pits (STPs)

Test excavations involved setting up two STPs each measuring 1 ×1m²; STP 1 was at the Kyazike landing site while STP 2 was at Kansyore Island. The discussion below shows the results from the two STPs. This is presented in the form of stratigraphic layers showing the findings from each layer, the disturbances encountered, the soil colour and texture as determined by the Munsell colour chart and artefacts recovered from the two STPs established during survey.

5.3.1 Nsongezi Shovel Test Pit 1

Nsongezi STP1 was at GPS reading 01° 00' 02.7"S, 030° 44' 31.4"E at a surface elevation of 1,229 meters above sea level. This was opposite the Kansyore falls on the Ugandan side. The STP was established after a number of considerations which included:

1) the need to examine the cultural chronology of the site
2) the enormous surface scatters of mainly lithics and pottery that were exposed
3) examining the stratigraphy of the area
4) crosschecking the contemporary occurrence of pottery and lithics and
5) to examine subsurface concentration of the area.

The STP surface had different elevation measurements and given this divergence the first level entailed leveling to 30 cm below surface. Thereafter excavation followed arbitrary 10 cm spit-levels. This was because the soil was too soft and loose to maintain the walls with less spits. The STP went up to a depth of 70 cm below surface with the western side as the deepest.

5.3.2 Material Finds from Nsongezi Shovel Test Pit 1

Nsongezi STP 1 yielded 1148 artefacts that were lithics 947 (82.5%), faunal remains 183 (15.9%) and pottery 18 (1.6%) (Table 2). The faunal remains were made up of bones 101 (8.8 %) and shells 82 (7.1 %). The lithics from

Nsongezi STP1 included geometrics or backed pieces (11) and Kansyore pottery (4) that suggested that the site was settled from the LSA or Neolithic period. The abundance of microchips meant that this was a Stone Age factory. The bones being dominated by fish bones suggested the predominance of fishing for subsistence in the past. The eastern side of the STP became sterile at a depth of 50cms due to the bedrock. However, excavation continued on the western side up to a depth of 70cms when the bedrock was touched throughout the STP. The entire STP having hit bedrock marked the end of the excavation.

5.3.3 Stratigraphy of Shovel Test Pit 1 Nsongezi

The stratigraphy as witnessed from the northern wall had three layers Figure 5.2.(1). Layer 1 comprised of levels; 1(0-30) cm and 2 (30-40) cm. The colour of the soils was very dark gray (3/1 HUE 5YR). The layer yielded: lithics (455), faunal remains (114) and pottery (18). Burnt hearth and crushed rocks were also obtained in this layer. This shows that all the pottery from the STP was in Layer 1. The sequence of pottery shows that there was interaction in the Iron Age but showing that Kansyore is earlier than the Iron Age.

Layer 2 stretched from 40-60 cm meaning that it was made up of levels 3(40-50cm) and 4(50-60cm). The soils were dark grey (4/1 HUE 5YR) loose loam clay. In this layer, the eastern side hit the bedrock at 50 cm below surface. Artefacts recovered from this layer were lithics (492) and faunal remains (69) that included bones (58) and shell (11). Therefore it was predominantly a lithics layer.

Layer 3 was made of Level 5 (60-70cm) with dark reddish gray (4/2 HUE 5YR) loam clay soils. The third layer was restricted to the northwestern corner because the STP reached the bedrock at 59 cm in the North East while it hit the bedrock at 70 cm below surface in the North West. At 70 cm below surface, the entire test pit bottom was covered by bedrock showing that it was sterile and excavation had to stop. The last layer was completely sterile with no artifact recovered.

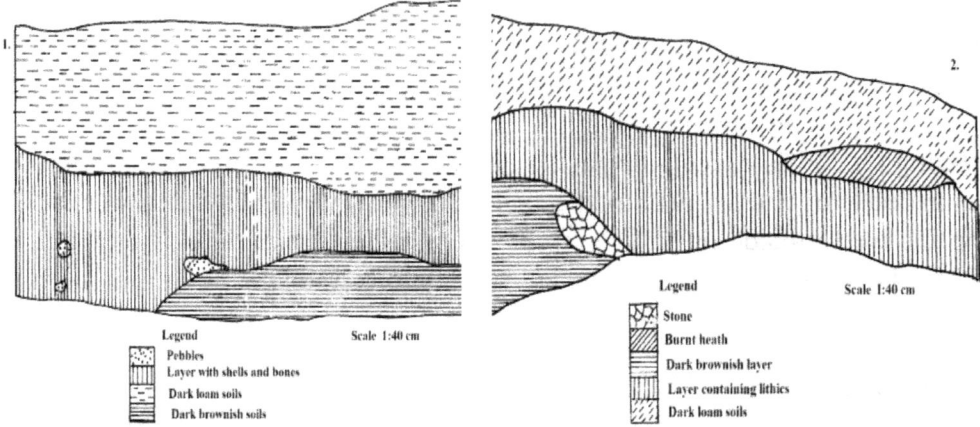

Figure 5.2: (1) Western Wall and (2) Northern Wall Profiles of Nsongezi STP 1

5.3.4 Kansyore Shovel Test Pit 2

Kansyore STP 2 was established at the north-eastern side of Kansyore Island. The STP was positioned at about 17 metres from the Kagera river banks. The GPS points for STP 2 were 01° 00' 05.4" S and 030° 44' 29.7" E at an elevation of 1,223 above sea level. The decision to have the STP at this location was dictated by surface scatters of Kansyore, EIW, LIA and roulette pottery and a dimple base; the desire to crosscheck and find out if the surface scatters were replicated below surface; to examine the stratigraphy of the area and the need to examine if the artefacts on the mainland will be replicated at Kansyore Island. The fact that most of Chapman's (1967) trenches were in the house foundation that area was avoided despite observation of high concentration of surface artefacts in the house rubble. The surface had lithics (10) and a bone (1) in the black (2.5/1 HUE 5YR) loose loam soils. Arbitrary 10 cm spit levels were followed in excavating STP 2 in an area that possessed minor disturbances of river cobbles.

5.3.5 Material Finds from Kansyore Island Shovel Test Pit 2

The findings from the entire STP 2 amounted to 1,481. The dominant finds were lithics 1,207 (81.5%), followed by pottery 26 (1.8 %), faunal remains 246 (16.6%) and metal objects 2 (0.1%) (Table 5.2). Faunal remains included shells amounting to 110 (7.4%). These were for both terrestrial and aquatic snails. A total of 136 (9.2%) bones were analyzed and identified as for both terrestrial animals and fish. This implied that the diet of the ancient inhabitants of the Island was based on both land and water creatures for their survival.

Level/Depth(cm)	Diagnostic pottery			Un.Di	Lithics						FR			Total
	Roulette	EIW	Channel	Kansyore		scr	Ba	others	CO	B/F	DEB	BO	SH	MO	
Nsongezi STP 1															
Surface (cm deep)									3	12	17				32
1(0-30)	2	5	4	3	3	8	6	1	33	46	106	24	31		272
2(30-40)			1			4	5		25	50	144	19	40		283
3(40-50)						8	5	1	6	37	237	42	10		346
4(50-60)						6	11	1	17	49	125	16	1		215
Total	2	5	4	4	3	26	11	3	84	194	629	101	82		1148
% age	0.2	0.4	0.3	0.3	0.3	2.3	1.0	0.3	7.3	16.9	54.8	8.8	7.1		100.0
Kansyore STP 2															
Surface						2		3	1	6	1	1			14
1(0-10)				4		7	1	4	16	66	125	6	14		239
2(10-20)		14	1			16	7		33	82	185	48		2	392
3(20-30)				1	2	17	4		27	136	133	26	64		410
4(30-40)		2				3			10	51	22	36	25		149
5(40-50)		2				10	12	3		31		15	5		78
6(50-60)						12	4	8	18	76	75	4	2		199
Total		18	1	5	2	67	28	18	105	448	541	136	110	2	1481
% age		1.2	0.1	0.3	0.1	4.5	1.9	1.2	7.1	30.2	36.5	9.2	7.4	0.1	100.0

Key: Un-di.=un-diagnostic pottery; CO= cores; B/F=blade/flakes; DEB=debitage; BO=bones; SH=shells; MO=metal objects; F.R=faunal remains; ba=backed pieces; scr=Scrapers

Table 5.2: Material Inventory for Nsongezi STP1 and Kansyore STP2

5.3.6 The Stratigraphy of Kansyore Shovel Test Pit 2

The stratigraphy from the western wall contained three layers (Figure 5.3). Layer 1 had loose brown (5/3 HUE 7.5 YR) dusty soils. The layer ranged from 10-50 cm and was composed of 5 levels spaced at 10 cm each. The layer yielded: pottery (26), lithics (1,014), bones (132), shells (108) and metals (2) (Table 5.2). This implied that the layer yielded all the pottery from the STP with Urewe dominating and appearing below Kansyore pottery. This implied coexistence of Urewe and Kansyore people.

Layer 2 had dark reddish brown (3/3 HUE 5YR) sandy gravel soils suggesting river deposition. The layer comprised of Level 6 with a depth of 10 cm (50-60cm). This layer yielded lithics (193), bones (4) and shells (2). The findings included microliths in association with faunal remains like a hippo tooth suggesting hunting and gathering of water resources such as hippo which is an indicator of the aquatic.

Layer 3 had yellowish red (5/6 HUE 5YR) gravel soils. This layer stretched from 60-70 cm. The eastern side of the STP became sterile at 50cms below surface due to the bedrock, however, excavation on the western side continued until the bedrock engulfed the entire test trench at 70 cm below surface that marked the end of the excavation due to sterility. The finds of Kansyore STP 2 and those of Nsongezi STP 1 show cultural affinity in this part of the Nile valley showing that rivers were not impediments to cultural interactions as the finds show close affinity despite the Kagera River separating the two STPs.

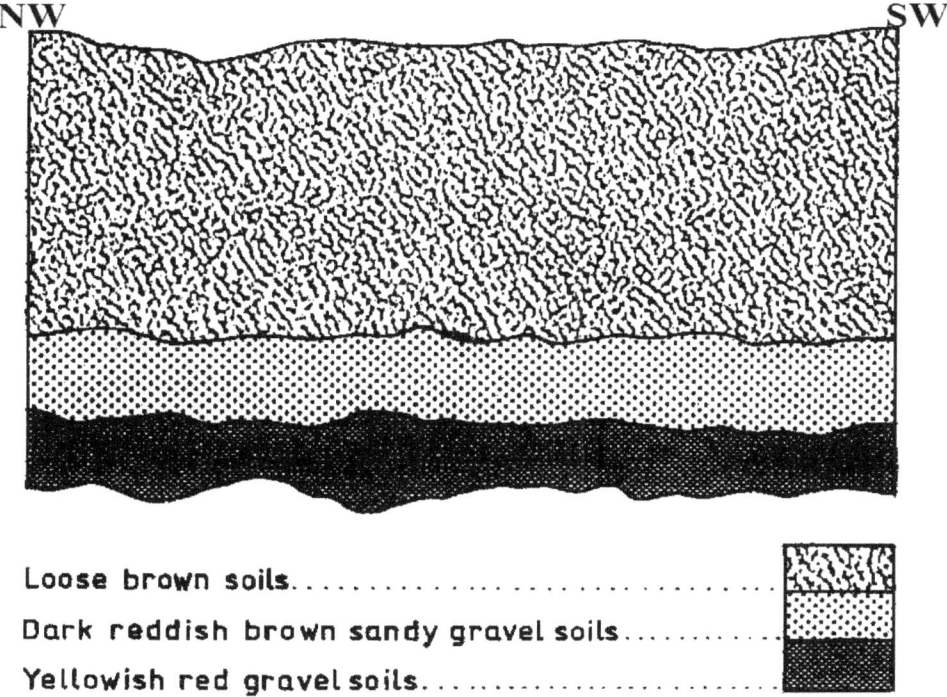

Figure 5.3: The Stratigraphy of Kansyore STP2

5.4. Excavation Finds

During excavation, large trenches were preferred in all areas of the research. This was because data from survey had revealed that despite signatures for the existence of cultural materials the areas lacked a deeper stratigraphy. Therefore, to attain the cultural layers needed for stratigraphic exhibition of cultural interactions bigger trenches were the available option to compensate for depth.

5.4.1 Kansyore Island Excavations

Three trenches were excavated at Kansyore Island where Trenches 1 and 2 had extensions as elaborated below.

5.4.2 Kansyore Trench 1

Trench 1 at Kansyore Island was 2×4 m² set up south of the datum point. The trench GPS reading was 01° 00' 05.2" S and 030° 44' 32.1" E. From the Kyazike landing site at Kansyore Island there are several terraces on the Island. These terraces are natural formations that appear like house foundations. Trench 1 was located at the uppermost terrace at the most elevated landscape with the hunch that it contained the oldest cultural materials. This is because the lower terraces were viewed as having materials eroded from the upper terrace and of secondary deposition. The rest of the main island was avoided due to disturbances caused by agricultural activities that were taking place and the prior excavations of Chapman (1967). The trench was also positioned at a place that had two Urewe potsherds on the surface. Excavation was done systematically following 5-10 cm arbitrary levels. The 5cm spits were used for the leveling and thereafter 10 cm spits were employed.

5.4.3 Kansyore Island Trench 1 Divisions

Trench 1 was divided into two portions where by the western side became Trench 1A while the eastern side became Trench 1B, each measuring 1 ×4 m² (Figure 5.4). The decision to divide the trench was due to the need to have adequate control of material recovery to examine its stratigraphic occurrence. However, even Trench 1A was further divided into two trenches each measuring 1 × 2 m² where the northern side was regarded as Trench 1A1 while the southern side was named Trench 1A2. The second decision to divide the trench further, was due to the need to use the part that became 1A1 as a control trench that could be used to study the occurrence of cultural materials and layers in the entire trench. Secondly, the decision to take a 1×2 m² portion of the trench was due to the observation that the southern part of the 1 ×4 m² (1A2) appeared to have a disturbance. Material evidence from this trench suggests a sequence from the aqualithic to the Iron Age.

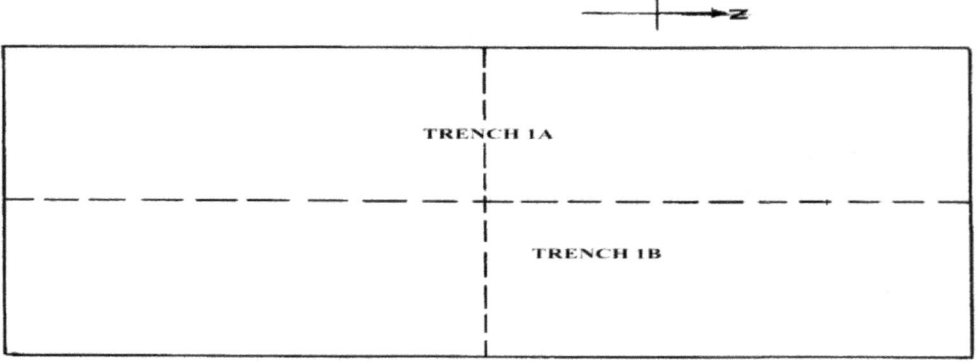

Scale 1:20 cm

Figure 5.4: The Plan of Trenches in Kansyore Trench 1

5.4.4 Material Finds for Kansyore Trench 1

Trench 1 yielded 6,852 artefacts that included lithics 3,913 (55.11%), pottery 738 (10.77 %), metals 12 (0.18%), red ochre pieces 19 (0.28%), faunal remains 2168 (31.64%) and 2 charcoal samples (0.03%) (Table 5.3). The diagnostic pottery comprised of almost all traditions including: roulette, Urewe, channel, and Kansyore pottery traditions. This was in association with lithic artefacts composed of backed pieces, scrapers, points, denticulate, burins, bec, pestle rubber, *outils escailles*, hammer stone and cores. The faunal remains included both aquatic (41) and terrestrial fauna (2127). The aquatic fauna suggested the presence of the aquatic civilization. The aquatic layer in this case may suggest the adaptation to the local environment other than interaction with Sudan since at Ishango on the Uganda/Congo border the use of aquatic resources dates far earlier than Sudan to about 99,000 years ago (Bushozi, personal communication). The data from material inventory, suggested cultural continuity.

Level/depth cm	Non flaked	Scrapers	Backed pieces	Other tools	Cores	Flake/blades	Debitage	Plain	Roulette	Urewe	Channel	Kansyore	Un-diagnostic Pottery	Bones	Shells	Red ochre	Metal objects	Charcoal	Total
	Lithics							**Diagnostic pottery**						**Faunal remains**					
1 (0-15)	1	15	14	5		102	372		6	37	14	15	181	114			4		880
2 (15-20)		42	25	7	91	176	694		5	35	13	14	132	226		1	4	1	1466
3 (20-25)		39	25	10	78	213	874	3	11	2	1	4	185	270		5	2		1722
4 (25-30)		3	11	2	19	38	38		2	32	9	8	10	271		2	2		447
5 (30-35)		13	12	6	25	74	297			14			1	258	13	3			703
6 (35-40)		1	3	2	9	14	53			2				111	26	8		1	209
7 (40-45)	1	3	5	3	4	21	177							241					489
8 (45-50)		7	4	1	1	18	83			2				176					292
9 (50-55)		5	1		2	33	94							203					338
10 (55-60)					2		28							194	2				224
11 (60-65)						4	13							63					82
Total	2	128	100	36	231	693	2723	3	24	124	37	41	509	2127	41	19	12	2	6852
% age	0.03	1.87	1.46	0.53	3.37	10.11	39.74	0.04	0.35	1.81	0.54	0.60	7.43	31.04	0.60	0.28	0.18	0.03	100.00

Table 5.3: Material Inventory of Kansyore Island Trench 1 and IA

5.4.5 Stratigraphy of Kansyore Trench 1

Trench 1 had four observable layers along the western wall (Figure 5.5). Layer 1 had very dark loose grey (HUE 7.5 YR) soils. This layer was made of Level 1(0-15) cm. The first layer was part of Trench 1 before any divisions that is the 4×2 m² cut. This layer yielded lithics (509), bones (114), metal objects (4) and pottery (253). Among the lithic finds was a pestle rubber. The layer had disturbances of rootlets and a barrow in a deposition that was natural.

Layer 2 was characterized by loose gravel black (2.5/2 HUE 5Y) soils. This layer on average was 15-30 cm comprising of levels 2 (15-20 cm), 3 (20-25 cm) and 4 (25-30 cm). The disturbances of rootlets reduced while barrowing disappeared completely. The findings in this layer included; pottery (466), lithics (2385), faunal remains (767), metals (8), red ochre (8) and charcoal (1). The fish bones were concentrated in this layer suggesting an aqualithic layer. The reduction in pottery in the aquatic layer raises concern in view of Haaland's (2009:213) suggestion that the invention of pottery occurred in connection with the exploitation of aquatic resources.

Layer 3 was the aqualithic layer proper (Plate 5.3). The layer was part of Trench 1A that ranged from 30-45 cm thick. Layer 3 comprised of 3 excavation levels; 5 (30-35 cm), 6 (35-40 cm) and 7 (40-45 cm). This layer produced charcoal (1), bones (610) and shells (39) that implied the existence of the aquatic civilization that stretched from Northeast Africa (Sutton 1974, 1977). Other artefacts obtained from this layer were lithics (723), pieces of red ochre (11) and pottery (17) showing reduction of pottery.

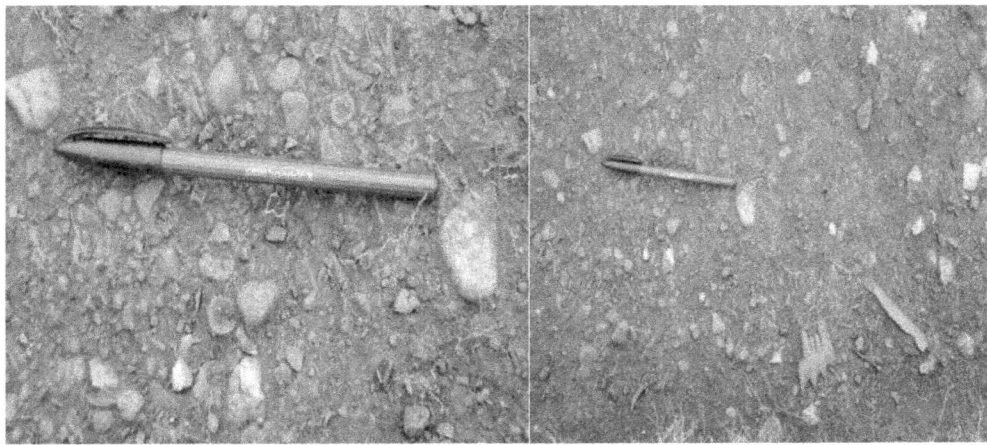

Plate 5.3: The Floor of the Aquatic Layer in Trench 1A

The soils of Layer 4 were reddish brown (5/3 HUE 2.5 YR) loose sandy soils mixed with small pebbles. This suggested that the bedrock was close from the soil coloration and texture. The fourth layer ranging from 45-80 cm below surface was the thickest layer. Layer 4 was part of Trench 1A1 that comprised of six levels; 8 (45-50 cm), 9 (50-55 cm), 10 (55-60 cm), 11 (60-65 cm), 12 (65-70 cm) and 13 (70-80 cm). This layer yielded lithics (296), faunal remains (638) and Urewe pottery (2). The faunal remains included mainly bones (636) and a few shells (2). The rootlet disturbances disappeared with the only disturbances observed being the river pebbles.

Trench 1A1 was less productive compared to 1A. The findings from Trench 1A1 generally were animal bones, lithics, red ochre, fish bones and a grinding stone worked by red ochre. Phillipson (2005) suggests that the presence of grinding stones may suggest cereal grains (presumably wild) were harvested and prepared for use as food. Despite that some were used to grind red ochre for human and pottery decoration. On the other hand the high concentration of small stones mixed with sandy soils suggested that the trench had become sterile. Therefore excavation seized at 80 cm below surface.

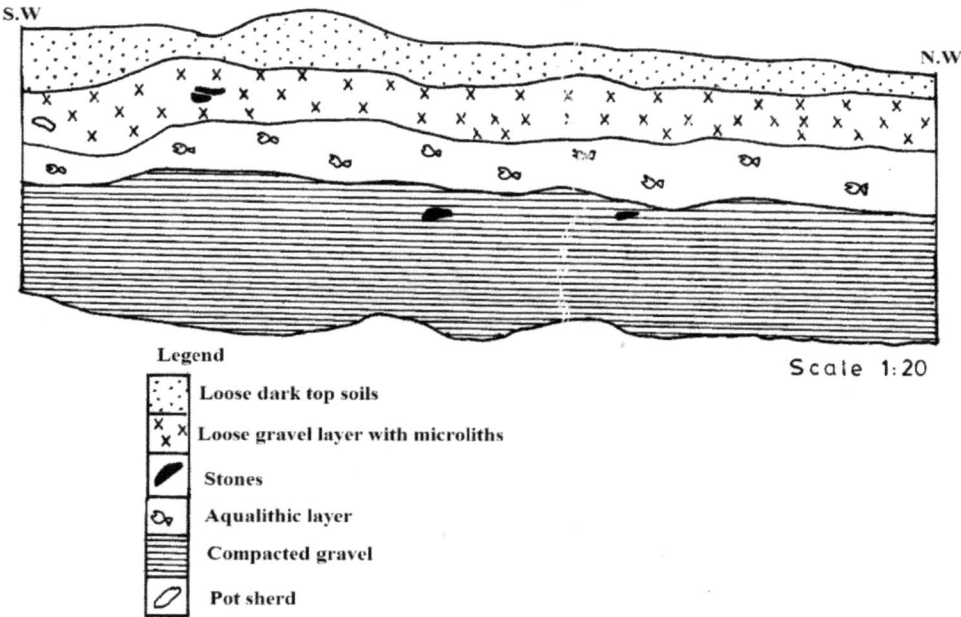

Figure 5.5: The Western Wall of Kansyore Island Trench 1

5.4.6 Kansyore Island Trench 1B

Trench 1B was the initial 1×4 m² western part of Trench 1 that was split to make two other trenches of 1 ×2 m² each, referred to as Trench 1B1 and Trench 1B2. The division was done at the beginning of level 4 (30-35) cm. The decision to divide Trench 1B followed the need to observe the sequence of material occurrence in an attempt to establish a sequence. A total of 7,375 artefacts were recovered from Trenches 1B, 1B1 and 1B2. These included lithics (5,353), pottery (849), faunal remains (1,154) and red ochre stones (14) (Table 5.4). The entire faunal collection in this trench was composed of bones meaning there was absence of shells unlike Trench 1A where shells and bones coexisted. The absence of shells may imply a time of reliance on fishing and probably environmental change that was not conducive for shellfish. Like in Trench 1A in Trench 1B Urewe pottery occurred in lower levels below Kansyore pottery. This may probably imply that crosshatching may have existed earlier than the Iron Age since the sorting of pottery per tradition was based on decoration motifs.

Table 5.4: Material Inventory of Kansyore Trenches 1B, 1BI and 1B2

Level (Depth) cm	Lithics						Pottery							FR	Metal objects	Red ochre	Total
	Backed	Scrapers	Others	Cores	Flake/blades	Debitage	Plain	Roulette	Urewe	Channel	Boudine	Kansyore	Un-diagnostic	Bones			
1(0-20)	41	60	19	49	255	938	1	10	98	27	1	23	492	232	4		2250
2(20-25)	34	55	10	48	168	739		2	24	15		6	123	120	1	3	1348
3(25-30)	20	34	6	47	150	733		1	9				13	64			1077
4(30-35)	4	11	1	8	35	109			1					58			227
5(35-40)	7	3	5	9	28	58			2					40		3	152
6(40-45)	6	2	1	13	29	77								70			201
7(45-50)	1	1		3	17	74								97			193
8(50-55)	1	1	1	2	27	213								95			340
9(55-60)	4	2		6	14	116								165			307
10(60-65)				7	11	79								118			215
11(65-70)	5				4	64								20		5	93
12(70-75)		2		1	6	53								7		3	74
IB2: 4(30-40)	17	32	8	33	73	356			1					43		3	566
5(40-45)	3	21	2	15	42	224								25			332
Total	143	224	53	241	859	3833	1	13	135	42	1	29	628	1154	5	14	7375
% age	1.94	3.04	0.72	3.27	11.65	51.97	0.01	0.18	1.83	0.57	0.01	0.39	8.52	15.65	0.07	0.19	100

Key: FR= faunal remains; others=other shaped tools

5.4.7 Stratigraphy of Trench 1B

The stratigraphy facing east had three observable layers (Figure 5.6). Layer 1 was made of only Level 1 (0-20 cm). The soil was very dark grayish brown (4/2 HUE 2.5 Y) loose gravel. The finds were lithics (1,362), pottery (652) and faunal remains (232). The latter were only bones. There were rootlet disturbances of short grasses in this layer.

Layer 2 was 10 cm deep stretching from 20-30 cm and comprised of Levels 2 (20-25 cm) and 3 (25-30 cm). The soils were dark grayish brown (4/2 HUE 2.5 Y) loose gravel. The finds were lithics (2,044), pottery (193), faunal remains (184) red ochre (3) and a metal object. Among the faunal remains was a hippo tooth that had secondary modifications and had been used as a tool in association with Iron Age and Kansyore pottery. Backed pieces, points, becs, outils escailles and denticulates characterized the lithics in this layer.

Layer 3 was made of both Trenches 1B1 and 1B2. It ranged from 30-75 cm and therefore consisted of nine levels; 4 (30-35 cm), 5 (35-40 cm), 6 (40-45 cm), 7 (45-50 cm), 8 (50-55 cm), 9 (55-60 cm), 10 (60-65 cm) and 11 (65-70 cm), 12 (70-75 cm). The soil was dark reddish brown (2.5/3 HUE 2.5YR) compacted gravel. This layer had the aqualithic layer that appeared from excavation Levels 3 (30-35) cm to 8(55-60) cm. The layer was characterized by a reduction of pottery as it was the tendency of aquatic civilizations in this area, with only four Urewe sherds found. Rootlet disturbances continued in this layer. Among the faunal remains (738) was a human premolar tooth and fragmentary pieces of a human skull. Other finds were lithics (1947), red ochre (11) and pottery (4). In the southern wall, section long bones were observed in Level 11(65-70) cm in the wall section but they were not excavated. In Level 4 (30-40) cm the part of Trench1B2 a fossilized bone was obtained. Unlike Trench1A that ended at 65cm below surface, excavation of Trench 1B ended at 75 cm below surface suggesting a slanting stratigraphy as observed from the sterile level.

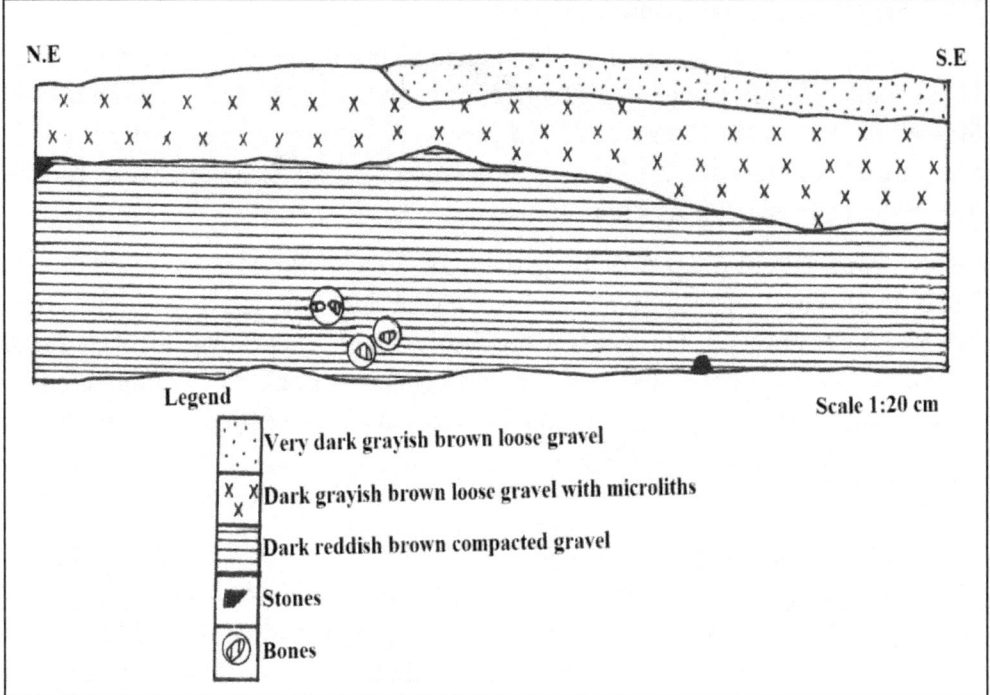

Figure 5.6: The Stratigraphy of Kansyore Trench 1B Facing East

5.4.8 Trench 2 Kansyore Island

This was a 2 ×1 m² trench aligned east at GPS reading 01° 00' 05.0"S and 030° 44' 32.7" E. This trench was established on the second terrace of the Island North east of Trench 1. It had a slanting stratigraphy and the bedrock was encountered at a higher level on the western side than on the eastern side. Therefore, the eastern wall had clear layers which partly contributed to the decision of making an extension of the trench in that direction to make Trench 2A (3× 1 m²) (Figure 5.7). Trench 2A was later divided into two trenches each measuring 3× 0.5 m². These were Trench 2Ai and 2Aii. A further extension was still made on Trench 2 that became 2B (Plate 5.4).

Plate 5.4: Trench 2 Kansyore Island Divisions and Extensions

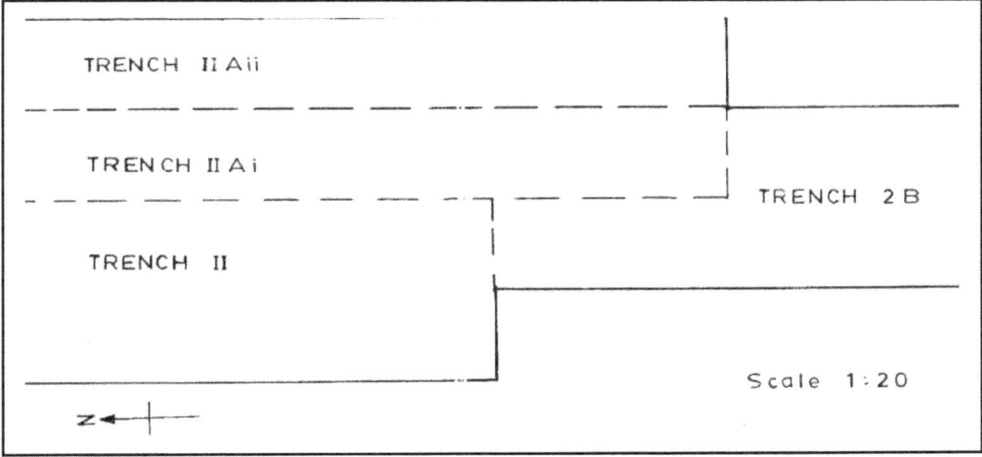

Figure 5.7: Plan of Kansyore Trench 2 Showing its Divisions

5.4.9 Trench 2 Kansyore Findings

Trench 2 had a total of 1,377 artefacts that included lithics 1,122 (81.5%), pottery 199 (14.5%) faunal remains 19 (1.4%) and metal objects 37 (2.7%) (Table 5.5). The diagnostic sherds based on decoration belonged to roulette 8 (0.6%), Urewe 22 (1.6%), bourdine 2 (0.1%), channel 2 (0.1%) and Kansyore

10 (0.7%) pottery traditions. Unlike Trench 1 (3,331), Trench 2 had limited faunal remains (19). The faunal remains were composed of shells and bones which is a similar occurrence as in Trench 1A. This further implied reliance on both aquatic and terrestrial resources by the hunter-fisher-gatherer community suggested by the finds in Trench 2.

The stone tools show a dominance of scrapers (41) followed by backed pieces (32) and other shaped tools that constituted a small amount (8). This was in line with the LSA sites in East Africa which suggests that similarity in cultural materials may not simply imply migration, diffusion or trade but ecological adaptability is also a possibility. That is to say people could make similar tools in response to a similar environment. This is as suggested by Julian Steward who rejects the view that all humans should pass through the same stages of development and instead suggested that similarities reflect similar adaptations to similar environments.

Level (Depth) cm	Lithics						Diagnostic pottery					Un-diagnostic pottery	Faunal remains		Metal objects	Total
	Scrapers	Backed	Others	Cores	Flake blades	Debitage	Roulette	Urewe	Bourdine	Channel	Kansyore		Shells	Bones		
1(0-10)				4	3	18	1					9	1	1	6	43
2(10-15)		1			9	12					1	20	1		27	71
3(15-20)								1								1
4(20-25)				1	2	18	2		2			6			3	34
5(25-30)		2	1	6	6	52		1				4				72
6(30-35)	3	2	1	9	12	115	3	15			1	25			1	187
7(35-40)	30	21	2	38	116	338					4	65				614
8(40-50)							2	5		2	1	23				33
9(50-60)	7	6		10	61	123					1	1		16		225
10(60-70)	1		4	3	30	55					2	2				97
Total	41	32	8	71	239	731	8	22	2	2	10	155	2	17	37	1377
% age	3.0	2.3	0.6	5.2	17.4	53.1	0.6	1.6	0.1	0.1	0.7	11.3	0.1	1.2	2.7	100.0

Key: scr=scrapers; bac = backed pieces; OT= other shaped tools; F.B=flake/blades; DT= debitage; ROT-roulette; Ur=Urewe; BDN-bourdine; CN- channel; Kans= Kansyore; Un-dia. =Un-diagnostic pottery; Sh= shells; Bo= bones

Table 5.5: Material Inventory of Trench 2 Kansyore Island

5.4.10 The Stratigraphy of Trench 2 Kansyore Island

The stratigraphy of Trench 2 as observed from the southern wall had four layers (Figure 5.8). Layer 1 was characterized by light brown (6/3 HUE 7.5 YR) soils whose texture was generally loose sandy. On average, the layer ranged from 0-10 cm comprising of level 1 (0-10 cm). Excavation followed 10 cm arbitrary spit levels. This was because excavating this layer intended to level the trench due to variations in the depth at the beginning of the trench. The finds in layer 1 were pottery (10), lithics (25), shell (1), a bone (1) and metal objects (6). The pottery from decoration belonged only to the LIA roulette which concurs well with the established sequence in this part of Africa.

Layer 2 was characterized by light gray (7/1 HUE 5YR) very loose sandy soils that had a relatively compact texture compared to the soils of Layer 1. The layer was on average 10-20 cm and comprised of Levels 2 (10-15 cm) and 3 (15-20 cm). The layer yielded 2 diagnostic sherds of Kansyore (1) and Urewe pottery (1) traditions in association was a backed piece (1), core (1), flakes (9), a shell (1) and metal objects (27).

Layer 3 was the widest layer with very dark grayish brown (3/2 HUE 10YR) compacted fine loam soils. Layer 3 was composed of six levels; 4 (20-25 cm), 5 (25-30 cm), 6 (30-35 cm), 7 (35-40 cm), 8 (40-50 cm) and 9 (50-60 cm). The artefacts obtained from this layer were pottery (163) of roulette, Urewe, bourdine, channel and Kansyore traditions; bones (16), metal objects (4), and lithics (982). Among the lithics was a grinding stone in level 9 (50-60 cm), scrapers (40), geometrics (31), a denticulate, a bec, a burin, flakes (197) and cores (64). The obtaining of pottery in this layer with the wavy line decoration elements characteristic of Sudan Mesolithic pottery suggested material affiliation in the Upper Nile catchment areas. The disturbances were restricted to rootlets, cobbles and a slate rock. A slate rock appeared in the north-western corner in level 5 (25-30 cm) that kept expanding eastwards towards the south-eastern corner. This led to the use of 10 cm spit levels to excavate due to the need to clear up the areas that had not yet been engulfed by bedrock. At the bottom of this layer, the bedrock covered three quarters of the trench.

Layer 4 was on the southeastern side that was still free from bedrock. The soils were yellowish red (5/8 HUE 5YR) gravel and stony. The layer was composed of only level 10 (60-70 cm). This layer yielded Urewe pottery that was red, an evidence of good firing. The pottery at the bottom was classified as Urewe because it had cross-hatching decoration characteristic of Urewe pottery tradition with flat rims or what Chapman (1967) regarded as squared rims associated to Kansyore pottery. This pottery could probably mean that crosshatching might be older than the Iron Age though attempts for radio-carbon dating were not fruitful due to lack of charcoal samples and the attempt to use a bone couldn't work either as the Waikato laboratory could not use it because the sample was too small. Though lithics (93) and pottery (4) were obtained in this layer, excavation had to stop as the whole trench was engulfed by bedrock at the bottom of layer 4. Trench 2 provided a clear stratigraphic sequence with Kansyore, Urewe (EIA) and roulette (LIA) from earliest to the recent.

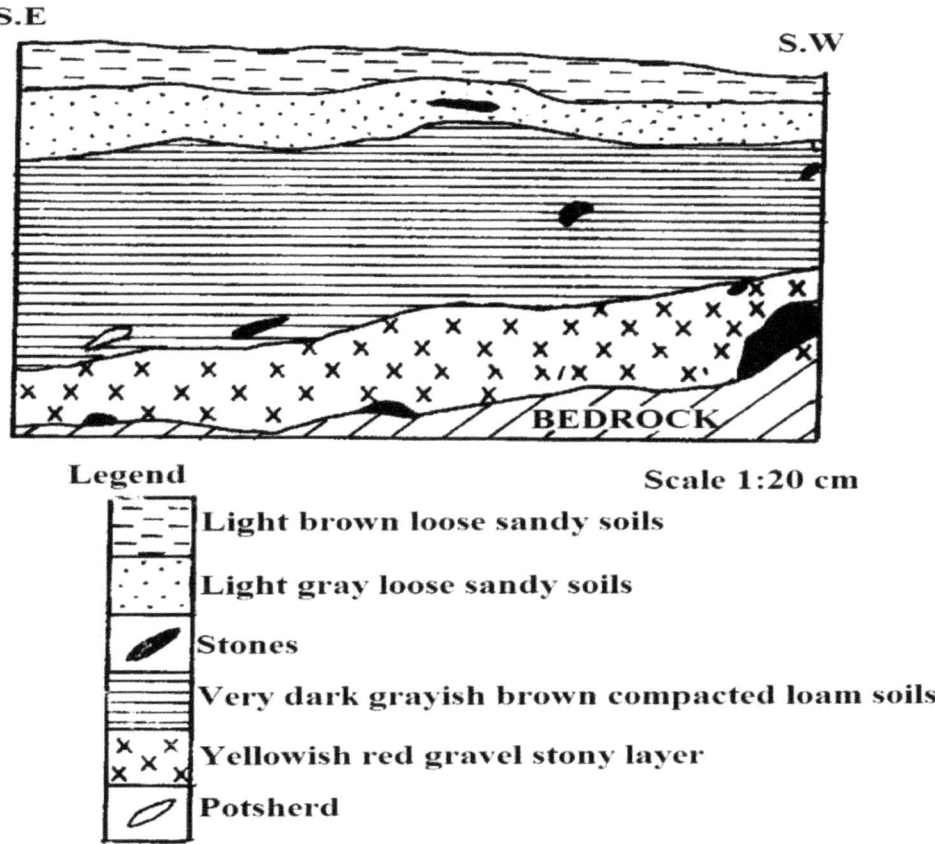

Figure 5.8: Southern Wall Profile of Trench 2 Kansyore Island

5.4.11 Trench 2A Kansyore Island

Trench 2A was an extension on Trench 2 that measured 3×1 m² along the eastern line of Trench 2. The reason for extension included: the need to find out whether the findings obtained in Trench 2 could be replicated and the desire to expand the sample size and check the sequence derived from Trench 2. Trench 2A was also split into two at level 4 as a control measure that led to the formation of Trenches 2Ai and 2Aii each measuring 50 cm ×3 m².

5.4.12 Trench 2Ai Kansyore Island

In the course of excavation of Trench 2A it was divided into two trenches of 3× 0.5 m². The eastern side that was regarded as Trench 2Ai was used as a control trench for examining the sequence. The division was based on the desire to have systematic material recovery that could be used to examine the sequence observed in Trench 2 that could further illuminate cultural connections in the upper Nile catchment. Excavation followed both 5 and 10 cm arbitrary levels.

5.4.12 Trench 2A and Trench 2Ai Findings

The trench yielded 1,566 artifacts, of these 1,498 were from Trench 2Ai, while 68 were from Trench 2A. The artifacts obtained were; lithics 1,236 (78.9 %), pottery 150 (9.6%), faunal remains 172 (11.2%), metal objects 4 (0.3 %) and charcoal 1 (0.1%) (Table 5.6). All the faunal remains were bones only that were obtained from Trench 2Ai. Fish bones however were not prominent as in Trench 1 that had an aqualithic layer. The trench surface yielded 9 artifacts: a lithic core (1), flake/blade (2) and pottery (4). The pottery from the surface was the typical roulette (3) characterized with knotted strips and in addition there was one piece of Urewe pottery. However, the entire trench produced pottery that belonged to the Iron Age that were LIA (6) and EIA (20) then bourdine (1) while others were the Kansyore pottery (14). These were in association with scrapers (17), backed pieces (43), denticulates and points (4).

Level/Depth (cm)	Lithics						Diagnostic Pottery				Pottery	CK	FR	MO	Total
	scr.	bac.	others	CO	F/B	DEB	ROT	UR	BOD	KAS	Un-dia.				
Trench 2A															
0 (5-10)				1	2		3	1			1			1	9
1 (10-15)	1			2		14					5				22
2 (15-20)		4				4					2			2	12
3 (20-25)				1	3	4									8
4 (25-30)		1		3	2	7					2		2		17
Trench 2Ai															
5 (30-35)		1			4	13					3				21
6 (35-40)						8							1		9
7 (40-45)	1				26	20		2		1					51
8 (45-50)						7	1				10	1	4		22
9 (50-55)				3	8	4		6			12			1	35
10 (55-60)	1			3	21	24	1	1		1	44		4		100
11 (60-65)		5		23	40	83	1	8		1	14		8		183
12 (65-70)	9	26	4	49	146	403		2		3	15		103		760
13 (70-75)	5	6		10	50	184				8	1		53		317
Total	17	43	4	95	302	775	6	20	1	14	109	1	175	4	1566
% age	1.1	2.7	0.3	6.1	19.3	49.5	0.4	1.3	0.1	0.9	7.0	0.1	11.2	0.3	100.0

Key: TR=trench; scr. scrapers; bac. =backed pieces; CO=cores; F/B=flake/blade; DEB=debitage; ROT=roulette; UR=Urewe; BOD=bourdine; KAS=Kansyore; un-dia-un-diagnostic; CK=charcoal; FR=faunal remains; MO=metal objects.

Table 5.6: Material Inventory of Kansyore Island Trenches 2A and 2Ai

5.4.13 Stratigraphy of Trench 2A and Trench 2Ai

The stratigraphy of Trench 2A and Trench 2Ai had four observed layers along the western wall (Figure 5.9).

Layer 1 comprised of the Surface Level (0-10 cm) and Level 1 (10-15 cm) of Trench 2A. This had light brown (6/4 HUE 7.5YR) very fine sandy soils. Despite the rootlet disturbances, the layer produced lithics (20) in association with an iron metal (1), LIA (3), EIA (1) and plain (6) pottery. Though small pieces of charcoal were observed in this layer, they were not collected as it was considered early to collect samples that could generate meaningful dates from a level so close to the surface.

Layer 2 had reddish brown (5/3 HUE 2.5 Y) fine loose sandy soils that were relatively compact compared to the top soils. This layer was on average 15-25 cm made of two levels; 2 (15-20 cm) and 3 (20-25 cm) and excavation followed arbitrary 5 cm spits. In this layer three quarters of the trench had darker sections while a quarter was sandy. The explanation for the sandy layer could probably be a period when the river waves were bringing in sand but without any river having existed in the place. The layer was generally not very productive compared to the previous one as it yielded lithics (16) among which were backed pieces (4); un-diagnostic potsherds (2) and metal objects (2).

The soils of Layer 3 were very loose fine sandy soils mixed with a small percentage of clay that made the soils a little compact though in the last two levels of this layer, it turned gravel and more compact. The northern side (1/4) of the trench was sandier compared to the southern side (3/4) of the trench. It was in view of this observation that eventually Trench 2A was split into two equal trenches referred to as Trench 2Ai and Trench 2Aii after Level 5 (30-35 cm). Excavation used 5 cm arbitrary spits. This was the widest layer (in depth) that ranged from 25-55 cm. This layer comprised of the last level of Trench 2A that is Level 4(25-30) cm and five levels: 5 (30-35 cm); 6 (35-40 cm); 7 (40-45 cm); 8 (45-50 cm) and 9 (50-55 cm) of Trench 2Ai. The layer yielded pottery (38) composed of roulette (1), Urewe (8), bourdine (1) and Kansyore (1) pottery traditions in association with a scraper (1), geometrics (2) and faunal remains (7). The squared rim cross-hatched pottery and unusual roulette (Neolithic roulette) (Plate 5.5a) with evidence of coiling appeared in association with Kansyore pottery. A charcoal sample was obtained in the southern corner.

Layer 4 had light brownish gray (6/2 HUE 2.5Y) gravel soils. A huge boulder was a source of disturbance. This layer comprised of five levels; 10 (55-60 cm), 11 (60-65 cm), 12 (65-70 cm), 13 (70-75 cm) and 14 (75-85 cm). The radiocarbon date from the charcoal sample taken at Level 12 (65-70 cm) yielded a date of 2710± 44 BP (WK- 31384). The dated sample was associated with rouletted pottery (Plate 5.7) which would suggest that roulette existed from the Neolithic period. The findings in this layer were pottery (100) that comprised of roulette (2), Urewe (11) and Kansyore (13) pottery traditions, though the majority (74) were un-diagnostic. The pottery was in association with lithics (1,092) and bones (168). The associated lithics were scrapers (15), geometrics (37), points (2) and denticulates (2). Kansyore potsherds obtained in this layer possessed horizontal dots and interlocked horizontal and vertical dotted lines (Plate 5.5) decorative elements related to the Khartoum Neolithic in association with macro crescents. Excavation ended at 85 cm below surface having encountered the bedrock.

Plate 5.5: (a) Neolithic Roulette

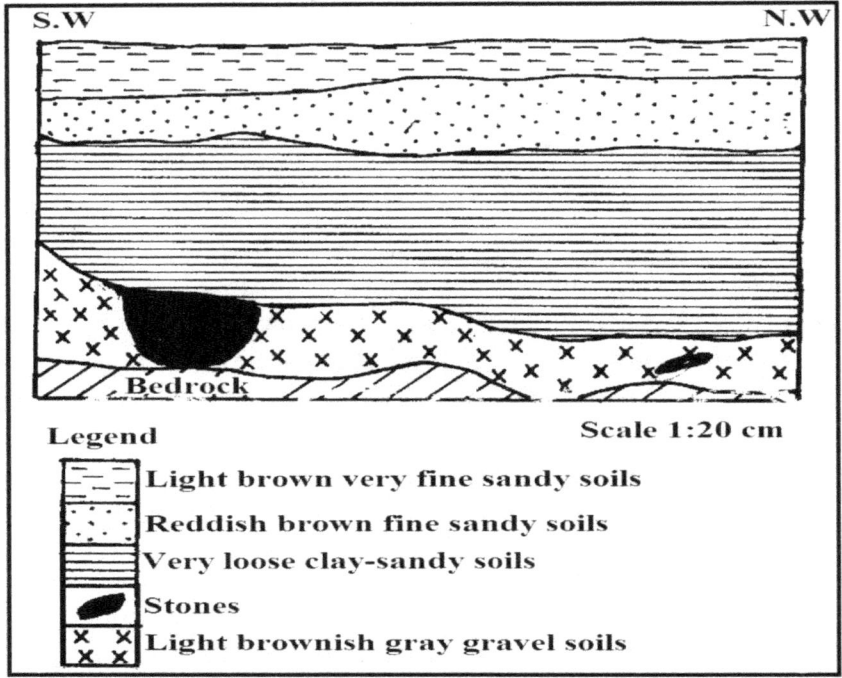

Figure 5.9: Western Wall Profile of Trench 2A Kansyore Island

5.4.14 Trench 2Aii Kansyore Island

Trench 2Aii like 2Ai started at 30 cm below surface following the division of Trench 2A. Excavation of Trench 2Aii followed arbitrary 10 cm spit levels. This followed the divergence in depth at the beginning of the trench that necessitated leveling.

5.4.15 The Findings of Kansyore Trench 2Aii

Trench 2Aii at Kansyore Island yielded 1437 artefacts ranging from the LSA to the LIA (Table 5.7). The finds were lithics 1,142 (78.8%), pottery 99 (6.8%), faunal remains 207 (14.3%) and red ochre 1 (0.1%). The faunal remains were all bones of terrestrial wild animals suggesting hunting. The pottery traditions detected from the decoration were; roulette 6 (0.4%), Urewe 7 (0.5%) and Kansyore 9 (0.6%). The lithic artefacts included geometrics (38), scrapers (18), denticulates (2) and a point (1) (Table 5.7). The scrapers, backed pieces and Kansyore potsherds illuminated the LSA while roulette and Urewe pottery suggested the LIA and EIA respectively. This suggested interaction between the Neolithic and Iron Age people.

Level/Depth (cm)	Lithics						Pottery					Fauna		Total
	Tools			Cores	Flakes/blades	Debiatge	Diagnostic pottery				Un-diagnostic	Bones	Red ochre	
	Scrapers	Backed pieces	Other tools				Plain	Roulette	Urewe	Kansyore				
1(30-40)				2	11	20						1		34
2(40-50)				2	4	15		1			6	10		38
3(50-60)	10	16	1	21	101	399	2	6	2	1	51	19	1	630
4(60-70)	6	16	2	16	82	289			4	8	18	173		614
5(70-80)	2	6		6	25	90						4		133
6(80-85)														
Total	18	38	3	47	223	813	2	6	7	9	75	207	1	1449
% age	1.2	2.6	0.2	3.2	15.4	56.1	0.1	0.4	0.5	0.6	5.2	14.3	0.1	100.0

Table 5.7: Material Inventory of Trench 2Aii Kansyore Island

5.4.16 Stratigraphy of Kansyore Trench 2Aii

The stratigraphy of Trench 2A facing east had five layers (Figure 5.10). The layers varied in thickness and material quantity production. This is the part that comprised of Trench 2Aii.

Layers 1 and 2 were discussed as part of the initial Trench 2 above. These ranged from 30-35 cm below surface.

Layer 3 and 4 were a weak sand depression with very loose sandy soils. The soil was dark grayish brown (4/2 HUE 2.5 Y) in colour with patches of light olive brown (5/3 HUE 2.5 Y). On average, the two layers were 30-70 cm thick comprising levels; 1 (30-40) cm, 2 (40-50) cm, 3 (50-60 cm) and 4 (60-70 cm). The bedrock appeared in the middle part of the trench and a weak sand depression in these layers. The patches of light olive brown (5/3 HUE 2.5 Y) soils encountered bedrock in level 3 (50-60 cm). The southern corner produced bone tools. The findings in this layer were lithics (1,003), pottery (99), faunal remains (203) and red ochre (1). The lithics had geometrics (32), scrapers (16) and other shaped tools (3). The faunal remains were all bone. The pottery exhibited a sequence of roulette (6), Urewe (7) and Kansyore (9) from latest to oldest though some plain but diagnostic pottery (2) was obtained. This means all the pottery and the only metal from the entire Trench 2Aii was from these layers.

The red ochre could have been for personal decoration as there was no evidence for its use on the pottery in Layers 3 and 4. The presence of red ochre, bone tools together with geometrics and Kansyore pottery may imply a contact phase of MSA/LSA period.

Layer 5 was a thin layer that was 70-85 cm thick comprising of the southern part in three levels; 4 (60-70 cm), 5 (70-80 cm) and 6 (80-85 cm). The soils were light brownish red (6/2 HUE 2.5 Y) rocky gravel. The findings of lithics (129) and bones (4) suggest a fishing-hunting subsistence strategy.

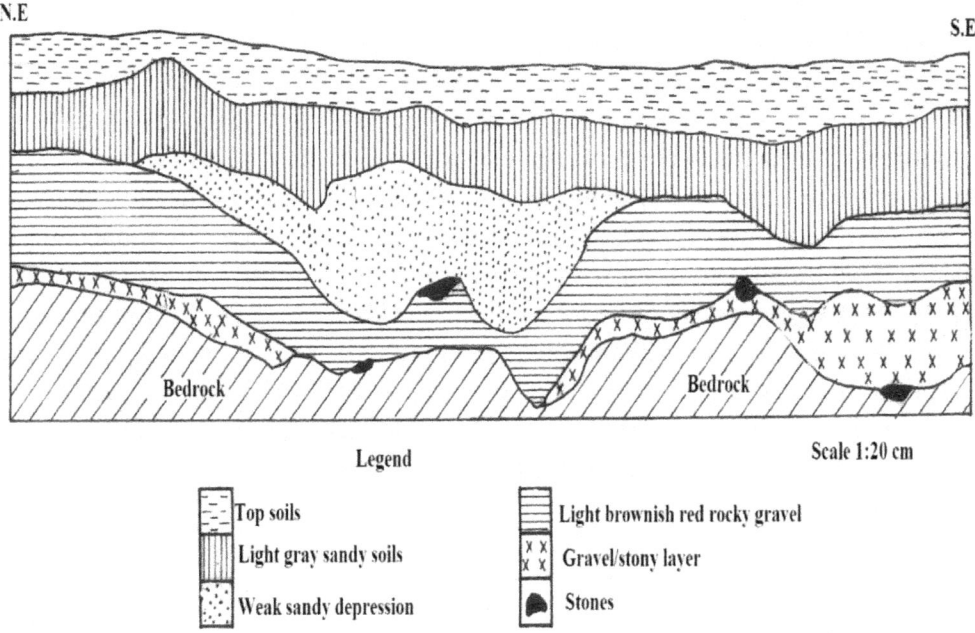

Figure 5.10: Stratigraphy of Trench 2A Facing East

5.4.17 Trench 2B Kansyore Island

Trench 2B was an extension of Trenches 2 and 2Ai. The extension was made to critically examine the sequence in Trenches 2, 2A, 2Ai and 2Aii, and since Trench 2Ai was very productive the need for more diagnostic artifacts to examine whether there was cultural interaction in the upper Nile catchment areas dictated the move for extension. The top layers as in all trenches at this site did not have plenty of material finds in the sandy soils. However, material production increased in the lower levels especially in the compacted darker soils with the gravel layers yielding more materials all the way up to bedrock.

This could be either due to site formation processes or the settlement patterns of Kansyore Island. Excavation of the first level utilized 10 cm spits as a way of leveling the trench but thereafter excavation was systematic following arbitrary 5 cm spit. The later was followed in Level 9 (45-50 cm) to level the trench to the same gravel layer. This was because the rest of the trench was gravel and so by Level 9 (45-50 cm) that was in the 50 cm×1 m² southwestern portion.

5.4.18 Trench 2B Findings

Trench 2B went up to 75 cm in depth below surface. A total of 2,331 cultural materials were obtained that included pottery, (309), lithics (1,715), faunal remains (307), metal objects (2), and red ochre (1). The pottery traditions identified basing on decoration were roulette (19), Urewe (30), channel (1) and Kansyore pottery (18) while among the lithics were geometrics (44) and scrapers (33), points (3) and denticulates (2) (Table 5.8). The charcoal sample at 50-55cm was dated 1671± 44 BP. The dated charcoal sample was in the same level with Urewe and Kansyore potsherds associated with geometrics and LSA scrapers. This may therefore imply that the coexistence of Urewe and Neolithic pottery traditions should not be simply dismissed as disturbances but could probably also imply interaction and coexistence. This therefore calls for examination of the transition from the Neolithic (Kansyore) to the Iron Age period in future in this area.

ARCHAEOLOGICAL EXAMINATION OF CULTURAL INTERACTIONS IN THE UPPER NILE CATCHMENT AREAS:

Table 5.8: Material Inventory of Trench 2B Kansyore Island

Level (Depth) cm	Lithics						Pottery					Charcoal	Faunal remains		Metal objects	Red ochre	Total
	Scrapers	Backed pieces	Others tools	Cores	Flake/blades	Debitage	Roulette	Urewe	Channel	Kansyore	Un-diagnostic		Bones	Shells			
1 (0-10)	1					26				2	5						34
2 (10-15)	1				5	18		2			5			4			35
3 (15-20)					1	1					2		2				6
4 (20-25)	3			1	4	7					2		1				18
5 (25-30)				1		16	1			2	4		3		1		28
6 (30-35)				5		14					9						28
7 (35-40)				1		10		2		1	10	1	1				26
8 (40-45)	2	2	2	2	6	25	8	2			25		4				76
9 (45-50)	8	2		5	19	39	4	3	1	1	29		3				115
10 (50-55)	5	5		38	55	176	6	5		2	28		26		1		342
11 (55-60)	5	14	3	39	142	423		13		8	99		124				877
12 (60-65)	8	18		9	93	312		3	1	2	19		129			1	585
13 (65-70)	2	2		1	33	86					4	1	11				147
14 (70-75)		1			3	9										1	14
Total	35	44	5	102	362	1162	19	30	2	18	241	2	304	4	2	1	2331
% age	1.50	1.89	0.21	4.38	15.53	49.85	0.82	1.29	0.04	0.77	10.34	0.04	13.04	0.17	0.09	0.04	100.00

5.4.19 Stratigraphy of Trench 2B

The stratigraphy of Trench 2B as seen from the southern wall had three observed layers, the fourth being the bed rock while along the western wall four layers could be observed minus the bedrock layer (Figures 5.11 and 5.12). The discussion is centered on the southern wall which had clearer layers.

Layer 1 was the widest layer characterized by dark grayish brown (4/2 HUE 2.5 Y) loose sandy soils that gained compactness by the end of the layer. Layer 1 was made up of five levels; 1 (0-10 cm), 2 (10-15 cm), 3 (15-20 cm), 4 (20-25 cm) and 5 (25-30 cm). The excavation used arbitrary 5 cm spit levels. The finds in this layer included; pottery (25) of which were roulette (1), Urewe (2) and Kansyore (4) pottery traditions. The lithics (88) included scrapers (4), cores (2) and flakes/blades (10) associated with faunal remains (9) that included shells (4) and bones (6). An iron nail was also obtained.

Layer 2 had dark gray (N/4 HUE 2.5 YR) compacted sandy loamy soils. The layer lay between 30-50 cm. The levels in this layer were four: 6 (30-35 cm), 7 (35-40 cm), 8 (40-45 cm) and 9 (45-50 cm). Excavation in this layer followed arbitrary 5 cm spit levels. Other artifacts obtained were similar to those in Layer 1 with the notable absence of shells and appearance of backed pieces. In Level 7 (35-40 cm), unique pottery (1) was obtained which had fine line marks as though it was made by a potter's wheel and this is instrumental in establishing the cultural interaction in the Nile catchment area since the potter's wheel was not known in the current area of study in ancient times. However it may not be plausible to rely on a single specimen to make a conclusive remark on it. Finding wheel-made pottery in this part of the Nile catchment would indicate cultural interaction. However the sample is too small to support the argument for now.

In Level 7 (35-40 cm), the gravel appeared on the south-western corner of the trench. Level 8 (40-45 cm) yielded roulette pottery below the Urewe layer that may imply coexistence and interaction between the Urewe and roulette makers and users rather than a disturbance. The entire layer yielded lithics (143), pottery (94) and faunal remains (8).

Layer 3 was 50-75 cm thick depthwise and was characterized by olive brown (4/4 HUE 2.5 Y) gravel soils. Therefore it was made up of five levels: 10 (50-55 cm), 11 (55-60 cm), 12 (60-65 cm), 13 (65-70 cm) and 14 (70-75 cm). Being a stony layer, the major disturbances were stones. The key feature in the layer was the bedrock that appeared in most parts of the trench. The lithics

(1,482) included a denticulate and all lithic types obtained from the previous layer but with differing quantities. The pottery (190) included Urewe with flat rims and crosshatched motifs and Kansyore ware among others. Besides pottery and lithics were bones (290), an iron metal (1) and red ochre (1). This layer marked the end of excavation when the bedrock encompassed the whole trench confirming sterility. The first level had a charcoal sample whose radio carbon date was 1671± 44 BP (WK-31383) associated with a metal object therefore dating to the Iron Age.

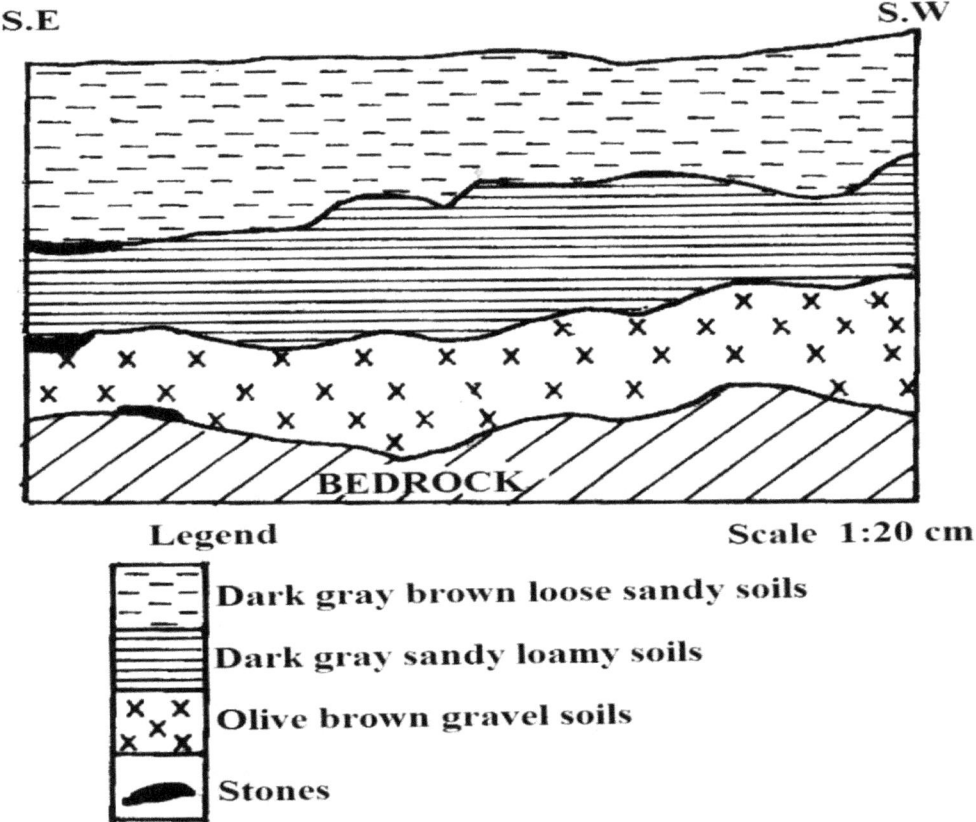

Figure 5.11: Southern Wall Profile of Trench 2B

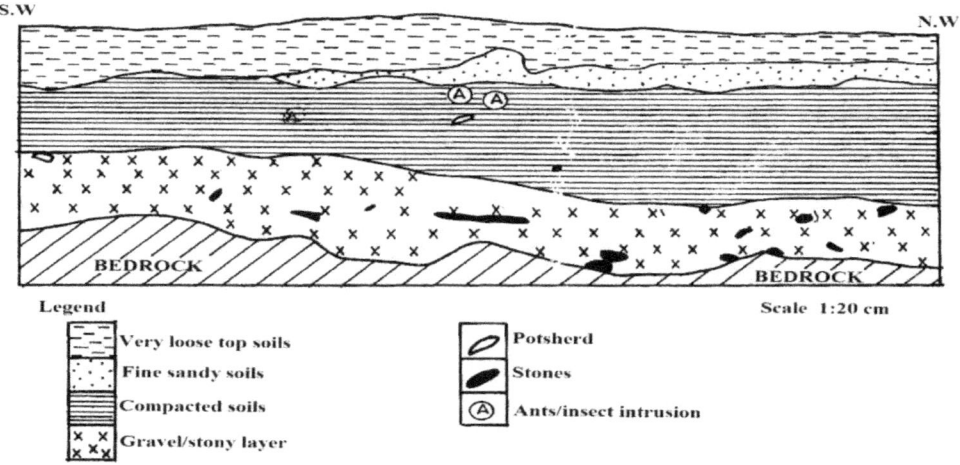

Figure 5.12: Straigraphy of the Western Wall of Trench 2B

5.4.10 Trench 3 Kansyore Island

Trench 3 was a 1 ×3 m² trench whose GPS readings were 01° 00′ 05″ S and 030° 44′ 32″ S. The trench was on a gently sloping landscape parallel to Trench 2 and on the eastern side of Kansyore Island. Excavation of the entire trench was systematic following 10cm arbitrary spit levels. Trench 3 (1,578) was the least productive trench compared to Trenches 1 (8,079) and 2 (6,696) at Kansyore Island (Figure 5.13). This could be due to the varying sizes of the trenches.

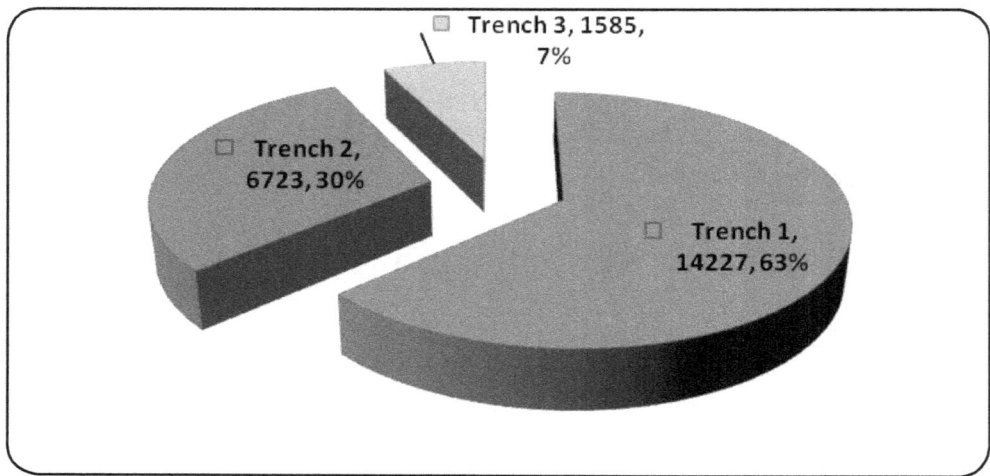

Figure 5.13: Frequency of Cultural Materials in Kansyore Trenches

5.4.11 Findings from Trench 3 Kansyore Island

A total of 1,585 cultural materials were retrieved from Trench 3. These included lithics 1,464 (92.4%), pottery 119 (7.5%) and metal objects 2 (0.1%) (Table 5.9). One of the metals was an iron nail suggesting construction. This implied that the dominant finds were lithics in this trench that were composed of scrapers 29 (1.8%), backed pieces 54 (3.4%), burins, points, and denticulates 6 (0.4%) (Table 5.9). Among the potsherds was the proposed channel pottery 2 (0.1%) that was obtained from the surface while the rest of the trench yielded roulette 2 (0.1 %), Urewe 11 (0.7%) and Kansyore pottery 2 (0.1%).This implied that Trench 3 did not yield any faunal remains or red ochre as the case was in the first two trenches.

Level/Depth(cm)	Lithics						Pottery Diagnostic				Un-diagnostic	Metal objects	Total
	Shaped tools			Cores	Flake/blades	Debitage	Roulette	Urewe	Channel	Kansyore			
	Scrapers	Backed	Others										
Trench surface						7					1		8
1(0-10)	1	1	2	4	5	42					10		65
2(10-20)	14	21	2	23	126	499	2	9	1	2	71	2	772
3(20-30)	13	17	1	18	157	232		2	1		19		460
4(30-40)	1	11	1	5	73	84					1		176
5(40-50)		4		2	19	79							104
Total	29	54	6	52	380	943	2	11	2	2	102	2	1585
% age	1.8	3.4	0.4	3.3	24.0	59.5	0.1	0.7	0.1	0.1	6.4	0.1	100.0

Table 5.9: Material Inventory of Trench 3 at Kansyore Island

5.4.12 Stratigraphy of Kansyore Island Trench 3

The stratigraphy of Trench 3 as observed from the western wall had two layers (Figure 5.14). The surface loose soils contained roulette (1), channel (1) and Urewe (2) pottery traditions. This suggests the site was last settled by iron-using people.

Layer 1 ranged from 0-30 cm meaning it was composed of three levels, 1 (0-10 cm), 2 (10-20 cm) and Level 3 (20-30 cm). The soils in Layer 1 were dark grayish brown (4/2 Hue 2.5 Y) loose gravel on the northern side and loose sandy on the southern side. The layer produced all the diagnostic potsherds (17) that belonged to roulette (2), Urewe (11), channel (2) and Kansyore (2) in the order of the proposed sequence of Great Lakes region by this research. All the metals (2) were also obtained in Layer 1. The lithic artefacts included; burins (2), points (2), denticulate (1), scrapers (28) and geometrics (39).

Layer 2 was on average 30 cm thick ranging from 30-60 cm. Therefore, it comprised of three levels; 4(30-40) cm, 5(40-50) cm and 6 (50-60) cm. The soil texture was gravel in nature. The soil colour was light yellowish brown (6/3, Hue 2.5 Y) on the northern side while the southern side had reddish brown (5/3 Hue 2.5 YR) soils. The layer almost exclusively yielded lithics (279) and one un-diagnostic potsherd. The cranial rock appeared on the southern end of the trench as the bedrock appeared on the northern side of the trench but eventually the bedrock appeared like a deep slope in the trench (Plate 5.6). The western side had a big rock with some pecked impressions where probably stone knapping took place. It also had a line of dots running down probably due to rock-formation processes (Plate 5.7). At bed rock, excavation ceased due to the sterility of the trench.

Plate 5.6: Trench 3 Kansyore Island at Bedrock

Plate 5.7: Pecked Impressions on the Bedrock of Trench 3 at Kansyore Island

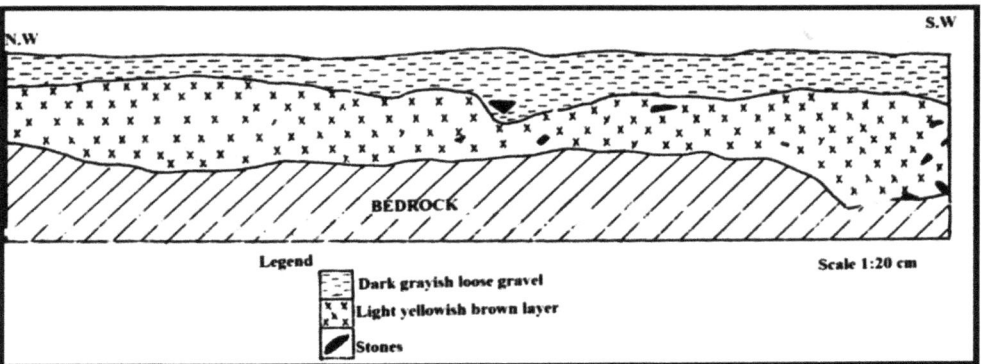

Figure 5.14: Stratigraphy of the Western Wall of Trench 3 at Kansyore Island

5.5. Island of Deserters

The final phase of excavation was executed at the Island of Deserters where five trenches were excavated.

5.5.1 Trench 1 Island of Deserters

This was a 2 × 2 m² trench at the quarry side of the Island of Deserters. It was established at the extreme southern part of the Island of Deserters. The trench was established close to the quarry site because it had exposed cultural materials and the fact that the spot chosen for sinking the trench was thought to have the least disturbance. Trench 1 was divided into two trenches each measuring 1×2 m² where the eastern side became Trench 1A while the western side became Trench 1B (Plate 5.7). This was in Level 4 (25-30 cm). The reason for the division followed the divergence in terms of cultural materials whereby the western side yielded pottery that was relatively older than the eastern side basing on the decoration. However, in Level 7 (40-45 cm) the two trenches were merged since they were now yielding materials of the same time period.

The surface of Trench 1 had soils that were hard and compact due to continuous trampling by people and animals since the area was used for grazing cattle. Excavation was systematic following arbitrary spit levels ranging from 5 to 10 cm.

Plate 5.7: Trench 1 divisions into 1A and 1B at the Island of Deserters

5.5.2 The Findings of Trench 1 Island of Deserters

The trench was excavated up to 75 cm below surface. This trench yielded three charcoal samples from Trench 1B. The cultural materials from the entire Trench 1 at the Island of Deserters were 4624 that included lithics 4156 (89.88%), pottery 442 (9.56 %), faunal remains 2 (0.04%), metal objects 3 (0.06%), daub 16 (0.35%) and red ochre stone 2 (0.04%) (Table 5.10). The lithics obtained suggested a LSA occurrence as evidenced from scrapers, backed pieces, burins, denticulates, *outils escailles* and discoids. The tool types auger well with the lithic types from Kansyore Island and some like denticulates with southern Sudan and the LSA industry of East Africa.

Pottery production was realized more in the top layers among which were nine ceramic pieces of Indian origin. These would suggest links with the East African coastal trade of the 19th century. The pottery including roulette (LIA), bourdine, Urewe (EIA), and Kansyore suggests settlement in this place from the Neolithic to the Iron Age period. Settlement is further confirmed by the existence of daub while the metal implied the Iron Age. However, the absence of slag, tuyeres and furnaces would suggest lack of iron smelting and probably outside acquisition of the metals possibly from the neighbouring Haya area suggesting regional cultural interactions.

Level (depth) cm	Lithics						Pottery							FR	MO	CK	DB	R/O	Total
	scr	bac	Others	CO	F/B	DEB	Plain	ROT	UR	BOD	FOR	KAS	Undi						
Trench 1																			
0 (0-5)				1		2		1											4
1 (5-15)	3	1			9	81	1	12	2		9		92	1					211
2 (15-20)	1	2	1		15	68	5	17	2	1			76	1					188
3 (20-25)	3	1		3	41	143		10	1	2		5	116		2				327
Trench 1A																			
4 (25-30)	7	1	1	10	50	119	1	1	11			3	53		1				258
5 (30-35)	3	1	1	6	26	133			2				1						173
6 (35-40)	5	2		5	21	102													135
8 (40-45)	2	1		14	29	224							3					1	274
9 (45-50)	19	2	5	24	81	336													467
10 (50-55)	19		3	40	93	140													295
11 (55-60)	10			17	33														60
Trench 1B																			
4 (25-30)	2	7	1	13	18	266			2				2			1			311
5 (30-35)	12	1	2	41	103	329							3			1			491
6 (35-40)	1	1	2	14	22	143			2			1	7			1	2		196
7 (40-45)	26				1	4											4		35
8 (45-50)	19	4	4	43	201	456											10		737
9 (50-55)		8	9	33	129	281													460
10 (55-60)						2													2
Total	132	31	28	264	872	2829	7	41	20	3	9	9	353	2	3	3	16	2	4624
% age	2.85	0.67	0.61	5.71	18.86	61.18	0.15	0.89	0.43	0.06	0.19	0.19	7.63	0.04	0.06	0.06	0.35	0.04	100.00

Key: scr=scrapers; bac = backed pieces; CO= cores; F/B=flakes/blades; DEB= debitage; Un-dia-un-diagnostic; ROT=roulette; UR=Urewe; BO=bourdine; FOR=foreign; KAS=Kansyore; FR=faunal remains; MO=metal objects; CK=charcoal; DB-daub

Table 5.10 : Material Inventory of Trench 1 Island of Deserters

5.5.3 The Stratigraphy of Trench 1 at the Island of Deserters

The trench had three observable layers along the southern wall (Figure 5.15). Layer 1 had loose dark reddish brown (3/2 HUE 5YR) loamy soils. The layer was on average 5-25 cm thick and made up of three levels; 1 (5-15 cm), 2 (15-20 cm) and 3 (20-25 cm). This means Layer 1 comprised the entire trench before the division. This layer was interrupted by grass rootlet disturbances which however reduced by the bottom of the layer. Artifacts from this layer included lithics (374) in association with pottery (352). The ceramics was both local and foreign including Indian ware (9) and the local roulette (40), Urewe (5), bourdine (3) and Kansyore pottery (5), faunal remains (2) and metal objects (2).

Layer 2 straddled Trench1A and Trench 1B. The soils were dark olive brown (3/3 HUE 2.5Y) loose loam. The layer ranged from 25-50 cm and was made up of five levels; 4 (25-30 cm), 5 (30-35 cm), 6 (35-40 cm), 7 (40-45 cm) and 8 (45-50 cm). Three charcoal samples were collected from the western side (Trench 1B). The first charcoal sample was at 30 cm below surface, the second sample at 36 cm below surface and was in association with daub and the third charcoal sample was at 41 cm in association with Kansyore pottery. Unfortunately, our budget did not permit the dating of all these samples. Slight disturbance was experienced from grass rootlets, small stones and termites. The layer had all the local pottery traditions (94) obtained in layer one, similar lithic tool types (3069), red ochre (1), daub (16) and a metal object (1). Pottery appearance stopped in this layer but just like the Kansyore Island pottery with the crosshatching decorative element typical of Urewe was collected in association with lithics which could make one presuppose that probably crosshatching predated the Iron Age.

Layer 3 had reddish yellow (6/8 HUE 7.5 YR) gravel soils. This layer was on average 50-75 cm meaning that it was composed of four levels; 9 (50-55 cm), 10 (55-60 cm), 11 (60-70 cm) and 12 (70-75 cm). Excavation exploited 5 cm to 10 cm spit levels. The 10 cm spits were used in Level 11 (60-70 cm) to ensure ultimate recovery of artifacts in a layer considered sterile. However, this could not be maintained in the last level whose end was conditioned by bedrock and marked the end of excavation. The bedrock explained why again a 5 cm spit was utilized. Layer 3 was an entirely lithics layer (817).

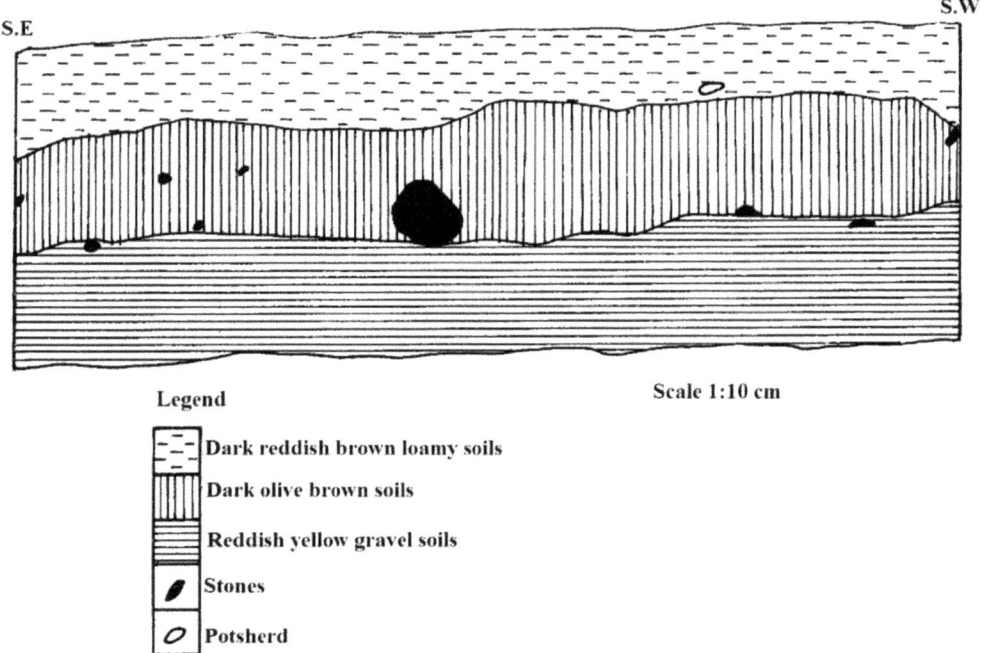

Figure 5.15: Southern Wall Profile of Trench 1 at Island of Deserters

5.5.4 Trench 2 Island of Deserters

Trench 2 at the Island of Deserters was a 2×1 m² trench. The setting of this trench was dictated by the pottery surface scatters obtained from the nearby banana plantation during survey and the need to have a balanced view of material production on this Island by having trenches spread out. Excavation of Trench 2 was systematic following 5 cm spit levels because of the need to have a critical examination of the recovered materials and the sequence in which they occurred. In the black (2.5/1 HUE 5 YR) surface soils plain potsherds and lithics were collected.

5.5.5 Trench 2 Island of Deserters' Findings

The trench went up to a depth of 75 cm below surface and yielded lithics (1,832), pottery (224), bones (54), charcoal (5) and a metal object (1). Among the lithic artefacts were some types that differed from those of other trenches, like a *levallois* denticulate (1), a pickaxe (1), the only composite tool in the entire assemblage of this research, a scraper-burin (1) and point preforms (3) with clear evidence of hafting on the butts. The ceramics from the decoration belonged to roulette (22), Urewe (25), bourdine (6) and Kansyore pottery (1) (Table 5.11). The distribution of material finds exhibited popularity and unpopularity of site activities (Figure 5.16). For instance in Levels 1 (0-5 cm) to 5 (20-25 cm) the finds, though few, progressively increased until Level 8 (35-40 cm) when they hit the maximum and then a tremendous fall is witnessed thereafter (Figure 5.16).

The findings from the trench further suggest interaction between MSA/LSA people. As noted by Phillipson (2005) the distinction between the MSA and LSA is superficial. Besides is the fact that though the *levallois* technology started in the MSA it continued into the LSA. The composite tools like the scrapers being general purpose tools could also imply an interaction phase.

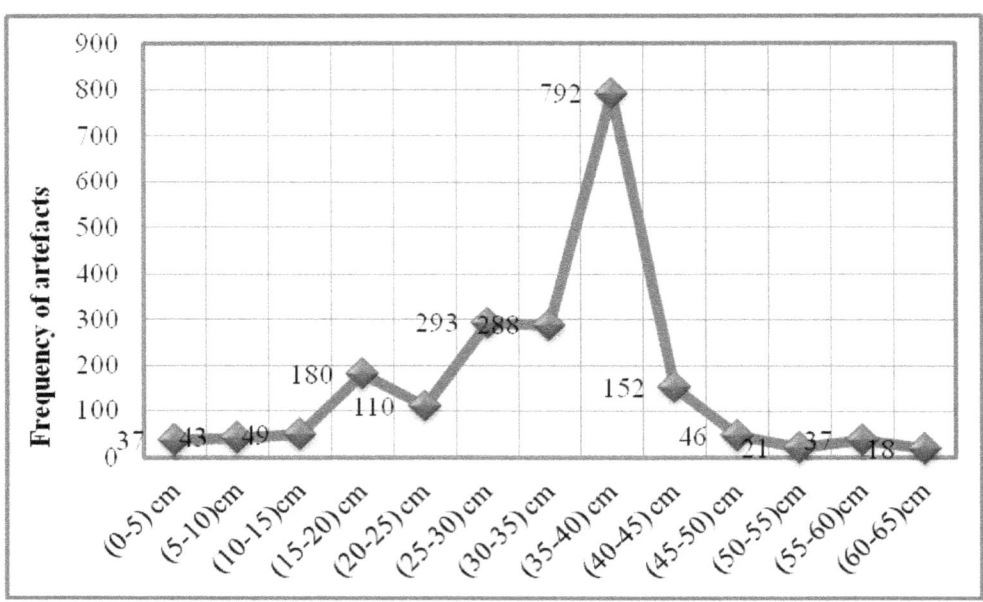

Figure 5.16: Distribution of Cultural Materials in Trench 2 per Level

Level Depth (cm)	Lithics						Pottery						Faunal remains		Total
	Scrapers	Backed pieces	Other tools	Cores	Flake/blades	Debitage	Plain pottery	Roulette	Urewe	Bourdine	Kansyore	Un-diagnostic	Charcoal	Bones	Metal objects	
Surface	1			1	3	4						5				14
1(0-5)	1			2	4	24						5		1		37
2(5-10)					16	25						5		5		51
3(10-15)			2	2	4	34		1				8		3		54
4(15-20)	2			6	16	67		21	1			67	1	7		188
5(20-25)	1		2		32	58		1	3	1		27		2		127
6(25-30)	7	3	1	11	67	166	3		15	1	1	3	2	12	1	293
7(30-35)	12	2	3	8	57	178	1			4		20	1	4		290
8(35-40)	24	8	3	30	189	493	4		5			21	1	12		790
9(40-45)	9	1	2	17	37	76						1		8		151
10(45-50)	1			4	12	29										46
11(50-55)				1	7	12										20
12(55-60)	2		1	4	5	25										37
13(60-65)	1	1		2	3	11										18
Total	61	15	14	88	452	1202	8	22	25	6	1	162	5	54	1	2116
% age	2.88	0.71	0.66	4.16	21.36	56.81	0.38	1.04	1.18	0.28	0.05	7.66	0.24	2.55	0.05	100.00

Table 5.11: Trench 2 Island of Deserters - Material Inventory

5.5.6 Trench 2 Island of Deserters' Stratigraphy

Trench 2 had three observable layers facing east and north (Figure 5.17a and 5.17b). However this discussion is based on the eastern wall.

Layer 1 had dark reddish gray (4/2 HUE 5YR) loam sandy and relatively compact soils that became gravel-like by the end of the layer. The first layer was 5-40 cm being composed of seven levels, 1 (5-10 cm), 2 (10-15 cm), 3 (15-20 cm), 4 (20-25 cm), 5 (25-30 cm), 6 (30-35 cm) and 7 (35-40 cm). Generally, this layer yielded; pottery (223), lithics (1,569), faunal remains (46) a metal object (1) and charcoal pieces (5). This means all the five charcoal samples were recovered in this layer and the same applies to the sole metal object. The concentration of charcoal samples would imply concentration of human activities. The disturbances in this layer were rootlets, stones and insects (beetles) the latter being in the north-eastern corner of the trench.

Layer 2 was in the gravel reddish brown (4/4 HUE 5YR) soils. The layer that stretched from 40-60 cm comprised of levels 8 (40-45 cm), 9 (45-50 cm), 10 (50-55 cm) and 11 (55-60 cm). In the north-eastern corner was an insect burrow (beetle) and a tree stamp in the south-east that formed a source of disturbance. There was a drop in artifact production in this layer compared to the previous layer from 1,806 to 256. This was basically a Stone Age phase with mainly lithics (263) and a single plain potsherd that could imply people earned a living by hunting as suggested by the bones of terrestrial wild animals (8).

Layer 3 possessed reddish yellow (7/7 HUE 7.5 YR) gravel soils. The layer was from 60 to 75 cm. Excavation in this layer was on the southeastern part of the trench as the rest of the trench had become sterile. The layer yielded only lithics (18) in level 13 (60-65) while the last two levels from 65-75cm did not have any material but were excavated to confirm that the trench was sterile though they yielded nothing and there after excavation seized.

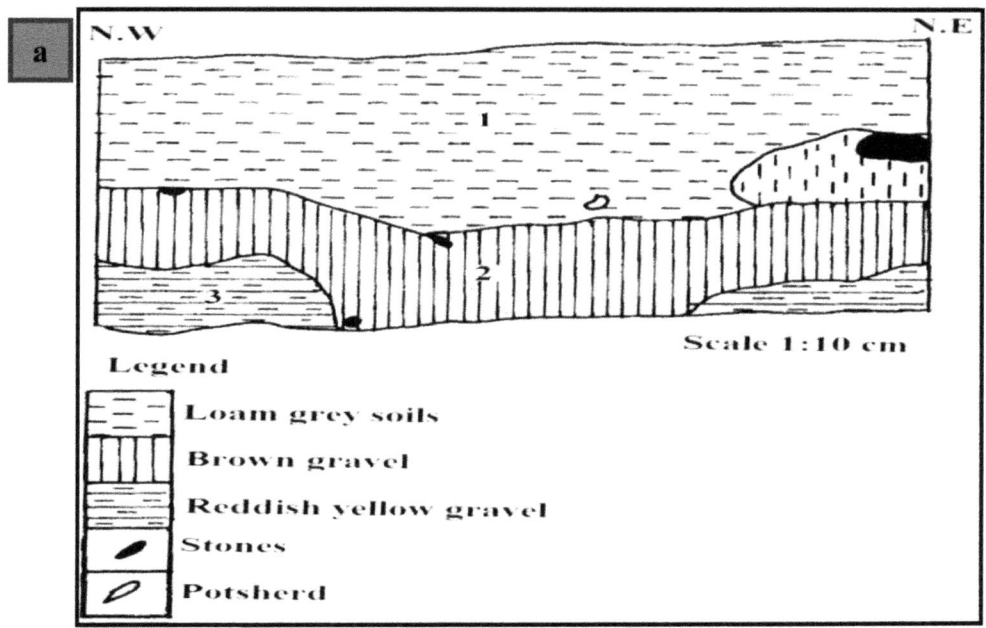

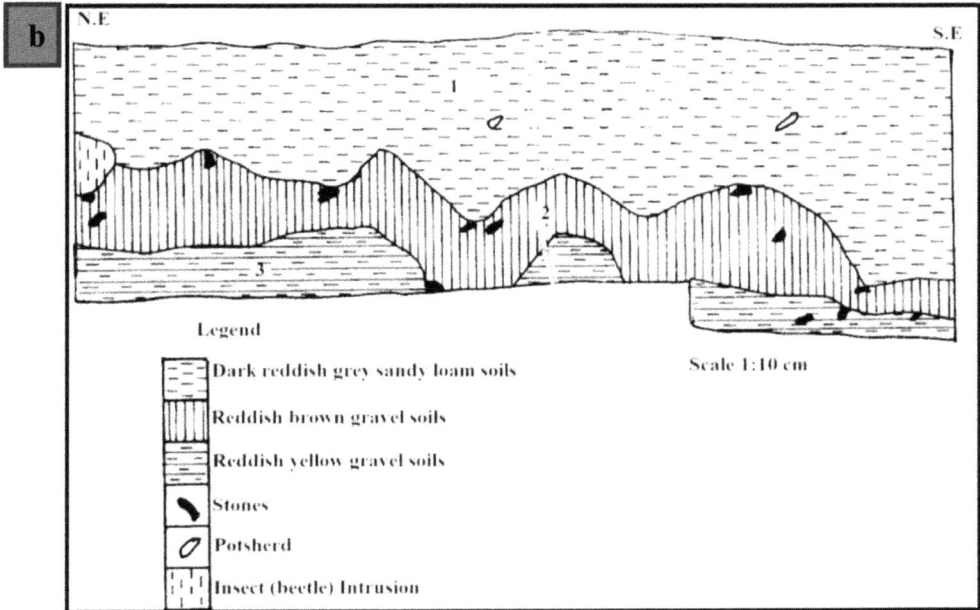

Figure 5.17: Stratigraphy of Trench 2 Island of Deserters

Key: (a) The Northern Wall   (b) The Eastern Wall

5.5.7 Trench 3 in Island of Deserters

This was a 2×2 m² trench set in an area with minimum disturbance close to the Kagera river banks. It was set on the north-eastern side of the site from the datum point. The consideration to sink the trench at this point was also due to its proximity to the garden where roulette and Urewe pottery were collected on the surface (Table 5.12). The excavation was undertaken systematically following 5 cm arbitrary spit levels. The use of 5 cm spit levels was preferred like as in the earlier trenches to control artifact recovery and to examine if they will portray characteristics that will show a relationship with the material from other trenches, sites and the entire upper Nile catchment under study to examine cultural interactions. This trench had the shallowest stratigraphy of all the excavated trenches at the site.

5.5.8 Trench 3 Island of Deserters' Findings

The trench went down to 65 cm below surface including the 10 cm for leveling. This means the excavated portion ended at 55 cm below surface. The cultural materials from this trench had affinity with those obtained from Trenches 1 and 2 at the Island of Deserters and even those from Kansyore Island apart from the difference in quantities. The trench yielded the same pottery types that were roulette, Urewe, bourdine, channel and Kansyore as Trenches 1 and 2 just like the lithic types as those in other trenches included scrapers and backed pieces. However, unlike Kansyore Island that had plenty of fish faunal remains at the Island of Deserters these were minimal with only one specimen obtained from Trench 3 and in association with all the finds was a single charcoal sample (Table 5.12). Generally a total of 941 artefacts were retrieved from Trench 3 at the Island of Deserters. As the general trend was, lithics were the dominant artefacts (770), followed by pottery (169), charcoal (1) and faunal remains (1). As noted, the sole faunal remains was a fish vertebrae and the only one retrieved from the entire site. The pottery exhibited a clear sequence from roulette, bourdine, Urewe and Kansyore from above to bottom (Table 5.12).

Level Depth (cm)	Lithics						Pottery					Un-diagnostic	Charcoal	Faunal remains	Total
	Scrapers	Backed pieces	Others tools	Cores	Flake/blades	Debitage	Plain	Roulette	Bourdine	Urewe	Kansyore				
Surface				1			1								2
1(0-10)				1	2	22	1	1				15			42
2(10-15)					2	12	1	2				8		1	26
3(15-20)				1	5	13				1		1			21
4(20-25)	1			1	48	26	2			5	2	26			111
5(25-30)	3	2	2	11	71	144	2				3	75			313
6(30-35)	10			15	31	208	2					17			283
7(35-40)	1	1	1	11	14	75									103
8(40-45)	1					22						4	1		28
9(45-50)						12									12
10(50-55)															
Total	16	3	3	41	173	534	7	4	1	6	5	146	1	1	941
% age	1.7	0.3	0.3	4.4	18.4	56.7	0.7	0.4	0.1	0.6	0.5	15.5	0.1	0.1	100.0

Table 5.12: Material Inventory per level for Trench 3 Island of Deserters

5.5.9 Trench 3 Island of Deserters' Stratigraphy

Trench 3 as observed from the eastern wall had three layers (Figure 5.18). The soils in Layer 1 were dark gray (3/1 HUE 5YR) sandy loam soils. The deposition in this trench was natural. Layer 1 was on average from 10 to 35 cm wide with five levels: 1 (10-15 cm), 2 (15-20 cm), 3 (20-25 cm), 4 (25-30 cm) and 5 (30-35 cm. There were grass rootlet disturbances in this layer that kept reducing as the trench progressed below surface. All the diagnostic pottery from the entire trench was in Layer 1 that was roulette (4), Urewe (6), bourdine (1), Kansyore (5) and plain (7) pottery. The lithics (632) included scrapers (14) and backed pieces (2), and the single fish bone vertebrae from the entire trench and site belonged to this layer. The occurrence of artifacts increased with the appearance of the gravel layer at the bottom of this layer.

However, the western side was more productive compared to the eastern side that was tending towards sterility.

Layer 2 had olive yellow (6/6 HUE 2.5Y) gravel soils. This layer lay between 35-40 cm thickness therefore it was composed of Level 6 (35-40 cm) only in a natural deposition. There were few rootlet disturbances. The layer only produced lithic artifacts (103) but with reduced quantity and increased size (macroliths) in comparison to the previous layer.

Layer 3 was characterized by yellowish (6/8 HUE 5YR) gravel soils. This layer was composed of five levels: 7 (40-45 cm), 8 (45-50 cm), 9 (50-55 cm). 10 (55-60 cm) and 11 (60-65 cm). In Level 7 (40-45 cm) the artifact concentrations dropped which was an indicator of nearing the sterile layer. The macrolithic artefacts (35) and un-diagnostic potsherds (4) were retrieved in the south-eastern corner associated with the single charcoal sample obtained from Trench 3. The last three levels (50-65 cm) did not yield any artifacts but were excavated to ascertain the sterility that led to stopping of the excavation at 65 cm below surface when the trench was proved sterile.

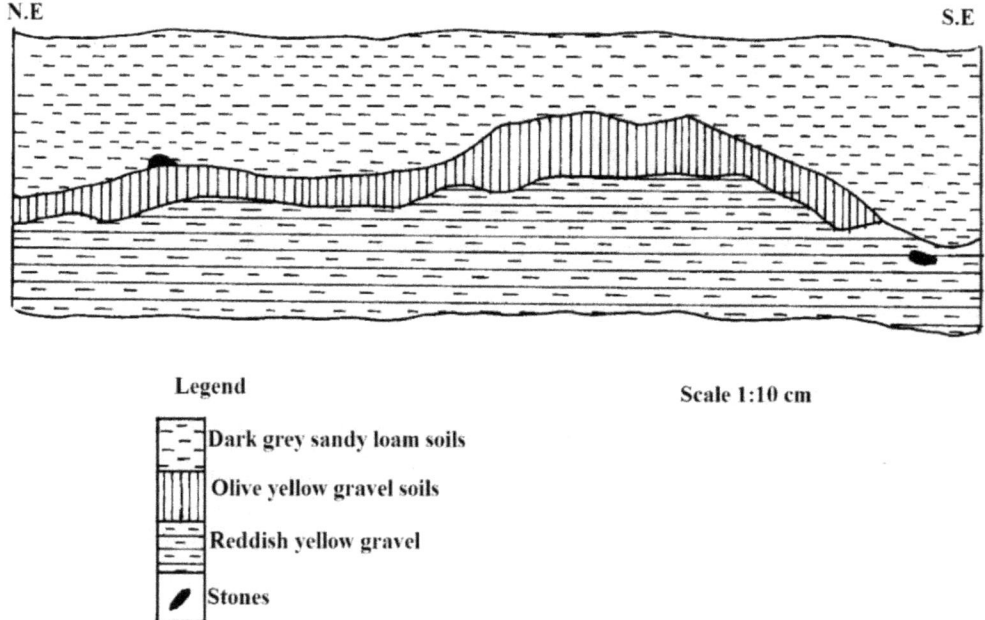

Figure 5.18: Eastern Wall Profile of Trench 3 at the Island of Deserters

5.5.10 Trench 4 Island of Deserters

The trench was set up at the most elevated and flat part close to the river bank. Trench 4 was 2× 2 m² whose excavation was done systematically following arbitrary 5 cm levels due to the desire to obtain a clear examination of material recovery from each level and examine their spatial relationship and distribution in relation to other sites and the entire Upper Nile catchment.

5.5.11 Trench 4 Island of Deserters' Findings

The trench was excavated to 85 cm below surface and had 3,422 artifacts. These included; charcoal 8 (0.2%), lithics 2,432 (71.1%), pottery 892 (26.1%), faunal remains 79 (2.3%), red ochre 3 (0.1%) and daub 8 (0.2%) (Table 5.13). The diagnostic potsherds were dominated by Urewe (61) followed by Kansyore (21), roulette (20) and bourdine (8) pottery traditions and plain diagnostic (49) pottery. Unlike all other trenches in the Nsongezi/ Kansyore area, Trench 4 was the only trench with additional evidence for the Iron Age in the area as it yielded iron slag pieces that could easily be mistaken for stones as they were heavy and highly magnetic. The lithic tool types from this trench had affinity with those from Trenches 1, 2 and 3 at the site and those from Kansyore Island. These included scrapers, backed pieces, burins, bec, point preforms, denticulates and a pickaxe. The faunal remains that included shells and bones were evidence of cultural material affinity with Kansyore Island. The fresh water shells obtained were similar to those from Kansyore Island.

Depth/Level (cm)	Lithics						Pottery						Charcoal	Daub	Faunal remains		Red ochre	Slag	Total
	Scrapers	Backed pieces	Other tools	Cores	Flake/blades	Debitage	Plain	Roulette	Urewe	bourdine	Kansyore	Un-diagnostic			Bones	Shells			
Surface						3													3
2(5-10)					3	10													13
3(10-15)		1	1			4													6
4(15-20)	1		1	1	2	2	46	1	11	2	1	2							107
5(20-25)	1	1	1	7	8	56	10	9	9		1	190	38	5	14	5			311
6(25-30)	1	2	3	11	10	66	31		35	4	13	382	4		26			5	588
7(30-35)		1		15	24	116	4		13	2	2	84	3	2	10	1		1	268
8(35-40)	1	5	2	20	57	101	3		3		3	32	1		11				238
9(40-45)	8	4	3	37	108	226					1	3			2		1		376
10(45-50)	13	6	6	20	109	263		1		2	1	1		1		6			442
11(50-55)	15	2		43	64	145		9	1									1	249
12(55-60)	18	2	8	44	60	224						1			2		1		359
13(60-65)	14	3	3	13	79	208									2				351
14(65-70)	4		1		15	75											1		111
15(70-75)					1	4													5
16(75-80)						2													2
Total	76	27	27	213	540	1549	49	20	61	8	21	733	8	8	72	7	3	7	3429
% age	2.2	0.8	0.8	6.2	15.7	45.2	1.4	0.6	1.8	0.2	0.6	21.4	0.2	0.2	2.1	0.2	0.1	0.2	100.0

Table 5.13: Material Inventory per level from Trench 4 Island of Deserters

5.5.12 Trench 4 Island of Deserters' Stratigraphy

The trench had four layers facing east (Figure 5.19) described below.

Layer 1 had very dark grey (3/1 HUE 5YR) loose sandy loam soils. This was the thickest layer of this trench made up of seven levels: 1 (0-5 cm), 2 (5-10 cm), 3 (10-15 cm), 4 (15-20 cm, 5 (20-25 cm), 6 (25-30 cm) and 7 (30-35 cm). Grass rootlets and animal burrows were the major disturbances in this layer. There was remarkable increase in artifact recovery in this layer from Level 4 (15-20 cm) that yielded lithics and typical roulette potsherds. Level 5 (20-25 cm) yielded 4 charcoal samples in association with lithics, pottery, bones and daub. The climax of the trench's production was observed in Level 6 (25-30 cm) with the highest number of artifacts recovered (588) and among which were 3 charcoal samples. Generally, this layer yielded pottery (841), lithics (381), and faunal remains (55) that were all bones, iron slag (6) and daub (5).

Layer 2 possessed dark grayish brown (4/2 HUE 2.5 Y) loose gravel soils. This layer was on average from 35 to 65 cm thick therefore it was made up of six levels: 8 (35-40 cm), 9 (40-45 cm), 10 (45-50 cm), 11 (50-55 cm), 12 (55-60 cm) and 13 (60-65 cm). This layer had disturbances of rootlets and stones but which ceased in Level 10 (45-50 cm). At the top of this layer in Level 8 (35-40 cm); there was a drop in pottery occurrence with an increase in lithic occurrence where the first oyster shells at the site were obtained. A bone in association with a potsherd in an ant-intruded area marked in the profile was obtained. Just like in other trenches at this site in this trench, material production was more in the gravel layers. This layer yielded pottery (51); scrapers and backed pieces among the lithics (1,936), daub (3), faunal remains (22) that were bones and shells fragments, slag (1) and red ochre stones (2). There was reduction in pottery production that completely ceased in Level 12 (55-60 cm). In Level 11 (50-55 cm), a rim with oblique cross-hatching decorative element typical of EIA had an abraded interior. The abrasion of the interior, according to Reid and Young (2000), could be attributed to the preparation of African grains. This is suggested as an alternative method of making inferences about agriculture due to the shortage of archaeo-botanical materials. A look at the preparation of sorghum and finger millet shows that it involved a lot of pounding, winnowing, roasting and grinding that contributed to interior abrasion of the container (cooking pot) (emphasis mine). Layer 2 shows a contact period between stone and iron users. This is derived from the high concentration of lithics where the Iron Age pottery especially Urewe also occurs. The Iron Age inference is further suggested by presence of iron slag. This could imply economic interaction of the stone and iron industry in the area. The daub fragments in addition to pottery suggested prehistoric settlements.

Layer 3 was made of light brownish grey (6/2 HUE 2.5 Y) loose gravel soils. This layer stretched from 65-75 cm. This meant it was composed of two levels, 14 (65-70 cm) and 15 (70-75 cm). The trench in this layer showed signs of approaching sterility with reduction of material occurrence and presence of small and relatively big stones suggesting a riverbed that constituted the geology of the area. The stones formed a source of disturbance in the excavation of this layer. The layer produced bones (2), red ochre (1) and lithics (113).

Layer 4 was the thinnest layer in the gravel olive yellow (6/6 HUE 2.5 Y) soils. The gravel in this layer engulfed the entire trench. In a natural deposition, small rootlets continued to this level as a disturbance though, stones were the major source of disturbance. This layer was made up of Levels 16 (75-80 cm) and 17 (80-85 cm). This means on average the layer was from 75-85 cm. Artifact recovery stopped in level 16 (75-80 cm) with only lithic debitage (2) derived from the entire layer. Thereafter one more level was excavated to check whether the trench was completely sterile, therefore Level 17 (80-85 cm) marked the end of the trench having ascertained that the trench was completely sterile.

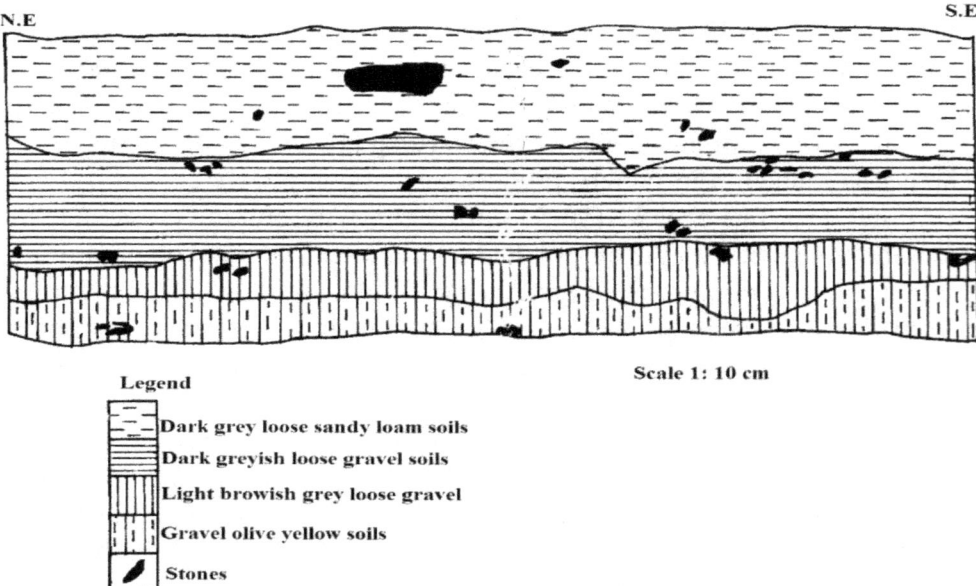

Figure 5.19: Stratigraphy of the Eastern Wall of Trench 4 Island of Deserters

5.5.13 Island of Deserters' Trench 5

Trench 5 was 2×1 m² and was excavated up to a depth of 60 cm below surface. Trench 5 was set up at the extreme northern end of the Island of Deserters to get a balanced view of the island. This was because the earlier trenches were mainly in the south, west and along the riverbanks. Therefore, it was pertinent to set up one trench in the north to examine the spatial distribution of cultural materials at the site. The top surface from the datum point was on average 5cm below surface. To level the trench the first layer went to 10 cm below surface and thereafter excavation was systematic following arbitrary 5 cm spit levels. The decision to use 5 cm spits was based on the desire to generate controlled artifact recovery and examination of the sequence of artifact occurrence on this part of the Island of Deserters.

5.5.14 Island of Deserters' Trench 5 Findings

Trench 5 had 784 cultural materials. The breakdown of the cultural materials was as follows: pottery 58 (7.40%), lithics 716 (91.33%), faunal remains 5 (0.64%) composed of only bones; daub 1 (0.13%) and red ochre stones 4 (0.51%) (Table 5.14). The appearance of red ochre in the lithics levels would imply that it was not entirely meant for pottery decoration as the evidence from Kansyore Island suggested but possibly for body painting as well. Though aware of Wreschner's (1980) view that body painting was of secondary interest and that red ochre was the sole symbolic vehicle from 6000 B.C used to enhance the potency of symbolic objects, the absence of symbolic objects will make this research suggest painting of bodies was as well crucial.

| Level/Depth (cm) | Lithics | | | | | Pottery | | | | | Faunal remains | Daub | Red ochre | Total |
| | Scrapers | Backed pieces | Others tools | Cores | Flake/blades | Debitage | Diagnostic | | | Un-diagnostic | Bones | | | |
							Plain	Roulette	Urewe	Kansyore					
1(0-10)					3	15	2	1			6	1	1		29
2(10-15)		1		1		13									15
3(15-20)	1			1		8					2				12
4(20-25)	2	1	3		3	30			2		11				46
5(25-30)	2			1	24	116				19	13	4		2	179
6(30-35)			1	20	59	261					1			2	348
7(35-40)				14	14	84									116
8(40-45)				4	8	24									37
9(45-50)						2									2
Total	5	2	4	41	111	553	2	1	2	19	34	5	1	4	784
% age	0.6	0.3	0.5	5.2	14.2	70.5	0.3	0.1	0.3	2.4	4.3	0.6	0.1	0.5	100.0

Table 5.14: Material Inventory per Level for Trench 5 Island of Deserters

5.5.15 Island of Deserters' Trench 5 Stratigraphy

The stratigraphy of Trench 5 had three observable layers along the western wall (Figure 5.20). The layers as detected from soil colour using a Munsell colour chart are discussed below.

Layer 1 was made of dark brown (3/3 HUE 7.5 YR) loose loamy soils. This layer was from 5-25 cm, with Level 1 (5-10 cm) for leveling the trench, level 2(10-15) cm, 3(15-20) cm and 4(20-25) cm. This layer yielded lithics (75), including a crescent, and cores associated with pottery (25) including roulette (1) and Urewe (2) pottery traditions, daub (1) and a bone (1). The layer had rootlet disturbances and a rodent burrow on the eastern part of the trench that appeared at the bottom of the layer in Level 4 (20-25 cm) and stones in the southern part of the trench. The artifact occurrence in this layer increased with the increase in depth below surface but towards the end, they regressed.

Layer 2 portrayed dark reddish brown (3/4 HUE 2.5 YR) sandy gravel soils. On average, it was from 25 to 35 cm thick that means that, it was composed of two levels: 5 (25-30 cm) and 6 (30-35 cm). Layer 2, like Layer 1, contained a backed piece and yielded scrapers (3). The pottery traditions from the decoration were of the Kansyore (19) type and in addition were faunal remains (4) and red ochre stones (2). The layer had a disturbance of a rodent burrow but that did not go beyond to the next layer. Occasional occurrence of stones was another source of disturbance.

Layer 3 lay on the bedrock that appeared in the southern part earlier than in the rest of the trench with yellowish gravel soils. This layer was on average ranging from 35-65 cm which means that it encompassed five levels: 7 (35-40 cm), 8 (40-45 cm), 9 (45-50 cm), 10 (50-55 cm) and 11 (55-60 cm). This layer yielded lithics (153) but whose occurrence kept declining progressively and red ochre (2), therefore Level 9 (45-50 cm) was the last productive layer. This meant that Levels 10 and 11 were excavated to ascertain that no artifact was left below surface. In the southwestern corner, the bedrock was formed by accumulation of crystalline materials or granules and excavation stopped at an average of 60 cm below surface.

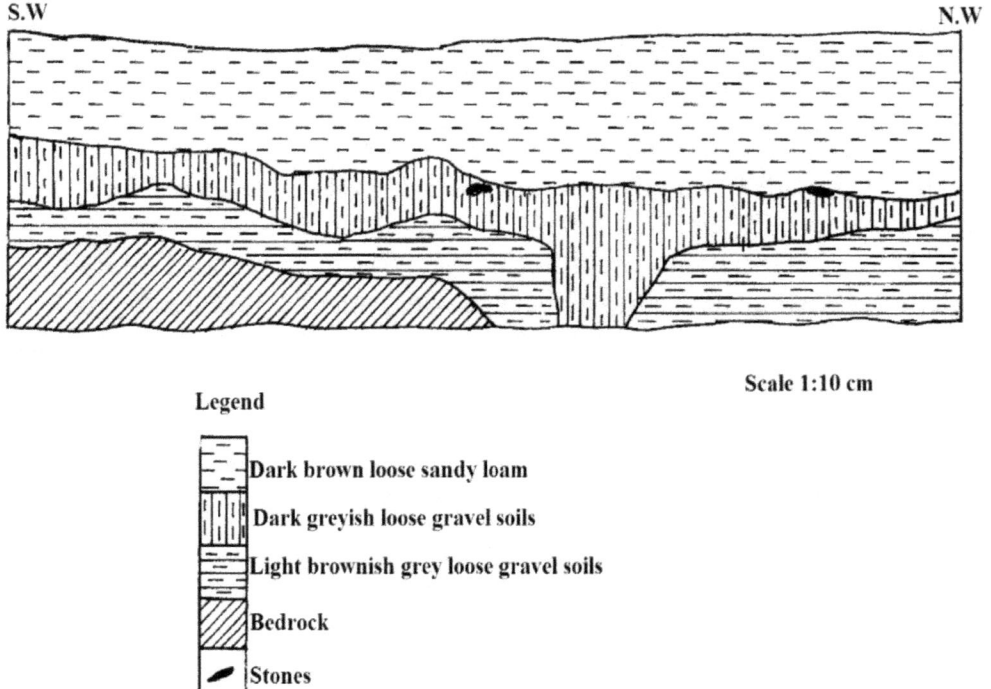

Figure 5.20: Stratigraphy of the Western Wall of Trench 5, Island of Deserters

5.5.16 Trench 5A Island of Deserters

Trench 5A was a 1×2 m² extension on the eastern side of Trench 5. The extension was in that direction because the western side of Trench 5 hit bedrock earlier than the east. Other considerations for the extension of Trench 5 to form Trench 5A included the desire to collect more cultural materials that could be used to examine the spatial distribution and interaction in the Upper Nile catchment area. The need to generate more samples of pottery whose decoration was only observed in Trench 5 and the thinking that Trench 5A might confirm the sequence obtained in Trench 5 also led to the extension. The need for datable materials to date the artifacts of Trench 5 in particular and the site generally was another objective that was realized by obtaining five charcoal samples in Trench 5A.

The excavation of Trench 5A was done with the use of 10 cm spits for Level 1 for leveling the trench. This was due to the divergence in the top surface elevation. However the excavation in the rest of the levels followed arbitrary 5 cm spits. This was due to the desire to have control over material recovery in order to examine the distribution of cultural materials that could assist to make an inference on interaction in the upper Nile catchment. A rim of the roulette pottery tradition, lithic cores and flakes, and a third phalange bone fragment were obtained from the surface of Trench 5A in the dark brown (3/4 HUE 7.5 YR) soils.

5.5.17 Trench 5A Findings

The trench went on up to a depth of 80 cm below surface. The total of cultural materials from Trench 5A was 834. These included: lithics 746 (89.4%), pottery 76 (9.1%), faunal remains 2 (0.2%), metal objects 1 (0.1%), red ochre 4 (0.5%) and charcoal samples 5 (0.6%) (Table 5.15). In comparison to all other trenches at the Island of Deserters, Trench 5A did not produce any backed piece but had core scrapers implying a core tool technology.

Level (Depth)cm	Lithics					Diagnostic pottery				Un-diagnostic pottery	Charcoal	Faunal remains	Metal object	Red ochre	Total
	Scrapers	Other tools	Cores	Flake/blades	Debitage	Plain pottery	Roulette	Urewe	Kansyore						
1(0-10)			2	7	11		1			3		1			25
2(10-15)					13			1		1		1			16
3(15-20)	1				6		1			9					17
4(20-25)			1	1	5					17					24
5(25-30)	4		2	20	82	1		2	1	19			1		132
6(30-35)	1	1	5	31	88				6	14	2				148
7(35-40)	1		6	17	67										91
8(40-45)	4		13	14	75									2	108
9(45-50)			4	6	57										67
10(50-55)	1		3		50										54
11(55-60)				32	55						1				88
12(60-65)			1	7	24						1				33
13(65-70)	1		3	6	17						1			2	30
14(70-75)			1												1
Total	13	1	41	141	550	1	2	3	7	63	5	2	1	4	834
% age	1.6	0.1	4.9	16.9	65.9	0.1	0.2	0.4	0.8	7.6	0.6	0.2	0.1	0.5	100.0

Table 5.15: Material Inventory per Level for Trench 5A Island of Deserters

5.5.18 Stratigraphy of Trench 5A

Trench 5A had four layers facing east (Figure 5.21) and north (Figure 5.22) that were identified according to soil colour; texture and moisture.

Layer 1 of Trench 5A comprised of dark brown (3/2 HUE 7.5 YR) loose sandy loam soils. Layer 1 was on average 0-45 cm that means it incorporated eight levels: 1 (0-10 cm), 2 (10-15 cm), 3 (15-20 cm), 4 (20-25 cm), 5 (25-30 cm), 6 (30-35 cm), 7 (35-40 cm) and 8 (40-45 cm). The deposition in this layer was natural but grass rootlets disrupted the excavation in Levels 1 (0-10 cm) to 4 (20-25 cm). There was progressive occurrence of artifacts in this layer whereby the first four levels yielded few artifacts (80) compared to the subsequent four levels (479). This was the general trend of all trenches at this site. The trench in this layer produced; a point, scrapers (11), cores (29) and flakes (90).

The pottery traditions in this layer were roulette (2), Urewe (3) and Kansyore (7). Other material finds were a metal object (1), red ochre (2) and faunal remains (2). This implied that all the pottery, metal objects, and faunal remains from the entire trench were found in Layer 1. There was steady progressive increase in material occurrence like in all other trenches that coincided with the appearance of the gravel soils. Two charcoal samples were obtained that were; one sample from the southwestern corner at 34 cm and the second one at 35 cm below surface. The third charcoal sample was abandoned due to its small size. The cultural materials in the layer suggested coexistence and contemporaneity of Kansyore pottery and Iron Age pottery.

Layer 2 of Trench 5A was composed of reddish yellow (7/6 HUE 7.5 YR) loose sandy gravel soils with a small patch of black loose soils on the northeastern side. The layer ranged from 45 to 65 cm that was 20 cm thick. This meant that in was composed of four levels: 9 (45-50 cm), 10 (50-55 cm), 11 (55-60 cm) and 12 (60-65 cm). Layer 2 of Trench 5A yielded lithic artifacts (240) that were an implication that this was a layer of Stone Age people. Two charcoal samples were obtained from Levels 11 and 12 of Layer 2 of Trench 5A. From level 12 (60-65 cm) excavations took place only in the northern 1×1 m^2 portion that still had dark soils as the rest had hit the sterile gravel.

Layer 3 of Trench 5A at the Island of Deserters was a layer that squarely touched the bedrock. The soils were olive brown (4/3 HUE 2.5 Y) in colour and loose sandy in texture. This layer was disrupted by the fourth layer therefore at one point it was 65-75 cm and then 85-90 cm thick. It had three levels: 13 (65-70 cm), 14 (70-75 cm) and 16 (80-85 cm) that made it 20 cm thick. (Note that Level 15 (75-80 cm) belongs to Layer 4.) The finds were one charcoal sample at a depth of 68 cm below surface in association with lithic artifacts (27) and red ochre (2). In Level 14 (70-75 cm), a black patch with loose silt texture caused by a probable anthill was observed. Level 16 (80-85 cm) did not yield any artifact but was excavated to check sterility of the trench and therefore excavation ceased at 85 cm below surface.

Layer 4 comprised Level 15 (75-80 cm) of Trench 5A. The soils were reddish yellow (7/6 HUE 5YR) sandy gravel. The disturbance in this layer/level was the anthive. No artifact was collected from this layer that marked the end of excavation since the layer proved sterile.

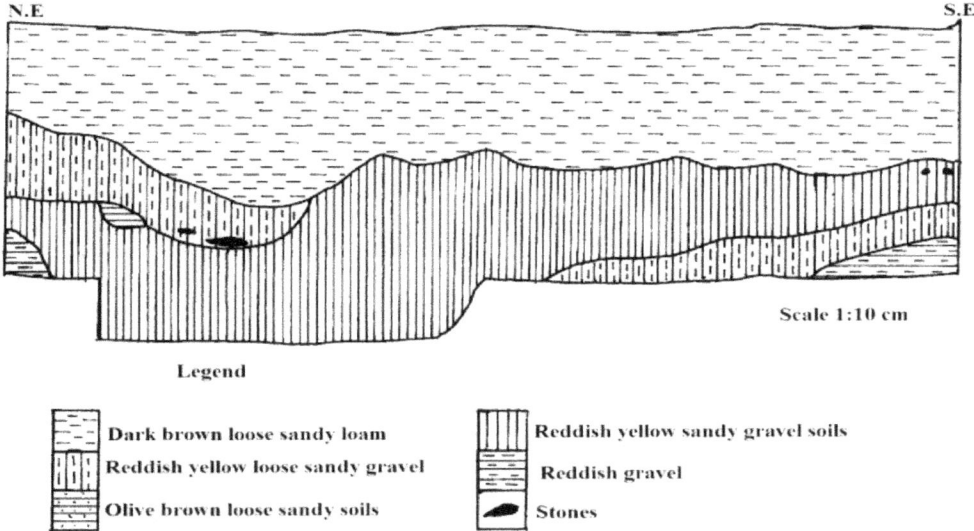

Figure 5.21: Eastern Wall Profile of Trench 5A at the Island of Deserters

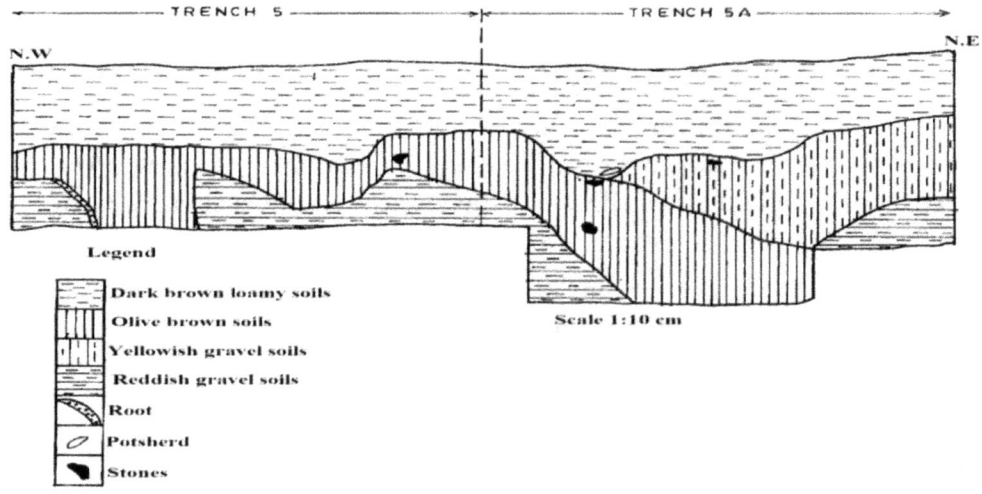

Figure 5.22: Northern Wall Profile of Trench 5 and 5A Island of Deserters

5.6 Dating Results

The dating results are for the two samples from Kansyore Island. The first sample from Trench 2B at a depth of 50-55 cm below surface dated wavy line pottery at 1671±44 BP (Table 5.16). This would imply that wavy line should not always be attributed to Neolithic pottery as this date was relatively younger. The second sample was obtained from Kansyore Island in Trench 2Ai at 65-70 cm below surface. The sample dated roulette pottery yielded at 2710±41 BP (Table 5.16). It should be noted that the date of sample two was a bit higher than normally expected for terrestrial herbivores. This date from Kansyore Island suggests that roulette begun in the Neolithic period. Chapman (1967) supported this argument by suggesting that roulette seems to be an ancient tradition since the Neolithic period.

Site name	Lab. Number	Trench number	Depth (cm)	Associated decoration	C14 age BP
Kansyore	WK-31383	Trench 2B	50-55	wavy-lines	1671±44 BP
Kansyore	WK-31384	Trench 2Ai	65-70	roulette	2710±41 BP

Table 5.16: Carbon 14 Dates

5.7 Data from Ethnographic Inquiries

The data from ethnographic inquiries was from five key informants and on aspects that arose from survey and excavation that required an input from contemporary knowledge. The sampling of informants did not much depend on the age of the informant but the time of stay in the area. This is because some of the areas of the research had experienced war for some time. This meant that age was not equivalent to being knowledgeable about the cultural history of the place due to displacements of war. Therefore, the ethnographic inquiries entailed in-depth oral interviews. The first question concerned the pottery decoration instrument and why pottery broke along coil lines. In this case the papyrus stem was established as the one used to execute the knotted strip roulette motif while the reason for pottery breakage along coil lines was due to use of the coiling, one of the oldest pottery making techniques.

The question of how the area was peopled generated various views but the dominant paradigm was migration. Most of the informants still held the view that prior to the migration of the Luo from the north the area was uninhabited by humans. This is in line with the migration theory propounded through the teaching of History in Ugandan institutions of learning at all levels. Those upholding the Hamitic myth claim that the Luo migrated from Bahr-el-Ghazel in South Sudan and settled in Uganda, especially northern Uganda, which hitherto was vacant according to the oral information obtained. The last question concerned interrogation to examine the nature of interaction. The response was that interaction in the Nile catchment areas was especially with Sudan through exchange of agricultural produce and game meat for the Sudanese products. This was supported by Kiyaga-Mulindwa (2006) who mentioned a place called Kampala within the MFNP that was used as a trading centre. Ethnographic inquiries also revealed the importance of the Nile that was taken to be water for domestic use and religious functions for instance at Bujagali close to Kikubamitwe that is regarded as an abode for the Basoga chief god *Budghali*.

In the Nsongezi/Kansyore area, the interviews intended to gather information concerning the pyramid (pyramidal site) and the house foundation at Kansyore Island (Table 5.17). The interviewees were drawn from people near the site identified with the assistance of the defense secretary Mr. Mungoni S. and Mr. Byaruhanga Peter. The data generated showed that the house foundation at Kansyore Island was for a hotel while the pyramidal structure was a burial site for a white man who drowned in the Kagera.

Names	Age	Village	Site	Designation
Neliko Kankyankula	65	Kagera	Nsongezi	Owner of slag site
Byaruhanga Peter	33	Ruyanga	Kansyore	Resident of Island next to Kansyore
Mungoni Slyveri	47	Nsongezi	Pyramid	Defense secretary
Kigambe Andrea	100	Katanga-Kikagati	Kansyore	Informant
Haruna Mukasa	68	Katanga-Kikagati	Kansyore	Former worker since 1960 at the hotel whose foundation stands at Kansyore Island

Table 5.17: List of Informants

5.8 Chapter Summary

The data from the field shows that there was continuity and discontinuity in site settlements especially at the Island of Deserters. This was deduced from the fact that material production was always low in the upper levels that was above 30 cm below surface. However below that depth there was a tendency for increment with the peak production in 40-45 cm below surface and then a progressive drop in artifact occurrence was witnessed as the trenches progressed towards the bottom. The examination of distribution of material production in relation to soil colour and texture showed that there were more materials in the gravel soils than in the loamy soils that implied that this was an old settlement.

Despite the earlier suggestion by Arkell (1949, 1953) that red ochre was principally for decorating pottery the evidence from the field suggested that red ochre in the southern part of the Upper Nile catchment could have had other roles and most likely body painting. This is because a look at the stratigraphic occurrence of red ochre showed that it appeared more in the Stone Age levels that were not associated with pottery. This was also suggested by the lack of a sizeable sample with evidence of pottery decorated with red ochre because only one potsherd from the entire assemblage had red painting but was plain and so could not be associated with any pottery tradition.

The aqualithic evidence had correlations with that from elsewhere with the exception of absence of the fishing gear in the form of bone harpoons or net sinkers. This suggests use of other means for fishing such as crescents (Seitsonen, 2010) or traditional fishing methods whose instruments could not be preserved in the archaeological context as some were made from grass or wood for instance nets. The research findings cast doubt on any direct relationship between aquatic resource utilization, pottery production and invention of pottery as suggested by Haaland (2009). This is because the tendency was less pottery recovered in the aqualithic layers. The association of lithic artefacts and EIA/LIA artefacts was not a surprise in the upper stratigraphic sequences because recent research in several areas in East Africa indicated that the production of lithic artefacts did not stop immediately after the spread of iron working but was maintained for many centuries later (Kessy, 2005, Kessy *et al*, 2011). This could be the same for the pottery traditions where Neolithic, EIA and LIA pottery appeared mixed therefore such a mixture should not just be dismissed as a disturbance but possibly was due to cultural interaction and continuity in the periods of transition.

The dates obtained indicated that roulette began in the Neolithic period while wavy line is not always an indicator of the Neolithic period from the dates obtained. The migration theory as derived from the ethnographic inquiries is still deeply rooted in the people's minds as responsible for the peopling of Africa. In line with this is the belief that Africa was an empty space prior to the coming of migrants who peopled Africa. However, this has been refuted by cultural materials predating Iron Age associated with the migrants. The exploitation of the locally available resources for decorating pottery showed that people utilized local resources and therefore adapted to the local environment.

CHAPTER SIX

ANALYSIS OF RESEARCH FINDINGS

6.1 Introduction

This chapter presents results from the data analysis that arose from a total of 16,085 artefacts (Table 6.1). The artefacts analyzed were from both surface collections, 892 (5.5%), and excavations 15,193 (94.5%). The excavations in this case included only artefacts from the STPs and the major trenches. All in all, Nsongezi had the least artefacts analyzed 723 (4.5%). This was mainly because field work in Nsongezi was restricted to survey that entailed surface collections and shovel test excavation. Therefore research concentrated on the Island of Deserters and Kansyore Island that yielded 4,013 (26.1%) and 11,171 (69.4%) respectively of the analyzed artefacts. This implies that Kansyore Island yielded the majority of the artefacts analyzed (Table 6.1).

The artefacts analyzed were: ceramics 1,637 (10.18%), lithics 9,619 (59.80%), faunal remains 4,650 (28.91%), metallurgical remains 78 (0.48%), charcoal samples 26 (0.16%), daub 25 (0.16%), red ochre 48 (0.30%), a smoking pipe fragment 1(0.01%) and a clay mace 1 (0.01%). The faunal remains included shells 286 (1.78%) and bones 4,364 (27.13%) while the metallurgical remains included metal objects 70 (0.44%), iron slag 7 (0.04%), and a tuyere 1 (0.01%). The two smoking pipe fragments were reconstructed into one artifact.

Artefact		Lithics			Pot	Faunal R		Metallurgical R			Others					Total	% age
Artefact type	NF	Tools	CO	F/B	Diag	Bo	Sh	MO	Slag	Tu	CK	DB	RO	S/pipe	clay mace		
Surface																	
Deserters	2	9	14	30	105	4	13									178	1.1
Kansyore	1	7	9	23	436		27	1						1	1	506	3.1
Nsongezi		25	57	71	55											208	1.3
Nsongezi STP 1		40	84	194	14	101	82									515	3.2
Island of Deserters																	
Trench 1		191	264	872	81	2		3			3		2			1,434	8.9
Trench 2		90	88	452	63	54		1			5					753	4.7
Trench 3		22	41	173	23	1					1					261	1.6
Trench 4		130	213	540	159	72	7		7		8	8	3			1,147	7.1
Trench 5		11	41	111	24	5						1	4			197	1.2
Trench 5A		14	41	141	13	2		1			5		4			221	1.4
Kansyore Island																	
STP 2		113	105	448	23	136	110	2			2					937	5.8
Trench 1	2	684	472	1,552	449	3,281	41	17					33			6,533	40.6
Trench 2		196	213	764	109	401	2	41			1		1			1,728	10.7
Trench 2B		84	102	362	66	304	4	2			1		1			926	5.8
Trench 3		89	52	380	17	1		2								541	3.4
Grand Total	5	1,705	1,796	6,113	1,637	4,364	286	70	7	1	26	25	48	1	1	16,085	100.0
% age	0.03	10.60	11.17	38.00	10.18	27.13	1.78	0.44	0.04	0.01	0.16	0.16	0.30	0.01	0.01	100.00	

Key: NF= non-flaked stones; CO cores; FB= flakes and blades; dia=diagnostic pottery; Bo=bones; sh=shells; MO= metal objects; Tu= tuyeres; CK= charcoal; DB= daub; RO= red ochre; S/pipe= smoking pipe and R= remains

Table 6.1: Inventory of Analysed Artefacts

6.2 Lithic Analysis

Lithic analysis aimed at examining the lithic typology and technology. This involved examination of typological variability and technological aspects that would trace human behaviour and organisation. Both the Nelson (1973) and Mehlman (1989) typological schemes were used in the analysis of lithic artefacts. Nelson's (1973) typology was utilised because he studied two of the sites also studied in this research that are the Nsongezi rock shelter and Kansyore Island. The use of Mehlman's (1979) typology was because it was used to study sites with Kansyore pottery that are Mumba-Höhle and Nasera. Masao (1979) and Kessy's (2005) lithic analysis approaches complemented Nelson (1973) and Mehlman (1989)' schemes. This is because Masao employs Nelson's scheme while Kessy uses Mehlman scheme.

Lithic analysis emphasised two attributes namely artifact type and metric attributes (length, breadth, and thickness). However, other attributes like raw material were vital as well. Raw material is vital because raw material sourcing gives clue on mobility systems, settlement patterns, and social interactions. These imply the human ranging patterns and social exchange systems (Waweru, 2007:52).

The instruments used in lithic analysis included: an electronic Vanier calliper and a magnifying lens to examine the metric attributes. The length of the long axis passing through the striking platform was used to measure the length of flakes/blades and shaped tools with flake features. The measurement of the maximum breadth was taken at widest points at right angle to length yet maximum thickness was done at the maximum dimension measured perpendicular to the ventral face of a flake (Kessy, 2005). Measuring crescents was done orienting the major axis passing through the crescent's ends. Therefore the length of crescents was the maximum distance between ends while the breadth was taken at the widest point at right angles to length while thickness was taken at the maximum dimension to the two main opposite faces. The length of triangles and points was oriented towards the longitudinal axis passing through the tips while breadth was at the widest points at right angles to length and thickness at maximum dimension perpendicular to the two opposite faces. Shaped tools with no flake features were measured using the main worked edges that run parallel to the observer and breadth at the greatest dimension at right angles to length (Kessy, 2005).

To determine the maximum length of cores measurements were taken perpendicular to the plane of the maximum striking platform and parallel to the flake release face. The maximum breadth was taken at the widest point at right angles to the length (Kessy, 2005:239). In the case of bipolar cores the length was oriented with the longitudinal axis passing through both platforms targeting the area of maximum projection. In single platform cores length measurements were oriented with the long axis passing through the platform along a line sub-parallel to the flake release surface. For cores with more than one platform and periphery-worked cores the length was taken targeting the maximum projection while the breadth was the greatest dimension at right angle to length. Amorphous cores that are irregular were not measured (Kessy, 2005). The unit of measurement was the millimetre (mm). The metric attributes were vital since some of the stone type classifications depended on metric attributes such as the blades. A combination of both the qualitative and quantitative approaches was essential for the interpretation of archaeological data but the degree of each depends on the problem under investigation (Masao, 1979:146). Therefore, since the current research, addressed cultural and economic interaction in the upper Nile valley then it only required use of the simple statistics using Microsoft Excel and Statistical Package for Software Systems (SPSS) in undertaking the quantitative approach.

The lithic artefacts analysed (9,619) were composed of shaped tools 1,705 (17.73%) out of which were composite tools (2) and non-flaked stones 5 (0.05%). Other lithic artefacts subjected to analysis were the cores 1,796 (18.67%) and flakes/blades 6,113 (63.55%) (Table 6.2). Kansyore Island had the highest number of lithic artefacts from both excavation and surface collection with a total of 5,658 (58.8%); followed by the Island of Deserters with 3,490 (36.3%) and Nsongezi 471 (4.9 %). This may reflect the importance of the stone artefacts in Kansyore industry. The lithics analysed were from surface collections 248 (2.6%), STPs 984 (10.2%) and excavation 8,387 (87.2 %) (Figure 6.1). That means more lithics were from excavation (97.4%) compared to surface collection (2.6%).

Artefact	Lithics					
Artefact type	Non-flaked stones	Shaped tools	Cores	Flake/blades	Total	% age
Nsongezi						
Surface		25	57	71	153	1.6
STP 1		40	84	194	318	3.3
Island of Deserters						
Surface	2	9	14	30	55	0.6
Trench 1		191	264	872	1,327	13.8
Trench 2		90	88	452	630	6.5
Trench 3		22	41	173	236	2.5
Trench 4		130	213	540	883	9.2
Trench 5		11	41	111	163	1.7
Trench 5A		14	41	141	196	2.0
Kansyore Island						
surface	1	7	9	23	40	0.4
STP 2		113	105	448	666	6.9
Trench 1	2	684	472	1,552	2,710	28.2
Trench 2		196	213	764	1,173	12.2
Trench 2B		84	102	362	548	5.7
Trench 3		89	52	380	521	5.4
Grand Total	5	1,705	1,796	6,113	9,619	100.0
% age	0.05	17.73	18.67	63.55	100.00	

Table 6.2: Analysed Lithics Artefacts

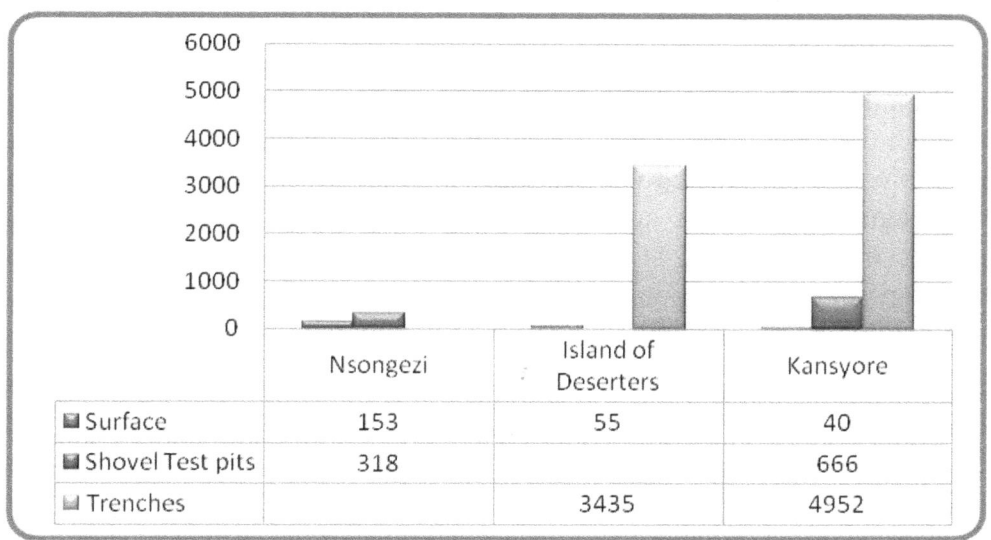

Figure 6.1: Frequency of Lithic Artefacts per Provenience and Site

6.2.1 The Typology

Classification is an analysis tool used to distinguish among different artefacts and other material objects. Archaeologists use various systems of classifying artefacts to organize data into understandable units. Archaeological classifications describe artefact types. Therefore, typology is the hierarchical classification based on artefact types and groupings. Odell (2003: 104) suggested that typology refers to a classification system that employs the type as the central unit of construction. Classification is part of everyone's life for to think one uses and forms categories of people, objects and events therefore typologies condense and communicate basic concepts in a given lithic assemblage (Whittaker, 1994). Lithic analytical typology could use either the morphological or the functional typology and the two are often related (Masao, 1979).

However, functional analysis is based on assumed intended use while morphological analysis focuses on shape, size, and modification. The research preferred the morphological analysis because by isolating industries on an implement based on morphological analysis one can follow their development and eventually detect their interaction by the regularity of proportions of the types and by their variations (Masao, 1979). This was done well aware of the weaknesses of typological analysis enumerated by Masao (1979:148) and Odell (2003). These include the type variety system's failure to take into consideration functional issues. David (1982) in the study of southern Sudan suggested that it is worthless to study typologies because quartz-based industries are un-diagnostic with no obvious change in their typology through time. On the contrary, Mehlman (1989:118) suggested that if quartz industries are not studied painstakingly then the assemblage would appear 'un-diagnostic' yet it is quite misleading to claim no marked typological change if a typological study has not been rigorously pursued. Therefore typology and classification lie at the very core of archaeology despite their critics (Willey and Sabloff, 1974:106).

Morphological analysis further informs about the prehistoric lithic tool kit (Bordes, 1969:2), this supports the approach used in this research. Typological classification was also crucial in this study because it examined similarities and variations among the stone tools. This assisted in evaluation of the level of interaction and variation. The emphasis on the metric attributes was due to the fact that these compensated for the asymmetrical frequency distribution curves which are typical of the LSA in East Africa (Nelson, 1973: 352). The size characteristic was regarded as vital to examine the relative abundance of raw material available, stage of artefact production and core reduction strategies (Odell, 2003). Classification of analysed lithic artefacts yielded six broad groups that were: retouched/shaped tools, composite tools, non-flaked stones, cores, flakes/blades, and debitage. However debitage was not subjected to deeper analysis.

6.2.2 Shaped Tools

Shaped/retouched tools are any chunk, chip, flake, or flake fragment having at least one edge of secondary modification as a retouched tool (Mehlman, 1989:127). These are characterised by deliberate and systematic modification resulting from modification, retouch or trimming which conform to some clearly recognised pattern of shape or size (Masao, 1979). The retouch may be alternate, direct, normal, inverse or invasive or various combinations of these and could be shallow, steep, casual, bidirectional or unidirectional (Nelson 1973: 137). Shaped or retouched tools have regular retouch patterns determined as additional modification after the flaking process that may be on any chunk, chip, flake, or flake fragment (Masao, 1979:95; Kessy, 2005: 240). Lithic classification takes into consideration the nature of retouches (Kessy, 2005). Retouches appear in several forms and that may be either unifacial or bifacial, normal or inverse, invasive or marginal and alternate or a combination of these (Mehlman, 1989:127; Masao, 1979; Kessy, 2005).

A total of 1,706 shaped tools were analysed. These included both heavy-duty tools 32 (1.9%) and light-duty tools 1,673 (98.1%). The heavy-duty tools were pick-axes 3 (0.2%), hand axes 2 (0.2 %). discoids 12 (0.7%) and core axes 15 (0.9%). The light-duty tools were composed of scrapers 914 (53.6%), backed pieces 578 (33.9%), points 74 (4.3%), denticulates 44 (2.6%), burins 29 (1.7%), *outil escailes* 12 (0.6%), becs 11 (0.6%), preforms 9 (0.5%) and composite tools 2 (0.1%) (Table 6.3). The study preferred to have the point preforms in the category of shaped tools. Many shaped tools were named to correspond to their morphology and technique of manufacture though at times without a clear view of its use (Whittaker, 1994:27) since emphasis was on morphological rather than functional typology.

Shaped tools were mainly from Kansyore Island 1,175 (68.9%) followed by the Island of Deserters 468 (27.4 %) and Nsongezi 62 (3.6%). While the Island of Deserters dominated production of heavy-duty tools (75%), Kansyore Island dominated the light-duty tools (70.5%). This tool variability may be due to the technological differences and subsistence patterns of the sites. For instance Kansyore had mainly the light-duty tools where for instance fishing was one of the subsistence strategies identified from the fish faunal remains that may not have required heavy-duty tools.

Lithic tool types	Sites						Total	% age
	Kansyore Island		Island of Deserters		Nsongezi			
	Trench /STP	Surface	Trench	Surface	STP	surface		
Scrapers	564		306	2	26	16	914	53.6
Backed	482	1	79	2	12	2	578	33.9
Points	61		13				74	4.3
Denticulate	22		20		1	1	44	2.6
Burins	21	1	7				29	1.7
Outils E	10		2				12	0.7
Becs	9		1		1		11	0.6
Composite			2				2	0.1
Preform			9				9	0.5
Heavy duty tools								0.0
Core axes			15				15	0.9
Discoids	4		7			1	12	0.7
Hand axe			1			1	2	0.1
Pick axe				2		1	3	0.2
Total	**1,173**	**2**	**462**	**6**	**40**	**22**	**1,705**	**100.0**
% age	68.8	0.1	27.1	0.4	2.3	1.3	100.0	

Key: Surf. = surface collections; Outils E=outils escailles; STP= shovel test pit

Table 6.3: Lithic Tool Types per site

6.2.3 Scrapers

Scrapers are retouched tools characterised mainly by unifacially flaked, Planoclinical edges (Nelson, 1973:175), though some are bifacially worked (Kessy, personal communication). Scrapers can be classified basing on the edge plan as; convex, concave, straight, notched, denticulate, or irregular (Mehlman, 1989). They are also divisible in a number of sub-classes according to the nature of the retouched edge or end as single side, double side, end and side, circular, nosed, small convex and notched scrapers (Clark and Kleindienst,

1974) (Figures 6.2 and 6.3). Scrapers were the major class of shaped/retouched tool in this assemblage (53.6%) (Table 6.3). This is not strange since quartz sites are typologically scraper dominated (Kusimba, 2001). The scrapers included those made on flake/blade blanks (flake scrapers) and those from cores (core scrapers). Therefore, scrapers were categorised basing on the nature of blank they were made from as either core scrapers or flake scrapers. Out of the 914 scrapers, core scrapers were 245. The core scrapers were mainly from the Island of Deserters just like all the core axes which would imply a core technology compared to Kansyore Island that exhibited a flake technology. The distribution of scrapers at the different sites in the order of frequency shows that Kansyore Island had the greatest occurrence (564) followed by the Island of Deserters (308) and Nsongezi (42) (Table 6.3). The existence of huge percentages of scrapers indicates a settled lifestyle especially at Kansyore with perennial activities such as food processing and tool manufacturing. The Kagera River made a settled life at Kansyore possible complementing a diet based on terrestrial food by providing an alternative aquatic diet dominated by fish and fresh water shells. Trench 1 with a well-preserved aqualithic layer at Kansyore Island had evidence for both these subsistence resources.

The scrapers in the entire assemblage were identified according to Mehlman's (1989) classification of scrapers. This was based on the location of the scraping edge and shape of the edge that defined most scrapers in the typology with the exception of the heavy-duty core scrapers that were classified under heavy-duty tools. The scraper types based on scraper edge were either side or end scrapers while those based on edge plan form included the convex, straight, concave or irregular or sundry scrapers. The description of scrapers based on size such as Mehlman Type 1 of small convex scrapers was dropped in this study because as suggested by Kessy (2005), the size did not indicate any pattern differences between sites suggesting no lithic technological variability and since they could fit in the other scraper types.

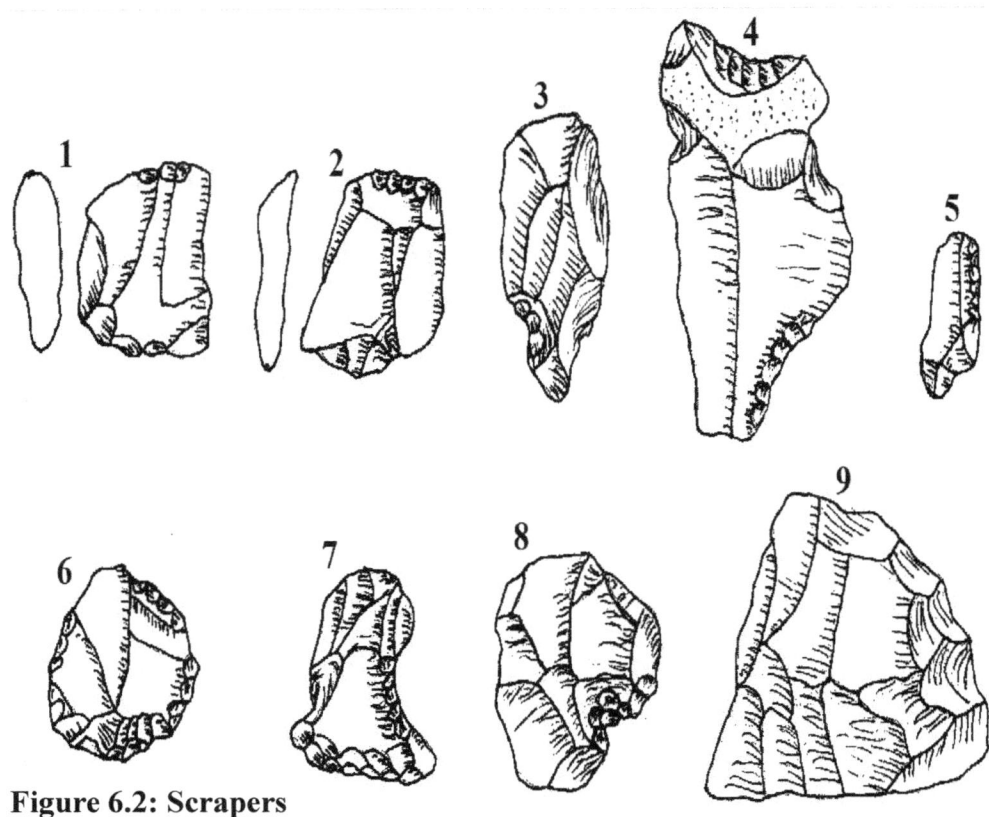

Figure 6.2: Scrapers

Key: (1) Double-sided End Scraper; (2) Convex Double End Scraper; (3) Nosed Scraper; (4) Notched Side and End Scraper; (5) Straight Side Scraper; (6) Circular Scraper; (7) Concave Side and End Scraper; (8) Notched Side Scraper; (9) Convex Side Scraper

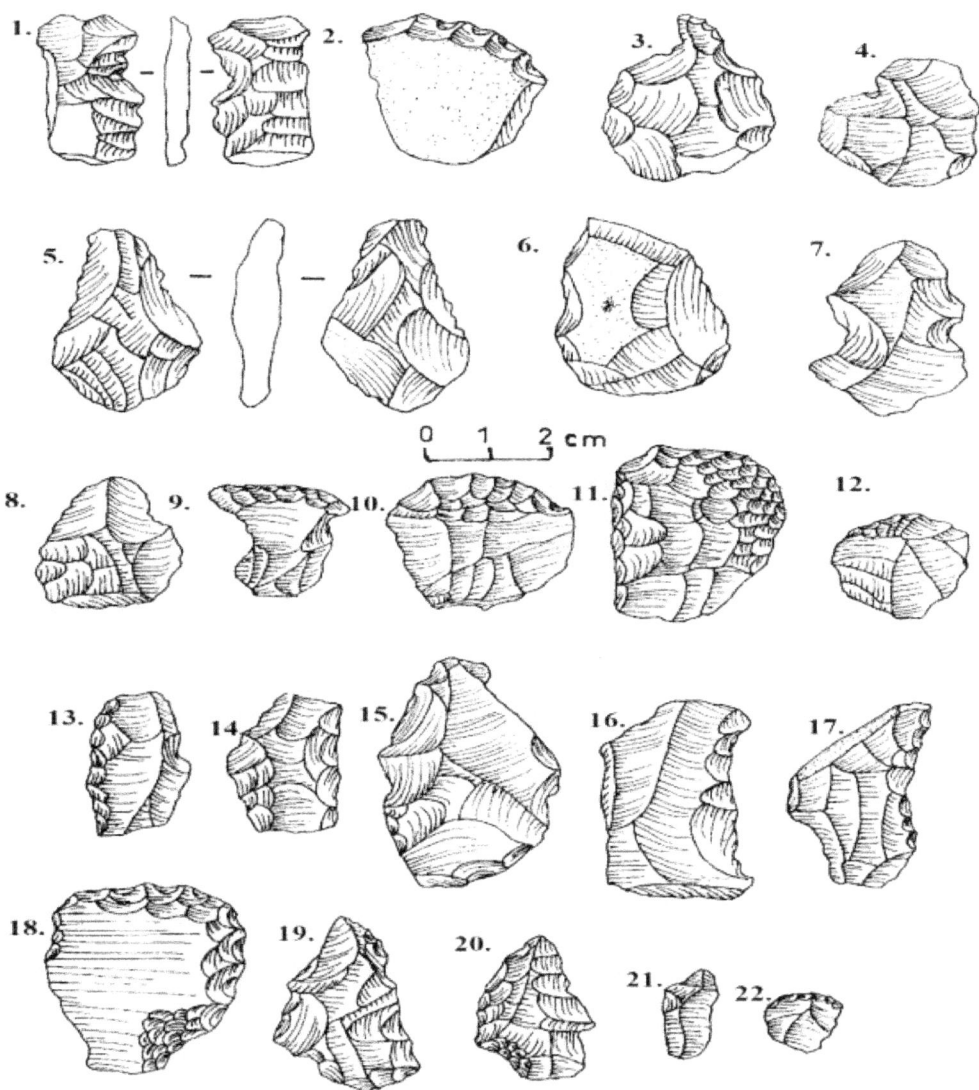

Figure 6.3: Scrapers, Utilised Flakes, Points and a Burin

Key: (1 &13) =Straight Double-side; (2, 9,10, 12)= Convex End Scrapers; (3)= Burin; (4)= Notched Scraper; (5, 6, 8, 15)= Utilised Flakes; (7)= Sundry Side Scraper; (11& 18)= Convex End and Side Scraper; (14)= Convex Double Side Scraper; (17)= Concave Side Scraper; (19 & 20)= Unifacial Points; (21&22)=Thumbnail Scrapers

6.2.4 Core Scrapers

Core scrapers are the oldest type of scrapers that started during the late Acheulian. The core scrapers have been categorised basing on a combination of attributes such as core shape, number of platforms, angle of relationship and number of faces associated with each platform (Mehlman, 1989:142). Core scrapers are highly retouched tools characterised by steep retouch, usually from the flat, ventral face, along some part or parts of the circumference to form a scraper edge that makes them scrapers. The core scrapers obtained were either one-edged, two-edged in different planes, three-edged in different planes, end, and side-edged, round or circular just like those from Kalambo Falls (Clark and Kleindienst 1974:98). The core scrapers were used as chopping and pounding tools showing signs of heavy usage (Bishop and Posnansky, 1960:54). That is why this research regarded them as heavy duty tools. Nelson (1973) warns against the overlap between core scrapers and cores, which requires careful scrutiny.

A total of 245 core scrapers were collected and analysed. These were from both surface collection (9) and excavation (236). These were subdivided into six core scraper types including: single-platform core scrapers (92), opposed double-platform core scrapers (61), adjacent double-platform core scrapers (52), multi-faceted platform core scrapers (8), platform-periphery core scrapers (29) and platform-bipolar core scraper (3). The first six core scraper types portrayed inter-site similarity and variability and evidence of interaction in terms of material culture since they appeared at all sites. However, the last category of core axe appeared only at the Island of Deserters. This implied that the Island of Deserters stretched beyond the LSA period.

6.2.5 Types of Core Scrapers

The first type was the single platform core scraper. These were cores that had small negative scars that were regarded as a form of retouch with a flat and a faceted platform (Mehlman, 1989:143). That implies that any core with a single platform and a scraping edge belonged to this type. A total of 92 single platform core scrapers were analysed whose spatial distribution showed that high frequency was recorded at the Island of Deserters (64) followed by Kansyore Island (25) and Nsongezi (3). The high percentage of single platform scrapers at the Island of Deserters could be due to the importance of this tool type in the general tool kit and the dominance of core technology at the site in comparison to Kansyore Island. The mean length, thickness, and breadth were 32.3mm, 17.01 mm and 25.8 mm respectively. The raw materials utilised were quartz (91) and basalt (1).

Another category of core scrapers was the opposed double-core scrapers. These were the cores with evidence of intentional trimming that had platforms at the two opposed edges (Figure 6.8o). These were a total of 61 from the Island of Deserters (45); Kansyore Island (14) and Nsongezi (2). The opposed double-platform core scrapers were common in the lower levels below surface especially below 40 cm unlike the single-platform core scrapers that were above the opposed double platform core scrapers. This may imply that while the single-platform core scrapers were mainly in the ceramic/stone contact phases the opposed double-platform core scrapers were preferred in the exclusively Stone Age periods that required the heavy duty tools. The mean length, thickness, and breadth were 36.3 mm, 19.7 mm, and 30.4 mm respectively. The raw materials used were still quartz (60) and basalt (1).

The third category of platform core scrapers was the adjacent double platform-core scrapers. These were core scrapers with two platforms that lay side by side. The 52 specimens were collected from the Island of Deserters (35), Kansyore Island (16), and Nsongezi (1). The mean length was 34.6 mm, mean thickness was 20.3 mm, and mean breadth was 30.3 mm. The preferred raw materials were quartzite (3) and quartz (49).

The platform-periphery core scrapers could be regarded as a mixed or intermediate type of core. This is because it had characteristics of a platform core and a periphery-worked core. Therefore, such cores had a platform and at the same time with part of the periphery worked on. Any such core with intentional retouches was analysed as a platform-periphery core scraper. This implied that there was a systematic relationship between the types of tools that cut across typological boundaries in the East African LSA assemblages (Masao, 1979:216). The similarity with the East African LSA industry would mean there was cultural and economic interaction in the upper Nile catchment areas that was not due to simply migration or diffusion but possibly due to ecological adaptability. This is because adaptation is a product of interaction between particular historical processes and human institutions (Mabulla, 1996:38). The 26 specimens were obtained from the Island of Deserters (19) Kansyore Island (7) and Nsongezi (1). The mean length was 40.8mm, mean thickness, 28.2 mm and the mean breadth was 37.2 mm. The platform–periphery core scrapers were all made of quartz raw material.

Another category of core scrapers analysed was termed as the platform-bipolar core scraper. In this category were core scrapers that had a platform and crushed edges as evidenced among the bipolar cores. Therefore, the platform bipolar core was any core with a single platform and evidence of bipolar that is having crushed edges. This is Mehlman's (1989:145) Type 77 in which the platform was not opposed to the bipolar edge and the bipolar morphology was complete but the two crushed edges were in opposition, with the remains of the platform situated along one of the lateral edges between the two bipolar edges. Three specimens were all obtained from Kansyore Island and made from quartz (2) and basalt (1). The limited occurrence of this tool type may make it rather hard to examine the extent of its impact in tracing the similarity and variability of this tool type in the Nile catchment areas. However it could possibly imply the use of both the bipolar and platform techniques at Kansyore Island. Another possibility could be the nature of the raw material utilised that was mainly quartz. The mean length, thickness, and breadth were: 26.3 mm, 17.6 mm, and 20.6 mm respectively.

A total of 8 multi-faceted platform core scrapers were analysed. These were named so because they had multiple facets on the platforms. They could not be classified as single-platform, opposed double-platform or adjacent double platform core scrapers. The existence of the multifaceted core scrapers would suggest the use of hard-hammer indirect-knapping. This is because the several facets had evidence of working edges which were not really crushed to be classified as bipolar core scrapers. The existences of facets would further suggest the preparation of core platforms for flake removal (Mabulla, 1996:416). The Island of Deserters and Kansyore Island each yielded four specimens. Quartz was the only raw material that is locally available. The mean length was 43.1 mm; mean thickness 24.3 mm and mean breadth was 37.7 mm.

The last category of the core scrapers were the bipolar-periphery core scrapers. A total of 2 specimens all from Kansyore Island made of quartz were analysed. These were characterised by two opposed sides of the circumference having evidence of the bipolar damages. The mean length was 41.5 mm, mean thickness 35.5 mm and mean breadth was 37 mm. The metric measurements of all the core scrapers gave insights into the nature of raw material utilisation and the size further shows that the core scrapers were initially used as cores but at a certain point one of the core edges was modified to perform other functions. There were variations among cores made of quartz and quartzite because of the variations of stone cobbles especially from the Island of Deserters where the cobbles seemed to be bigger than at Kansyore Island.

6.2.6 Flake Scrapers

A total of 669 scrapers were analysed that were made of flake/blade blanks and in this analysis they were termed as flake scrapers. Three major scraper types belonged to flake scrapers. These were the side scrapers (516), end scrapers (148), and other scrapers (5). Therefore the side scrapers were the most frequent (77.1%) followed by the end scrapers (22.1%) and the rest (0.9%) of the scraper assemblage other than core scrapers (Table 6.1). There was site variability in the production of scrapers with Kansyore Island having the highest percentage (74.1%), Island of Deserters (21.1%) and Nsongezi (4.8%). This implies that though the Island of Deserters had dominated the production of core scrapers, Kansyore Island dominated the production of the flake scrapers which could suggest presence of a flake technology at Kansyore Island and an LSA people who used the scrapers. Therefore, on the basis of typological difference, the assemblage at Kansyore is suspected to be younger than that from the Island of Deserters. Though inference of age based on typological similarities or differences is not always a reliable measure of contemporaneity (Masao, 1979:127-8), it was awareness of this fact that led to attempts to date the site of Kansyore but samples from the Island of Deserters were not dated due to financial constraints.

6.2.7 End Scrapers

Scrapers with the scraping edge truncating the distal end or proximal end or both ends were scored as end scrapers (Masao, 1979; Nelson, 1973). Nelson (1973) divided the end scrapers into simple, double, triangular, oblique, carinated, nucleaform and miscellaneous end scrapers. In this analysis, the end scrapers (148) analysed were categorised as convex single end (29), convex-concave combination (19), straight side and end scrapers (2), nosed end (36), convex side and end (38) and circular scrapers (24) (Table 6.4).

Sites	Island of Deserters		Nsongezi		Kansyore Island			Total	% age
Scraper Types	Trenches	Surface	STP 1	Surface	Surface	STP 2	Trenches		
Side Scrapers									
Concave Single Side Scrapers	2				2	3	35	42	6.3
Concave Double Side Scrapers							1	1	0.1
Convex Single Side Scrapers	61	1	15			22	206	305	45.6
Convex Double Side Scrapers	11	1	1	1		1	27	42	6.3
Straight Single Side Scrapers	14			1		6	58	79	11.8
Straight Double Side Scrapers	1						6	7	1.0
Sundry Single Side Scrapers	4		1			2	11	18	2.7
Sundry Double Side Scrapers	1						2	3	0.4
Notched Side Scrapers	6		1	1	1	6	4	19	2.8
End Scrapers									
Convex End Scrapers	5			3		1	20	29	4.3
Convex End Concave Side Scrapers	1			1		3	14	19	2.8
Convex End And Side Scrapers	12		1	2		4	21	40	6.0
Nosed End Scrapers	10		2			5	19	36	5.4
Circular Scrapers	8		1	1		3	11	24	3.6
Other Scrapers									
Concavity	3						2	2	0.3
Thumbnail Scrapers	3						3	3	0.4
Total	139	2	22	10	3	56	437	669	100.0
% age	20.8	0.3	3.3	1.5	0.4	8.4	65.3	100	

Table 6.4: Scrapers other than Core Scrapers per site and provenience

a) Convex Single End Scrapers

Convex single end scrapers were scrapers with a single scraping end situated on either the distal end or the proximal end (Figure 6.3-2, 9, 10, 12). These are the same as Masao (1979) and Nelson (1973:186)'s simple end scrapers with a single proximal, distal or a convex scraper end. Mehlman (1989:12) regards them as convex end scrapers with the convex scraper edge approximately perpendicular to the long axis of a flake or chunk. A total of 29 specimens were analysed mainly from Kansyore Island (21), followed by the Island of Deserters (5) and Nsongezi (3). The specimens had either a straight scraping end (1) or distal scraping end (9) or proximal end scraping edges (9). Two of the scrapers for this type were made on *levallois* flakes. The mean length was 30.2 mm, mean thickness was 8.8 mm, and mean breadth 27.7 mm. The only raw material was quartz.

b) Convex Double-End Scrapers

Double-end scrapers are almost the opposite of the single end scrapers (Figure 6.2-2). Scrapers scored in this category had two scraping ends. Mehlman (1989) described them as scrapers with opposed scraping edges equivalent to Merrick's type A-3-c. These were scrapers with the distal and proximal scraper ends on the same blank. That meant that they had double truncation on both the distal end and the proximal end (Masao 1979a). They were like single end scrapers in all respects (Nelson 1973, 189) only that these had two scraping ends. Three types of scrapers were analysed and classified as having double ends and these were the convex concave combination (190), convex end and side (38) and straight end and side scrapers (2).

The convex-end and side combination scrapers were regarded as double-end scrapers (Figure 6.3-11, 18,). This is because in this mixed type of scraper it is the end which is more pronounced (Mehlman, 1989:130). The scrapers analysed in this class were those with a convex scraper edge on one end with a convex, straight, or irregular scraper edge along either or both sides. One specimen had a notched side and end scraping edge. The analysis identified 40 scrapers with at least a convex side and one end having scraping edges. These included the convex end and side scrapers (37) and straight end and side scrapers (3). Among the convex end and side scrapers were two made on *levallois* flakes. All these were generally classified as end and side scrapers that were collected from Kansyore Island (25), Island of Deserters (12), and Nsongezi (3). Quartz was the raw material preferred for their manufacture.

The mean length, thickness, and breadth were 29.9 mm, 8.2 mm, and 23.8 mm respectively.

The last category of double end scrapers was the convex end and concave side scrapers. The scrapers in this type had scraping edges on either the distal end or the proximal end combined with a hollowed out scraping edge while one had the distal end with a convex scraping edge at the same time with a concave scraping edge on the lateral. These are also termed as the convex concave combination scrapers. This is because the tool had the distal end with a convex scraping edge combined with a concave scraping edge on the mesial. The 19 scrapers that belonged to this type were mainly from Kansyore Island (17), followed by Nsongezi (1) and Island of Deserters (1). The maximum length, thickness, and breadth were 29.4 mm, 7.2 mm and 22.2 mm respectively. This scraper type was manufactured using quartz.

c) Circular Scrapers

The scrapers close to the discoid in plan form (Figure 6.2:6) were categorised as circular scrapers. A total of 24 scrapers with at least three scraping edges were analysed. Nelson (1973) classified them as semi-circular convex and circular convex scrapers but herein they are circular scrapers. Kansyore Island yielded (2), Island of Deserters (14) and Nsongezi (8). To differentiate them from discoid cores the criteria used entailed identification of characteristics of a flake on a circular scraper unlike a discoid that is made on a core. The raw material used was quartz. One of the analysed specimens in this type was more of a convex double side and end scraper. The scraper had two lateral scraping edges and the end with a scraping edge too. The convex double side and end scraper made from quartzite was from Kansyore Island. The mean length was 27.2 mm, thickness 8.6 mm, and breadth 25.1 mm.

d) Nosed End Scrapers

Nosed end scrapers possessed a narrow, constricted convex or sub-rectangular edge that has been produced by extensive lateral trimming or retouch along one or both adjacent edges (Figures 6.2-3; 6.8k). Nelson (1973:192) outlines five factors responsible for the occurrence of the nosed scrapers. These are: notches or concave lines of trimming constriction along the margins of a relatively thin piece of waste; notches or deep concave lines of steep trimming could constrict the convex edge, retouching, or trimming a naturally occurring spur. It could also result from utilising the intersection of two converging lines of trimming or retouch along the convergent lines of a flake and lines of steep trimming or naturally a vertical surface forming a narrow, deeply U-shaped specimen which is often thicker than it is wide. Mehlman (1989) regards them as nosed end scrapers since the convex edge is tightly flexed making an ogive shape without notches. Nelson and Posnansky (1970:145) have two types of nosed scrapers that are the convergent-nosed scrapers and narrow highly backed nosed scrapers. The former have convergent straight edges while the latter have convex edges that make them close to burins. The analysis identified two types and these were the nosed side and end scrapers and the convergent-nosed scrapers. The former were the dominant (32) compared to the latter (4). These had a single side with a scraping edge converging with a non-retouched side forming a tip or nose. These shouldn't be mistaken for the convex side and end scrapers as the nosed side and end scrapers had a side and the end forming the nose or tip trimmed. The convergent nosed end scrapers had a convergent end forming a tip on the distal end with both laterals having scraping edges. These could be termed as convex double -nosed scrapers or nosed double side scrapers. Some had the nosed end forming the scraping edge. Quartz was utilised for the manufacture of all the nosed scrapers. The mean length, thickness, and breadth were 30.4 mm, 7.6 mm, and 21.4 mm respectively.

6.2.8 Side Scrapers

Based on morphology the side scrapers (516) analysed were either single side or double side scrapers. The types of scrapers characterised by a single side scraping edge were the convex single side scrapers (305), the straight single side scrapers (79), concave single side scrapers (42), sundry single side scrapers (18), and notched side scrapers (19). On the other hand those with double or two scraping sides were classified as convex double side scrapers (42), straight double side scrapers (7) sundry double side scrapers (3), and concave double side scraper (1). Therefore, side scrapers were frequent (77.1%) in the scraper assemblage than end scrapers (22.1%) or the other scrapers (0.4%). Any scraper whose dominant scraping edge was on the mesial side was analysed as a side scraper. The analysis regarded a side scraper as any scraper with a scraping edge covering a side totally, a side partially, either sides or the side that was notched. Kansyore Island had the majority (393) followed by Island of Deserters (102) and Nsongezi (21).

(a) Convex Single Side Scrapers

The convex single side scrapers were scrapers with one slightly convex scraping edge (Figure 6.2:9). These were the dominant scrapers with a total of 305 analysed. Kansyore Island dominated the production (228) followed by the Island of Deserters (62) and Nsongezi (15). Quartz (245), quartzite (56), and gneiss (4) were used for the manufacture of convex single side scrapers. The mean length, thickness, and breadth were 28.2 mm, 7.1 mm, and 20.7 mm respectively.

The convex double side scrapers had convex scraper edges on the opposing long sides of the flake or chunk (Figure 6.3:14). The 42 specimens in this research had two scraping edges on the opposing long sides or mesial sides. Kansyore had 28 specimens, Island of Deserters (12) and Nsongezi (2). The raw material types utilised in this tool category was quartz. The mean length, thickness, and breadth were 29.5 mm, 6.9 mm, and 21.5 mm respectively.

(b) Sundry/Irregular Side Scrapers

The 18 scrapers analysed were classified as sundry single side scrapers because they had one irregular scraping edge (Figure 6.3:7). The edge was simply irregular but not as indented or serrated as for the denticulates. One of these specimens had evidence of platform preparation and could be regarded as a *levallois* sundry side scraper. These were obtained from Nsongezi (1), Kansyore Island (13), and the Island of Deserters (4). The raw materials preferred for this tool was quartz only. The mean length, thickness, and breadth were 34.3 mm, 9 mm, and 25.4 mm respectively.

Sundry double side scrapers were the scrapers characterised by double irregular working or scraper edges. These were on the two opposed long sides of the flakes that appeared more as straight. The irregular scraper edge was where the length measured back from the midpoint of the retouch arc was less than the width at right angles (Mehlman, 1989: 131). These were 3 specimens whereby 2 were identified from Kansyore Island and 1 from the Island of Deserters, all were made from quartzite. The mean length, thickness and breadth were; 40.6 mm, 8.6 mm and 22.6 mm respectively.

(c) Straight Side Scrapers

This was a category of scrapers with a relatively straight scraping edge (Figure 6.3-1, 13 & 6.2-5). Two categories were identified that were the straight single side scrapers (79) (Figure 6.2:5) and straight double side scrapers (7)

(6.3:1,13). All these scrapers had at least one straight scraping edge on the longest sides of the flake. However, the straight double side scrapers had at least two scraping edges along the two long opposed sides of the flake (Figure 6.3:1&13). The majority (70) specimens of the two types were identified from Kansyore Island followed by the Island of Deserters (15) and Nsongezi (1). The raw material utilisation analysis showed that quartz was preferred. The mean length, thickness, and breadth were 27.8 mm, 6.4 mm, and 18.2 mm respectively.

(d)   Concave Side Scrapers

A total of 42 scrapers characterised with a single side hollowed out or curved in along the mesial side (Figure 6.2-7 & 6.3-17) were analysed. These scrapers were mainly from Kansyore Island (40) while the Island of Deserters had the least (2). Quartzite was the major raw material (39) as quartz had only 3 specimens. The mean length, thickness, and breadth were 29.6 mm, 7.14mm, and 20.9mm respectively.

(e)   Concave Scraper

Though not common, one scraper possessed curved-in scraping edges on two sides unlike the concave single side scrapers with one curved-in scraping edge. This was termed as the concave scraper. This could as well be taken as a concave double-sided scraper. According to Nelson (1973), scholars like (Leakey, 1931; Leakey, 1945; Gabel, 1969) have also regarded concave scrapers as hollow scrapers. The concave scraping edge appears anywhere on the piece extending for most of the length or width of the periphery. That is the length across the arc from end to end is greater than twice the depth of the arc (Mehlman 1989).

This means it is neither a side nor end scraper as the scraping edge may be on the distal end, proximal end or the mesial side. The one analysed conformed to the latter category that is having the concave scraping edges on both sides of the mesial that is why it was analysed as a side scraper. The scraper was from Kansyore Island made of quartz. The length of the scraper was 30mm, thickness 5 mm, and breadth 18 mm.

(f)   Notched Scraper

This was any scraper with one or more concave scraping edges that were shorter than 1.0 cm (Nelson, 1973). The notched scrapers discussed here had both multiple notches and single indentations (Figures 6.2: 4, 8; 6.3:-4 &

6.8j). One of the specimens in this category had notches on the side and end. Notched scrapers were a total of 19 scrapers that were all manufactured from clear quartz. Analysis of spatial distribution was as follows: Nsongezi (2), Island of Deserters (6), and Kansyore Island (11). The mean length, thickness, and breadth were 33.5 mm, 8.4 mm, and 22.7 mm respectively.

(g) Concavity

The concavity is a scraper type with a concave edge anywhere along the periphery, usually extending less than half the length or width of the piece. That is the length across the arc from end to end is greater than the depth of the arc (Mehlman, 1989:131). Two scrapers of this category obtained from Kansyore Island were made from quartz. The mean length was 22.5 mm, mean thickness of 5 mm and 16 mm as mean breadth.

6.2.9 Thumbnail Scrapers

Thumbnail scrapers are small double ended scrapers that are characteristic of the Wilton industry in East Africa (Cole, 1964: 223). They are termed thumbnail because they are small and their circumference is as if they were made by pressing a thumbnail (Figure 6.3-21 &22). Three thumbnail scrapers were recovered from the Island of Deserters. They were all made from quartzite raw material. The mean length, thickness, and breadth were 15.3mm, 4mm, and 12 mm respectively. The size of all the scrapers analysed suggested local manufacture just like the raw material utilised that were quartz and quartzite and gneiss that were locally available. This therefore means that the similarity of the scraper types with those of other East African industries and Sudan Neolithic cannot be explained by migration per se but it was an attempt where people's subsistence was dictated by the resources available, for instance the utilisation of the river cobbles as lithic raw materials.

6.2.10 Denticulates

In this research denticulates were not regarded as scrapers since they have variability, as it is usually a single edge considered in the definition and can and often do occur on any blank form (Marks 1991:183). Denticulates are serrated or tooth-edged tools that were emphasised by the Mousterian tool kit (MSA) usually made on large flakes (Whittaker 1994, 30). Masao (1979) noted that denticulates are flakes or cores with at least one of the edges serrated. The specimens analysed were 44 and constituted 2.6% of the shaped tools. They were made on flakes with a saw blade edge-like or toothed edge. One specimen among the 44 was made on a *levallois* flake blank that could be termed as a *levallois* denticulate. Denticulates appeared at Kansyore Island (22), Nsongezi (2), and the Island of Deserters (20). Quartz was preferred as the raw material for denticulates. The mean length was 30.1 mm, thickness 9.4 mm, and breadth 20.5 mm.

6.2.11 Points/*Percoirs*

Points are made on flakes; they are generally lanceolate or triangular in plan form and may be bifacially, or unifacially retouched. Bushozi (2011) identified three types of points that were unifacial points (Figure 6.3:19&20; Figure 6.8p), bifacial points and *levallois* points while Clark and Kleindienst (1974) identified points as either unifacial or bifacial like the current research. Nelson (1973: 227) regarded a point as a convergent flake trimmed or retouched to a sharp point with shallow, invasive flaking, or a bifacially flaked, sub-triangular implement. Therefore a point was retouched along two convergent sides to give a spear- head/arrow morphology (Mehlman, 989:135). The points could converge in an angle that is usually less than 45° and appear as either triangular or lanceolate in plan form (Kessy, 2005: 269). In this research two types of points were identified that were the unifacial points (72) and bifacial points (2). The bits of the points analysed were pointed and rounded while the butts were flat and showed signs of preparation for hafting especially at the Island of Deserters (13), unlike the points from Kansyore Island (61). This shows that points were 74 and were more frequent at Kansyore Island.

Unifacial points have pointed/arrow-like distal ends with retouches on one surface usually the distal (Bushozi, 2011: 219). Kessy (2005:270) takes the unifacial points as the ones with retouched edges though some have basal thinning to facilitate hafting. Mehlman (1989:135) defined unifacial points as shaped tools with unifacial retouch near the tip at the distal edge. The analysed unifacial points had retouch on one edge that was either on the ventral side or the dorsal side.

Bifacial points were less frequent with only two specimens. These were the points with bifacial retouch along one or both edges up to the point tip (Mehlman, 1989).Therefore the bifacial points analysed had two faces retouched. These two faces /edges were at the bit side or the distal end. The two edges could be retouched differently that is one edge retouched from the ventral while another was retouched from the dorsal but once both edges at the tip had a retouch then it was regarded as a bifacial point. The Island of Deserters and Kansyore Island each yielded one specimen. The raw materials utilised was quartz with clear quartz used for the 72 unifacial points. The mean length of the points was 25.3 mm, while the mean thickness was 5.7mm and 16.2 mm for the mean breadth.

6.2.12 Becs

These are small stone tools made on flakes or flake fragments having a flat beak or bec formed by the intersection of two trimmed notches. These later may be flaked from the ventral face but could also be done alternately, that is one from the ventral and one from the dorsal face. Where the notches intersect, the tool equates with the bec (Clark and Kleindienst, 1974). Becs contain thick, robust points or projections formed by minimal, steep retouch.

The retouch appears on a natural spur on a piece of waste, with the retouch casual and discontinuous (Nelson, 1973). Masao (1979) associated becs with borers where the point of modification was formed by the distal intersection of two converging sides. Masao (1979) concurs with Nelson (1973) that since becs were made on waste they could be regarded as unshaped stone tools. Clark *et al* (1984) also takes becs and borers as similar. Becs have also been referred to as "burin-like tools "(Nelson and Posnansky, 1970:143). Despite that, becs in this assemblage had evidence of intentional retouches therefore they were regarded as shaped tools. Becs were characterised by notching and retouching which was either normal or alternate to form a short awl-like point that could be used for piercing. The eleven becs were from Nsongezi (1), Island of Deserters and (1) Kansyore Island (9) that were all made from quartz. The mean length, thickness, and breadth were 30.1mm, 7.3 mm and 20.7 mm respectively.

6.2.13 Geometrics

Geometrics were characterised by an edge formed by either unifacial or bifacial trimming and in the case of microliths, the edge was meant to facilitate hafting. This is termed as backing. Backing was also regarded as intentional blunting (Clark and Kleindienst, 1974). The backed side was usually characterised by blunt/ steep retouch approximating 90° (Mehlman, 1989: 132). The backed pieces also regarded as microliths or geometrics were small stone tools that acted as a hallmark for the LSA in the area under study. The LSA industry was dominated by backed tools, micro burins, and geometrics (crescents, triangles, and trapezes). The backed pieces were categorised basing on the shape, angle, and alignment of retouch on the backed sides (Kessy, 2005: 259). A total of 578 backed pieces were analysed. These included curved backed pieces 206 (35.6%), crescents 200 (34.6 %), diverse backed pieces 91 (15.7%), triangles 28 (4.8%), angle backed pieces 17 (2.9%), backed drills 13 (2.2%), straight-backed pieces 11 (1.9%), trapezes 6 (1.0%), oblique truncated pieces 4 (0.7%) and orthogonal truncated pieces 2 (0.3%) (Table 6.5). The frequency of the backed pieces at the three major research areas was as follows; Kansyore Island 483 (83.6 %), the Island of Deserters 81 (14 %) and Nsongezi 14 (2.4 %) (Figure 6.4). This implied that Kansyore Island with the highest frequency of backed pieces had a predominant microlithic industry unlike the Island of Deserters. The existence of evidence of wild fauna could suggest that some of the geometrics were used for hunting.

Sites	Island of Deserters	Surface	Kansyore Island	Surface	Nsongezi	Surface	Total	% age
Angle Backed	1		16				17	2.9
Backed Drills	2		11				13	2.2
Crescents	26		169	1	3	1	200	34.6
Curve Backed Pieces	32	1	166		6	1	206	35.6
Diverse Backed	5		83		3		91	15.7
Oblique Truncated	3		1				4	0.7
Orthogonal Truncated	1	1					2	0.3
Straight Backed	5		6				11	1.9
Trapezes	1		5				6	1.0
Triangles	3		25				28	4.8
Total	79	2	482	1	12	2	578	100.0
% age	13.7	0.3	83.4	0.2	2.1	0.3	100.0	

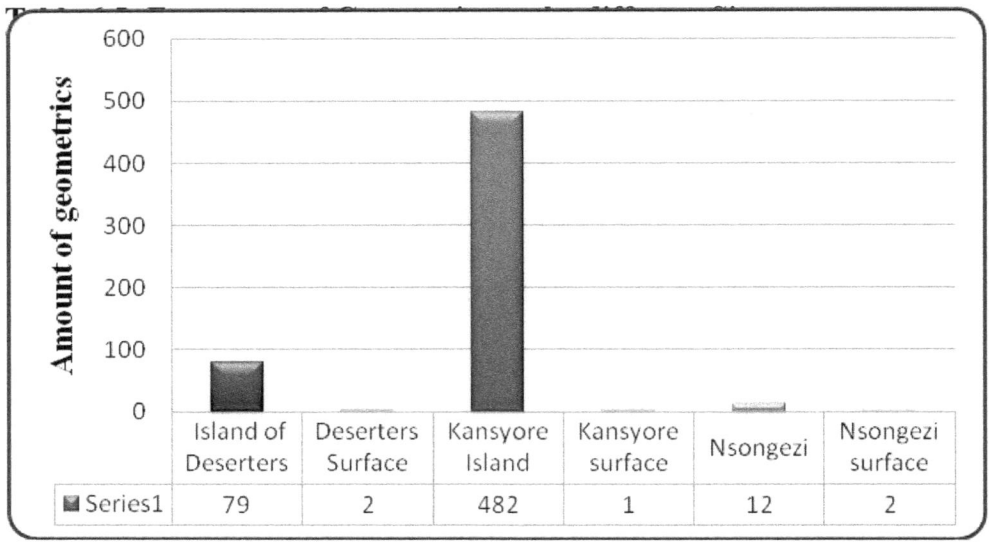

Figure 6.4: Geometrics per site from both surface collections and excavation

6.2.14 Crescents

Crescents are also known as lunates (Clark and Kleindienst, 1979:99; Phillipson 1976a: 27; Marks and Mohammed, 1981; Sutton, 1981; Marks, 1991) or circle segments (Honegger, 2006). Mehlman (1989) described crescents as microliths with a backed edge that was not continuous from end to end. This was because the retouches (backing) were usually heavy at the ends and lighter in the middle (Masao, 1979:103). The crescents analysed were characterised by absence of a flake talon but with straight sharp cutting edges and a curved blunted back (Figure 6.5, m, n, p and q). These were designed not for holding into the hands and use as complete instruments but for hafting and gluing into handles of bone and wood (Sutton, 1981: 476).

The 200 crescents came from Kansyore Island (170), the Island of Deserters (26), and Nsongezi (4) (Table 6.6). The preferred raw material for making the crescents was only quartz. This may be because quartz fractures with sharp edges that can easily be backed. The mean length of the crescents was 23.8 mm. The mean thickness was 4.5 mm and the mean breadth was 11 mm. In Kansyore Island where the crescents were dominant, they were characterised by mainly proximal oblique truncations. The crescents signify the period when the bow and arrow begun to be used in hunting.

The crescents in this assemblage varied in size with some being small while others were quite big. This would probably imply that crescents were multi-functional tools. Honegger (2006) suggested that, these Holocene tools have been considered as either arrow heads (weapon elements) or as sickle blades. This could probably mean that the small sized ones were used as projectile tips or barbs (arrow heads) while the relatively bigger ones served as sickle blades. In the latter case in the study of Nubian lunates, Honneggar (2006) suggested lunates were to fit knives for cutting vegetal materials. While in the previous case Lampard (2007) and Lampard and Phillipson (2010) suggested that they were used as hunting devices sometimes, though Seitsonen, (2010) is of the view that crescents were used as fishing arrows. However, the crescents especially from Kansyore Island call for further investigation to situate them in the debate of being multi-functional tools.

6.2.15 Curve Backed Pieces

These constituted the biggest proportion of all the geometrics with a total of 206 out of the 578 specimens. Curve backed pieces according to (Kessy, 2005:264 and Mehlman, 1989:133) had a convex backed edge that intersected with the opposite lateral with one end having a non-modified edge (Figure 6.5 k, i, r). Though quite similar to the crescents what differentiates the two is that the curve backed pieces have a flake/blade talon and yet the backing is not as deep as that of a crescent (Masao, 1979: 99-101). Nelson (1973) refers to them as curve backed flakes that are any microliths having a uni-terminal convex truncation. The truncation may be oblique, diagonal, or re-curved. The frequency of curve backed pieces at the sites was as follows: Nsongezi (7), Island of Deserters (33), and Kansyore Island with the majority (166) curve backed pieces. The mean length, thickness, and breadth were 24.7mm, 5.03mm and 14.2mm respectively. The raw materials utilised were quartz (176), and basalt (27), and aplite dyke (3).

6.2.16 Straight Backed Pieces

Any backed piece where the backed edge was close to a straight line was taken as a straight-backed piece in this study (Figure 6.5; c, e, f and s). The backed edge that formed the length of the piece intersected with the opposite edge to form an acute angle of <25° at the point of intersection with the un-retouched edge having a flake/blade talon (Mehlman, 1989: 189; Kessy, 2005: 265). They have also been regarded as straight-backed flakes those that have a retouched edge that is straight, although the opposite edge may show signs of concavity (Masao, 1979:188). Nelson (1973:168) used the term "microliths with longitudinal truncations parallel to the flake axis" that he categorised under "miscellaneous forms". The straight-backed pieces analysed were at times triangular and at times quadrilateral. The 11 straight-backed pieces were obtained from Kansyore Island (6) and the Island of Deserters (5) and were all made of clear quartz. The mean length was 30.6mm; mean thickness as 5.7 while the mean breadth was 13.5mm.

6.2.17 Triangles

A triangle is a geometric microlith consisting of three points, called vertices, connected by three sides that may be straight or circular. To qualify as a backed piece the artefact with the triangular shape had to have at least two sides backed while the third was a naturally cutting edge (Figure 6.5 b and d). Mehlman (1989:133) defined the triangles as, a plan form with two of the three edges at least partially backed. Nelson (1973:156) noted that the edge opposite the truncation is usually unmodified and may not exhibit any degree of modifications greater than retouch. Therefore the triangles had a sharp angle of 90° unlike the angle-backed pieces that had an obtuse angle with the third side sharper (Kessy, 2005:263). The backed edges are usually straight though some have concavity or convexity. The triangles analysed showed signs of convexity. I concur with Nelson who suggests that by triangles intergrading with the crescents it makes them rare. A total of 28 triangles were analysed from Kansyore Island (25) and the Island of Deserters (3). These were all made from quartz. The mean length, thickness, and breadth were 23.2mm, 4.7mm and 14.8 respectively.

6.2.18 Trapezes

These are microliths of trapezoidal/trapeziform outline. The central portion of the modified edge may or may not be modified (Nelson 1973:157). Mehlman (1979:133) noted that the backing appears on the two least parallel opposing edges where the shorter of the two approximately parallel edges may be backed while the long one is not (Figure 6.5-1). Therefore, the tool was retouched on the distal and proximal and rarely on the sides (Fernandez, 2003). The trapezes analysed displayed mainly the proximal oblique truncations. Trapezes are usually intermediate between crescents and triangles (Masao, 1979) and he cited Fagan (1971:88) who regarded any quadrilateral pieces that were backed with naturally two sharp parallel edges as trapezes. The 6 trapezes analysed were identified from Kansyore Island (5) and the Island of Deserters (1). The trapezes in this assemblage were the asymmetrical type having been made on truncated flakes just like the Masao (1979:173) type (Figure 6.5-1). Quartz was the only raw material utilised where 3 were in clear quartz. The mean length was 22.8mm, mean thickness 5.5mm while mean breadth was 20mm.

6.2.19 Angle Backed Pieces

These are backed tools characterised by two lines of backing intersecting to form an obtuse angle along one side of the piece. One line intersects the opposite sharp edge in the same way as for an oblique truncation (Mehlman, 1989:134). Kessy (2005:267) noted that some angle-backed pieces have partially backed edges that do not terminate at either the distal or proximal end of the flake and appear similar to the triangles as earlier on noted. The angle backed pieces analysed were a total of 17 obtained from Kansyore Island 16 (94.12%) and the Island of Deserters 1 (5.88%). The preferred raw material for this tool type was clear quartz. The mean length was 25.1 mm, mean thickness was 6.9 mm, and mean breadth being 20.6 mm.

6.2.20 Diverse Backed Pieces

These were the backed pieces that did not conform to any of the categories above as also suggested by Mehlman (1989:134). Nelson (1973:172-173) classified them under the miscellaneous backed pieces with no formal plan or edge arrangement. The backed edges are either irregular or circular (Kessy, 2005: 268) (Figure 6.5-a, j, o, and t). A total of 91 diverse backed pieces were analysed that were from Kansyore Island (83), Nsongezi (3) and the Island of Deserters (5). The mean length, thickness, and breadth were 25.2mm, 5.6mm, and 17.4mm respectively. The tool-makers for this type preferred to use quartz for all tools in this category.

6.2.21 Backed Drills

Backed tools that were included in this category were those that had an acuminate needle like projection created by backing (Figure 6.5g). Much as Mehlman (1989) noted that the piece does not have to be elongate however, those analysed were the elongated type that appeared very pointed with chisel–like ends. Clark and Kleindienst (1974) referred to them as backed awls. Nelson (1973:172) also regarded them as awls with two major categories: that were, the narrow sharp-pointed awls having truncations formed by two converging lines of blunting while the second category was that of the narrow sharp-pointed forms with a low angle oblique or diagonal truncation. It was the first category that was referred to as points by Sampson and Sampson

(1968) and Jones (1932) cited by Nelson (1973:172). The backed drills in the current assemblage had chisel like distal ends. These were 13 that were from Kansyore Island (11) and the Island of Deserters (2). All backed drills were made from the clear quartz. The mean length was 32.07 mm; mean thickness as 7.30 mm and mean breadth 11.84mm.

6.2.22 Oblique Truncated and Orthogonal Truncated Pieces

The oblique truncated pieces (4) and orthogonal truncated pieces (2) (Figures 6.5u; 6.8n and 6.4h & v) respectively though without steep backing had evidence of truncation. The raw material utilised was quartz. Kansyore Island (2) and the Island of Deserters (4) were the source of this tool type. The mean length, thickness, and breadth were 24.8mm 7.5 mm and 19.1mm respectively.

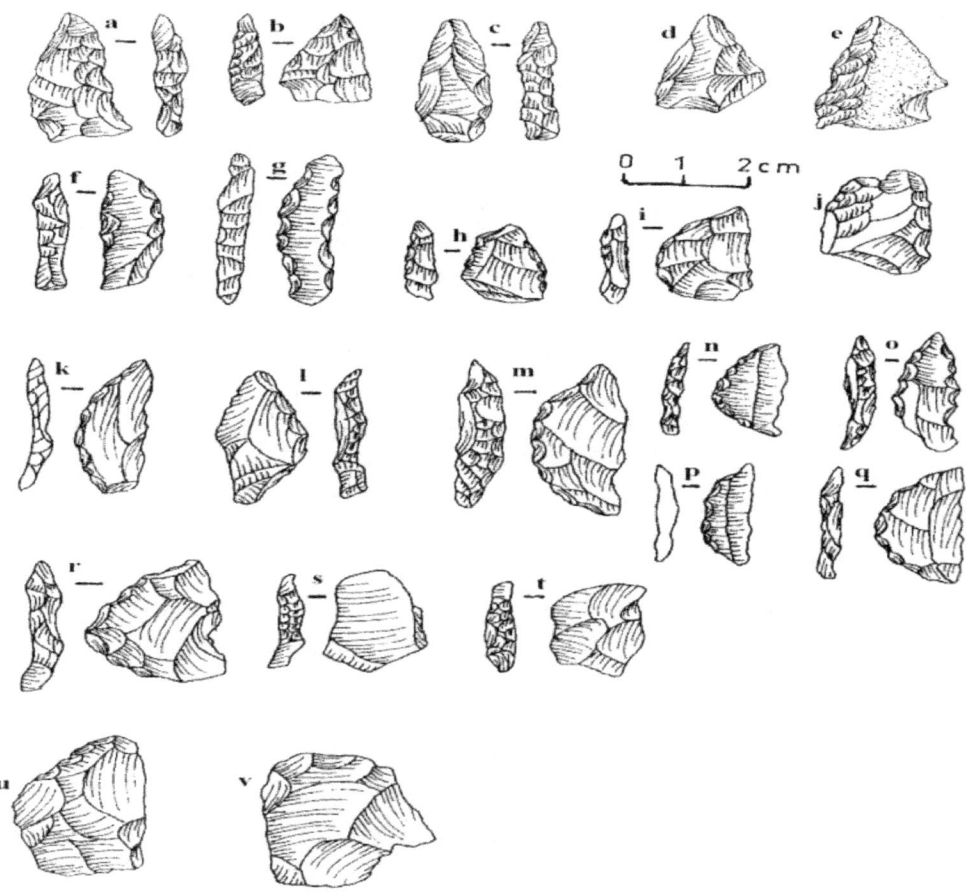

Figure 6.5: Geometrics

Key: Crescents= (**m, n, p, q**); Straight Backed Pieces= (**c, e, f, s**) =; Diverse Backed Pieces= (**a, j, o, t**); Oblique Truncated= (**u**); Orthogonal Truncated= (**h, v**); Triangles= (**b, d**); Trapeze= (**l**); Backed Drill= (**g**) and Curve Backed Pieces (**k, i & r**).

6.2.23 Burins

Burins were stone tools made by striking off a retouch flake that runs along the edge of the flake and removes the edge leaving a steep or even right-angled edge (Figure 6.3:3). The strong steep edges and sharp points of burins were good for scraping and engraving hard materials such as bone, antler, and wood (Crabtree, 1973). They are also tools with a characteristic burin facet or facets formed on the thickness of the artefact, which was generally a flake or flake fragment (Clark and Kleindienst, 1974). Though aware of Nelson (1973: 229) and Masao (1979: 230-233)'s classification of burins into technical and significant burins, the analysed burins (29) were placed under dihedral burins (single facet) (12), angle burins (14), and other burins (3). This followed Kessy (2005: 271) and Mehlman (1989:138-9) classification of burins basing on number of spalls removed, number of edges altered, angle of spall removal, and type of modification resulting from the knapping process. The greatest percentage of burins came from Kansyore Island (75.9 %) in comparison to the Island of Deserters (24.1%).

Dihedral burins were burins whose bit had two sets of intersecting facets where the bit was either symmetrical or asymmetrical to the flake axis (Nelson, 1973:237) formed. Dihedral burins in East Africa were termed as bec-de-flute by the Leakeys (Nelson, 1973). Mehlman (1989) and Masao (1979) were of the view that dihedral burins had scars removed at two intersecting edges of a piece leading to the formation of an acute angled working edge. Burins considered as dihedral burins in the study were the burins with spalls and a dihedral platform. The 12 dihedral burins from Kansyore Island were made of clear quartz. The mean length, thickness, and breadth were 30.9 mm, 7 mm and 15 mm respectively.

Angle burins were burins with multiple spalls removed from one edge normally at the proximal or distal running parallel the flakes' long axis with or without retouch on the edge of the spall (Kessy, 2005: 272). Mabulla (1996) considers them as burins with single or two symmetrical burin facets on the burinated edge. The burin blow often forms an angle close to 90° (Mehlman, 1989: 137). The platform from which the burin spalls are struck must truncate the proximal or distal end of the flake, but it may be oblique to the flake axis generating specimens occasionally with symmetrical bits. A total of 14 angle burins were obtained from Kansyore Island (7) and the Island of Deserters (7) made on quartz raw material. This implied that, all burins from the Island of Deserters were angle burins. The mean length, thickness, and breadth were 35.2 mm, 7.3 mm, and 17.9 mm respectively.

The last category of burins was the other or mixed burin type. Nelson (1973) regarded these as miscellaneous burins while Mehlman (1989) regarded them as mixed burins or sundry. In the analysis they were taken as mixed burins because they combine characteristics of the dihedral and angle burins, therefore they are a composite or mixed burin type. This was because they were neither dihedral nor even purely angle burins but they fall in between the two types above. The 3 specimens were all got from Kansyore Island and made of clear quartz. The mean length, thickness, and breadth were 21.3 mm, 9 mm and 17 mm respectively.

6.2.24 Composite Tools

Any tool that combined characteristics of more than one retouched/shaped tool was taken as a composite tool. These were multi-purpose tools that served more than one function such as chopping or digging (Joukowsky 1980:321). The composite tools were 2 (0.1%) out of the 1,706 lithics artefacts. These were from the Island of Deserters in Trench 2, level 3 (10-15) cm. The composite tools were both notched side dihedral burins. That is other than the burin spall they had a side with a clear notch of a notched side scraper. The raw material exploited was quartz. The mean length was 38 mm, mean thickness was 13 mm, and mean breadth was 27 mm.

6.2.25 Outil's Escaille's

These shaped tools were characterised by the presence of tiny step flake scars that served as evidence of crushing or shattering along the edges. Most of them had bifacial retouch and crushing at opposed ends. The fact that they are crushed at both ends takes us into the debate as to whether they were bipolar cores or shaped tools as raised by Kessy (2005:272-274). They can however be distinguished from bipolar cores by the more regular forms of the faceted edges (Clark and Kleindienst, 1974: 92). Kessy (2005) further noted that several names were used to refer to these tools. For instance Masao (1989) and Nelson (1973) regarded them as outils e'cailles'; Clark and Kleindienst (1974) as outils esquille and less correctly as 'outils écailles' and yet Leakey (1931) referred to them as fabricators. Despite the earlier discrepancy in names in this analysis they were viewed as outils écailles that were regarded as any tool that had evidence of the use of the bipolar technique on both the distal and the proximal evidenced by crushed edges. A total of 12 outils écailles' were recovered from Kansyore Island (10) and the Island of Deserters (2). This implied the use of bipolar technique especially at Kansyore Island. The raw material preferred was exclusively clear quartz. The mean length was 25.8mm; mean thickness at 7.3 mm and mean breadth was 20.6 mm.

6.2.26 Heavy Duty Tools

The heavy-duty tools analyzed were the discoids 12 (0.7%), hand axes 2 (0.1%), pick axes 3 (0.2%) and core axes 14 (0.8%). This implied that the heavy-duty tools were 32 (1.9%) in the lithic assemblage of 1,706 (100%).

6.2.27 Discoids

These were bifacially modified pieces that were radially flaked with a flat, bi-convex or lenticular section (Figure 6.8-1). These tools may have been hafted as blades of the adzes or used as circular knives (Clark and Kleindienst, 1974). According to Mehlman (1989), discoids were bifacially modified pieces that were flat, ovate, and almost circular with some or most of the periphery bifacially retouched. They were differentiated from the disc cores by the fact that the discoids were too thin and heavily retouched. The analysed discoids were small, flat, and roundish made from river cobbles. The analysed 12 discoids were unearthed from Nsongezi (1), Kansyore (4), and Island of Deserters (7). The raw material for the discoids was entirely clear quartz. The mean length was 28.8mm; mean thickness at 13.2 mm while the mean breadth was 27 mm.

6.2.28 Hand Axes

Hand axes were bifacially retouched heavy duty tools that were more rarely unifacially retouched. They were characterised by a flat, biconvex, or Plano-convex cross section and a cutting edge around the whole circumference though at times it was near the butt (Clark and Kleindienst, 1974). The hand axe is a hallmark of the Acheulian industry between 1,500,000 and 300,000 years ago (Bushozi, personal communication) and thus a typical tool for the Lower Paleolithic in Eurosia and Africa (Joukowsky, 1980:321). Some, especially the earlier ones were made by hard hammer percussion though later the Acheulian relied as well on soft hammer percussion for the production of hand axes. The latter would produce hand axes that were wider and flatter. This therefore implied that the hand axes under consideration were made using hard hammer percussion. The hand axes were general purpose tools used for butchering, but they were also suitable for digging, shaping wood and a variety of other tasks (Whittaker, 1994:27; Keeley, 1980) but they also served as multipurpose tools (Joukowsky, 1980:321). Two hand axes were analysed that were obtained from Nsongezi area.

The Nsongezi hand axes were made out of basalt and quartz. The mean length was 91 mm; mean thickness was 45.55mm and mean breadth 71.66 mm. Though specimens made from cores are plentiful those from flake forms predominate and the side struck flake being the most popular (Lowe, 1952:38). Bishop and Posnansky (1960:58) described Uganda's hand axes as mainly of a pointed form and include the 'duck-head' variety which has a heavy butt and a thin blade giving a duck head profile in cross section. Those analysed conformed to the latter description. The hand axe culture is said to originate from the Congo Lupemban 11 culture that influenced the hand axe culture of the Horn of Africa and the Still Bay culture of eastern and southern Africa. Therefore, the hand axe shows evidence of cultural interaction.

6.2.29 Pick-Axes

These were core tools that were pointed though at times they were round-edged. They have a minimum of unifacial primary retouch, even at the distal end. They usually exhibit a high-backed, plano-convex or triangular cross section; the ventral face being usually un-flaked. If the ventral face was flaked then the artefact was a trihedral pick. Picks may be single or double-ended (Clark and Kleindienst, 1974: 98). However, Whittaker (1994: 37) regarded them as very small stone artefacts usually made from sections of small blades usually hafted and made to make composite tools. However the 3 pick axes in this study exhibited a triangular cross section (Figure 6.6) that were made from big but elongated pebbles that could be seen from the metric attributes.

They were from Nsongezi (1) and Island of Deserters (2) made of quartz. Two of the pick axes were from surface collections. The mean length, thickness, and breadth were 143 mm, 51.3 mm, and 67 mm respectively.

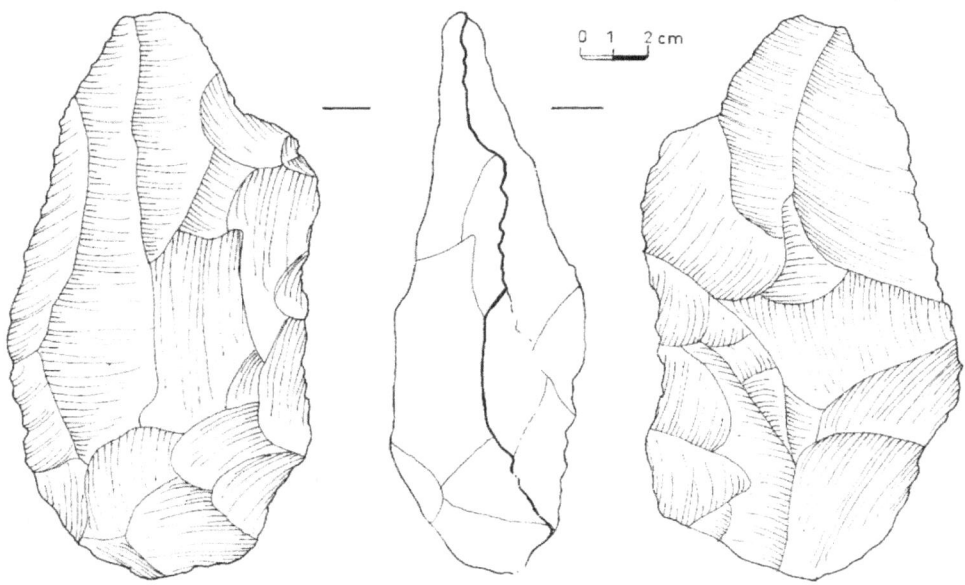

Figure 6.6: Pick Axe

6.2.30 Core Axes

A total of 15 core axes were analysed that were all from the Island of Deserters. The core axes are heavy-duty tools where those analysed had convergent or parallel edges made on cobbles. They were bifacially worked with the butt left completely un-worked that differentiated them from core scrapers. The retouch appeared on the distal end. Mehlman (1989:139) described them as biface/picks that have a thicker cross-section that are not classifiable as cores or bifacially modified pieces. It is the trimming of the distal end that gave them a symmetric or axe edge. In earlier publications they were described as chisels and adzes. However while the former had a concave-convex the latter were asymmetric yet core axes have symmetric edges (Clark and Kleindienst, 1974:4).

The mean length, thickness and breadth were; 44.5 mm, 27.9 mm and 39.5 mm respectively. The core axes from the Island of Deserters were made of mainly quartz (13) of which 5 were in crystal clear quartz. Other raw materials utilised were basalt (1) and quartzite (1) with a single specimen each.

6.2.31 Preforms

The specimens in this category were termed as preforms because they were un-finished or lacked all attributes of the actual tool form. Preforms to Odell (2003) are any blank that had been partly but not completely shaped into a finished tool. In the current assemblage preforms were flakes that had shapes of points with a proximal that was tanged and a pointed distal but without any retouches to qualify as points (figure 6.8i). The former were regarded as point preforms (9) whose one specimen had evidence of radial technology. These in the analysis were taken as point preforms (9) and were all from the Island of Deserters made in quartz raw material. The mean length, thickness, and breadth were 35.4mm, 9.6 mm, and 24.5mm respectively.

6.2.32 Non-Flaked Stones

The 6 non-flaked stones of the entire tool assemblage were stone tools that had no evidence of secondary modification by man but with evidence of utilisation. These included the hammer stones (2), pestle rubber (1), grinding stones, (2) and a mortar stone (Figure 6.7).

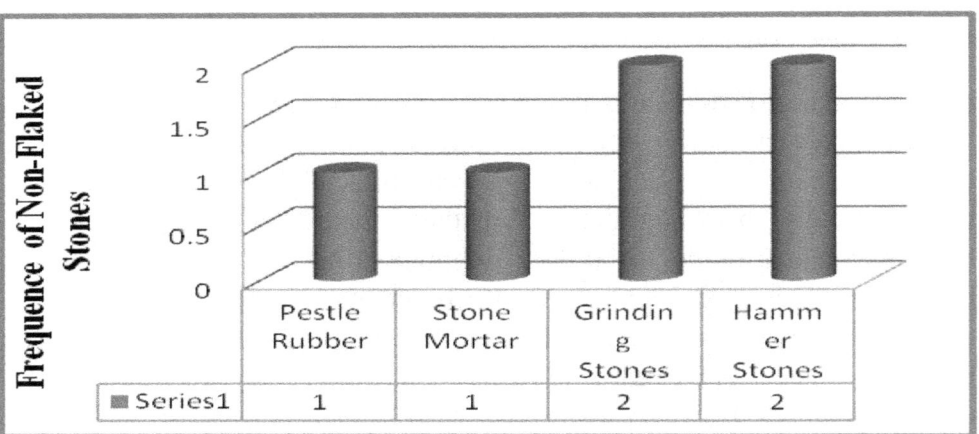

Figure 6.7: Non-Flaked Stones and Preforms

6.2.33 Pestle Rubber

This is a shaped tool used for grinding or crushing material. One pestle rubber was identified from Kansyore Island Trench 1A in level 1(0-15) cm. Mehlman (1989:152) defined a pestle rubber as an oblong sub-hemispherical cobble sized stone with one or more ground facets. Two types of pestle rubbers were distinguished that were; a pestle rubber with a pecked and bruised extremes due to usage and then one with a prominent pecked depression within one or more of the rubbed facets. The pestle rubber analysed belonged to the former category and was made from quartz raw material. The pestle rubber was 67mm, 32mm and 51mm in length, thickness, and breadth respectively.

6.2.34 Hammer Stones

The two hammer stones analysed were from Nsongezi and Kansyore Island. The Nsongezi specimen came from Test Pit 1 at (40-50 cm) in association with scrapers and backed pieces while the Kansyore hammer stone was obtained from Trench 1A Level 7 (40-45 cm). The Nsongezi hammer stone was in basalt while the Kansyore hammer stone was made on quartzite raw material. These hammer stones were made from roundish river pebbles. The Kansyore hammer stone could as well be regarded as a grinder as it had stains of red ochre due to probable grinding of red ochre common at Kansyore Island.

6.2.35 Grinding Stones

A grinding stone is any stone with at least one flat surface used for grinding foodstuffs, medicine, cosmetics or colourants (Darvill, 2008). The grinding stones analysed herein had flat surfaces. The grinding stone from the Island of Deserters had some black marks probably food residues (Plate 6.1). Two grinding stones were analysed that were all made out of quartzite raw material. The grinding stone from Kansyore Island was from trench 1A1 at a depth of (50-55) cm. This grinding stone had a reddish surface showing that it was probably used for the grinding of red ochre also collected from the same place. It weighed 500 grams. Grinding stones are one of the *fossiles directeurs* confirming the existence of pre-iron food producers as they were used for the processing of domestic grains for consumption (Karega-Munene 2003:23).

The grinding stones that occur in some LSA sites crushed red ochre but also probably served a more basic economic purpose of pounding vegetable foods (Sutton, 1981: 476). Besides that on the surface at Kansyore Island is what could be termed a stone mortar. In the view of Cole (1964) these are like stone bowls of the Gumban B type before detachment by a sharp blow. The stone mortar appears on a rock boulder with a deep depression made of quartz (Plate 6.1).

Plate 6.1: A Grinding Stone from the Island of Deserters

6.2.36 Flake/Blades

The flake blade category had 6,113 artefacts. These were flake and blade types. The flakes included whole flakes (4,274), utilised flakes (565), *levallois* flakes (63), core rejuvenated flakes (5), utilised *levallois* flakes (14). The blades analysed were the whole blades (1,069) and utilised blades (123) (Table 6.6)

Sites	Kansyore		Island of Deserters		Nsongezi			
Provenience	S/B	S	S/B	S	S/B	S	Total	% age
Whole Flakes	2,346	14	1,708	28	133	45	4,274	69.9
Levallois Flakes	1		62				63	1.0
Core Rejuvenated Flake	5						5	0.1
Utilised Flakes	387	4	139		13	22	565	9.2
Utilised *Levallois* Flakes			14				14	0.2
Whole Blades	680	5	334		48	2	1,069	17.5
Utilised Blades	82		39			2	123	2.0
Grand Total	3,501	23	2296	28	194	71	6,113	100.0

Key: S/B= Sub-Surface/ Excavation; S= Surface Collections

Table 6.6: Blade/Flake Types

6.2.37 Whole Blades

A blade is any flake with a length that is (at least) twice its width (Mehlman, 1989) (Figure 6.8m). Blades are typical of the upper Palaeolithic industry and were made using the indirect hammer percussion (Whittaker, 1994:33) but also appear in the Middle and Lower Acheulian (Bordes, 1968). The Upper Palaeolithic blades with straight cutting edges were excellent tools (Whittaker, 1994, Masao, 1979), even without retouches they were ideal blanks for making other tools especially end scrapers, spear points and burins. Basing on morphology and overall outline 1,192 blades were analysed and classified into whole blades (1,069) and utilised blades (123).The criteria for the identification of blades were the length and breadth irrespective of thickness, any specimen whose length was twice as long as the breadth were classified as blades (Figure 6.8m).The site statistical frequency for whole blades variability was as follows; Kansyore (685), Nsongezi (50) and the Island of Deserters (334). The mean length, thickness, and breadth were 31.5 mm, 6.5 mm and 14.1 mm respectively. The raw materials utilised were quartz (979), quartzite (61), gneiss (5), and basalt (24).

6.2.38 Utilised Blades

The utilised blades (123) had all the metric criteria as the whole blades but in addition to that, they had evidence of irregular edge modification. Mehlman (1989) regards them as trimmed utilised blades. The utilised blades constituted 2.0% of the blade/flake collection (6,113). The raw materials utilised were gneiss (1) quartz (116) and quartzite (6). The mean length, thickness, and breadth were 30.2 mm, 6 mm, and 13.5 mm respectively.

6.2.39 Whole Flakes

According to Mehlman, flakes are all un-retouched pieces preserving some part of the talon (Figure 6.8a, b, c, e, f and g). In this assemblage flakes were categorised into whole flakes (4,274), *levallois,* and kombewa flakes (63), core rejuvenated flakes (5) and utilised flakes that were utilised whole flakes (565) and utilised *levallois* flakes (14). The utilised flakes were predominantly of quartz raw material which could be due to the nature of quartz fracturing mechanism that could make it easy to use the blank even without further modification. The whole flakes that amounted to 4,274 were obtained from Kansyore Island 2,360 (55.22%), Nsongezi 178 (4.16%) and the Island of

Deserters 1,736 (40.62%). The raw materials for the analysed whole flakes were as follows: quartzite (263), quartz (3,899) basalt (59), gneiss (30) and, aplite dyke (3). The mean length, thickness, and breadth were 29.4 mm, 7.4 mm and 20.3 mm respectively. This implies that Kansyore Island had a flake industry where quartz was preferred since it was readily available in the form of the river cobbles from the Kagera River.

6.2.40 Utilised Flakes

The whole flakes that contained some form of marginal edge trimming/modification resulting from use were classified as utilized flakes (Figures 6.3:5,6,8 and 15). This means the edge modifications were not intentional. This flake type was regarded as trimmed/utilised flake by Mehlman (1989). A total of 565 utilised flakes were analysed. The raw material utilised for utilised flakes were: quartz (511), quartzite (46), gneiss (6), and basalt (2). The distribution of utilised flakes per site was as follows: Nsongezi (51), Island of Deserters (157), and Kansyore Island (395). The mean length, thickness, and breadth were 28.7 mm, 7.3 mm, and 21.0 mm respectively.

6.2.41 Levallois Flakes

Levallois flakes were whole flakes that had evidence of core preparation. These define the Middle Paleolithic of Eurosia and North Africa and the Middle Stone Age of sub-Saharan Africa (Bushozi, 2011:1). A total of 63 *levallois* flakes were analysed out of which one had two bulbs of percussion and this was termed as a Kombewa flake. The Kombewa striking platform had positive bulbs on both sides and plain flake faces that intersected on a high-domed arc round the line of intersection (Lowe, 1952:55). A Kombewa flake derives its name from the Seme Hamlet in the central Kavirondo district of western Kenya, a name first used by O'Brien (1938). The two bulbs of percussion are termed as two convex surfaces on the ventral, (Iliana, 2010:127). This is an MSA indicator (Iliana, 2010) as Kombewa flakes exist next to the *levallois* flakes. The Kombewa flake analysed was from the Island of Deserters manufactured from basalt. The mean length, thickness and breadth were; 66mm, 13mm and 50.5 mm respectively.

The *levallois* flakes (62) analysed still exhibited differences within the same technology. This is because 27 were radial *levallois* flakes. *Levallois* flakes appeared mainly at the Island of Deserters (61) than Kansyore Island (1). The raw materials utilised were quartzite (11), basalt (14) and quartz (37).The mean length was 43.4 mm, mean thickness 12.2 mm, and mean breadth as 33 mm. The frequency of *levallois* flakes at the Island of deserters may imply that the Island was settled from the MSA while the occurrence of a *levallois* flake at Kansyore Island may suggest cultural interaction of the MSA/LSA people though the evidence is minimal.

6.2.42 Core Rejuvenated Flakes

Core rejuvenated flakes were regarded as specialised flakes by Mehlman (1989:150). They are either core rejuvenated flakes or core redirecting flakes that are elongate to blade length shapes of small sizes with a triangular cross section. These flakes are a product of extending the life of a core that has become uneven or difficult to work but which still has the potential to yield further blades (Darvill, 2008). The core platform is rejuvenated or re-surfaced due to flake removal errors or it could be a single core from which a single flake is removed (Andrefsky, 2005:301). The core-rejuvenated flakes were all manufactured from quartz and from Kansyore Island. The mean length, thickness, and breadth were 34.5mm, 7.4mm, and 17.6 mm respectively. The core rejuvenated flakes testify to the degree of core maintenance (Odell, 2003:121).

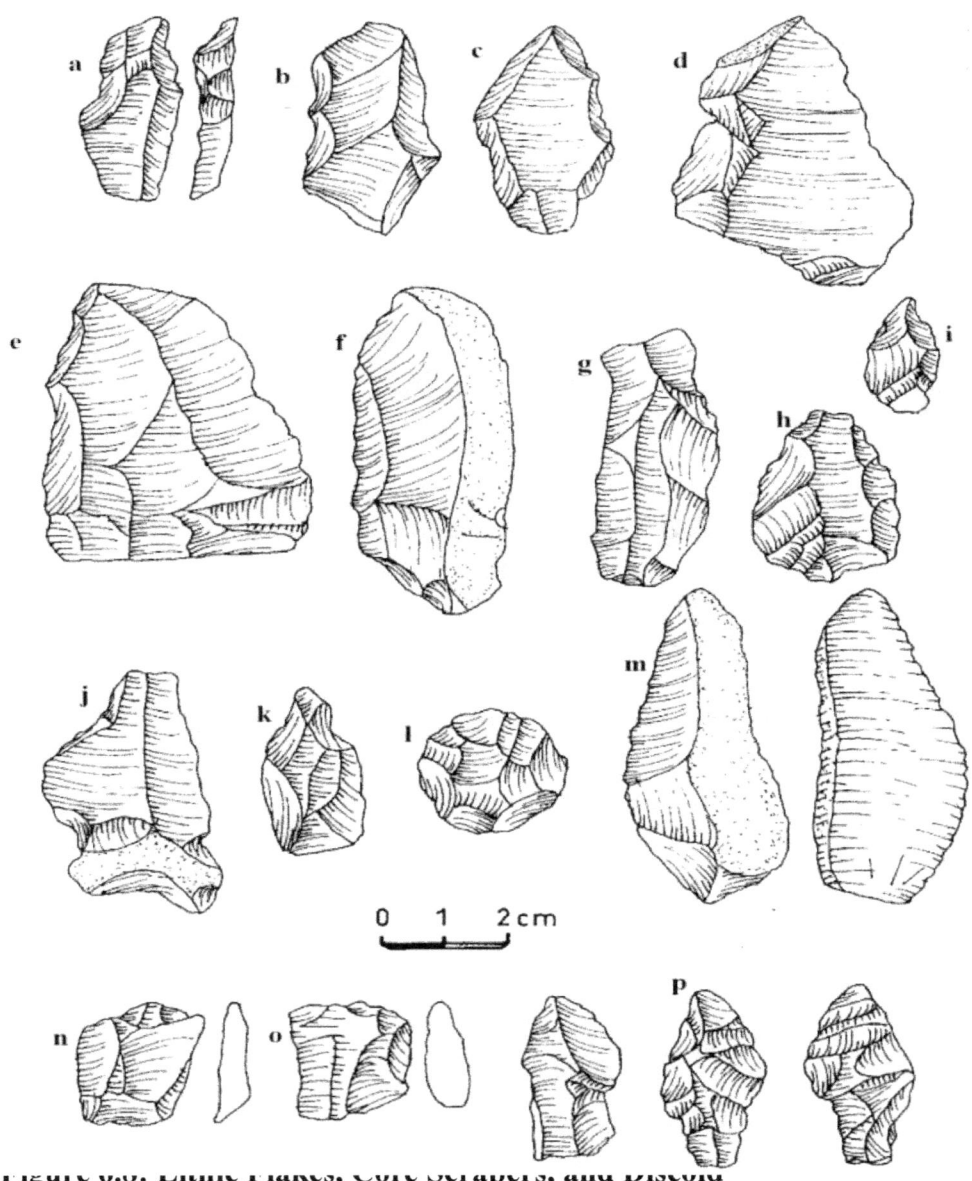

Figure 6.8: Lithic Flakes, Core Scrapers, and Discoid

Key: (**a, b, c, e, f, g**) = Whole Flakes; (**l**) = Discoid; (**m**) = Blade; (**o**) = Opposed Double Platform Core Scrapers; (**p**) = Unifacial Point; (**d**) = Opposed Double Platform Core; (**h**) = Disc Core; (**i**) = Preform; (**j**) = Notched Scraper; (**k**) = Nosed Scraper; (**n**) = Oblique Truncated Piece

6.2.43 Cores

Cores are the Chunky pieces that have flake negative scars of sufficient size that yield flake/blade blanks (Mehlman, 1989). That means that cores are sources of flakes/blades that make shaped tools (Kessy, 2005; Nelson, 1973). There are several types of cores more less characteristic of the large divisions of the Paleolithic period, they start by being shapeless, or globular, then become discoid or *levallois* and then pyramidal or prismatic. Clark and Kleindienst (1974:90) divided cores into two that are the unspecified cores that are classified according to the number of platforms and specified cores where the flake release faces/ face show signs of core preparation. These include the *levallois*, prismatic and discoidal cores. The cores that were analysed were divided into the following broad core types: platform cores (1,235) 68.8%, periphery worked cores 140 (7.8%), amorphous cores 50 (2.3%), bipolar cores 274 (15.3%), and intermediate cores 97 (5.4%) (Table 6.7). The division followed Mehlman's (1989) typology that classified cores basing on the number of platforms, relative position of platforms, flaking distribution pattern, and general morphology. Core scrapers were regarded as shaped tools in this study despite awareness of Mehlman's (1989:141) suggestion that incorporating them under scrapers would inflate the scraper types.

Core Types	Kansyore Island	Island of Deserters	Nsongezi	Total	% age
Periphery Worked Cores					
Part periphery	39	46	2	87	4.8
Radial biconic	7	8	4	19	1.1
Disc	5	12	3	20	1.1
Levallois core	5	9		14	0.8
Platform Cores					
Pyramidal Single Platform Cores	30	78	1	109	6.1
Diverse Single Platform Cores	56	31	2	89	5.0
Opposed Double Platform Cores	101	103	42	246	13.7
Adjacent Double Platform Cores	52	57	11	120	6.7
Multi-Platform Cores	316	219	55	590	32.9
Single Platform Cores	18	37	13	68	3.8
Prismatic Cores		11	2	13	0.7
Intermediate Cores					
Platform Periphery Cores	25	65	2	92	5.1
Platform Bipolar Cores	5			5	0.3
Other Core Types					
Bipolar Cores	267	2	5	274	15.3
Amorphous Cores	26	24		50	2.8
Total	951	702	142	1,796	100.0
% age	53.0	39.1	7.9	100.0	

Table 6.7: Broad and Specific Core Types

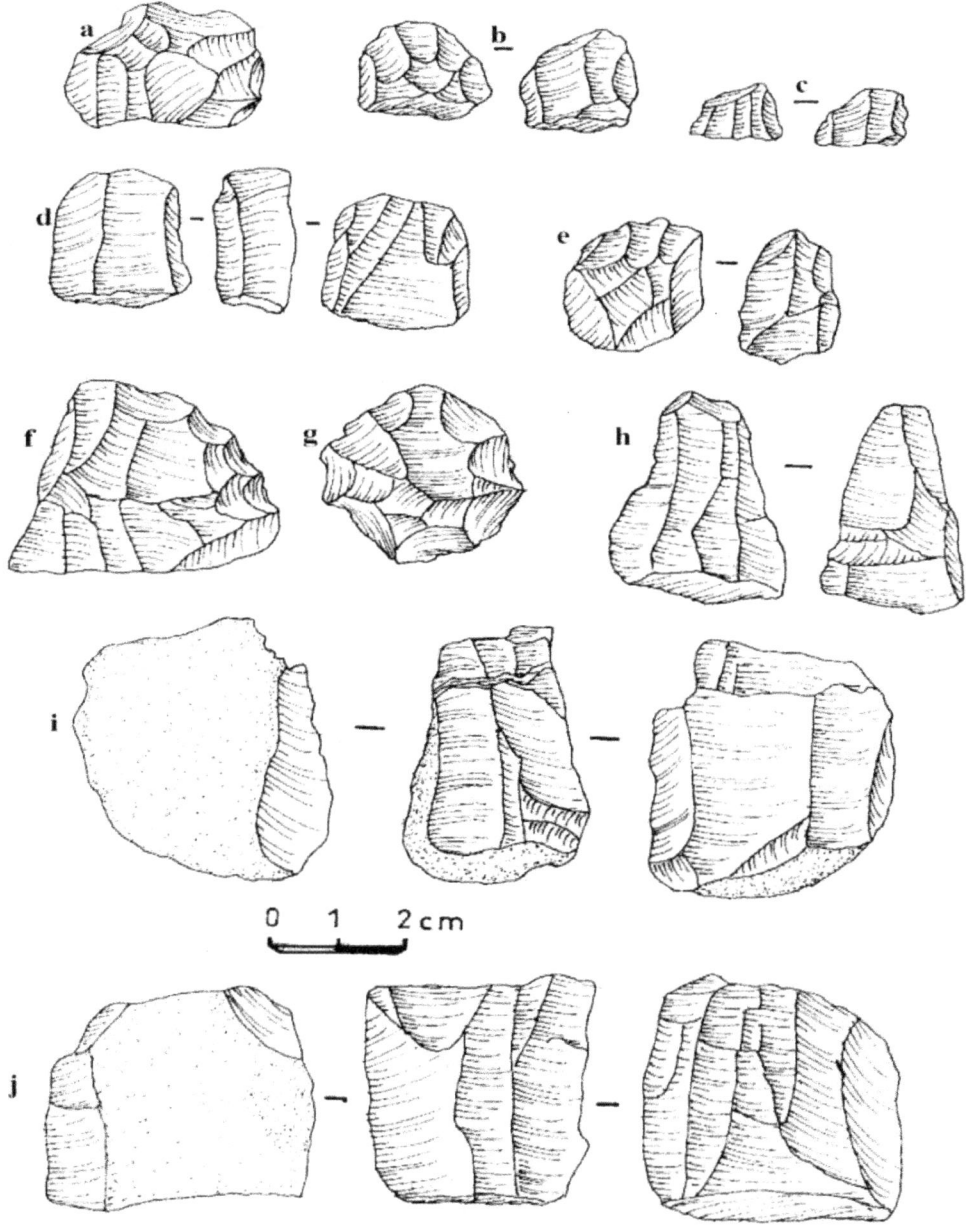

Figure 6.9: Cores

Key: Multiplatform Cores (**a & b**); Prismatic Cores (**c & d**); Single Platform Core (**e**); Opposed Double Platform Core (**f**); Pyramidal Core (**g & h**); Part Periphery Core (**i,**); Adjacent Double Platform Core (**j**)

6.2.44 Platform Cores

These were cores classified basing on the position and number of platforms. The platform cores were mainly made from river cobbles which is contrary to the view of Clark and Kleindienst (1974: 90), that, 'they are usually made on chunks or angular fragments and less commonly on cobbles'. The platform cores were classified into: single platform cores 68 (3.8%), diverse single platform cores 89 (5%); pyramidal single platform cores 109 (6.1%); opposed double platform cores 246 (13.7%), adjacent double platform cores 120 (6.7%), and multiplatform cores 590 (32.9%) (Table 6.7). An examination of all these shows that the platform was either one or several hence the type depended on the pattern and number of platforms. In the analysis three broad groups were identified among platform cores that were; single platform cores, double platform cores and multiplatform cores. The single platform cores encompassed single platform cores, pyramidal single platform cores, prismatic cores, and diverse single platform cores. The double platform cores on the other hand included the opposed double platform cores and adjacent double platform cores. Generally platform cores constituted the majority of the cores collected with 68.8% of all the total cores analysed (1796).

6.2.45 Single Platform Cores

Single Platform cores had flake negatives running from a single destination or platform (Figure 6.9 e). These were referred to as any core with a single, well-defined platform area that is neither sufficiently regular nor symmetrical (Mehlman, 1989:143). Kessy (2005), like Mehlman, regarded them as diverse single platform cores. In the current analysis, a line was drawn between single platform cores and diverse single platform cores. The single platform cores were cores with one platform that was un-faceted while the diverse platform cores had a single platform from which flakes/ blades were struck in two directions. The 68 single platform cores were taken from the Island of Deserters (37), Kansyore (18), and Nsongezi (13). The raw materials utilised were quartzite (2) and quartz (66). The mean length was 32.9 mm, thickness 16.1 mm, and breadth 25.3 mm respectively.

The diverse single platform cores were cores that had broad negative scars unlike the single platform cores. They were also regarded as informal cores (Nelson, 1973) or angle platform cores (Clark and Kleindienst, 1974). This is because the flaking surface is often at right angles. The 89 specimens conform to Nelson and Posnansky's (1970) type from the Nsongezi rock shelter. These had a single platform with few flake/blade scars on the flake release faces. Kansyore Island had the majority (56), followed by the Island of Deserters (31) and Nsongezi (2). The raw materials utilised were quartzite (1), quartz (87), and gneiss (1). The mean length, thickness, and breadth were 32.8 mm, 16.5 mm, and 24.6 mm respectively.

Pyramidal single platform cores or Nelson's (1973) conical cores were characterised by a conical shape where the cone serves as a platform (Mehlman, 1989). The scars created by the removal of flakes/blades met at an apex of an inverted pyramid (Kleindienst, 1974) (Figure 6.9: g ,h). Nelson and Posnansky (1970:149) regarded them as conical cores that have an ovate outline and definite equators from whence flake scars converge towards central poles. The 109 pyramidal cores analysed had a single platform at which flake scars were converging. The pyramidal cores analysed in some cases had a cone at the platform tip that was pointed while in other cases, the platforms were flat topped. The Island of Deserters dominated the other sites (78), followed by Kansyore (30) and Nsongezi (1). Of rare occurrence in the research, area was a single core made from a chert raw material core belonging to this core type. Therefore the raw materials utilised were quartzite (2), quartz (107), and chert (1). The mean length, thickness, and breadth were 28.7 mm, 18.9 mm, and 24.5 mm respectively.

Prismatic cores are cylindrical in shape with either of the ends serving as a platform (Mehlman, 1989:143) (Figure 6.9:c & d). They have a circular striking platform or nearly circular (Kleindienst, 1974). These had the least occurrence with 13 specimens and they intergraded with the pyramidal cores. These were obtained from the Island of Deserters (11) and Kansyore Island (2). The raw materials used were quartz (12), and basalt (1).The mean length, thickness, and breadth were 38.2mm, 21.2mm and 29 mm respectively.

6.2.46 Double Platform Cores

The double platform cores are the same as what Clark and Kleindienst (1974) defined as the two platform cores. In this case, the platforms are either opposed or adjacent. The first type of double platform cores were the opposed double platform cores (246). The opposed double platform cores are usually blocky with planes of the platform often approximately parallel (Mehlman, 1989) (Figures 6.8d & 6.9 f). However, the platforms were well defined on the opposing ends of the piece. The site distribution for these cores was as follows: Island of Deserters (103), Kansyore Island (101), and Nsongezi (42). A variety of raw materials were utilised and these were: quartzite (7), gneiss (3), and quartz (236). The mean length, thickness, and breadth were 33.9 mm, 16.8 mm, and 25.2 mm respectively.

The adjacent double platform cores were the other type of double platform cores. These cores had platforms that lay side by side (Figure 6.9j). These amounted to 120 (6.7%). The site distribution for these cores was as follows: Island of Deserters (57), Kansyore Island (52), and Nsongezi (11). The dominant raw material was quartz (115), followed by quartzite (2), basalt (2), and gneiss (1). The mean length, thickness, and breadth were 32.9 mm, 16.1 mm, and 25.3 mm respectively.

6.2.47 Multiplatform Cores

Cores in this type were cores that possessed more than two striking platforms that were casually struck with a few flakes struck from each platform (Figure 6.9: a, b). According to Mehlman these cores should have three or more platforms and since those that approach six platforms attain shape of a polyhedron they should be regarded as formless or worked out and classified under the amorphous cores. Therefore in this study 590 cores with more than two platforms but with clear negative scars were classified as multiplatform cores. These were obtained from Kansyore Island (316), Island of Deserters (219), and Nsongezi (55). The raw materials utilised were quartzite (428), quartz (159), and gneiss (3). The mean length was 33.9 mm, thickness was 20.4 mm, and breadth was 28.2 mm.

6.2.48 Periphery Worked Cores

The cores that had flake/blade negatives on the circumference were classified as periphery worked cores (Figure 6.10). Therefore core types in this category were based on the extent to which the periphery had been worked, the types of flakes removed and the cross section (Kessy, 2005:284; Mehlman 1989:141). It should be noted that the periphery could be worked on one face or both faces but any core in this category should have had at least ¾ of the periphery flaked. 140 (7.8%) periphery worked cores were identified out of the 1,796 cores analysed. The periphery worked cores included the part periphery cores 87 (4.8%), radial biconic cores 19 (1.1%), disc cores 20 (1.1%), and *levallois* cores 14 (0.8%) (Table 6.7).

The part periphery cores as implied by the name were any cores whose circumference was partially worked. That is with the flaked area not covering the entire core (Kessy, 2005) (Figure 6.9i). These were termed as proto-biconical cores by Clark and Kleindienst (1974) and as semi-radial cores by Nelson (1973). These were mainly on river cobbles. In this category were a total of 87 cores analysed that were obtained from Kansyore Island (39), Island of Deserters (46), and Nsongezi (2). The raw material utilisation for this core type was as follows: quartzite (3), quartz (81), gneiss (2), and basalt (1). The mean length, thickness, and breadth were 34.1 mm, 23.7 mm, and 29.4 mm respectively.

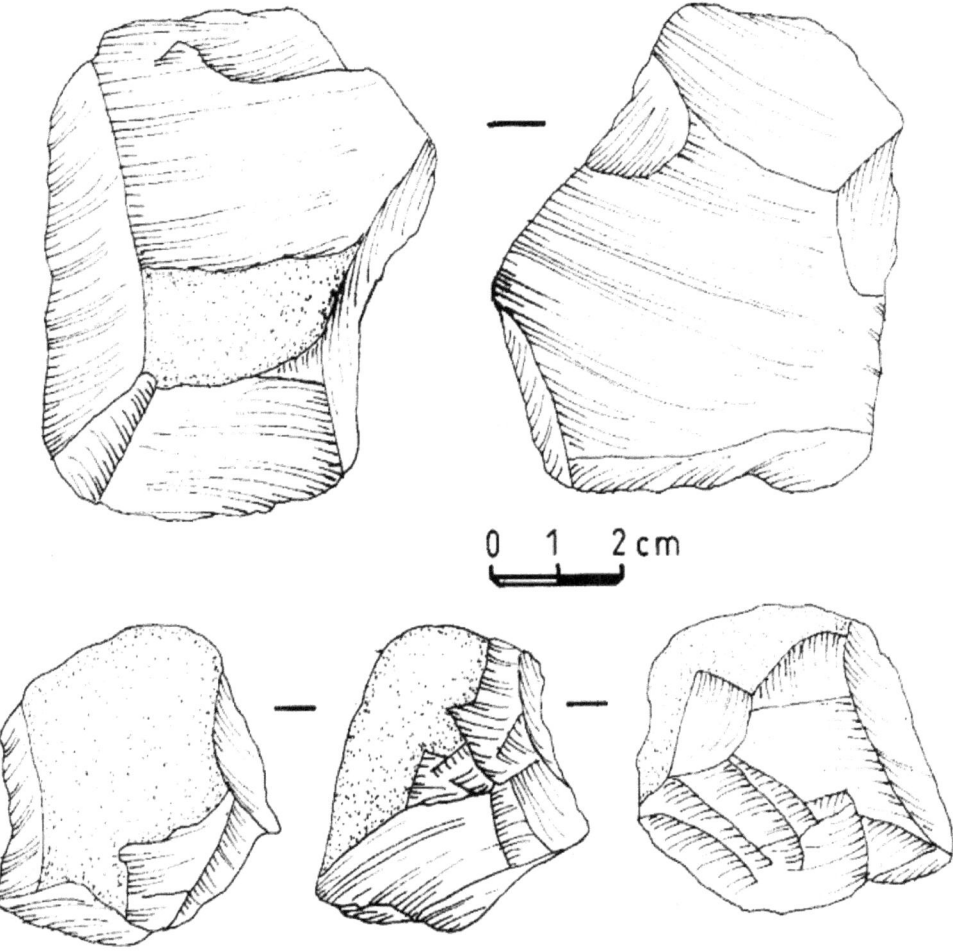

Figure 6.10: Periphery worked Cores

Cores with a specially prepared platform for the removal of a single flake/blade of a predetermined form (Clark and Kleindienst, 1974) were regarded as *levallois* cores. O'Brien (1966) commenting on the Nsongezi industry noted that the *levallois* culture has its hallmark as the tortoise cores and flakes with a prepared platform (Levalloisoid). The 14 specimens were obtained mainly from the Island of Deserters (9) and others from Nsongezi (5). These cores were mainly manufactured from basalt (6) and quartz (6) while others were made of quartzite (1) and gneiss (1). The mean length was 63.6 mm, mean thickness 30 mm while the mean breadth was 48.8 mm. The metric measurements implied that these cores were made of large blanks. *Levallois* cores were an indicator of the MSA industry.

Radial biconic cores are also periphery worked cores that were angular chunks or cobbles that had been flaked alternately on both faces using the previous platform on the one face for the removal of the next flake from the opposite face (Clark and Kleindienst, 1974). Mehlman (1989) described them as cores with flakes removed from the entire circumference that range from diamond to domed or triangular shape. The cores analysed for this core type were circular with one face flatter than the other with flakes removed almost from the entire circumference. The 19 specimens were identified from Kansyore (7), Island of Deserters (8), and Nsongezi (4). The preferred raw materials were quartzite (14), quartz (3), aplite dyke (1), and gneiss (1). The mean length, thickness, and breadth were 27.3 mm, 18.5 mm, and 24.1 mm respectively.

Disc cores were any radially prepared core that had evidence of flake removal from round the periphery or from both faces (Figure 6.8h). The diameter reduced as flakes were removed usually in a stage of exhaustion or at the time of abandonment. These were 20 specimens got from Nsongezi (3), Kansyore (5), and the Island of Deserters (12). The raw materials used were quartz (3), basalt (4), gneiss (1), and quartz (15). The mean length, thickness, and breadth were 41.8 mm, 23.2 mm, and 20 mm respectively.

6.2.49 Intermediate Cores

Intermediate cores were core types that combined characteristics of more than one core type. Therefore, these cores combined characteristics of two of the main core types. In other words, intermediate cores are the mixed cores that lie in between two major core types. These included platform periphery cores (92) and platform-bipolar (4) cores.

The platform-periphery cores (92) were neither exclusively platform nor periphery worked cores hence the name platform-periphery cores. This implied that any single core that partially had the flake/blades removed from the circumference while at the same time having a platform or platforms was classified as a platform-periphery core. It is worth noting that these cores had at least one main platform from which flakes/blades were struck with the periphery bifacially worked (Kessy, 2005). The Island of Deserters had the majority (65) followed by Kansyore Island (25) and Nsongezi (2). The preferred raw materials were quartzite (1) and quartz (91). The mean length was 32.5 mm; mean thickness 21.5 mm and mean breadth 28.3 mm.

The platform-bipolar cores were cores with either a single or double platform while in the latter case the platforms were either opposed or double but with battered edges that served as evidence for the use of the bipolar technique. These according to Mehlman (1989:145) have two varieties: the distinguishable platforms may be opposed to the characteristic bipolar edge or the platform may not be opposed to the bipolar edge but where the two bipolar edges are in opposition with the remains of the platform situated along one of the lateral edges between the two bipolar edges. The 5 specimens conformed to the first category that is having two bipolar edges that were opposed to a platform. Four were platform bipolar while one was a bipolar-periphery core. These constituted 0.3 % of the core assemblage. This is because the bipolar is a crushing technology that would rarely leave a recognisable platform or periphery as in the five cases identified. The cores in this category were all obtained from Kansyore Island and made from quartz. The mean length, thickness, and breadth were 39.8 mm, 24 mm, and 35.8 mm respectively.

6.2.50 Bipolar Cores

These were cores of a special form of opposed platform core and products of the bipolar technique. They are pillow shaped with the two opposed edges crushed, battered or step flaked on one or both sides (Mehlman, 1989:145). The bipolar cores like the outils écailles have battered edges but are distinguished by the size of the initial blank (Kessy, 2005: 287). Just like the outils e'cailles' the 274 bipolar cores had numerous short stepped flakes and fractures but as opposed to the outils écailles they were worked bifacially and had opposed working edges or platforms from which narrow, parallel flake scars frequently originated as those described by Nelson and Posnansky (1970:149). Though aware of the debate whether they are cores or tools this will not constitute the discussion of the current research whose aim was examining cultural interactions. Bipolar cores were mainly from Kansyore Island (267) followed by Nsongezi (5) and the Island of Deserters (2). Though all sites were represented it seems the bipolar technology was chiefly employed at Kansyore Island. The raw materials utilised for manufacture of the bipolar cores were mainly quartz (264) and a few cases of gneiss (4), and quartzite (6). The mean measurements in length, thickness, and breadth were 30.1 mm, 15.9 mm, and 22.9 mm respectively. The bipolar cores would imply the tool makers used a smashing technology with no specific form of flakes but ending up with smashed implements later on improved to make stone tools most common in the LSA.

6.2.51 Amorphous Cores

Cores that had random negative scars with flakes removed from any convenient point as noted by (Kessy, 2005) were classified as amorphous cores. These are the same as (Clark and Kleindienst, 1974)'s formless cores or Nelson (1973)'s informal pebble cores. Amorphous cores have all the characteristics of a core especially flake negatives but did not fall in any of the other discussed core types (Mehlman, 1989:148). Therefore any core that did not have meaningful flakes removed and no clear pattern of platform or periphery worked edges was graded as an amorphous core. The 50 amorphous cores were obtained from the Island of Deserters (24) and Kansyore Island (26). The raw materials utilised were quartzite (3) and quartz (47). The mean length, thickness, and breadth were 37.3 mm, 22.3mm, and 31.6 mm respectively. The amorphous character of the cores does not reflect amateurism but rather the easy availability of good and plentiful raw materials especially from the steep slopes of western Uganda. However, the presence of amorphous cores could also imply the application of casual technology (Mabulla, 1996).

6.2.52 Debitage

This broad category included all the by-products of tool making exclusive of cores (Mehlman, 1989). However, in this analysis debitage included core fragments 3,063 (15.5%), scraper fragments 99 (0.5%), blade fragments 258 (1.3%), backed fragments 157 (0.8%), flake fragments 1,174 (5.9%) and the dominant type of debitage the angular fragments 14,990 (75.9%). The angular fragments included pieces without a flake talon, retouch, and features of a core edge that did not belong to any of the other categories of debitage. Therefore the entire debitage assemblage consisted of 19,741 specimens. Kansyore Island had the greatest number of debitage with 11,155 (56.5%), followed by the Island of Deserters with 7,322 (36.8 %). The greatest percentage (93.6%) of debitage was obtained from the trenches since STPs only yielded 6.4% (Table 6.8). The analysis identified most flake fragments as proximal ends. The comparison of debitage weight in grams from Kansyore Island and the Island of Deserters revealed that debitage from the Island of Deserters was heavier (617.2 grams) compared to the one of Kansyore Island (490.8 grams). This could be due to the nature of raw materials used and tool types where by the Island of Deserters had many cores and used basalt more than any site which could explain the weight variability. The angular fragments had more weight (531.7 g) since they were dominant followed by core fragments (467.9g), flake fragments (77.4g), blade fragments (2)' scraper fragments (7 g) and backed fragments (2) (Table 6.9).

Debitage Type	Shovel Test Pits	Kansyore Island	Island Of Deserters	Total	% age
Core Fragments	29	1,658	1,376	3,063	15.5
Angular Fragments	1,143	8,145	5,702	14,990	75.9
Scraper Fragment	1	58	40	99	0.5
Blade Fragments	12	229	17	258	1.3
Backed Fragments		124	33	157	0.8
Flake Fragments	79	941	154	1,174	5.9
Total	1,264	11,155	7,322	19,741	100.0
% age	6.4	56.5	37.1	100.0	

Table 6.8: Total Debitage Collected from all Sites

Debitage	Kansyore Island	Island of Deserters	Total
Core Fragments	278.3 Grams	189.6 Grams	467.9 Grams
Angular Fragments	307.7 Grams	224 Grams	531.7 Grams
Scraper Fragment	5 Grams	2 Grams	7 Grams
Blade Fragments	4 Grams	18 Grams	22 Grams
Backed Fragments	2 Grams		2 Grams
Flake Fragments	20.2 Grams	57.2 Grams	77.4 Grams
Total Weight	617.2 Grams	490.8 Grams	1,108 Grams

Table 6.9: Weigth of Debitage in Grams

6.2.53 Raw Materials

The best raw materials are those that are non-crystalline, have a high degree of plasticity, elasticity, and brittleness, and break with a conchoidal fracture (Seitsonen, 2004: 122) or those that lack cracks or inclusions and other flaws (Whittaker, 1994). Highly rich siliceous cryptocrystalline rocks such as chert, flint, chalcedony and other metamorphic rocks such as quartz, quartzite, and fine-grained basalt, and rhyolite have been widely used as sources of raw materials for stone tool making (Yohe II, 1996). The examination of lithic raw material utilisation on tools, cores, and flake/blades revealed that the dominant raw material in the focus area was quartz (91.96%) of which 25.52% was clear quartz. Other highly rich siliceous cryptocrystalline rocks were also observed.

These included: aplite dyke (0.07%), gneiss (0.74%), chert (0.01%), quartzite (25.52%), and basalt (1.56%) (Table 6.10 and Figure 6.11). Quartz occurs in veins in the ridges and hilltops of Ankole and as pebbles in the Kagera River. Mabulla (1996) pointed out that quartz is a hard rock (7 on the Mohs scale) whose fracture resulted in sharp cutting edges that would not call for further modifications which explains the presence of many utilised flakes. Therefore while quartz produces tools with sharp edges quartzite would produce durable tools. This implied that in the southern Upper Nile catchment areas, lithic raw material procurement and use were localised since local resources were abundant and distributed in the area. The one piece of chert obtained can be used to suggest interaction and the probable reason could have been cultural and symbolic values such as gift giving or social status (Mehlman, 1989).

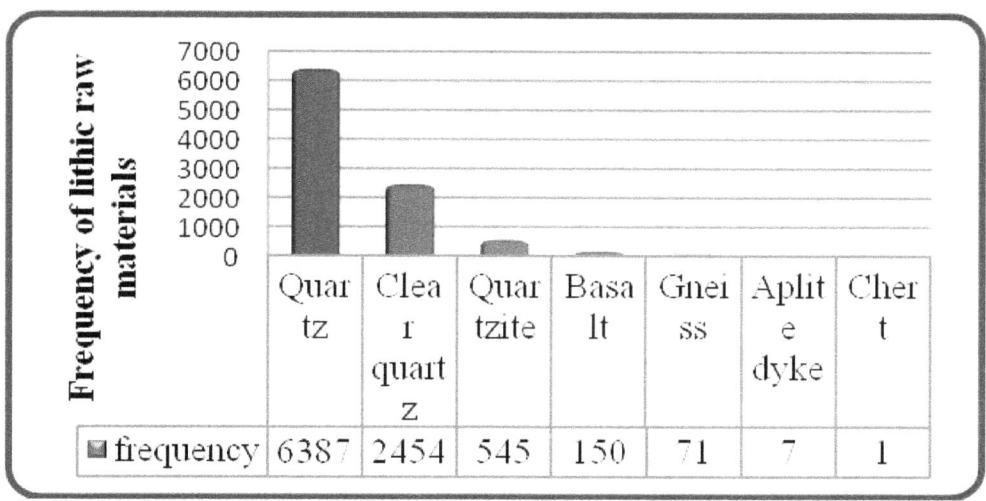

Figure 6.11: Frequency of Lithic Raw Material Utilisation

Raw Material Type	Cores		Tools						Blade/Flake	
	Quantity	% Age	Other Tools	Geometrics	Scrapers	Non-flaked	Total of Tools	% Age	Quantity	% Age
Quartzite	37	2.1			98	2	100	5.9	408	6.67
Gneiss	16	0.9	9		4		13	0.8	42	0.69
Basalt	14	0.8	1	27	2	1	31	1.8	105	1.72
Aplite Dyke			1	3			4	0.2	3	0.05
Chert	1	0.1								
Other Quartz Types	1,253	69.8	17	465	487	2	971	56.9	4,163	68.10
Clear Quartz	475	26.4	181	83	323		587	34.4	1,392	22.77
Total	1,796	100.0	209	578	914	5	1,706	100.0	6,113	100.00

Table 6.10: Frequency of Lithic Raw Material Types

6.2.54 Pottery Analysis

The pottery analysis, discussion, and conclusions are purposely restricted to the pottery from Kansyore Island, Nsongezi, and the Island of Deserters. This leaves out pottery data from Chobe and Kikubamitwe. This is because it was in Kansyore Island, Nsongezi, and the Island of Deserters where data that addressed the research problem was obtained. The aim of pottery analysis within the framework of the current study was to identify pottery attributes on the southern part of the Upper Nile catchment area (Ugandan side) that showed parallels with the Khartoum Neolithic pottery. This would permit comparison with Khartoum Neolithic pottery based on earlier studies carried out such as at Lokabulo by Robertshaw and Shaqadud by Marks and Mohammed-Ali. The smallest unit of analysis was the potsherd. Pottery was analysed because the local manufacturing programs and production processes provide an understanding of an area's internal communication routes and its foreign contacts (Joukowsky, 1980:332).

Thus, it was envisaged that the analysis of pottery would give clues on the prehistoric contacts and interactions in the upper Nile catchment areas. The pottery that was obtained amounted to 4,961 sherds. The pottery was from both surface (596) and sub-surface collection (4,365). The majority were plain un-diagnostic potsherds that amounted to 3,324 (67 %) while the diagnostic potsherds were 1,637 (33%). The diagnostic potsherds were from both surface (596) and subsurface (1,041) collections. Kansyore Island dominated the production of diagnostic pottery (1,100) compared to the Island of Deserters (468) and Nsongezi (69). The diagnostic pottery further included plain ware 129 (2.6%) and decorated pottery 1,508 (30.4%) of the entire ceramic assemblage (Table 6.11).

Pottery	Local pottery						Foreign pottery	un-diagnostic pottery	Total	% age
	Diagnostic									
Pottery traditions	Plain	Roulette	Urewe	channel	Bourdine	Kansyore				
Surface collections										
Kansyore	31	87	212	40	17	49			436	8.8
1.D	13	35	51		1	5			105	2.1
Nsongezi		41			7	7			55	1.1
Kansyore Island and Nsongezi sub-surface										
STP 1 Nsongezi		2	5	3		4		3	17	0.3
STP 2 Kansyore			17	1		5		2	25	0.5
Trench 1& 1A	3	24	123	37		41		509	737	14.9
Trench 1B	1	12	135	42	2	29		635	856	17.3
Trench 2		8	22	2	2	10		155	199	4.0
Trench 2A		6	20		1	14		109	150	3.0
Trench 2Aii	2	6	7			9		75	99	2.0
Trench 2B		19	28	1		18		241	307	6.2
Trench 3		3	10	2		2		102	119	2.4
Island of Deserters sub-surface										
Trench 1	12	40	8		3	9	9	355	436	8.8
Trench 2	8	22	25		6	2		162	225	4.5
Trench 3	7	4	6		1	5		146	169	3.4
Trench 4	49	19	62		8	21		733	892	18.0
Trench 5	2	1	2			19		34	58	1.2
Trench 5A	1	2	3			7		63	76	1.5
Total	129	331	736	128	48	256	9	3,324	4,961	100.0
% age	2.6	6.7	14.8	2.6	1.0	5.2	0.2	67.0	100.0	

Table 6.11: Pottery Inventory

6.2.55 Local Pottery

The local pottery was analysed by using attributes that scholars use to solve archaeological problems. Among such scholars are Shinnie (1960) who examined pottery from the excavations at Bigo which he categorised as either coarse or fine ware and concluded that the Bigo population was African based. Sheppard (1963) utilised attributes of surface finishing, weight, colour, temper, shape, decoration, metric dimensions, and fabric in the classification of pottery. Posnansky (1968b) examined decoration, form, firing and temper while analysing the Bweyorere capital site (Ankole) pottery. Through this, two pottery traditions were identified that were roulette especially knotted grass roulette and bourdine that the author noted had been found in the Kagera valley and on Kansyore Island hence highlighting regional cultural connections.

Chapman (1967) examined decoration in the analysis of pottery from Kansyore Island and divided it into six types. Further distinctions were suggested due to the existence of atypical fragments. Following Chapman's analysis, a suggestion was made that Kansyore pottery had resemblance with the Sudanese ware. Pearce and Posnansky (1963) examined pottery decoration, form, and surface finishing and identified three pottery traditions that were Kansyore ware, dimple-based pottery and 'recent' pottery from the re-excavation of the Nsongezi rock shelter. The study concluded that dimple-based pottery follows Kansyore ware and that both must belong to the same time within the second millennium A.D. Soper (1971a) used shapes of bases, rims, decoration techniques, and decoration elements among other characteristics to make a comparative study of the pottery assemblages of East Africa. Soper (1971b), in an attempt to examine whether Urewe pottery extended as far as northern Uganda, analysed the material from Chobe with emphasis on decoration and rim-type. On these grounds, the pottery was divided into: Urewe ware, bourdine (finger-marked wares) and roulette wares. The latter included both cord and curved wooden roulette. Bower (1973) analysed decorations, paste, and shapes of Seronera pottery in the Serengeti National park and identified four pottery traditions among which was Kansyore pottery. Connah (1997) in the examination of pottery from the area between Kibiro on Lake Albert and the northern bank of the Victoria Nile below Murchison Falls examined decoration and vessel form. The analysis revealed similarity in spite of some local differences in pot forms and decoration.

Kiyaga-Mulindwa (2004, 2006) mainly examined decoration with minimal attention on surface finishing and form in examining pottery from Kikubamitwe and Mutunda respectively. While Mutunda ceramics were made by the coiling method, the analysis of surface finishing revealed use of both burnishing and graphite-slip while the commonest decoration was the string cord roulette. The analysis of the pottery from Malindi, Naminya, and Kikubamitwe identified dimple based vessels, globular short-necked pots with rounded or squared rims. The decoration was characterised by grooving or channelling, cross hatching, and varieties of impressed or incised decorations, triangular pendants and embossed decorations were also observed just like the rocked zigzag bands at Kansyore for Urewe (Chapman, 1967) and Kwale ware (Soper, 1967). Nakaweesa (2011) in the study of the Nyero pottery used decoration elements, decoration placement, and vessel shape as the key attributes and identified Kansyore pottery for the first time in eastern Uganda.

In Sudan, several ceramic classification schemes have been used to identify and examine cultural connections of the Khartoum Neolithic and Mesolithic. These include the pioneer scheme of Arkell (1949, 1953) who considered decoration with emphasis on motifs, decoration placement, and fabric. The latter laid emphasis on temper, ware, and firing. Arkell's scheme identified two modal ceramic components characterised by a decorative motif that were the Khartoum Mesolithic associated with 'wavy line' and Khartoum Neolithic the 'dotted wavy line' (Mohammed- Ali and Khabir, 2003). It was assumed by Arkell that wavy line evolved into dotted wavy line (Arkell, 1949: 84-85; 1953:68). The Arkell scheme was later moderated by scholars like Caneva (1988). Caneva (1983, 1987) regarded Arkell's scheme as subject to visual impression hence the emphasis on decorative technique and the implement before the finished product in the latter's scheme.

The Arkell scheme was later used by Camps (1982) at Amekni. The latter was able to classify the "Sahara-Sudanese Neolithic by considering the technique and implement as dependent variables. In a further attempt to trace the Nilo-Sahara Neolithic ceramics, Hays (1974) used the type variety classification scheme and ended up with one ware made of five decorative techniques each associated with one or more decorative motif (Mohammed-Ali and Khabir, 2003). Hays (1974) suggested a "Khartoum Horizon style" on the basis of lithics which unfortunately generalised similarities and failed to account for the divergences. Nordstrom's (1972) classification scheme combined fabric, techniques, and patterns of decoration that classified the Neolithic ceramics of Sudanese Nubia into a single ware with two types of temper. Though this came up with a taxonomic model with new technological attributes it did not provide a technological index due to lack of stratified data (Mohammed- Ali and Khabir, 2003).

David et al (1981) examined decoration, colour, decoration techniques, and implements as pottery attributes. The research studied the Lokabulo rock shelter that produced pre-ceramic and ceramic Later Stone Age phases, Jebel Tukyi rock shelter where a population of iron users succeeded pottery-making LSA pastoralists and Dhang Rail mound that gave evidence of traces of ceramic LSA underlying the Iron Age sequence. Robertshaw and Mawson (1981), examined material from Itohom rock shelter on the eastern fringes of Imatong mountains in Southern Sudan which yielded a ceramic LSA and recent Iron Age levels through examining colour, texture, vessel shape and decoration. Marks and Mohammed-Ali (1991) in the analysis of pottery from Shaqadud laid emphasis on fabric, surface treatment, and decoration though not neglecting other attributes like colour, hardness, and firing conditions.

Caneva (1988)'s scheme aimed at addressing weaknesses of the earlier schemes used in the Nile valley for scholars like: Arkell (1949, 1953), Choldnicki (1984), Haaland (1981), Hays (1971, 1974), Mohammed Ali (1982) and Nordstrom (1972). This led to development of a scheme used for the analysis of pre historic pottery in the Nile valley that was hierarchical using the *chaine operatoire* approach. This involved the identification of technique, implement, element, and motif respectively. This means the analysis diverted from the general attributes to the particular ones. The major shortfalls of the Caneva scheme are that there are always fewer techniques compared to motifs and the technique is not always identifiable and cannot always be recognised from motifs (Mohammed-Ali and Khabir, 2003:31). Despite that the Caneva scheme was employed by Dale (2007) to study Kansyore pottery from Siror (Western Nyanza, Kenya).

On the other hand are ceramic studies that have examined inter and intra-regional interaction of the Khartoum Mesolithic and Khartoum Neolithic using physiochemical analyses. This therefore implies these studies centred on the analysis of ceramic fabric. Such studies at Shaqadud in western Butana and the 6th Cataract identified use of non-plastic inclusions, quartz and sandstone (De Paepe, 1991) cited by (Mohammed-Ali and Khabir, 2003). In the petrologic studies it was concluded that most samples were made using the local raw materials and samples were mainly sand-tempered (overwhelmingly feldspar and quartz) (Mohammed-Ali and Khabir, 2003). This implied that, as suggested by the current study, cultural similarities were promoted by ecological adaptability where people utilised the available resources and being in the same environment ended up with similar cultural materials. This therefore means that cultural connections were not due only to migration, diffusion, or just trade.

Outside the Nile valley, Pikirayi (1993:122), in his study of the Mutapa state, examined the shape/vessel profile, the material it was made from, its metric dimensions, surface treatment and colour, temper and decoration as basic attributes to trace for evidence of human interaction employing historical and archaeological records. The current study selected visual stylistic attributes and generated a scheme that combined decoration, decoration placement, decoration techniques, and shape (Appendix). Besides that was the examination of technological attributes such as surface finishing, colour, firing conditions and temper that illuminate the technology of pottery making between traditions presented in the pottery assemblage. This is because the shapes result in a functionally oriented classification while decoration would lead to a cultural stylistic classification as noted by Phillipson (1976b:21).

Pikirayi (1993:121) noted that in ceramics, shape and decoration technique/motif illustrate cultural contact. On the other hand, colour illuminates the firing atmosphere, ceramic technology, and source of the clay. Temper also indicates the function of the vessel and the source of the raw materials for pottery making. Decoration indicates the cultural values and can help in estimating the dates. This is because the stylistic patterns represent culturally guided choices (Ashmore, 2000:123). The rim profiles were also emphasised because they give an indication of the pottery forms. The pottery analysed was both foreign 9 (0.2%) and local 1,628 (32.8%) (Figure 6.12). This implied that the local pottery constituted a bigger percentage (32.8%) of the total pottery collection compared to foreign ceramics (0.2%) and hence intensive site use. The pottery analysed had various decoration types, surface treatments, vessel shapes, and decoration placements that led to classification of pottery traditions.

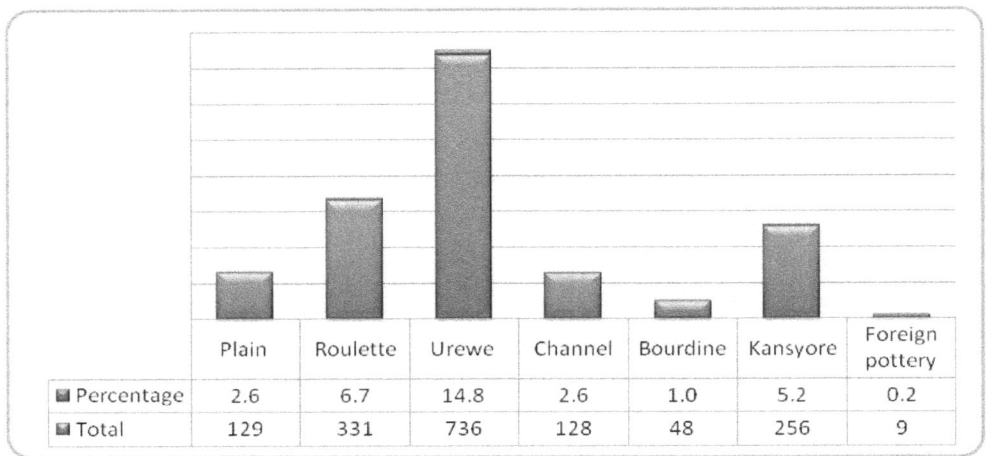

Figure 6.12: Diagnostic Pottery

The local pottery traditions identified basing on decoration and vessel form included roulette (331), Urewe (736), channel (128), bourdine (48), and Kansyore (Figure 6.12). This implied that the sites were used by different prehistoric groups with the predominance of iron users compared to the ceramic using hunter-fisher- gatherers. This may help to explain ceramic variation and mixing of levels (Dale, 2007:253).

6.2.56 Kansyore Pottery

A total of 256 potsherds of Kansyore ware were analysed that were 5.2% of the total pottery assemblage (4,961). Kansyore pottery was obtained from both surface 61 (23.8%) and sub–surface collections (76.2%). Kansyore Island provided the majority (177) of the specimens followed by the Island of Deserters (68) and Nsongezi (11). Despite earlier reports that Kansyore pottery predates Urewe and is associated with intensive hunter-fisher-gatherer populations of the mid-late Holocene (Posnansky *et al* 2005:83) the examination of chronology in the current study suggested that Urewe and Kansyore in some cases appeared in the same excavation levels where they co-exist. Kansyore pottery has been described from a number of sites in East Africa and Sudan (refer to a table showing published sites with Kansyore Pottery in East Africa in Dale (2007:17) modified basing on Collet and Robertshaw (1980: 139) and Prendergast (2008: 36-39) and a map showing Kansyore Sites (Open Circles) in Prendergast (2008:2).

Chapman (1967) classified Kansyore pottery into six types basing on decoration. The first type is one whose decoration is characterised by dots or indistinct lines made through stab and drag. The second type is similar to type one but had a uniform design with small shallow impressions made possibly with a rough roulette. The third type had roughly parallel lines of impressions made by a straight edged instrument such as the Etheria shells. The latter forms a zigzag impression that occurs still on both the dimple-based ware and roulette at Kansyore Island. The fourth type had impression patterns set at right angles appearing like small finger impressions. The fifth type, just like the fourth, had parallel lines of impressions with rounded and squared dots. The last type identified was one with deep indentations that are rounded or squared. The seventh type was the atypical due to failure to identify them by decoration though they could be regarded on grounds of texture and rims as Kansyore ware. Dale and Ashley (2010) divided Kansyore ware into three variants that were Early Kansyore (c.6000-5000 cal. B.C), Late/Terminal Kansyore (c. 1000 A.D cal B.C- cal A.D 500), and Middle Kansyore falling between the 5th and 3rd Millennia B.C. The late/terminal Kansyore phase is considered by the authors as a period that was characterised by increased contact.

The Kansyore pottery analysed was in form of sherds as no complete pot was obtained. The sherds appeared as single parts or a combination of different parts as follows: rim (1), bodies (194), rim/neck/shoulder (6), shoulder/body (5), rim/body (45), rim/shoulder/body (3), and unidentifiable parts (2). This implied that no base sherds were identified and the body sherds being the majority could be due to the size of the Kansyore vessel types being small vessels probably emphasis was placed on bodies making them durable than rims and bases.

6.2.57 Decoration

Pottery decoration entails any internal and external addition on pottery that does not change its original design. Therefore, Chirukure *et al* (2002) defined pottery decoration as the art executed on the vessel for functional and non-functional reasons. While to Phillipson (1976b:22), the term decoration denoted any intentional, primarily non–functional, elaboration of the surface of the vessel wall involving designs either in intaglio or in relief. The key decoration attributes analysed were the decoration elements, decoration placement, decoration techniques, and decoration instruments.

6.2.58 Decoration Elements

Decoration elements are the independent diagnostic decorative parts that either singly or with others constitute motif (Chami, 1994). This study hoped to benefit from the analysis of decoration elements to examine the nature of cultural and economic interactions in the Upper Nile catchment areas by identifying elements that could have parallels with the Khartoum Neolithic pottery. Decoration elements can also trace the evolutionary pattern of ideas from their small adaptations (Joukowsky, 1980) and to identify and distinguish traditions (Chami 1994; Kwekason 2010). Highly decorated ceramics are the distinguishing features of the Kansyore archaeological entity since it is identified by the intensity and variety of decoration (Dale, 2007:17). The decoration of Kansyore pottery is best described as vertical, horizontal, vertical/horizontal and horizontal bands of impressed motifs, including walked punctates, comb impressions, and zig-zag motifs (Dale, 2007; Robertshaw, 1991; Mehlman, 1989; Soper and Golden, 1969; Chapman, 1967).

A total of 59 decoration elements were identified (Figure 6.13). The decoration elements are constructed through the use of dots (Figure 6.13:1-10,12,23,24,30,33,47,56); dashes (Figure 6.13:8) and lines (Figure 6.13: 25,27,35,48,50,52,53,55,57,59).

These appear in form of parallel rows, impressed dots, and lines that are closely spaced. The dots are rectangular (Figure 6.13: 25,27,35,40,48,59), squared (Figure 6.13: 6, 7), circular, oval (Figure 6.13: 40-41,46); triangular (Figure 6.13: 2, 3, 6, 38, 43 and 45), crescent-like (Figure 6.13), hoof-like (Figure 6.13:27) or teardrop-like (Figure 6.13: 27). Some dots were executed in the form of stippled lines (dashes) that appear deeply combed (Figure 6.13: 29, 32, 33, 44-48, 54). The lines were mainly impressed (255) and rarely boldly incised (1) (Figure 6.13:50). The decoration was executed also in horizontal bands (Figure 6.13: 9, 15, 22, 28, 36, 38, 39, 41, 42, 43), or interlocked vertical and horizontal bands (Figure 6.13: 1, 6, 10, 12, 24, 30, 37, 47, 56), interlocked horizontal and oblique lines (Figure 6.13: 7, 11), short oblique (diagonal) bold lines (Figure 6.13: 25, 55), alternating incised = impressed Vs (Figure 6.13:16) while others were irregular (Figure 6.3: 26, 39), some dots were packed with stippled lines like the first row of Figure 6.3: 54; archical dots (Figure 6.13: 23), comb-stamped horizontal bands that were similar to Chapman (1967) Type IV (Refer to Chapman, 1967: 175-177 and Mohammed-Ali, 1991:78 and Figure 6.13: 1, 6, 11), banded motifs (Chapman 1967, Type 1; Mohammed-Ali, 1991:78) (Figure 2,9,13 (Refer to Chapman,

ARCHAEOLOGICAL EXAMINATION OF CULTURAL INTERACTIONS IN THE UPPER NILE CATCHMENT AREAS: | 205

1967: 175-177 and Mohammed-Ali, 1991:78), mat-like impressions (Figure 6.13:54), para saw-tooth (Figure 6.3:49). Besides the above motifs were the wavy lines (Figure 6.13: 51, 52, 53, 57, 59). These appear as bold (Figure 6.13: 52, 53) while others are double (Figure 6.13: 57); the seeming zigzag in Figure 6.13: 49 was made by stippled lines and referred to as the dotted zigzag, a common element in the Khartoum decoration motifs. Mohammed-Ali (1991:75-76) refers to them as dotted zigzag motifs made by rocker stamping, and those that are wider as fishnet. The one analysed fits in the dotted zigzag motifs that Hays (1975: 87) referred to as the wolf saw-tooth and irregular chevrons (Figure 6.13: 31).

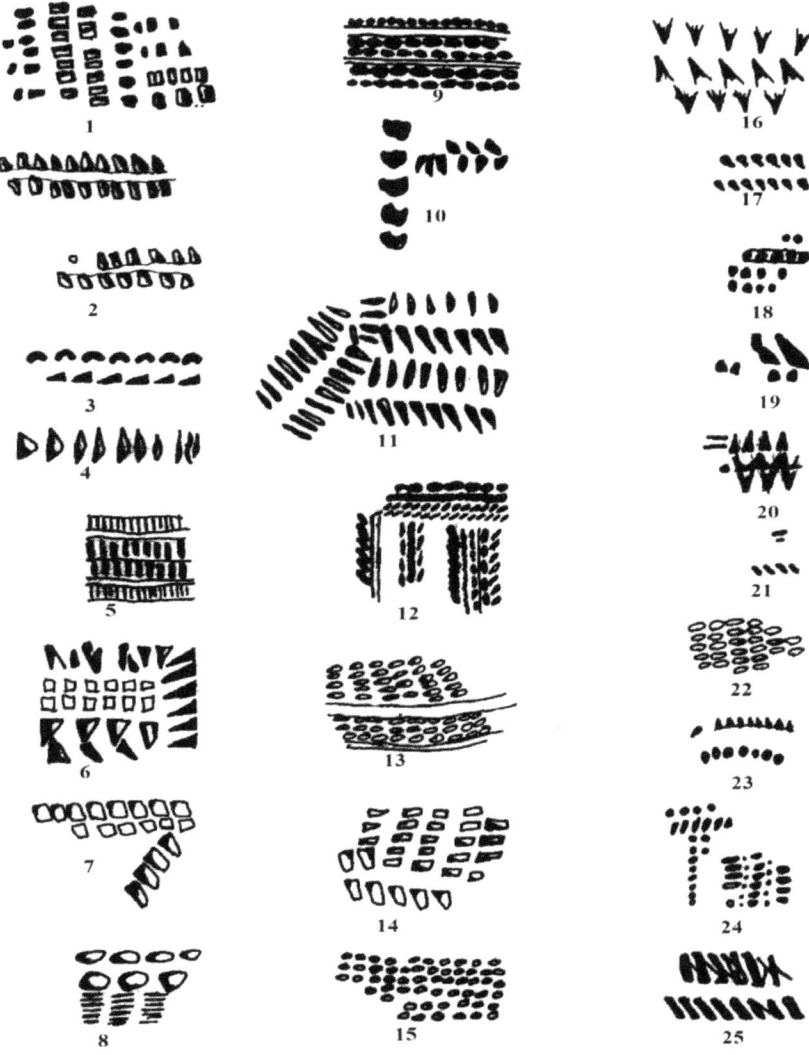

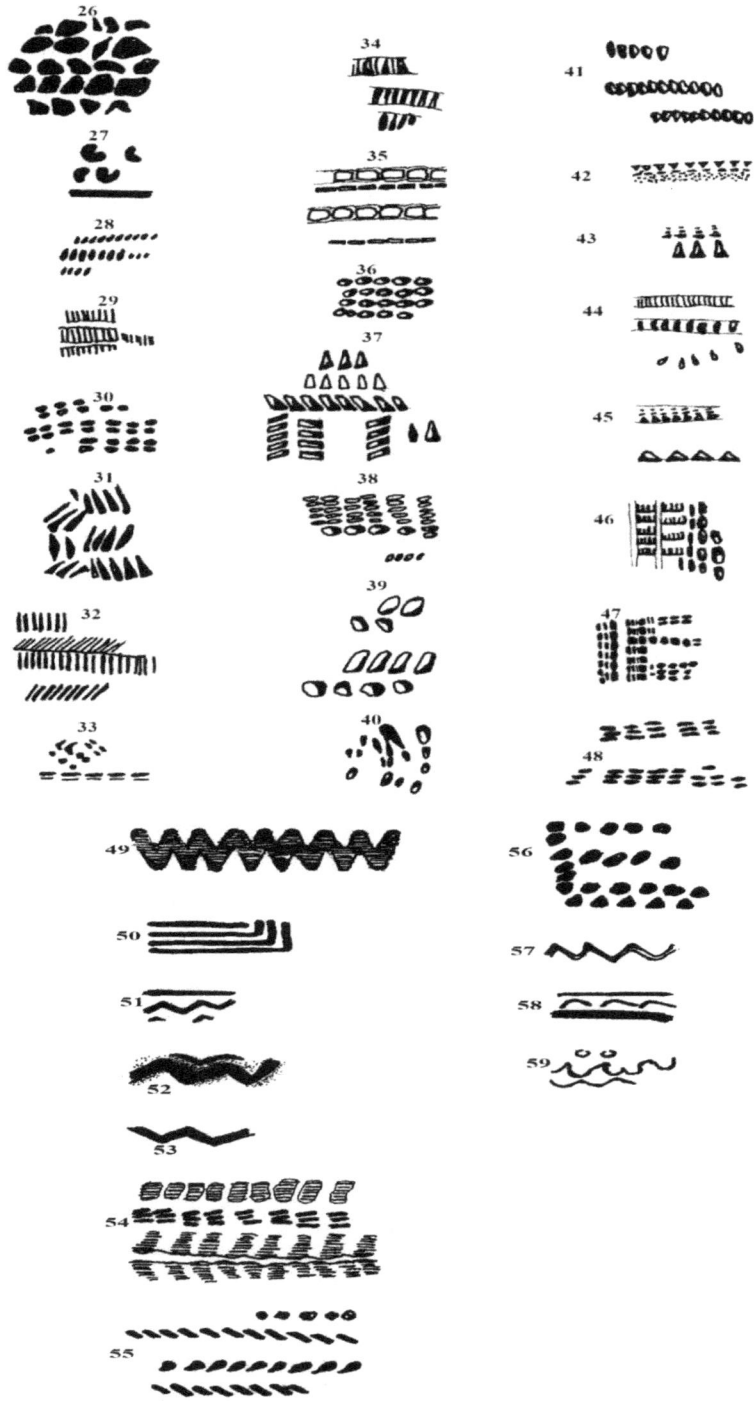

Figure 6.13 Kansyore Pottery Decoration Elements

Key for Figure 6.3

1, 6, 10, 12, 14, 24, 30, 37, 47, 56= Varieties of Interlocked Vertical and Horizontal Dotted Lines

2, 9= Banded Double Paired Dotted Lines

3= Row of Crescent Dots

4= Straight Dotted Inverted Crescents

5, 29, 34= Rows of Stippled Banded Lines

7, 11, 33, 44= Varieties of Interlocked Horizontal and Oblique Dotted Lines

8= Double Rows of Round Dots and Triple Bands of Dashes

13= Banded Several Dotted Lines

15, 22, 28, 36, 38, 39, 41= Varieties of Horizontal Dotted Lines

16= Rows of Impressed Incised Vs

17, 55= Row of Horizontal Tear Drop Dotted Lines

18, 19, 21= Variations of Irregular Dotted Lines

20, 43, 45= Rows of Triangles

23= Dotted Archical Lines

25= Rows of Bold Oblique (Diagonal) Stippled Lines

26= Impressed Dotted Irregular Lines

27= Banded Rows of Hoof-Like Dotted Lines

31= Alternating Moulded Wedges

32= Alternating Bands of Fine Oblique and Vertical Incisions

35= Horizontal Banded Rectangular Dotted Lines

40= Irregular Vertical Rounded Dots

42= Inverted Triangles Underlined by Dashes and Fine Dots

46= Banded Vertical Dashes (Ladder-Like) and Dots

48= Triple Rows of Oval Dotted Lines

49= Dotted Zigzag Lines

50= Bold Vertical and Horizontal Converging Lines

51= Banded Wavy Lines

52, 53= Bold Single Wavy Lines

54= Mat Impression

55= Rows of Oblique Bold and Tear Drop Dotted Lines

57= Double Wavy Lines

58= Banded Chevrons

59= Dots Underlined By Zigzag Lines

Decoration elements	Total	% age
Fern Branch Dotted Lines (Stippled Lines)	24	9.4
Wavy Lines	22	8.6
Alternating Fine Incisions	9	3.5
Interlocked Vertical And Horizontal Lines	24	9.4
Horizontal Crescent/Hoof-Like Dotted Lines	12	4.7
Arch-Like Lines	9	3.5
Mat Impression	8	3.1
Horizontal Dotted Lines	54	21.1
Dashes	24	9.4
Banded Dotted Lines	18	7.0
Dotted Zigzag Lines	18	7.0
V's And Triangles	13	5.1
Vertical Dotted Lines	9	3.5
Chevrons	12	4.7
Total	256	100.0

Table 6.12: Frequency of Decoration Elements

Decoration elements appear either as single elements or several elements (motifs). Table 6.12 gives a summary of the 59 decoration elements identified. The statistics given in Table 6.12 showed that the major decoration elements were in form of horizontal dotted lines (21.1%) while those with the least occurrence were the mat impressions (3.1%)

6.2.59 Kansyore Ceramic Decoration Techniques

The decoration of the analysed Kansyore pottery was executed using the following decoration techniques that are rocker-stamping 55 (21.5%), impression 78 (30.5%), comb-stamping 85 (33.2%), and incision 38 (14.8%). Therefore stamping was either by rocker or comb. Mohammed-Ali (1991:69) defined rocker-stamping as pressing either a tool with a continuous edge or one with multiple teeth (a comb or a cord-wrapped stick) into the surface of the vessel at one end of the tool and then transpiring the pressure across to another end until the whole length of the tool edge has been impressed into the clay. Then one end is lifted and the tool is pivoted from the end still in the clay since this is repeated several times it creates a rocker motion hence the term rocker stamping. The decorative elements produced by rocker stamping are usually continuous lines, dots, dashes or a combination of triangles and dots. The basic fundamental pattern of rocker stamping is a zigzag that manifested itself in the dotted zigzag lines (Figure 6.13: 49). Comb stamping was mainly executed with a multi toothed comb and the shapes of the comb differed leading to the production of diverse dots such as circular, oval, rectangular, and squared dots. The incisions were not very common but led to the appearance of the dashes and some zigzag lines (Figure 6.13:32). The impressions on the other hand would create several patterns such as those that appeared in form of impressed mats and the varieties of dotted motifs (Figure 6.13).

6.2.60 Kansyore Ceramic Decoration Placement

Decoration placement refers to where the various designs are placed or put on the vessel. The decoration as earlier noted mainly appeared in bands below the rim on either a single vessel part or a combination of various vessel parts as follows: rims (6), shoulder (3), body (194), rim/neck/shoulder (6), neck/shoulder (2), rim/body (36), rim/shoulder/body (2), and shoulder/body (4). This therefore implies that the Kansyore ceramic-using fisher-hunter-gatherers preferred to place decoration mainly on the vessel bodies. The analysis of decoration placement on Kansyore sherds revealed that majority were decorated on the body exterior (200) than the interior (50) with a few cases of interior and exterior decoration (6). Chapman (1967) noted that interior decoration of any kind on Kansyore sherds was rare but existed at Kansyore Island. Interior decoration was a practice applied as a test in the interior before eventual decoration of the exterior (Dale, 2007:230). At Kansyore Island interior decoration was executed on the rim interior and appeared in the form of parallel vertical lines. Decoration did not appear on the rim/lips which could probably be because Kansyore pottery rims are thin and some are tapered that could not allow placement of decoration on the rim/lips compared to the EIA pottery with the thickened and flayered Iron Age pottery rims. The research did not obtain any complete vessel to examine the extent of decoration but it appeared to be covering the entire vessel bodies (157) while others were in bands (99) that did not engulf the entire vessel.

6.2.57 Technological Attribute Analysis

In the examination of technological attributes that could be used to examine the nature and state of cultural interaction in the upper Nile catchment areas the key attributes were paste, temper, colour, and surface finishing. To examine the ideas and craftsmanship of the Nile valley cultures it was also seen as important to examine the colour and surface finishing on the vessel parts obtained. According to Chami (1994), visual attributes reflect ideas and fashions of certain periods and may easily be copied over long distances but the raw material seems to have a much more limited range of distribution. This implies the raw material utilisation has a lot to do with the local environment therefore similarity being due to ecological adaptability rather than diffusion or migration and trade.

6.2.58 Kansyore Ceramic Paste and Temper

The inclusions in clay intended to assist in reducing the shrinkage and warping of the vessel during firing and drying were analyzed. The aim was to identify the temper and its source that could be used to make inference on contact/interaction. The analyzed Kansyore sherds had paste that was rated as mainly coarse (194), coarse-fine (60) and fine (2). The majority of the Kansyore sherds analyzed being coarse is not strange as it is similar to Kansyore sherds elsewhere in East Africa. For instance Chapman (1967); Collet and Robertshaw (1980); Robertshaw (1991), and Soper and Golden (1969) described Kansyore ceramic paste as coarsely tempered with large primarily quartz inclusions.

The analyzed ceramics showed that the inclusions or temper were applied in combinations that included sand, quartz, vegetal materials, and mica. The commonest temper was a combination of quartz and mica (159) followed by sand and quartz (78), sand/vegetal materials (18), sand/quartz/shell (1). The variability of tempering material could be attributed to technological and ecological variation rather than migration or diffusion. This use of mica made the sherds to glitter. The use of mica has been recorded elsewhere for instance, Mehlman (1989) at Mumba-Höhle rock shelter and Nasera in a few cases while in Siror it was noted that the presence of mica in temper in Kansyore ceramics is uncommon (Dale, 2007). Interestingly, Arkell (1949:89) described one of the ceramic categories from Khartoum as micaceous ware. This therefore implied that cultural interaction could be traced in the use of same tempering materials in the Upper Nile catchment areas.

6.2.59 Firing Conditions and Surface Colour

The colour of a potsherd largely depends on the composition of its clay, the temperature during firing, duration under firing and the general firing conditions. In case of reduced oxidization, a black colour is produced that is attributed to smudging which means that the fuel is not fully burnt generating the black soot that taints the surface. In case of full oxidization almost going to vitrification then bright colors are produced, like yellowish red. The colors identified from the pottery assemblage were identified with the assistance of a Munsell colour chart and a magnifying lens. Kansyore pottery consisted of various colors (Table 6.13). What can be deduced from the vessel colors was that they appeared mostly in the dark colors (gray) that constituted 132 (51.6%) followed by brown 78 (30.5%) and red and black 46 (18%). The tendency has been to think that lighter colours indicate good firing conditions, but this is contrary to the Kansyore ceramics. Despite the dark colours almost in and out they appeared strong and wellfired. This was also noted by Mehlman (1989) at Mumba-Höhle and Nasera. The existence of more than one colour on the vessel was attributed by Dale (2007), to variable oxidation associated with open firings rather than differences in clay composition or sources.

Brown	Total	Grey	Total	Red	Total	Grand Total
Strong Brown	1	Reddish Grey	12	Reddish Yellow	8	21
Dark Brown	3	Very Dark Grey	15	Yellowish Red	2	20
Reddish Brown	15	Light Grey	13	Weak Red	1	29
Dark Brown	4	Dark Grey	74	**Others**		78
Reddish Brown	8	Reddish Grey	8	Black	32	48
Light Brown	11	Grey	10	Pinkish White	3	24
Brown	4					4
Dark Reddish Brown	21					21
Light Yellowish Brown	11					11
Total	78		132		46	256
% age	30.5		51.6		18.0	100.0

Table 6.13: Colours of Kansyore Ceramics

6.2.60 Wall Thickness

The vessel wall thickness was analysed by examining the rim thickness, maximum length and body thickness. Walls that were 4mm or less were described as thin while those that were 10 mm or more as thick (Joukowsky, 1980: 338). The intention was to identify the variability of thickness among traditions and to examine differences and similarities among traditions and also establish links with the Khartoum Neolithic ceramics. The measurement of length was used to establish the size of fragmentation as well. This revealed that the Kansyore specimens had the thinnest walls compared to Urewe and roulette traditions in the area of research. This was judged by the analysis of the Kansyore ceramic mean length (27.49mm) and mean body thickness (7.11mm) and mean rim thickness (8.2mm). The thin walled vessels might mean they were mainly domestic utensils probably cups and plates that did not require thick-bodied vessels.

6.2.61 Kansyore Ceramic Surface Finishing

A thorough examination of the surface of the vessel parts obtained revealed that varieties of methods were employed on the vessels. These entailed using a slip (174), burnishing (5), smoothing (13), rough-smooth (28), slip-burnish (2), slip-smooth (12) and rough (22) (Figure 6.14). Surface finishing judged on the exterior was mainly characterised by slipping (68%) done by the application of a thin black/grey slip. Slip is regarded as a form of painting by (Pikirayi, 1993: 126) contrary to the current study. Painting was rare as it appeared on only one potsherd from the Island of Deserters that had a red-like paint which was also taken as a slip. The fact that surface fishing partially depends on the function of the vessel could imply that the dominance of slipping means that most of the vessels were used for domestic purposes. Soot coating however was regarded as a secondary surface appearance rather than a finish (Pikirayi, 1993:123).

Surface finishing served a number of functions such as making aesthetically pleasing kitchenware (Sasoon, 1980:39); correcting any mistakes that may spoil the beauty of the vessel (Sheperd, 1963) and improving durability (Joukowsky, 1980). Burnishing on the other hand was done with a stone pebble, rubbing the wet clay. Existence of sherds with significant distinction in surface finishing is an evidence of functional utility probably controlled by the market demand for the consumer community and is seen to have a connection to craftsmanship (Nassor, 2010:98).

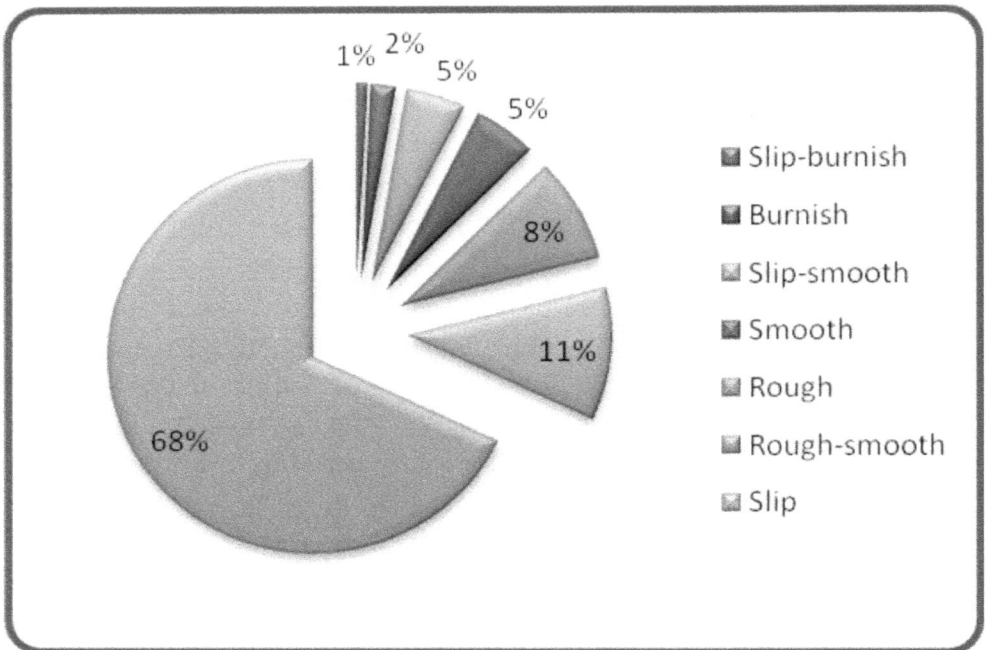

Table 6.14: Frequency of Surface Finishing

6.2.62 Kansyore Ceramic Rim Profiles

The analysis of rim profiles was based on any sherds that contained a rim part. Kansyore rims were rare since majority of the recovered Kansyore potsherds were bodies (194). The 55 sherds with rim parts had the following rim profiles; in-turn (12), upturn (19), slightly out-turn (9), tapered (7), squared (3), plain roundish (3), slightly flayered (1), un-identifiable (4) (Figure 6.14 and 6.15). The use of tapered rims could probably be due to the need to ensure comfort when one is sipping from the vessel. Rim forms have always been associated with vessel shapes for instance up-turn rims suggest open bowls, in-turn rims suggest restricted or hemispherical bowls while flared rims indicate restricted pots. This therefore implies that the Kansyore ceramic assemblage was composed of mainly open and hemisperical bowls (45) with an isolated case of a restricted pot (1).

Figure 6.14: Kansyore Rim Profiles

Key: **a,b&d**= Slightly In-Turn Rims; **c&e**= Up-Turn Rim; **g**= Tapered Rim; **h**= Flat and Squared Rims

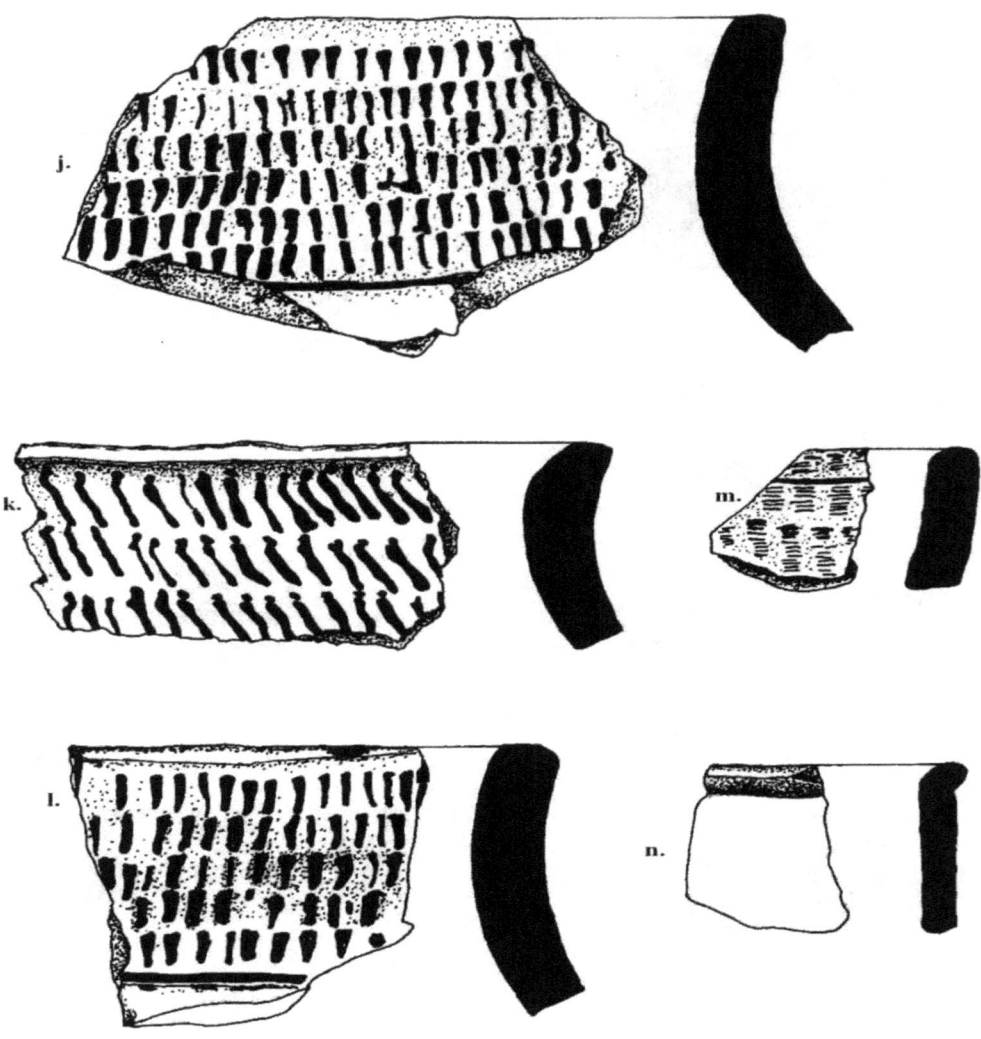

Figure 6.15: Rim profiles for Pots (j, k, l) and Bowls (m,n)

Key: **j, k, l**= Slightly Out-turning Rims; **m**= Everted Rim, **n**= Flayered Rim

6.2.63 Other Pottery Traditions Other than Kansyore Ceramics

A total of 1,372 potsherds were analysed other than the Kansyore pottery (256) that were obtained from Kansyore Island, Nsongezi and the Island of Deserters. Those identified to traditions included EIA/Urewe (736), roulette (331), channel (128), bourdine (48) and diagnostic plain (129) potsherds not attributed to any tradition (Figure 6.12 and Table 6.11). However these are not presented in this work as they were not addressing the research problem but will form basis of future publications.

6.2.64 Foreign Pottery

Nine pieces of foreign pottery were obtained from the Island of Deserters Trench 1 Level 1 (0-10 cm) (Plate 6.2). They were all body parts whose decoration appeared on the body too. The decoration element was characterised by horizontal grooves. The thickness implied that they were dishes and not cup fragments. Surface finishing executed with a glaze did not appear among the local pottery traditions. The hardness of the fabric suggested that they were fired inside a high-temperature kiln. The existence of foreign pottery of Indian origin suggested links between the interior and the East African coast through the Indian Ocean trade during the 19th century.

Plate 6.2: Foreign Pottery

6.2.65 Faunal Remains

Faunal remains formed one of the categories of the analyzed cultural materials. A total of 4,650 faunal remains were analyzed. The faunal remains were bones (4,364) and shells (286) mainly retrieved from Kansyore Island 4,307 (92.62%) followed by Nsongezi 183 (3.94%) and the Island of Deserters 160 (3.44%) (Table 6.15).

6.2.66 Shells

Shells constituted 6.2 % of the faunal remains. These were collected from Kansyore Island 184 (64.3%), Nsongezi 82 (28.7%), and the Island of Deserters 20 (7.0%) (Table 6.15). In the analysis of shells, the study only considered the shell type that led to identification of shells as either freshwater or land snail shell artefacts. The habitat and uses were also identified and the tentative conclusion was that in the latter case they were mostly for food basing on the current use. Bushozi (2011) cited Bower (1985, 2005; McBrearty and Brooks 2000; Yellen, 1996) who argued that MSA humans utilised diverse food resources including aquatic organisms. The shells analysed were from both surface collections (40) and excavations (246). The 246 shells from excavations were obtained from Kansyore Island: Trench 1 with 41 (16.7%), Trench 2 yielded 6 (2.4%) and STP 2 had 110 (44.7%) while at the Island of Deserters, Trench 4 yielded 7 (2.8%) and the Nsongezi STP1 yielded 82 (33.3%) (Table 6.15). Shells belonged to two major groups and these are fresh water shells and land snail shells. The fresh water shells constituted the majority (268; 98.17%) while the land snail shells were only 5 (1.83%). The fresh water shells identified were the *Pila ovata* and *Etheria* while the land snail shells were the *Limicolaria, Burtoa,* and *Edouardia* (Plates 6.3, 6.4, 6.5). The shells implied that the prehistoric people partially depended on aquatic resources for their dietary needs in the Upper Nile valley catchment areas.

Trench/Test Pit	Bones	Shells	Total	% Age
Nsongezi STP1	101	82	183	3.94
Kansyore Island				
Surface		27	27	0.58
STP 2	136	110	246	5.29
Trench 1	2,127	41	2,168	46.62
Trench 1B	1,154		1,154	24.82
Trench 2	17	2	19	0.41
Trench 2A	2		2	0.04
Trench 2Ai	175		175	3.76
Trench 2Aii	207		207	4.45
Trench 2B	304	4	308	6.62
Trench 3	1		1	0.02
Island of Deserters				
Surface	4	13	17	0.37
Trench 1	2		2	0.04
Trench 2	54		54	1.16
Trench 3	1		1	0.02
Trench 4	72	7	79	1.70
Trench 5	5		5	0.11
Trench 5A	2		2	0.04
Total	4,364	286	4,650	100.00
% age	93.8	6.2	100.0	

Table 6.15 : Faunal Remains

6.3.1 Pila Ovata, Fresh Water Gastropod Snail

This is edible though not so commonly eaten or palateable to many people. The practice of eating snails is not so common in Uganda as it is on the Congo side. The *Pila ovata* can live in muddy places with poorly oxygenated water though it likes staying in fresh waters. This can survive in muddy places but even when it gets dry they can survive up to the next rainy season.

6.3.2 Ethreria

The second category was the *Etheria* another fresh water snail that is well oxygenated and edible as it is very rich in proteins. It is risky getting this kind of snail since it often grows where rapids are located like at Kansyore Island. The *Etheria* shell peels off some kind of white powder. The powder is calcium carbonate ($CaCo_3$). Humans exploit this for instance; in some instances men and women use the powder for beauty purposes and during the circumcision seasons since it has a shining element. However the practice of circumcision is not common in south-western Uganda where they were obtained, this left beauty and food purposes as the available options for the existence of *Etheria* shells in this area. The *Etheria* is one of the most common species at Kansyore Island (Plate 6.3).

Plate 6.3: *Etheria* Shells

6.3.3 Limicolaria and Burtoa

The *Limicolaria* and *Burtoa* are widely found in most parts of Uganda especially in dumpy areas. They are edible but not so palatable to many people because of their strange taste although they are rich in protein. These are a type of land snails (Plate 6.4). These shells were perforated and presumably worn in Esh Shaheinab (Arkell, 1953). The *Limicolaria* is a land snail that favours swampy, seasonally flooded grasses (Krzyzaniak, 1978:172). The existence of similar shell types at Esh-Shaheinab shows cultural similarities in the Upper Nile catchment areas which is attributed to the ecological conditions.

6.3.4 Edouardia

Edouardia is similar to the *Limicolaria* though slightly fatter (Plate 6.5). It is an edible land snail rich in protein. This stays in various habitats especially the dumpy localities but can also survive in arid places.

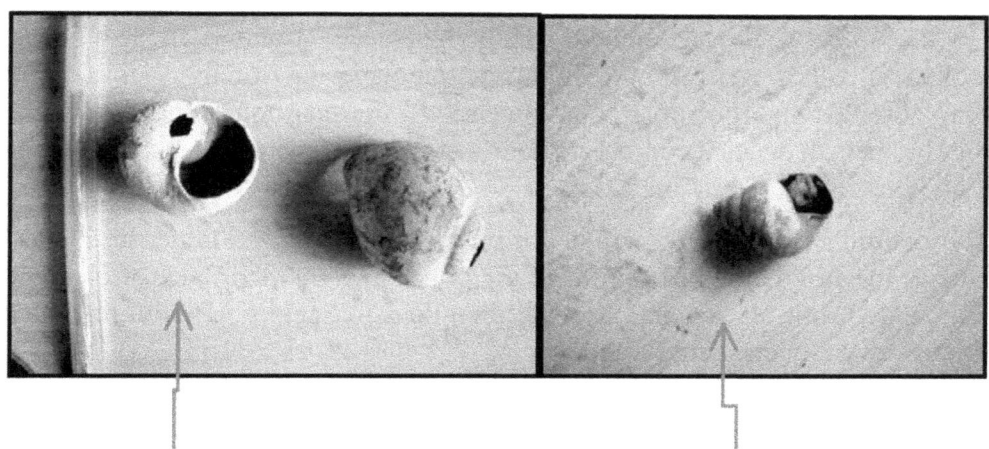

Plate 6.4: Limicolaria Shells **Plate 6.5: Edouardia Shells**

All over the world, besides their food value, snails/shells are used as decoration and for ornaments. To date in Uganda, shells generally provide material for decoration and ornaments/jewellery. Due to the tropical nature of Uganda, all the land snails mentioned above appear in most parts of the country. The difference comes in size because of seasonality and sometimes in colour because of the nature of the soils. Therefore this means their presence may be due to the suitability of the environment. The presence of plenty of shells, especially the freshwater shells, implied that snails were part of the prehistoric diet and the Kagera River was the chief source. This was derived from similar species elsewhere that have been suggested to be part of the diet, like at Esh-Shaheinab. Therefore the presence of similar cultural materials like shells in Uganda and Sudan (Esh- Shaheinab) was not a product of migration, diffusion or trade but rather similar riverine ecological zones.

6.3.70 Bones

A total of 4,364 bones were analyzed. Kansyore Island had the highest frequency of bones 4,121 (94.43%), followed by the Island of Deserters 140 (3.21%) and Nsongezi 103 (2.36%) (Table 6.16). The analyzed bones composed of piscine bones 1,461 (33.5%); mammalian and avian bones 527

(12.1%). Some were modified into bone tools 276 (6.3%) while others 5 (0.1%) had cut marks. The piscine bones were mainly the body vertebrae (1,457) with one case of an operculum and three fish head bones. Kansyore Island was the major contributor of fish bones with Trench 1 having a complete aqualithic layer. This would suggest the aquatic civilization (Sutton, 1974, 1977) at Kansyore Island. From their size and structure, the fish bones looked as if they were from a similar or same species of fish. According to Mary Prendergast (personal communication), the fish bones analyzed were for Barbus fish species commonly found at Kansyore sites. Pneumatic avian long bones appeared in one case.

The mammal bones were mainly for bovines or small and large ruminants. Due to the fragmented condition of the bones and shells or lack of element uniqueness, not all specimens were identified to species. Therefore 2,095 (48.0%) were unclassified fragments.

The bones included a wide range of mammalian long-limb bones, teeth, corneal processes and, in one case, badly-fragmented pieces of a skull. Short bones such as digital bones of large and small ruminants (herbivores such as buffalo, kob) were identified. Large and small carnivore teeth and claws; and large and small ruminant teeth as well as omnivore teeth possibly of monkey were analyzed. Elephant tusks, hippo tusks, and cheek teeth were identified. Bone tools were especially from Kansyore Island (Plate 6.6). Kansyore Island is rich in fauna remains and further excavations and detailed analysis may possibly yield exciting results.

Most of bones recovered from the Nsongezi area were well preserved and nearly complete compared to Kansyore Island. This divergence may be explained by the nature of the sites whereby Kansyore being an island the preservation of bones might have been affected by water unlike Nsongezi that is located on land. The bones from the entire collection belonged to carnivores, herbivores and omnivores. Some of those identified were for animals such as; monkeys, elephants, hippo, buffalo, and warthog; fish; primates with evidence from the human incisor tooth and skull fragments and probably domestic animals that could either be sheep or goat. Some bones also belonged to large and small ruminants, while others belonged to carnivores. The teeth and claws identified the carnivore species. The bone elements identified were ulna, teeth, pelvis, vertebrae, metacarpals, phalanx, ribs, skull, calcaneus, epiphysis, tusks, horn (corneal process), capeoleous, trunk, scapulae, a condyle of a femur, and tibia.

Frequency of bones per trench							
Trench/Test Pit	Mammal/Avian	Fish	Fragments	Bone Tools	Cut Marks	Total	% Age
Nsongezi TP1	1	100				101	2.31
Surface	2					2	0.05
Kansyore Island							
Test pit 2	68	67			1	136	3.12
Trench 1	178	838	1,010	101		2,127	48.74
Trench 1B	172	264	595	123		1,154	26.44
Trench 2	3		9	5		17	0.39
Trench 2A	2					2	0.05
Trench 2Ai	16	7	128	19	3	173	3.96
Trench 2Aii	12		179	16		207	4.74
Trench 2B	25	132	136	10	1	304	6.97
Trench 3			1			1	0.02
Island of Deserters							
surface	2		2			4	0.09
Trench 1			2			2	0.05
Trench 2	23	1	28	2		54	1.24
Trench 3			1			1	0.02
Trench 4	20	52				72	1.65
Trench 5	2		3			5	0.11
Trench 5A	1		1			2	0.05
Total	527	1,461	2,095	276	5	4,364	100.00
% age	12.1	33.5	48	6.3	0.1	100	

Table 6.16: Frequency of Bones per Trench

The bones also exhibited secondary modifications in the form of cut marks, being burnt, engraved or shaped as bone tools (Plates 6.6a and 6.6b) and in one case from Kansyore Island Trench 2B, a fossilized bone was recovered. Some of the cut marks were very sharp suggestive of a very sharp instrument in use (Plate 6.6c). This could probably be a stone used to cut in preparation of a blank for making a tool. The existence of bone tools may imply the use of bones in prehistoric time either for cracking nuts or as needles. The faunal remains are not strange in the area since Nsongezi rock shelter and a nearby open air site yielded fauna including fish identified as the Ripon Falls barbell (Plate 6.7a) and molluscs that included *Etheria elliptica, Caelatura hauttecoeuri Humorous, Pila ovata, Mutela* and *Parreysia bakeri* (O'Brien, 1939, Lowe, 1952, and Pearce and Posnansky, 1963). Some of the teeth were for bovids the size of a bushbuck, small gazelle, or sheep or goat while others were for big game such as hippo (tooth) (Plate 6.6b) and elephants (Plate 6.7b).

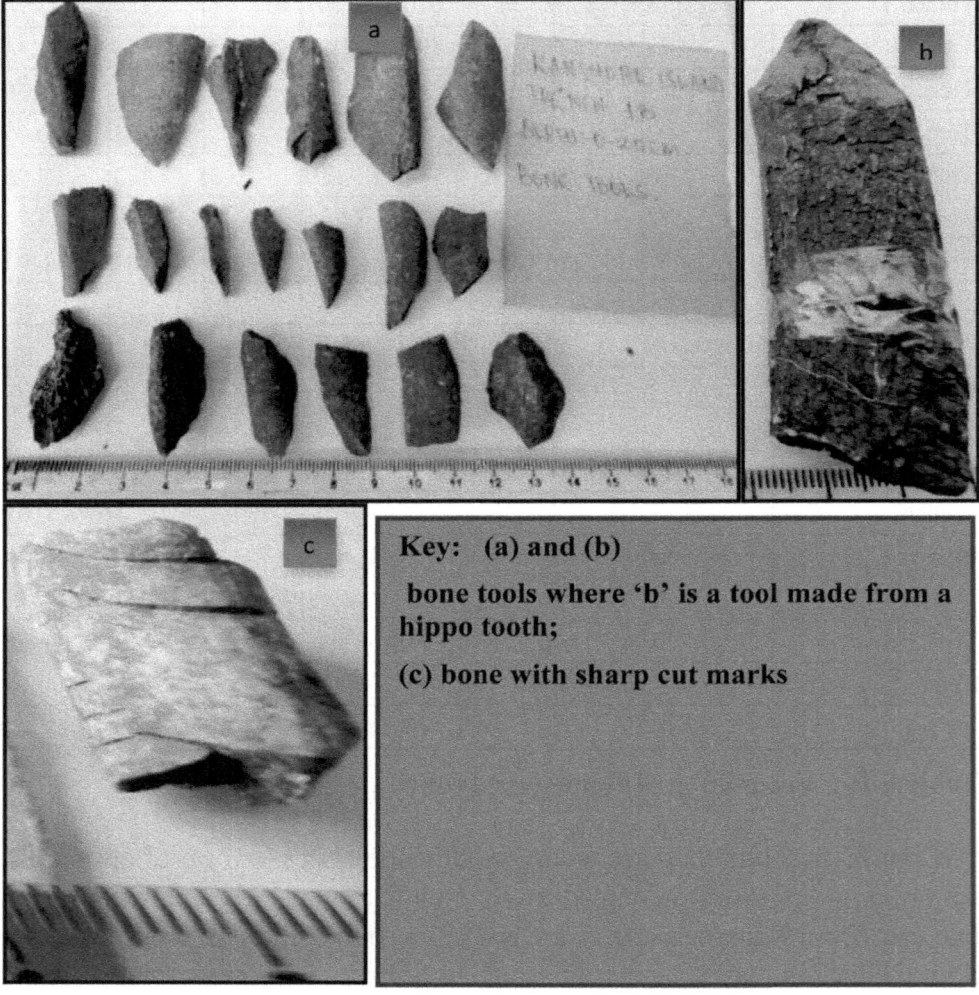

Plate 6.6: Bone Tools from Kansyore Island

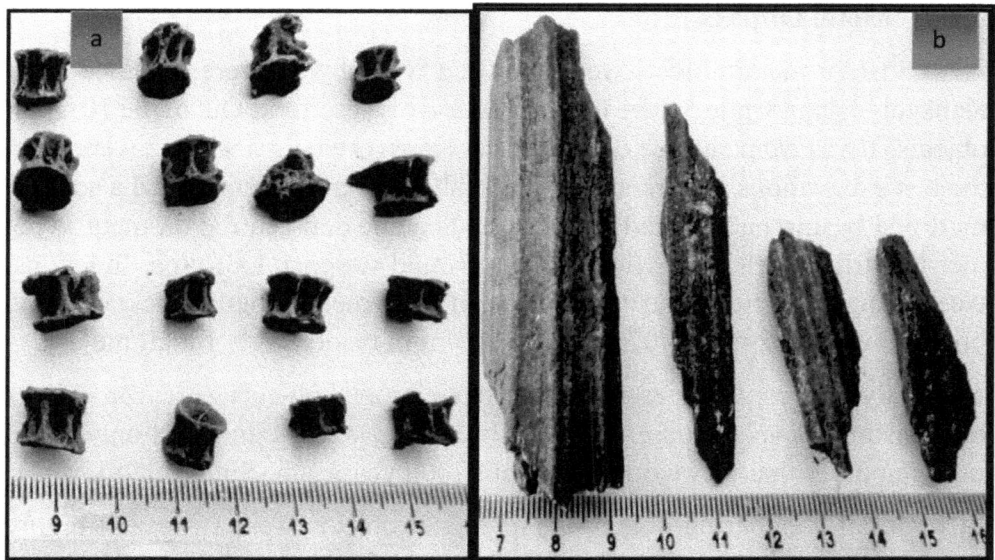

Plate 6.7: (a) Fish Vertebrae (b) Elephant Tusk Fragments

6.5   Metallurgical objects

A total of 78 metallurgical remains were analysed that consisted of metal objects (70), iron slag (7), and a tuyere (1).

6.5.1   Iron Slag

The seven pieces of iron slag analyzed were obtained at the Island of Deserters in Trench 4. These were the only slag pieces obtained from the entire excavation. In the analysis of iron slag, the following attributes were examined; morphology; thermal conditions, lustre, colour/streak; inclusions, fragmentation, raw materials and surface conditions basing on Mapunda's Analysis Scheme. In terms of thermal conditions the slag had melted meaning they had no floor marks with a smooth surface typical of common slag. The shapes were amorphous. All iron slag pieces had a ceramic luster. The color was gray. The surface condition was smooth yet the raw material proved that it was real slag. The slag occurred in the stratigraphic levels between 25 and 55 cm below surface, associated with EIA and LIA pottery. The presence of tuyeres and Iron Age pottery in association with the metal objects and iron slag implied a fully-fledged Iron Age.

6.5.2 Metal Objects

A total of 70 metal objects were analyzed whereby 65 were obtained from Kansyore Island while 5 were from the Island of Deserters. Out of the 70 metal objects, 1 was from surface collections at Kansyore Island while 2 were from the test excavations and trenches. The analysis of metals employed a scheme modified basing on Mapunda's Analysis Scheme and centred on metal type, metric attributes (length, width, thickness and weight), tool type, functions, weathering conditions and fragmentation. The mean length, thickness, and breadth were 34.2 mm, 5.07 mm, and 11.4 mm respectively for all metals.

The analysis of metal types concluded that all metal objects were iron objects after testing for magnetism. In East Africa, iron was the first and only metal used regularly that was worked at about 2000 years ago (Sutton, 1981: 453).

In terms of weathering conditions all metal objects were rusty and highly corroded with only one that was still plain implying they were iron metals. An examination of fragmentation that was taken as a major breakage but not just peeling off due to rusting established that 5 metals had one edge broken; 59 with two broken edges, 2 with three edges broken, 2 with all sides broken and 3 were not fragmented at all. The tool types identified from the metal objects showed that they were mainly adornment gear including bangles (18) and rings (9) and yet others included; an arrowhead (1), pieces of nails (5), a needle (1), metal hunks (6) and indeterminate (31) fragments. The functions therefore derived from the tool types were: construction, hafting, ornamentation and weaving (Plate 6.8). Jewelry is important in the trace of the path of ideas but can also show the choice by society and the maker's artisanship.

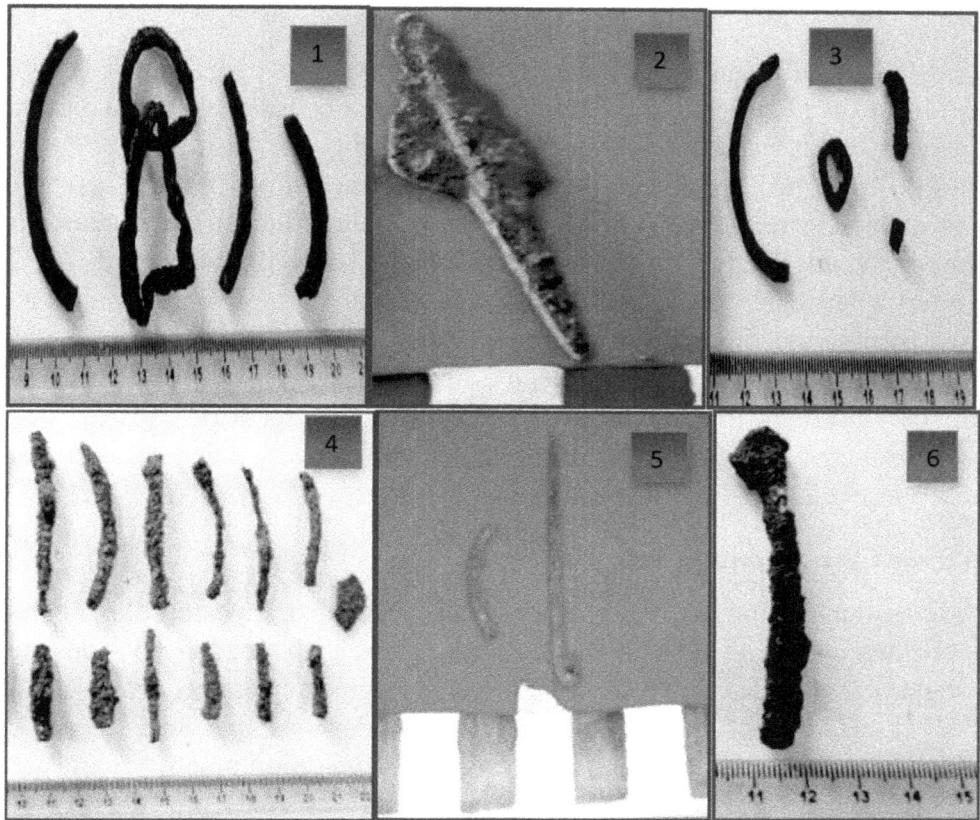

Plate 6.8: Some of the Metal Objects

Key: 1= Bangle Fragments, 2= Arrowhead, 3= Bangle Fragments and a Ring in Set, 4= Bangle and Nail Fragments, 5= Needle for Weaving, 6=Bangle Fragment.

6.6　House Daubs

The daub fragments (25) were from the Island of Deserters in Trench 1 (16), Trench 4 (8) and Trench 5A (1) respectively. The size varied with only one huge piece while the rest were small. The colors also ranged between brick red and dark red. One daub piece was hollow-like. The presence of daub implied the existence of house structures probably of mud and wattle. However, an insight into the shape of the structures could not be obtained since no postholes were observed.

6.7 Red Ochre

Forty eight red ochre stones were obtained from Kansyore Island (35) and the Island of Deserters (13). The source of the red ochre was not established. The red ochre was used for painting pottery as one potsherd had red slips and probably for beautification, which is painting human faces. There was evidence of grinding red ochre as seen from one grinding stone recovered as elaborated under lithic analysis. Clark (1988:299) cited by Bushozi (2011:58) argues that ochre was used for adornment and that sometimes red ochre was used for decorating tools and equipment. New studies on technological organisation and microscopic residue analysis suggest that ochre powder mixed with other ingredients was used as a hafting agent (Lombard: 2007) while others (Bushozi, 2011; Mehlman, 1989) suggest that red ochre was taken as one of the symbolic revealing objects.

6.8 Clay Mace and Smoking Pipes

Among the specimens analyzed was a clay mace that appeared like a bored stone with a round hole in the middle that was obtained from Kansyore Island. Besides the mace were smoking pipe fragments obtained from surface collections (Plate 5.1a and b) typical of modern Ankole smoking pipes (Chapman, 1967). Smoking of tobacco is still a common practice in the area of research and both men and women indulge in the practice. The smoking pipe fragments were identified as parts of the socket stems and the bowl of the smoking pipes. The smoking pipes analyzed can be correlated to the types of Connah (1997; 51) and Phillips (1983:303) that were associated with tobacco smoking that have been dated to the 7th century A.D in the lower Victoria Nile.

6.9 Data from Ethnographic Inquiries

In the Nsongezi Kansyore area, the oral interviews revealed that the house foundation at Kansyore Island was formerly a hotel constructed in the 1950s, though different dates are given ranging from 1955-1957. The hotel is said to have been destroyed during the 1979 war with Tanzania on suspicion that it might be harbouring rebels. The owners domesticated a number of animals including; *enjaza, empeewo* and *Ngaali*. Kansyore Island is said to have been a ritual place for the Ankole Kingdom with several stones used by the kings as utensils (Stone mortar). The pyramidal structure overlooking the Nsongezi rock shelter was said to be the grave of a white man who died while fishing in the Kagera River.

6.10 Chapter Summary

The data that was analysed revealed that the lithics were either light-duty or heavy-duty tools. While Kansyore Island dominated the production of light-duty tools, the Island of Deserters dominated the production of heavy-duty tools. This therefore implied that the lithic industry at Kansyore Island was a flake industry while the one at the Island of Deserters was a core industry. The toolkit at Kansyore, like Nsongezi, showed that they were LSA/IA sites while that at the Island of Deserters was an MSA/LSA/IA site. The examination of raw material utilization shows an attempt to exploit the locally available raw materials that were mainly in terms of river cobbles of quartz and quartzite though other raw materials such as gneiss and aplite dyke were utilized. The only exotic raw materials were basalt and chert. Stratigraphically the distribution of cultural materials showed intensive site use in the middle strata compared to the top and bottom and along river banks. This implied that the water bodies acted as catchment areas where activities concentrated.

The pottery traditions identified show that it is no longer acceptable to simply equate ceramics with ethnicity or to use them as chronological tools (Ashley, 2010:158). This is because stratigraphically there was at times coexistence of different pottery traditions. This means that pottery styles can and do cross diagnostic boundaries just as economic specialization can spread without wholesale migration (Stewart, 1993). There has been denial of evidence especially where Kansyore ware has been taken to have persisted into recent times (Miller, 1969; Chami, 2006).

Furthermore, the presence of EIA wares associated with stone tools and Kansyore ware have been attributed to a mechanical mixture yet it could be interpreted as evidence of cultural continuity of Stone Age ways of life after settlement by Iron Age food-producing societies as has been documented in southern central Africa. The problem of the transition from Kansyore to the Iron Age is out the scope of this study but it is an area recommended for future research. This is because it would possibly answer the issue of dating Kansyore sites, which has been a source of confusion that has made it to be given a long stretch of time due to the failure to sort out variants within the tradition. There has been denial of the existence of interaction between the hunter-gatherers and farmers and also stereotypes that take transition to be unidirectional from simple to complex that is to say from hunter-gatherer to farmer and not the reverse (Reid, 2005:358). It is all too easy for archaeologists to slip into the assumption that sites dominated by stone tools were inhabited by hunter- gatherer peoples and farmers occupied sites with pottery (Denbow, 1999 cited by Reid, 2005:370). This can subconsciously lead them to ethicize these economic activities. Archaeologists must take care to consider the possibility of multi-ethnic populations within a site.

Section 3
CONCLUSION

CHAPTER SEVEN

COMPARATIVE DISCUSSION

7.1 Introduction

This chapter is the comparative analysis of the material excavated from Kansyore Island and the Island of Deserters in Uganda, and written literature on central and southern Sudan that all constituted the Upper Nile catchment areas in this work. The purpose of the study was to find out if there was cultural affinity between Uganda and Sudan.

The cultural materials used for this task are only from Kansyore Island and the Island of Deserters because it was only at these sites where material recovered identified with Kansyore tradition, while material from other sites such as Chobe and Kikubamitwe will be reported elsewhere. This is because Kansyore pottery, more than any other pottery tradition analysed, was comparable to the Khartoum Neolithic pottery. Yet comparison should be made among assemblages within the same major time periods and where possible within comparable radio-carbon dates (Marks and Mohammed-Ali, 1991b).

The materials analysed in this work which are compared with those of Sudan are the lithic artefacts, pottery identified as Kansyore, faunal remains especially the aspect of the aqualithic, red ochre and dating evidence. This is because earlier studies have emphasised affinity between other parts of Africa and Khartoum pottery basing on mainly pottery especially its decoration and decorative instruments (Chapman, 1967) and which is why this work used even other artefacts besides pottery as enumerated above.

The first aspect of comparison is the conceptualization of the term Neolithic in the Upper Nile catchment areas. The Sudan Neolithic was, for instance, viewed as consisting of two components one of which was the 'Early Khartoum' (Khartoum Mesolithic) and the second as the central Sudanese Neolithic or Shaheinab Neolithic tradition (Khartoum Neolithic) (Krzyzaniak, 1978). The Early Khartoum tradition was defined by Sutton (1974) as the aquatic way of life which has been dated as far as 20,000 BP (Yellen, 1998) in sites like Ishango, though in Turkana, Batheleme (1977) had dated it with three dates of ca 9500, 6500-6000 and 3500 BP but since the samples dated were mollusca they should be regarded with caution. The existence of the aqualithic was also identified at Kansyore Island which had a broad spectrum of fishing evidence in Trench 1B. Here a complete aquatic/aqualithic layer was recovered.

The term Neolithic in Sudan has been controversial with some scholars identifying two phases (Usai, 2005; Mohammed-Ali, 1984 and Krzyzaniak, 1978) while others suggesting three phases (Fekri, 1986). The two phases of the earlier category included Phase 1 of the Early Neolithic or the gouge culture of Arkell (1953) with evidence obtained from Khartoum Hospital, Sagai, Sorourab I, and the lower assemblage at al-Qoz dated between 5500 and 4500 B.C (Mohammed-Ali, 1984). This first phase was regarded as the classic Neolithic by Marks *et al* (1985) dated 5600 BP – 5000 BP. The second is the late Neolithic phase of Kadada type (Usai, 2005) and Shaheinab, al-Geili, the upper component at al-Qoz, Kadero I and Zakyab, dated from the late 5th to the early 3rd millennium B.C (Mohammed-Ali, 1984).

On the other hand, scholars such as Fekri (1986) and Marks & Mohammed-Ali (1991b) considered the Khartoum Neolithic as having had three phases. These were the Early Khartoum Neolithic with four sites of Rabak (4905±90 BC), Umm Direiwa (4800 ±100), Islang (4745±40 BC) and El Ghaba (4540 ±150 BC). The second phase was the middle Neolithic with mainly Shaheinab, Kadero 1, Zakyab and Nofalab whose average age was 4200 BC and the third Late Neolithic phase that had evidence from El Khadada (Kadada) (3530±60 BC) and Shaqadud cave (2595±75 BC). These divergent views imply that the Neolithic in Sudan is rather obscure (Usai, 2005).

The story is not different in East Africa concerning the Neolithic terminology. Collet and Robertshaw (1983) state that the Neolithic stage in East African prehistory was first posited by Louis Leakey in 1931. Leakey (1931) thought that the presence of stone bowls, mortars, and grinding stones indicated some form of agriculture hence the term Stone Bowl Culture. However Sutton (1966:38) abandoned the term 'Neolithic' as 'cumbersome and subjective', for 'Late Stone Age' (LSA). However, though not favoured by Sutton, the term 'Stone Bowl Culture' gained popularity for several years (Cohen, 1970). The mid-1970s saw the return of the term 'Neolithic (Onyango-Abuje, 1976) and since 1977 'Pastoral Neolithic' has become the norm (Prendergast, 2008). The latter term was adopted due to the preponderance of domestic cattle and sheep/goat in faunal samples from concerned sites (Bower, 1977).

This therefore means the LSA in East Africa with pottery and elements of domestication have been termed as either Late Stone Age (LSA), Neolithic or Pastoral Neolithic (Chami and Kwekason, 2003). These definitions were, however, confined to the Rift Valley and the adjacent highlands (Chami & Kwekason; 2003:67)) on two grounds. The first one was the view that the Rift Valley with its lakes and proximity to the Nile valley where the aqualithic civilisation occurred was prone to a similar Neolithic tradition through diffusion and migration. Secondly was the conception that the Neolithic/ Pastoral Neolithic (PN) traditions were for southern Cushitic speakers (Phillipson, 1993). However the current research considered the Neolithic to exist even outside the Rift Valley and in that regard considered the Kansyore tradition as Neolithic.

7.2 Lithics

In lithic analysis of the material from the Ugandan side of the upper Nile catchment areas it was discovered that the type of artefacts and attributes had similarities with those that had been reported in Sudan.

Comparison of the lithics is at the level of the lithic industry, tool, and core typologies. The first aspect showing cultural affinity is the lithic industry. Though the LSA industry is usually characterised by a blade core technology (bipolar) (Mehlman, 1989; Mabulla, 1996; Kessy, 2005), the lithic industry at Kansyore Island had a microlithic flake industry as flakes were dominant in comparison to blades where out of the 6,113 blade/flake assemblage, flakes comprised 4,921 (80.5%) compared to 1,192 (19.5%) blades. The bipolar cores comprised 274 (15.3%) of the 1,796 core assemblage as opposed to platform cores 1,235 (68.8%). The least occurrence of bipolar cores implied that the lithic industry was not predominantly a blade industry.

Though blades occurred, they may not have been necessarily a result of the blade industry; whereas the stone industry at the Island of Deserters showed that the LSA is underlain by the MSA lithic industry. This was evidenced from the levallois flaking technique with a toolkit characterised by tortoise-shaped cores, pyramidal, discoidal and biconical varieties and evidence of the use of an early levallois technique for production of flakes of predetermined shape (Howell and Clark, 1964: 494). Another line of evidence for the MSA at the Island of Deserters was the flakes, and well-trimmed triangular points that were common south of the equator during the MSA (Phillipson, 2005).

Therefore the lithic industry at the Island of Deserters was of a core type. For instance, all the core axes (15) were obtained from the Island of Deserters. In addition, while production of light-duty tools was dominant at Kansyore Island with 1,673 out of the 1,705 lithic artefacts, the production of heavy-duty tools was dominant at the Island of Deserters with 23 of the 32 heavy-duty tools and yet Kansyore Island had only 4 specimens.

In comparison, the Neolithic industry at Sorourab 1 (Mohammed-Ali, 1984) and the Shaqadud cave and shell midden (Marks, 1991:173) in Sudan was also technologically a microlithic flake industry where blade production was minimal like at Sorourab 1, while at Shaqadud any blades found were either a result of importation from the Nile valley or were fortuitously produced (Marks, 1991). This was attributed to the size of pebbles utilised and the availability of raw materials that made cores to be discarded. Testing at Sorourab 1 showed no evidence of specialised activity (Mohammed-Ali, 1984) contrary to the Island of Deserters with the *levallois* core preparation to produce specialised flakes. On the other hand, in Southern Sudan, Jebel Tukyi rock shelter in Western Equatoria, Lokabulo rock shelter in Eastern Equatoria and Dhang Rial mound had an un-diagnostic flaked quartz industry (David, 1982) while sites like Lulubo and Itohom in south-east Sudan had a microlithic quartz assemblage (Robertshaw, 1982).

Another area of cultural affinity was in terms of lithic artefact types. The lithic tool typology in the southern part of the Upper Nile Catchment was dominated by scrapers with the dominant type as the side scrapers (77.1%) followed by end scrapers (22.2%) and concave and thumbnail scrapers (0.7%). The scrapers were single-side, double-side, notched, nosed, straight-side or sundry-side. There was also affinity in backed pieces that were either straight-backed, angle-backed, diverse-backed, chisel-like drills/awls or truncated pieces. The dominant backed tool was the curve-backed piece though even the crescents featured prominently in Uganda. All lithic tools were well made. Other tool types identified were the burins (dihedral, angle and mixed), unifacial points, outils écaillés, becs, and denticulates. Blades and flakes also featured as either whole flakes or blades some of which were utilised flakes or blades mainly from Kansyore Island.

Scrapers, the most dominant tool type on the Ugandan side of the Nile catchment, were also reported in Sudan. In the latter case end scrapers made on flake and core fragments were common where straight-sided, convex, and thumbnail scrapers were identified in Sorourab 1 (Mohammed-Ali, 1984). In Southern Sudan at Lokabulo, Itohom, and Lolubo numerous scrapers including the thumbnail scrapers appeared (Robertshaw, 1982) just like at Kansyore Island and the Island of Deserters. Other lithic types reported in Sudan were denticulates, notched and truncated pieces and lunates, a common Neolithic artefact in the region and points. All these tool types also appear in the south (Uganda) though in varying quantities. However the borers, picks, and proto-gouges in Sorourab 1 did not feature in the south (Uganda). Blades and flakes and bifacially narrow lanceolate points (David *et al*, 1981) in Sudan have been identified in Uganda too. The concave scrapers constituted 6.4% of the finds on the Ugandan part of the Nile catchment yet they were prominent in the Khartoum variant industries examined by Shiner (1968).

The LSA culture of using backed tools was highly evident at Kansyore Island just like in southern Sudan at Lokabulo and Lulubo. This is similar to Shaqadud where Marks (1991:178) noted that the majority of the tools involved some form of backing where the dominant backed tool was the lunate (crescent). Yet from Kansyore Island and the Island of Deserters there were more curve-backed pieces (206) compared to crescents (200). The curve-backed pieces, also termed as typical traverse arrows, were described as a modification of the lunate form, having a short length:width ratio and somewhat concave edges where the back meets the un-retouched sharp edges (Marks, 1991) appear in both areas.

Comparison was also seen in metric attributes where by the crescents had varying sizes. Although all crescents were of a microform, some were small, others medium, and the rest slightly bigger on the Ugandan side of the Upper Nile catchment. This could probably reflect functional differences. For instance the small size could have been used as points for spearing fish (Soitesonen, 2010) while the bigger size could be sickle blades (Honnegar, 2006). A similar situation reported from Shaqadud showed that the crescents tended to be small, elongate but some were big with a mean length of 14.74 mm and a width of 5.94mm (Marks, 1991:178). The Shaqadud crescents slightly differed from those of Uganda in terms of measurements where the latter had a mean length of 23.8 mm and a breadth of 11mm. These indicated an early Neolithic period. It was a Neolithic tendency to haft crescents on wood or bone to make specified tools. The purpose of these specified tools was harvesting cereals in the same way sickle blades came to be used later and to date, though at times they were used to hunt (Honneggar, 2006). Some crescents might have served as an arrow or fishing spear (Seitsonen, 2010).

Other geometric tool types besides the crescents such as trapezes and triangles identified at Kansyore Island, Nsongezi, and Island of Deserters also appeared at Shaqadud 150 km northeast of Khartoum (Marks and Mohammed-Ali, 1991) and Lokabulo (Robertshaw, 1982). The triangles and trapezes appear to be well-made but smaller than the lunates at Shaqadud. However in Kansyore where these appear in great proportions compared to the Island of Deserters they were slightly shorter in length but broader than the crescents. This is suggested by the mean length of triangles and trapezes which was 23.2 mm and 22.8 mm respectively while the mean breadth was 14.8mm and 20mm respectively. In comparison the mean length of triangles and trapezes from Shaqadud was 15.27 mm and 13.11mm respectively. Another backed tool type was the perforator that appeared with single or double side backing in Sudan. These were replicated with the existence of straight-backed pieces on the Ugandan side of the Kagera.

The examination of core types revealed the dominance of platform cores, though bipolar, amorphous, and intermediate cores obtained too in Uganda. Similarly in Sorourab 1 single cortex cores and opposed platform, discoidal and opposite (adjacent) platform cores were in use (Mohammed-Ali, 1984). This also implies that even in Sudan at Sorourab 1 platform cores were manufactured. On the contrary, the Lokabulo lithic industry in South Sudan included cores with prepared platforms like those at the Island of Deserters in Uganda.

Another tool type worth according comparison was the denticulate. As Marks (1991) states that denticulates are not merely poorly-made scrapers or discontinuously retouched and used flakes, this study also regards them similarly which is why they are not considered scrapers. The current research did not consider denticulates as scrapers despite being aware that they can often and do occur on almost any blank form, from fragments of blades to large flakes, a view supported by Marks (1991:183). Denticulates were also among the best-made and prevalent at Shaqadud and appeared at Sorourab 1, while at Kansyore and Island of Deserters, denticulates were either straight or circular. In a similar manner, notches were viewed as products of intentional human activity and not a result of human presence that may cause unintentional notches. This was confirmed by the fact that, like at Shaqadud cave, at Kansyore Island where these occur in great proportions there was little indication of human occupation that would have caused unintentional notches.

Affinity was also identified in the frequency of some tool types, for example the fewer occurrences of becs. Even Marks (1991:183) noted that becs were very rare and probably not intentionally produced in Sudan. But in spite of that they are typical in the sense that they conform to the definitions. The rarity of becs was also clear from the lithic tool assemblage obtained from Kansyore Island and the Island of Deserters where 11 becs were obtained out of 1,705 shaped tools. Still, though *outils écaillés* are the most pronounced retouched tools resulting from bipolar reduction they had a low percentage (0.7%) in the assemblage which indicated that, they were occasionally used at Kansyore where they appeared. On the contrary, despite the mention of the use of the bipolar technology in the Khartoum Neolithic the *outils écailles* do not feature among the tool types identified at Shaqadud or Sorourab 1.

Affinity also existed in terms of the lithic raw material utilised. The major lithic raw material utilised in the south of the Upper Nile catchment areas was almost exclusively quartz (8841) followed by quartzite (545), basalt (150), gneiss (71), aplite dyke (7), and chert (1) respectively. Apart from chert the rest of the raw materials are locally available, especially from the Kagera river that probably received basalt pebbles from the volcanic rocks of neighbouring Rwanda. The dominance of quartz in the LSA industry of East Africa has been reported elsewhere (Kessy, 2005); hence consistency in intra-assemblage distribution of raw material types may exhibit resource proximity and quartz forming the bulk of the lithic assemblage affirms its ubiquitous presence (Marks and Mohammed-Ali, 1991b).

In a related development the use of quartz as a raw material in the Khartoum Neolithic in Lokabulo and Itohom was reported by Robertshaw (1982). Other raw material types such as quartzite and chert that appeared in the Shaqadud assemblage were also identified in the Ugandan lithic industry considered herein. Still in Sudan at the Jebel Kathangor ash mound despite having a sparse microlithic industry, chert was the dominant raw material (Kleppe, 1982) and yet only a single specimen was identified at the Island of Deserters in Uganda. On the other hand, raw materials like rhyolite, agates, fossil wood, ferrocrete and sandstone that appeared in Khartoum Neolithic sites were not evident in the south Upper Nile catchment areas (Uganda).

Another area where affinity was identified was in the use of specialised raw materials for particular lithic artefacts. For instance, quartz was for mainly making microliths and rhyolite for large tools at Sorourab1 (Mohammed-Ali, 1984) and still while quartz was used for lunates it was rare for scrapers that were mainly on rhyolite and basalt at Shaqadud in the north.

Similarly in Uganda, quartz was for mainly microliths yet quartzite was for larger tools in the southern part of the Upper Nile catchment areas. For instance, all the grinding stones analysed from Uganda in this work were made on quartzite yet basalt was used for most of the *levallois* flakes. The choice of certain raw materials for specific tool types may imply they were either not desirable or obtained where distance from the source is one of the possible reasons though cannot single handedly explain it (Marks and Mohammed-Ali, 1991b). This was because the percentage of rhyolite correlated poorly with its total presence in the Shaqadud tool assemblage which had almost no rhyolite tools despite being the same distance away from the 6th Cataract as are Kadero 1 South and Zakyab. The raw materials seemed to be abundant as in the case of the Ugandan sites where cores were rarely exhausted as similarly reported from Sorourab 1 by Mohammed-Ali (1984).

However, some slight differences were identified in lithic artefact types in the Upper Nile catchment areas. For instance at Shaheinab a wide range of stone implements were in use such as borers, flaked and ground gouges and axe heads, small ochre grinders, rare mace heads, infrequent saddle querns, harpoons, chisels, needles and bone, stone axe heads and fish hooks (Krzyzaniak, 1978). This means that lithic artefacts such as disk mace heads of sand stone, grooved fishing line sinkers, ochre grinders, and cylindrical stone rubbers for making shell fish hooks for working ivory and bone did not feature in the Nsongezi-Kansyore toolkit.

While the most common Stone Age tools in the Khartoum Neolithic were the polished gouge probably for making dugout canoes; bone and stone axes used as scrapers; and fishing and hacking tools, it was not the case in Uganda. Among the bone axes, the most important was the barbed bone harpoon, with at least three barbs, sandstone rubbers, scrapers, trihedrals and borers (Arkell, 1949b) which was identified at several Khartoum Neolithic sites but not in Uganda.

Lithic technology also had aspects of cultural affinity in the Upper Nile catchment areas. The toolmakers majorly employed the techniques of direct percussion in the southern part of the Upper Nile catchment areas. This involved using both hard and soft hammer techniques. The presence of bipolar flakes and *outils écaillés* exhibited use of the direct percussion technique especially at Kansyore Island. Kansyore Island did not differ from other sites in Africa where the bipolar reduction strategy is evident (Muwonge, 2009) as in all the LSA sites of East Africa. Whereas direct percussion was used in the process of producing flakes, pressure flaking was most preferable for the production of retouched tools. This was evident through the numerous shaped tools which included geometrics, scrapers, points, becs, discoid and burins in the stone assemblage. In comparison, Shaqadud had a bipolar core reduction strategy as the dominant technology in the cave (Marks *et al*, 1985).

Further cultural correlations could be identified from the core reduction strategies. Marks (1991) reported the use of the platform core reduction strategy that yielded single and opposed platform cores. Secondly is the bipolar or *sur enclume* technology that resulted in bipolar cores and *outils écaillés*.

The Island of Deserters exhibited use of the *levallois* technology. This is a MSA attribute where stone technology was no longer a matter of knocking flakes off a core but it involved a more complex technique of preparing the core by precise flaking to a required shape and size and then finally striking off the finished tool (Sutton 1981:473). The *levallois* technology though may have started as an Acheulian flaking technique was a technique that eventually formed the most characteristic feature of many flake industries of the MSA (O'Brien, 1966: 207). However since the study was restricted to a comparison of the Neolithic aspects, the discussion of the MSA will stop at that.

It should be noted that technological similarities between the southern and northern part of the Upper Nile catchment areas were not restricted to stone artefacts since Lokabulo tradition had similarities with the south that encompassed at least subsistence, dating (Robertshaw, 1982) and pottery.

7.3 Pottery

A comparison of pottery showed that cultural affinity existed in terms of pottery decoration, form and in some instances the fabric. The decorative shared attributes dealt with here include decoration elements, instruments, and placement.

The first attribute in decoration was its placement. This involved the examination of the position of the decoration to check whether it was on the interior or exterior part of the vessel. This revealed that the southern Upper Nile catchment potters preferred decorating the exterior. Kansyore pottery exhibited exterior decoration especially on the body and at times covering the entire vessel. Internal decoration though not so common on Kansyore pottery was identified (Chapman, 1967) which correlated with the Itohom pottery. The vessel bodies for Kansyore pottery were preferred for decoration compared to other vessel parts. This may be because the Kansyore potsherds at times had tapered rims that did not have enough space for decoration on the rim and since no complete vessel was obtained it was not clear as to whether the decoration was placed on the bases as the dimple based potters did. Internal decoration identified in Kansyore pottery was also identified from two sherds from Itohom in Southern Sudan.

Comparable internal decoration on the rim was also identified on Khartoum Neolithic (Arkell, 1949: Plate 71). For example Kansyore Types I and II can be compared to Arkell's Plate 71, while Kansyore Type III with Arkell's Plate 79.3. Kansyore Type III can yet be compared with Plates 31 and 32 of Arkell (1953) and Kansyore Type IV with plate 38 of the same book (Refer to Chapman, 1967 for the Types). This likeness is partly due to the use of similar tools in decoration, in particular the *Etheria elliptica* shells, though this did not explain the similar rims and base (Chapman, 1967).

Affinity was also identified in terms of vessel form, also taken as vessel shape by Sheppard (1963). Following analysis of the various forms or parts that constitute the structure of a vessel, i.e. the rim, neck, and shoulder profiles, vessel forms were determined. The use of vessel parts to determine the vessel form was based on Pikirayi (1993:121) and Pwiti (1996:81)'s view that isolation of vessel parts is crucial in defining shape profiles on the basis of vessel contour. Therefore, Pikirayi's (1993) model was employed in determining vessel forms. Two broad vessel forms were identified that were pots and bowls. The two terms, as Pikirayi (1993:122) notes, are not employed from a functional point of view but in reference to the general vessel contours or shape form.

Basing on this model, the research concluded that the Upper Nile vessels were mainly small-sized bowls that were unrestricted open or restricted and hemispherical bowls with the rare occurrence of a single short-necked pot. Similarly in south-eastern Sudan, Robertshaw (1982) identified restricted mouthed pots. These vessels had tapered, flat/squared, slightly out-turned, slightly flayered and upturned rim profiles that showed that these were medium vessels probably used as household utensils. The rims of Esh Shaheinab vessels also had flattened tops (Arkell, 1949b). Similarity of both Kansyore ware and the Early Sudan pottery could be viewed in terms of straight tapering rims: Arkell (1949a) Plate 74 (Chapman, 1967:177). However, the Kansyore polygonal bowls did not appear among Lokabulo pottery (Robertshaw, 1982).

Cultural affirnity also existed when pottery decoration was examined. The research identified 59 Kansyore decoration motifs. These were characterised by dots, lines, and dashes. The motifs appeared with surfaces that are intricately decorated characterised by horizontal and vertical bands of impressed dots, walked punctates, comb impressions and comb stamps. The horizontal and vertical dotted bands are usually interlocked though at times appeared oblique or diagonal. The banded motifs appeared with either single bands, widely-spaced bands or narrowly-spaced bands.

The few occurrences of zigzag showed that these were either single-lined or several zigzags and at times banded by horizontal incisions. In cases of decoration on the vessel interior this was on the rim and appeared as marks left following smoothing of the vessel. The dots were diverse as the diversity of the combs. Therefore some of the dots on the Kansyore vessels were round while others were circular, rectangular, triangular or V-shaped. In one incident the decoration was identified as the dotted zigzag type that is common on Khartoum Neolithic pottery. On the other hand, the assemblage from the type site of Esh-Shaheinab decorations were made of impressed varieties of dots, triangles, straight lines, Vs and zigzags in various combinations or alone.

This work also identified wavyline pottery at Kansyore Island which showed links with the Khartoum Mesolithic. It should be noted that, though the wavy-line pottery is well-known from Sudan (Arkell, 1972) it had a single excavated occurrence in the Lake Turkana Basin (Bartheleme, 1977) just like at Kansyore Island.

In comparison with the pottery from the Khartoum type site at Shaheinab, dotted wavy-line ware was usually decorated with a pattern of 5 or 6 wavy lines on which dots have been superimposed, alternating with 5 or 6 straight lines of dots (Arkell, 1949b). In the view of Robertshaw (1982:92) as earlier stated the Lokabulo pottery tradition shared decoration modes with Kansyore pottery. The shared decoration modes included alternating vertical and horizontal panels of impressions and alternating bands of vertical and horizontal impressions as well as presence of circular motifs (Figure 7.1). Despite such similarities Kansyore and Lokabulo pottery had differences; for instance, Lokabulo vessels with deep horizontal incisions did not appear on Kansyore pottery (Robertshaw, 1982:92).

Plates 7.2, 7.3 and 7.4 show some of the shared decoration motifs. A comparison between Kansyore pottery initially from Gogo Falls and the Lokabulo tradition show similar patterns of dots that are interlocked (refer to Robertshaw, 1982:92 in numbers 3, 9, 11, 12, 14); round, (refer to Robertshaw, 1982:92 number 13); or horizontal (refer to Robertshaw, 1982:92 number 1, 5, 10). Horizontal straight double-dotted bands (refer to Mohammed-Ali, 1991:77 item-o and Plate 7.1) also show similarity. These were executed in what at times is referred to as 'fern branch' style in Khartoum Neolithic pottery. The nature of dots in all examples presented by Mohammed-Ali (1991:77) show similarity with Plate 7.2 of the ovalish impressed dots but only differ in the manner in which they were executed where some are interlocked horizontal and oblique, such as those presented by Mohammed-Ali (1991:77) as (i) and (f) and Plate 7.3:4 in this work.

Similarity was also witnessed from the material illustrated by Mohammed-Ali (1991:73) that showed affinity with my Plate 7.3 and one potsherd from the Khartoum Neolithic sites at Um Direiwa in Haaland (1992:56) and a dotted zigzag potsherd from Jebel Tukyi adapted from David *et al* (1981) by Halaand (1992:56). The dotted zigzag was evident in the Shaqadud assemblage and it was what Hays (1975) regarded as a wolf tooth for the Khartoum Neolithic which is similar to Plate 7.5.

Plate 7.1: Kansyore Banded Motifs

Key: Banded Straight Paired Lines (4) and Horizontal Crescents and Vertical Double Dots (5).

Plate 7.2: Kansyore Banded Motifs

Key: Alternative Pivoting (4, 7), Rocker Stamping (1-3), and Impression (8-10), Alternating Vertical and Horizontal Bands of Stippled Lines or Dashes (11)

Plate 7.3: Kansyore Dotted lines

Key: Interlocked Vertical and Horizontal Dotted Lines (1-3) and Rocked Horizontal Vertical and Horizontal Line (4), Impressed Vertical Dotted Lines (5) and Impressed Horizontal Dotted Lines (6-8)

Plate 7.4: Rows of Horizontal Dotted and Impressed Lines

Plate 7.5: Dotted Zig Zag Lines

Robertshaw (1982) rightly summed up the decoration of Kansyore pottery in relation to the Khartoum Neolithic pottery. Although the Lokabulo pottery was highly fragmented, decoration modes shared with Kansyore ceramics included; alternating vertical and horizontal panels of impression as well as presence of circular motifs (Collet and Robertshaw, 1980). At the type site of Shaheinab, Arkell (1949b) noted that the pottery was characterised by dotted wavy lines where dots alternate after every five to six lines. Though the pottery was un-burnished the pattern was impressed (Arkell, 1949b). Yet among the Khartoum variants the ceramics had dotted wavy lines and decorated below the rim with fingernail impressions and punctate designs (Shiner, 1968). Besides that they shared the dotted zigzag (Plate 7.5), the horizontal dotted lines (Plate 7.4), horizontal and vertical interlocked dotted lines (refer to Robertshaw, 1982:92), and banded motifs (Plates 7.1).

Affinity in decoration techniques was initially identified by Chapman (1967) who identified some of the shared attributes between Kansyore pottery and Khartoum Neolithic pottery in terms of the use of a common decoration instrument. The common decorating instrument in the view of Arkell (1949) was the spine of a catfish (*synodontis*). Yet Dale (2007) held that shells that were used as tools for decoration, especially the aspatharia shell was used for executing the straight and serrated edges.

The shared decoration techniques include rocker stamping, alternative pivoting and simple impression (Dale, 2007:184) basing on Caneva (1988)'s typology for El Geili in addition to that of Collet and Robertshaw (1980) which is the *chaine operatoire*. In the current study the decoration techniques identified were stamping that was either comb stamping (33.2%) or rocker stamping (21.5%); impression, and incision (14.8%).

(a) Rocker Stamping

Rocker stamp may occur as a single motif or varying from widely spaced to continuous zigzag to very fine overlapping ones (Robbins, 1977). For instance Chapman (1967) noted that her Kansyore Type III at Kansyore Island was dominated by rock zigzag. The decoration implement used was either with a plain edge, evenly serrated or unevenly serrated. In the end this created decoration elements like dots, lines, dashes, and triangles. Rocker stamping thus uses a multi-toothed comb that is rocked from end to end and never leaves the surface producing rows of impressions in grid like panels (Dale, 2007:156) (Plate 7.3: 1-3). Alternate pivot stamping that involved use of a double-pronged implement that yields pairs of dots as decorative elements was regarded as part of the rocker stamping in this research (Plate 7.2: 4 & 7). In this technique, one used a two-pronged instrument as a tool that produced round impressions or dots in pairs of lines when it was rocked or pivoted across the clay body (Dale, 2007).

(b) Impressions

Kansyore pottery impressions are simple impressions (Dale, 2007:154), because they are executed using a stylus that creates decorative elements of single dots. The comb impression technique was the major decoration technique used in making the dotted line decorations for Kansyore pottery (Plate 7.2: 8-10). This technique was also found in Neolithic contexts from the North of Khartoum to the Lake Victoria areas (Robertshaw, 1982:92).

Similarly, Kansyore and Lokabulo pottery shared decoration techniques of walked punctates and rocked zigzag. In a related development, the Dhang Rial mound in southern Sudan had traces of a ceramic LSA characterised by rocker-stamped comb-impressed pottery (David, 1982). It should be noted that, the comb had a varying number of teeth, shape and spacing and could be applied in the clay body in a variety of ways creating different decorative results (Dale, 2007:166).The instrument such as a stylus was pressed into the clay body, lifted, pressed again and so on producing impressions of different shapes that may be round, square, oblong, herringbone, or finger nail shaped. The impressions could be cuneiform shaped like the Kansyore pottery from Lwala in Uganda (Kessy *etal*, 2011).

(c) Incisions

This entailed the use of a fine point identified as a fish spine (Arkell, 1949; Chapman, 1967). The incisions could be U-shaped or V-shaped grooves, horizontal, vertical, combination of horizontal and vertical grooved lines or incised lines. Though the shared decoration techniques included walked punctates and rocked zigzag, Kansyore and Lokabulo pottery differed in the use of impression and incision (Robertshaw, 1982). The common pottery at Jebel Kathangor associated with ceramic LSA had deep horizontal incisions or ribbing which were combined with bevels, decorated rims, lugs and handles. Some decoration modes of Jebel Kathangor pottery such as the deep incisions and bevels taken as grooves and bevels appeared in the channel ware and EIA pottery at Kansyore Island.

An analysis of the Kansyore pottery fabric revealed that the dominant colours were grey (51.6%), followed by brown (30.5%), and red-and-black (18.0%). Despite such colours the vessels were strong and appeared well-fired. They were tempered with sand, quartz, mica and in isolated cases of vegetal material and grog.

In terms of surface finishing while burnishing was rare in the Kansyore material, Esh-Shaheinab had both burnished and un-burnished dotted wavy-line ware with angular quartz grain inclusions (Dale, 2007). The burnished dotted wavy lines are a typological link between the Khartoum Mesolithic and Khartoum Neolithic (Arkell, 1949a, 1953). The surfaces of Kansyore pottery were mainly slipped (68%) and rarely burnished (2%) though others were smoothed.

Coiling was another common characteristic in the Upper Nile catchment areas. The vessel walls were thin (7.1 mm) and usually broke along the coil lines implying the use of the coiling technique in their manufacture of Kansyore pottery like in the Khartoum variant industry (Shiner,1968). In Sorourab coiling was also apparently the technique of manufacture yet thickness of the ceramics was 7-8mm, tempered with quartz, sand, mica, or infrequently vegetal material. The fabric was hard and well-fired, the pottery partly slipped and or smoothed.

7.4 Faunal Remains

The faunal remains included both bones and shells. The bones identified to specie were for both animals (12.1%) and fish (33.5%). This shows that the prehistoric peoples at Kansyore Island mainly depended on fishing. Fishing is evidenced from the several fish bones at Kansyore Island (1308) and a complete aqualithic layer that was obtained in Kansyore Trench 1. The Island of Deserters on the other hand had limited fishing (53) compared to Kansyore Island from. This implied that the Kansyore tradition was characterised by a fishing subsistence strategy.

On the contrary, in Shaqadud despite abundant fauna there was no evidence, faunal or otherwise that fishing was practiced (Robertshaw, 1982). Similarly in Kadero the most significant finds were domestic fauna (88.14%) compared to wild fauna (11.85%), but had no fish or remains of reptilia, amphibian, and molluscs (Kzyazaniak, 1978). The faunal remains act as living floors in the absence of food residues in the sites that contain stone tools they act as indicators of man's ways of life (Bishop and Posnansky, 1960). Some of the bones at Kansyore Island and the Island of Deserters had cut marks and yet the frequency of bone cut marks is a characteristic of MSA (Bushozi, 2011:64). However, the bones with cut marks appeared at Kansyore Island that is an LSA site with no other evidence for the MSA. This could probably imply that some MSA culture continued in the Neolithic and since the Island of Deserters had MSA characteristics on the mainland would imply that rivers did not hamper cultural interaction.

The several bone tools are another indicator of cultural affiliation. According to Aldred (1961:67) the bones could be used as needles in the Egyptian prehistoric period. The presence of secondary modifications on the bones such as cut marks, burning and breakage patterns can be used to reconstruct the culinary processing. In this case the burnt bones would suggest exposure to high heat probably due to roasting or at times burning of detached heads or singe hair from the skin before further processing. Therefore cut marks indicate the butchery patterns as well. Bone breakage may indicate habitual practices concerning butchery and extraction of bone nutrients. All in all, the culinary processing marks can help one to assess how fauna were utilised as human food (Gifford-Gonzalez, 2003). Besides food processing creating cut marks, in Siror, Dale (2007) identified weathering and gnawing. Another form of secondary modification was engraving in Kansyore faunal remains where some bones were flute-like as those from Siror (Kenya). The faunal remains identified were for mainly wild fauna such as warthog, buffalo, hippo, monkeys, and kob and in one case an avian bone while the fish bones were mainly for the barbus fish type.

At Lokabulo in southern Sudan the fauna also comprised only wild animals and bivalve molluscs that indicated that the LSA environment was more humid. Lokabulo like Kansyore did not yield domesticates and from the fauna remains it could be deduced that they hunted a wide range of species. The lack of domesticates in both Lokabulo and Kansyore sites has been attributed to the distribution of the tsetse fly by Robertshaw (1982). On the contrary, Itohom - still in southern Sudan - had no fauna remains at all (Robertshaw, 1982) while at Esh-Shaheinab remains of fish, reptiles, game mammals like porcupine, elephant, rhinoceros, hippopotamus, antelopes and domesticates were recognised (Peters, 1986). The faunal remains at Esh-Shaheinab indicated a mixed hunting-gathering-herding economy. But, unlike at Kansyore where fish bones were dominant, at Esh-Shaheinab they were few.

Shells were another part of the faunal remains from Kansyore Island. The Molluscan shell has proven to be a powerful tool in paleoenvironmental reconstruction of both local habitats and climate. Shell shape, species' ecology, and shell chemistry can all inform on local terrestrial and aquatic conditions, and regional hemispheric or global climate (Claassen, 1998:142). The species' ecology, shell shape and shell chemistry are the three main aspects of molluscs that are used to retrodict paleoenvironments around a site (Claassen, 1998:122). The shells were identified as belonging to both land (terrestrial) and water (aquatic) species. The species were mainly the *Limicolaria* and *Pila ovata* though *Edouardia* and *Burtoa* also featured in Uganda in this work. The presence of a varied molluscan assemblage indicated that during the Holocene high lake stands had shallow fresh water throughout this area (Harvey and Grove, 1982). The presence of freshwater shells indicated that during the LSA occupation, effective participation must have been more or less seasonal.

The *Limicolaria* shells also reported in several sites in Sudan including the type site Shaheinab and Sorourab 1 that had *Limicolaria caillandi* and *Burtoa nilotica* among others, whose presence suggested the existence of a better climate then in Sudan than that of today (Mohammed-Ali, 1984), were also obtained from Kansyore Island. In this case we see creatures that adapted to a similar environment that couldn't be limited by the water body hence cultural interaction did not necessitate people to migrate for such creatures could move freely along the Nile which would account for their presence in the different parts of the Upper Nile catchment areas.

Despite the evidence of fishing at the Ugandan sites the usual fishing gear of bone harpoons and net sinkers was not obtained just like at Lokabulo in southern Sudan. A similar situation was identified in the study of fishing at the junction of the Nile and Atbara where, though evidence of fishing equipment was limited to fragments of bone points, the spectrum and size distribution of fish implied a more diversified set of fishing gear including nets and rafts (Peters *et al* 1993; Peters, 1991). It should be noted that fishing can be carried out using a number of implements but archaeological evidence is limited for the reconstruction of the traditional fishing equipments that were constructed from grass, fibres, reeds or wood and at times bare hands could be used (Peters, 1991:10). This leaves the possibility of the people of that time having fished using some of these traditional methods none of which are preserved under normal conditions, or using crescents as fishing spears in the studied sites in the south. In East Africa however harpoons were obtained from the Lake Edward area (Sutton, 1974) and in the Turkana area (Barthelme, 1977).

The appearance of shellfish hooks and barbed bone harpoons showed dependence on fishing but with improved techniques since barbed harpoons have been obtained from a number of Neolithic sites in Sudan including the type site Esh Shaheinab (Arkell, 1949b). The evidence for the exploitation of aquatic resources at Lokabulo are the bivalve shells, at Itohom were the crocodile bones yet at Kansyore sites studied herein were fish bones and shells. These would imply a fisher-hunter strategy. According to Robertshaw (1982), therefore the Lokabulo was a variant of the aquatic techno-complex that adapted to savannah conditions and yet the concept of an aquatic subsistence and settlement system within the Sudanese region is open to question and it is best to disassociate it from the Lokabulo tradition. This is because at Shaqadud in Butana despite the abundance of faunal remains there was no evidence of fishing hence the emphasis on fishing may be misplaced.

Human remains were represented by a single tooth and fragments of a skull. However, although human remains are common on Kansyore sites they are represented by isolated bones like in Gogo Falls, Kanjera, Kansyore Island, Nyangoma, Ugunja 1 and 2, Usenge, Wadh Lango and White Rock (Prendergast, 2008). This is contrary to the Sudan Neolithic sites where some were located in graveyards. No wonder Arkell (1949) according to Haaland (2009) likened pots to pillows since they appeared beneath heads of skeletons.

7.5 Chronology

A discussion of the chronological aspects was vital to review the theories of the origin of the Khartoum Neolithic tradition and its affinity with the Kansyore tradition. This included the examination of the stratigraphic layering of the material, the stratigraphic association of artefacts for relative and absolute dating from the carbon14 samples derived from the different cultural layers. This is because to clear out the issue of Kansyore connections with the north there is a need to address origin (Prendergast, 2008) which concerns dating. Most of the dates are derived from the carbon-14 dating method based on the principle of association. Dating is crucial to sort out artefact mixture and any hiatus in a given tradition. To examine if there was interaction in the Upper Nile catchment there was need to come up with clear sequences. It is this that can assist to identify cultural materials that belong to the same traditions, variants and those that differ. Kansyore dates are full of dates attributed to wrong contexts, due to contamination or intrusion of samples or due to dates attributed to wrong contexts that are simply too old or too recent (Chami, 2006:94).

The use of relative dating has been carefully checked with both the existing dates of the local sequences and the new radio carbon results. The research used four dates that were obtained from different sites and Trenches. The small chunks of charcoal collected from the different levels and units made it unlikely that all would be from the same trunk of a tree (Chami, 1994). The same applied to the bone samples since they were from different levels it was unlikely that they were from the same animal. Contamination and poor handling was prevented by not touching the samples and wrapping them in aluminium foil and using tweezers to clean them before sending them to the laboratories.

7.6 Stratigraphy

An examination of the Kansyore stratigraphy showed a multi component site characterized by mixing of ceramic traditions. There were mainly two major occupation phases of Kansyore and Iron Age. The Iron Age entailed both the Early Iron Age and the Late Iron Age. Besides that there was a transitional period in between the Iron Age and the Kansyore period characterised by channel ware. However, what should be noted is that for most of the trenches there was the coexistence of the Early Iron Age and the Kansyore material. In this case sometimes the Kansyore period appears to have persisted to the late period and where it was overlain by Urewe it was just by a few levels. In all trenches it is clear that the appearance of pottery does not lead to a reduction of lithics, instead at times even the lithics increase in the ceramic levels. This implies that the inhabitants did not abandon use of stone with the adoption of ceramics, meaning that there was coexistence of stone and ceramic users. The Island of Deserters had MSA, LSA, and Iron Age occupation periods. Since the study was restricted to the Neolithic, the MSA material will not be discussed.

A look at the stratigraphic layering showed the coexistence of Urewe/EIA and Kansyore cultural material. Therefore, despite the contemporaneity of the material it should not be dismissed as disturbance or shouldn't be taken that the Kansyore might have been a variant of the EIA but this implies people of the different time periods stayed in one place and as they carried out their activities the materials mixed up and in the same way stone use persisted in the ceramic period, the same happened with the EIA and Kansyore coexisting. Therefore the stratigraphic sequence of the artefacts from the three sites should begin with Kansyore at the bottom followed by Channel, EIW and LIA traditions respectively.

A similar situation was identified in Southern Sudan at Jebel Tukyi rock shelter that contained a mixture of Ceramic LSA and Iron Age material that David (1982:51) attributed to natural depositional processes and animal and human disturbances. This showed that the LSA/IA interface could not be established on the basis of the chronology of the Kansyore sequence obtained but is still subject to future research.

Dating has been a key problem for the Kansyore pottery tradition which in turn generates problems of sequence. Despite attempts on the Tanzanian coast by Chami (2006) the interior of Africa still has a problem of dating

(Table 7.1). For instance the Lokabulo tradition at the time of its comparison with Kansyore pottery by Robertshaw (1982) was dated from about 2000 BC-AD 1000 yet a single date existed of 690 BC for Kansyore in the Lake Victoria region (Soper and Golden, 1969). Table 7.1 shows an attempt to establish a comparative sequence of East Africa and the Middle Nile. While this is a welcome move it shows that the Kansyore Type 1 was still blank and questionable (Table 7.1). Despite the suggestion of a Kansyore Type 2 being contemporaneous with the Khartoum Mesolithic, the evidence from the current study suggests that the Kansyore tradition belonged to the Khartoum Neolithic due to dating gaps where the Khartoum Mesolithic's oldest date was 9500 BP (Haaland, 2009) and yet the Kansyore dates are up to 6000 BP (Prendergast, 2008, 2010) despite the early date from Luanda of 8240±245 BP (Robertshaw et al, 1983). Haaland (2009) dated the Khartoum Neolithic to 6000 BP yet Sadiq (2009) dated Neolithic settlements in the Nile valley at 6800 BP which would possibly rhyme with the Kansyore dates.

Victoria/North Uganda/Turkana/Rift valley	Middle Nile
Early Iron Age	Late Neolithic
Turkwell/Akira	Late Neolithic
Narosura	Late Neolithic
Nderit/Ileret	Neolithic
Kansyore Type 1	?
Kansyore Type 2	Khartoum Mesolithic

Table 7.1: Ancient Pottery Sequence Sequence for Eastern, Central, / Southern Africa and Middle Nile; Adapted from Chami: 2006

Dating therefore is a crucial aspect in trying to establish connections in the Nile catchment. This is because in Egypt, following the work of Sir Flinders Petrie, almost all potsherds could be dated while half the sherds in Anglo-Egyptian Sudan can be dated. In the A-E Sudan borders of French Equatorial Africa, Belgian Congo, Uganda, Kenya, and Abyssinia, it is by getting connections with pottery that has been dated in the Sudan that pre-historians in those countries will be able to work out and date the pottery cultures of these countries (Arkell, 1950:61). Kansyore earlier on was dated ranging from 4000 BC to 500 AD which received critics from scholars like Mehlman (1977), Collet and Robertshaw (1980), Bower and Nelson (1978), Kwekason and Chami (2003) and Chami (2006) who suggested that the lengthy dating was indicative of either a very conservative tradition or large dating errors. Collet and Robertshaw (1980:139) gave a third possibility for the long dating of Kansyore that some of the assemblages associated with Kansyore units may be belonging to different units so they require sorting to generate a complete cultural sequence that will clearly tell the variants of Kansyore. This means that the Kansyore wares are still poorly dated and imperfectly characterised (Bower *et al*, 1977:139). On the contrary the wide range of dates and geographical locations associated with early ceramics show that pottery first emerged in a variety of social and economic contexts (Dale, 2007).

The date for Kansyore from Nyang'oma was in the middle of the first millennium B.C (Soper and Golden, 1969; N-493, 2640±120 B.P) while the date of 2315±185 B.P (GX-1100) was from Raging in the Seme Location (Gabel, 1969). However, the pottery from the latter site was not well described and the stratigraphy was unclear (Collet and Robertshaw, 1980:141; (Prendergast, 2008:38). The Kansyore dates (Refer to Dale, 2007:23 for a table showing the dates of Kansyore sites in East Africa) show long dating periods. The long dating may be attributed to interaction of hunter-gatherers and food producers (Dale, 2007). The dating of Kansyore in south eastern Sudan (4000-2000 B.P) might mean that the culture spread out of East Africa rather than into it (Bower, 1991:67).

The dates from Mumba-Höhle were much earlier being dated to the third Millennium B.C (Mehlman, 1989; UCLA-1913, 4860±100 B.P., FRA-1, 4890±70 B.P). The dates of the Kansyore levels at Nasera were of a similar order, 4720±150B.P, and 5400±150 B.P (Mehlman; 1977, 1989). The date for Kansyore pottery from Lukenya Hill (Gv Jm14) was in the first millennium AD (Gramly, 1975) but to Collet and Robertshaw (1980) this material did not belong to either Kansyore or Nderit traditions and was thus irrelevant. At Salasun, Kansyore was stratified above Nderit and below Narosura in association with a carbon date of 2680 B.P ± 150 (GX-4421) (Bower et al 1977:139). The Kansyore from Salasun had a number of dates, two of which are 6595 B.P ± 235 (GX-4469/A) and 7225 B.P ± ??(GX-4422/A) (Prendergast, 2008; Bower and Nelson, 1978). This means that these latter dates are earlier than dates from Mumba-Hohle. These Salasun dates indicate that Kansyore pottery was unlikely to be present in that assemblage (Collet and Robertshaw, 1980:142). The Gamble cave date offered by Leakey was 10,000 BC which might be the oldest date for pottery suggesting that pottery making was invented in Africa and East Africa in particular despite views by Arkell (1953) about its improbability.

Therefore timing is a big question with Kansyore dates covering nearly 6000 years with the earliest dates from Luanda (8240±245 BP/ bone apatite/GX-8743, calibrated to 7819-6590 cal BC and the latest dates from Wadh Lang'o (1989±28BP (OxA-14506) cal. AD 1-120 (Dale and Ashley, 2010; Ashley, 2005) and Mumba (1843±60 BP: AA699111) cal. AD 28-335 (Prendergast et al 2007). This could suggest that the origin of the Kansyore pottery tradition was Nyanza in Kenya or it may be because research on Kansyore has concentrated in Kenya and better dates could be obtained in future (Refer to Dale, 2007:23 for detailed dates of published Kansyore sites).

A look at the Table presented by Dale (2007:23) shows that no dates were available for Kansyore Island the type site. In the current research, the datable materials obtained were charcoal and bones. For instance the Island of Deserters yielded 22 while Kansyore Island had 4 charcoal samples. In the entire research, 6 samples were analysed from the four sites excavated (Table 7.2). The first four samples in Table 7.2 were collected from Chobe and Kikubamitwe in levels that were associated with purely Iron Age material therefore these would not form part of the current discussion but will be considered in future publications. That means the current discussion will concentrate on the two samples from Kansyore Island. It should be noted that both samples were bones where all isotope values were measured on bone gelatine. The use of bones was due to the fact that no charcoal samples were obtained in these levels and as noted earlier charcoal samples were scarce in Kansyore with 4 samples compared to the Island of Deserters that had 22 samples.

Site	Lab. Number	Level depth	Associated decoration	C14 age BP
Chobe	Ua-41115	80-90 cm	zigzag/microliths	436 ±30
Chobe	Ua-41116	70-75 cm	zigzag	391±30
Kikubamitwe	Ua-41117	70-80 cm	roulette	799±31
Kikubamitwe	Ua-41118	40-50 cm	channels/grooves	924±30
Kansyore	WK-31384	65-70 cm	roulette	2710±41 BP
Kansyore	WK-31383	50-55 cm	wavy-lines	1671±44 BP

Table 7.2: Carbon 14 Results

The first date obtained from Trench 2Ai from a herbivore tooth was 2710±41 BP (WK-31384) associated with roulette that was regarded as Neolithic and hence appeared under the Kansyore pottery. In association still were Urewe pottery and microliths. The second date of 1671± 44 BP (WK-31383) was obtained in a layer associated with wavy line pottery in Trench 2B in association was Urewe pottery and lithics. These dates suggest that despite Kansyore Island being the type site for the Kansyore pottery it does not seem to be the earliest place for making this pottery tradition. The dates though rhyme with dates from Wadh Lang'o (1989 ±28 BP OxA-14506 Cal AD 1 - 120) that had been regarded as the youngest Kansyore pottery dates (Dale and Ashley, 2010; Ashley, 2010) and Mumba (1843 ±60 BP: AA699111) cal. AD 28-355 (Prendergast *etal*. 2007). Another implication from the date associated with roulette was that roulette started in the Neolithic period. It should be noted that Kansyore ware existed at Kansyore Island though the dates are still problematic (Soper and Golden, 1969; Collet and Robertshaw, 1980).

According to Chapman (1967) the site of Esh- Shaheinab, the type site of Khartoum Neolithic was dated around 3300 B.C and yet other Neolithic sites were earlier. This means that single dates are almost useless at the level of temporal resolution required (±50 years) (Fekri, 1986:96).

Initially the Khartoum Neolithic was dated from its type-site locality Shaheinab, but there are other dates from Umm Direiwa, El-Ghaba, Islang, Kadero, Zakiab, Nofalab, Rabak, Guli, Shaqadud, and El-Kadada some of which are older than those from Shaheinab. Es- Shaheinab was first dated by Libby (1955) with two dates of c-754 and c-753 which had a large standard error (Hays, 1975; 90). Two other dates were obtained by Haaland of T-3222 and T-3223. The average of the four dates of Esh-Shaheinab was 4160 ± 100 BC and 3200 BC-2800 BC (Close, 1988). Peters (1986) dated Esh-Shaheinab at 6000-5000 BP. This means that Shaheinab is coeval with the Badarian and older than Gerzean showing that there is no chronological justification to assume that domestication was introduced into Sudan from Egypt in the Gerzian period hence no cultural interaction directed to the north.

Umm Dereiwa (Haaland, 1979) on average was 4465-3185 BC from its initial three dates. El Ghaba was assigned to the Khartoum Neolithic by Geus (1982,1983,1984) cited by Hays (1975), from four dates whose average was 4500-3800 BC; El-Ushara was dated 4000 ±105 BC, the fishing camp of Islang Island was dated 4745 ±140 BC that meant it could be contemporaneous with Umm Dereiwa and El Ghaba. The oldest level at Rabak (Kosti) 200 km south of Khartoum was 6020 ± 130 B.P (T-5134) calibrated to 3215 ± 135 B.C. This means the latter was older than Kadero I but as old as El Ghaba, Kadero II and I were dated by Krzyaniak (1982) whereby Kadero I southern midden was 4015 ± 85 B.C. while the northern midden was 4330 ± 95 B.C. and Kadero II was 4220 ± 140 B.C. The average of the two dates from Zakyab was 4345 ± 125 BC (Haaland, 1978, 1981), Nofalab north of Omurduman was dated by El Anwar, (1981), and the average of the two dates was 4230 ± 130 BC while Guli was dated by Adamson *et al* (1974) at 4350 ± 200 BC. Shaqadud in Butana had one date equivalent to the Khartoum Neolithic of 4460 ± 195 BC (SMU-1134) (Marks *et al* 1982). El Khadada had five dates with one too old compared to the four (5170 ± 110 BP) therefore the average of the four dates was 3530 ± 60 BC. Therefore the dates in the southern part of the Upper Nile catchment were younger compared to the North.

7.7 Aquatic Civilization

The aquatic civilization refers to the late Palaeolithic assemblages that are also referred to as the Mesolithic, Neolithic of Capsian Tradition, Neolithic of Sudanese Tradition, Sahara Sudanese Neolithic, aqualithic, and ceramic Late Stone Age (LSA) (Holl, 2005). The aquatic civilisation was Sutton's

(1974, 1977) model to account for the distributional patterns of Early Holocene archaeological sites. It has also been viewed as an attempt to frame a robust and parsimonious explanation for a series of events that led to the explanation of the wetland lifestyle. According to Sutton (1977:321), the aqualithic civilisation characterised the wet period of 5000 to 10,000 years ago which he attributed to African origin. The aquatic civilisation spread across eastern and northern Africa during the wetter climatic conditions of the early mid Holocene (Nicoll, 2004). The aquatic way of life is known from the archaeological sites in the Saharan highlands and southern fringe of the upper Niger, through the Chad basin to the Middle Nile and southwards as far as the East African Rift valley and the equator (Sutton, 1981: 481-2) (Also refer to the map showing the geographical distribution of the aquatic in Haaland, 1992) and in the western rift, it has been recognised at Isangho on the Zaire shore of Lake Edward (Rutanzige). The evidence from Ishango suggests that the adaptation may have developed in the late Pleistocene and diffused to other regions (Nicoll, 2004). This implied a south-north diffusion of cultural developments. At Ishango the first mathematical artefact of a bone harpoon with mathematical base 12 and sub bases was identified. In the eastern rift aqualithic sites are found along the ancient highland shorelines of Lakes Turkana and Nakuru with the most important site being Gamble cave lying by Lake Nakuru whose aqualithic layer was dated 6000 B.P. by Leakey in the 1920's (Sutton, 1981:482). Ti-n-Torah in the Libyan part of the Sahara had a date of 9300 B.P (Haaland, 1992) while Talalegal in the Niger was dated 9500 BP.

The aquatic tradition was characterised by fish-bones and mollusc shells and bones of reed rats and turtles, and sometimes for crocodiles and hippos, which provide economic insights (Haaland, 1992). The aquatic resources were made into liquid foods (porridge) which had an impact on the kind of vessels made. This explains the diversity of the pottery types; variety of small vessels such as cups probably used to serve liquid foods and drinks which were related to social differentiation where drinking was part of social display (Krzyzaniak, 2004 cited by Haaland, 1992). Therefore the LSA of central Sudan consisted of two components the Early Khartoum/Khartoum Mesolithic and the central Sudanese Neolithic or Shaheinab Neolithic/Khartoum Neolithic and the LSA assemblage of the former was described as the aquatic way of life (Krzyzaniak, 1978:159).

Deducted from Arkell's (1949, 1953) modal sites, the specie composition indicates that they used nets and deep water fishing. This implies that they must have had boat technology and small disk-shaped pottery could have been used as net sinkers. In addition the bone harpoons were fixed to the ends of wooden spears with line attachments. These were used for catching fish and other aquatic animals either in boats or from the water's edge. LSA people have been regarded as highly specialised societies of hunters and fishermen who used barbed bone points for catching fish like at the Ishango fishing site on the mouth of the Semliki River and Lake Edward. The Ishango Negroid Skeleton is associated with cultural materials indicating an economy based on harpoon fishing dating to 9000-6500 B.C (Kessy, 2005:85). However from about 5000 years ago the effects of widespread drying out of the climate led to the drying and fall of lake levels which led to the decline of the economy based on harvesting aquatic resources (Sutton 1981: 483-4). On Kansyore Island, the numerous fish bones at the floor of Trench 1A (Plate 5.3) that was covered with fish bones and shells would suggest the aquatic civilisation. Similarly in Southern Sudan at Lokabulo, David (1982) identified what he termed as the aquatic techno-complex.

7.8 Red Ochre

Red ochre is any mineral substance that contains iron oxide, such as red haematite or brown goethite or yellow limonite. Like in Esh-Shaheinab red ochre was obtained from Kansyore Island and the Island of Deserters. It should be noted that red ochre could have been put to diverse uses and does not necessarily represent the direct outcome of specific functional or symbolic behaviours (Refkin, 2011). Its uses included as a pigment in symbolic contexts during the LSA and MSA and an ingredient for hide tanning; personal decoration, from the upper Palaeolithic it was known for cave paintings and ritual burial contexts, mundane or domestic uses derived from modern hunter-gathers that included; medication, food preservative, tanning hides, adhesive for hafting and insect repellent. In the south Nile catchment the available evidence suggests that red ochre was used in the decoration of pottery and for personal adornment. According to Arkell (1950:58), in an attempt to associate like with like, man associated the red colour of ochre stones with the blood seen when an animal is killed in the hunt. Since an animal lost its life with the loss of its blood, the painting of bodies with the red ochre would imply one would have a longer life, which has been carried on using red lipstick (Arkell, 1950:58).

The evidence from the comparative analysis shows that it is possible that some societies adopted use of pottery and the apparent Neolithic stone industries without developing a farming economy. This was derived from the lack of direct or indirect evidence of agriculture in Lokabulo in southern Sudan (David, 1982) and lack of domesticates in both the Kansyore sites examined in this work and at Lokabulo. Therefore technical developments especially adoption of pottery can define the Neolithic in an economy based on hunting and gathering. This is because the traditional view considered grinding and polishing of stone tools as criteria for the Neolithic simply based on technological and artistic grounds. Therefore as stated by Renfrew and Bahn (1998:543), the Neolithic was an old world chronological period characterised by the development of agriculture and an increasing emphasis on sedentism. This means it is a socio-economic development rather than a technological one. Therefore the absence of domesticates should not be used to rule out the presence of Neolithic cultures where evidence of sedentism existed.

7.9 Chapter Summary

The comparison of the Khartoum Neolithic, lithic assemblage and those in the southern part of the Upper Nile valley show that both had a microlithic flake industry in which blades did not feature prominently. The lunate was a common tool in the Upper Nile catchment though differences emerged in the way they were backed for instance in Sorourab like in the south they were well-backed. Similarities were identified in terms of lithic typology and technology. In ceramics the decoration, vessel shapes, inclusions tended to be similar with slight divergences in the appearance of the final products. The faunal remains, aqualithic civilisation, and use of red ochre all address the specific objective of the research as they show the nature of cultural and economic interaction in the Nile catchment areas. Despite the similarities, differences appear especially in the dates between the south and north Upper Nile catchment areas. The historical connections suggest that the Nile was not an end as attempts to discover its source suggest contacts between the north and the south.

CHAPTER 8

DISCUSSION

8.1 Introduction

The aim of this study was to examine cultural connections and affinity in the Upper Nile Catchment areas from 6000 to 1500 BP. This was therefore a comparative study examining data from Kansyore Island, Island of Deserters, and Khartoum Neolithic sites. The objective was to examine and compare cultural material from archaeological works.

8.2 Cultural affinity and correlations

Looking at archaeological materials and works from the two areas cultural affinity was demonstrated to exist. The cultural materials looked at were; pottery, lithics, and faunal remains. The existence of such affinity had earlier on been theorised by Chami (2006) who came up with a comparable sequence of ancient pottery sequences of eastern, central and southern Africa with that of the middle Nile (Table: 7.1). Similarly, Robertshaw (1982) identified similarity between Kansyore pottery and Lokabulo pottery in southern Sudan in terms of decoration, subsistence, and dating. Chapman (1967) worked at Kansyore Island and named pottery from the type site as Kansyore pottery that was identified as having similarity with Sudan pottery but was cautious on the relationship due to the long distance and differences in dates. The same pottery has been identified in several sites in East Africa all the way to southern Sudan.

Excavation work at Kansyore Island demonstrated a very credible archaeological stratigraphy which had a very clear cultural sequence; from above was roulette (LIA), underlain by Urewe (EIA) down to typical Kansyore ceramics. What is very clear is that still the cultural sequence below the layer of Kansyore in an undisturbed cultural context several potsherds of rouletting tradition were found that had nothing with the upper LIA rouletting tradition and had been either at the beginning of Kansyore or even before Kansyore. By that thinking therefore I am going for the first time to propose that the rouletting tradition existed at the beginning of or before the Kansyore period.

The charcoal sample collected in association with these rouletted potsherds was dated to 2710±41 BP (WK-31384). This was a major discovery of the research that challenges views that claim no rouletting had been identified in the East African Neolithic (Soper, 1985:148). The identification of Neolithic roulette also implies that there was no correlation between race/ethnicity and pottery traditions therefore it is no longer plausible to attribute Kansyore pottery to the Sahelians, Urewe to the Bantu speakers or roulette to the Luo speakers since the existence of roulette in the Neolithic meant that it was used much earlier than the Luo existence.

At this juncture I want to introduce the issue of wavy-line pottery. In my excavation at Kansyore Island in the Neolithic context, I recovered one clear wavy-line potsherd. This is a major discovery because this pottery has been identified with the Mesolithic tradition in the North. Therefore, it was not expected to be found in the Neolithic context of East Africa. Despite arguments by Chapman (1967) that the distance between Kansyore Island and Sudan makes it unwise to posit any correlations between Sudan pottery and Kansyore pottery and in some circles suggesting that water bodies were a cul-de-sac, this research demonstrates that there was cultural interaction and that the River Nile was not an impediment to interaction. This study breaks down such boundaries. It has been a tradition in African archaeology to establish boundaries for cultural affiliations. The general notion has been that some cultures were bounded to some areas and could not spread to other regions. For example Paul Lane bounded the Neolithic to the Rift Valley and Serengeti arguing that it could not go south of this area. Similarly, Chapman (1967) argues that the distance could not warrant interactions despite the similarity in decoration motifs between Sudan and Kansyore pottery. It is my argument that boundaries established by archaeologists should be dismissed as the existence of wavy line pottery at Kansyore Island showed the crossing of boundaries by pottery traditions.

Another issue I would like to raise concerns faunal domesticates. At both Kansyore Island and the Island of Deserters, I did not find any evidence of domesticates such as cattle, sheep, goat, chicken or dogs in association with my Kansyore cultural materials. This observation is important because Kansyore pottery and similar culture in Sudan is of Neolithic tradition. Since the Neolithic is associated with domesticates this makes me wonder if Kansyore tradition was Neolithic and if they did domesticate animals. This similar problem has been identified at several Kansyore sites in East Africa and even at Lokabulo in south-eastern Sudan (Robertshaw, 1982) but some Kansyore sites had domesticates. Similary in Sudan sites without domesticates were dubbed as Mesolithic. Kansyore pottery characterised by dominance of impressed motifs that are dotted and the use of the coiling method, one of the oldest pottery-making techniques, shows that I am dealing with the Neolithic tradition. However, this area still calls for further research where for instance soils could be analysed to identify if plant remains did exist.

David (1981) was of the view that any study interested in examining the similarity between the Sudan Neolithic and Kansyore tradition should account for the absence of domesticates at Kansyore sites. In my scholarship, the lack of domesticates has been attributed to tsetse-fly distribution as far as the Lake Victoria sites (Robertshaw, 1982:96). The evidence from this research supports the earlier suggestion by Chami and Kwekason (2003) that the existence of Neolithic pottery suggests evidence of domestication and challenges the earlier assumption that prehistoric people south of the Sahara relied only on hunting and gathering before the Iron Age.

The debate on the absence of domesticates and direct evidence for agriculture at the Kansyore Neolithic sites is ongoing. Reid and Young (2000) advocated for alternative methods of making inferences about agriculture such as the recovery of grain impressions from walls of ceramics from Sudanese sites (Haaland, 1995). That in case of failure to obtain permanent artefacts, alternatives could be sought from those that were used in the preparation of the food stuffs or containers used for their storage, grinding stones and harvesting knives, pits and packed-stone features identified with storage functions or storage vessels (pots). For instance, in the preparation of African grains the constant stirring of the grains or flour during heating, heats the vessel walls and not the base leading to heavy abrasion of the interior and this could be used to recognize grain preparation in antiquity. It is these that will enable one establish the links. At Kansyore Island such abraded pottery was obtained which was an indirect evidence of domestication.

The debate concerning the definition of Neolithic is another issue in this discussion. Arkell (1953) suggested that the Kansyore sites can be classified as Neolithic despite the absence of domesticates. Arkell suggested that this showed people who were food gatherers but who were not aware of agriculture. For instance despite the limited occurrence of grinding stones they infer farming though some were also used for grinding ochre for personal adornment rather than corn (Shinnie, 1950:10). However, though no direct evidence of cultivation was recovered from these sites in southern Upper Nile catchment areas the subsistence option cannot be ruled out (Gifford-Gonzales, 2003). This dismisses views that existence of both LSA remains and dimple-based pottery suggest that the pottery is later than the stone industries and thus Iron Age (Soper, 1967). Suggestions like these are dismissed on the grounds that they are racist views established in 19th century Europe reasoning that Africa south of the Sahara was populated by people who could not have innovated and hence remained hunter-gatherers until innovations were spread by immigrants (Chami, 2009; Harris, 1971). This is because cultural similarity had been attributed to either linear transmission or diffusion between cultural units (Binford and Binford, 1968).

An examination of chronometric dates obtained showed that chronologically the Kansyore pottery dates were younger compared to the Sudan Neolithic dates. However older dates had been identified at other Kansyore sites in East Africa with the oldest date from Luanda (8240±245 BP; GX-8743 calibrated to 7819-6590 cal BC), (Dale and Ashley, 2010). Other relatively older dates were from Pundo (7000±40 BP) (Lane *etal*, 2006) and Siror with 6194 ± 47 BP (Dale 2007). It should be noted that Sudan pottery was known before Kansyore pottery but the findings show close affinity. The aim of the study was to examine cultural affinity therefore chronological issues were taken as part of future research. Though Kansyore pottery does not have as good dates as those of Sudan, the Kansyore tradition from the areas investigated had affinity with the Sudan Neolithic and should be regarded as belonging to the second phase of the Khartoum Neolithic of the El Khadada type based on the dates so far obtained in the current research. However, areas like Luanda with the earliest Kansyore dates could fit well in the Early Khartoum Neolithic phase. Kansyore pottery was associated with microliths and this contemporary association of microliths and pottery manifests a Neolithic tradition (Chami, 1996). This evidence gives ample basis for the argument that there was interaction during the Neolithic period and existence of the Neolithic outside the Rift valley. This means the Kansyore people should not be simply treated as hunter-gatherers but from the pottery evidence they had a sedentary lifestyle and practiced domestication implying it was a Neolithic culture.

Heavy tools like querns, pounders, grinders, and pestles are another indicator of agriculture. The grinding stones imply the grinding of some grain whether imported or home grown (Monod, 1964:196). The worked axes were probably hoes. The evidence of grinding stones and core axes from the Island of Deserters and Kansyore respectively supports this. Therefore, this area in the Nile valley just like Khartoum Neolithic sites qualifies to have Neolithic sites. For example, Early Khartoum (Mesolithic) was an LSA site that contained no traces of domesticates while Esh-Shaheinab a Neolithic site yielded traces of goats and/or sheep (Monod, 1964: 200). No confirmed evidence of domesticates was identified from the Ugandan sites as in many Kansyore sites elsewhere.

Chapman dated Kansyore pottery to 3000 BC but my expectation was to fill the missing gaps which still I could not do. Dating is still one of the problems of Kansyore sites that require further research. Chami (2006) pointed out that Kansyore ware from the available dates was given a very long time period for a single tradition of over 3000 years. Hence, the need for further research which could possibly sort out this long period and identify variants within the same tradition. This would require further excavation and finding material in proper layers in sequence. This gap also indicated a conservative tradition or dating errors which needed to be fitted. Collet and Robertshaw (1982) also pointed out the dating problem which was suggested to have been aggravated by the lack of charcoal samples in most sites and resorting to the use of bones for dating. Unfortunately, dating the bones is problematic and unreliable. It should be noted that a lot has been done in dating the Sudanese Neolithic which calls for a similar approach on the southern part of the upper Nile catchment areas. Only proper and widespread dating will sort out the aspect of origin that is paramount in understanding the north-south interaction.

In relation to dating is the issue of chronology. An examination of the stratigraphy and material inventories in Kansyore Trenches 1, 1A, 1B, 2Aii and Island of Deserters Trenches 2 and 4 revealed that, Urewe pottery was contemporary with Kansyore pottery and for instance in Kansyore Island Trench 1 and the Island of Deserters Trench 4 Kansyore pottery was underlain by Urewe pottery. The results therefore would suggest the popularity of Urewe and its co-existence with Kansyore pottery. In addition the occurrence of limited artefacts in the upper levels and then reaching a climax in the middle and then decreasing towards the bottom of the excavation trenches was due to site use and re-use or continuities and discontinuities. The fact that much as we encounter pottery there was no reduction in lithics was a sign of settlement patterns which contributed to the co-existence of material. Coexistence of Neolithic and Iron Age material calls for questioning earlier assumptions if actually the LSA were replaced or absorbed by the Iron Age agro-pastoralists (Kessy, 2005). So the question remains: were the Kansyore people the same asthose who adopted the EIA cultural traditions (Chami, 2006:95). The findings suggest they are the same and hence counter the earlier thinking that Africa was peopled by migrants rendering the migration theory weak.

Another discovery was the aqualithic where a complete layer existed in Trench 1 on Kansyore Island. The aqualithic being at Kansyore Island demonstrated that not all inventions emanated from the north as some had origin in the south such as the aqualithic. This is because sites like Ishango in the south were much older compared to those in the north. Therefore, the possibility of emerging from a much more ancient eastern African tradition is not ruled out (Sutton, 1977). This challenges the use of the unidirectional model of always accounting for innovations using diffusion and migration where all major inventions were falsely attributed to migrants from the north.

Having established that cultural interactions existed, the next question is "how did this happen?". Similar adaptive strategies were suggested by Sutton (1974) for cultural similarity and in the case of the aquatic civilisation. This implies that innovations could have diffused from the south to north and therefore diffusion was not a one-way colonial development. Evolutionary explanations regarded Khartoum as a core area for the spread of Sudanese cultural tradition specifically the wavy-line and dotted-line pottery decoration elements (Arkell, 1949, 1953) though it could have been a combination of migration and diffusion (Hays, 1971, 1974; Clark, 1965). However, the existence of Khartoum Neolithic sites such as Talagal (ca. 9500 B.P.), Tin Torha (ca. 9000 B.P.) (Branch, 1987); Nabta Playa ca. 8800 B.P. that were older than wavy line (Khartoum Mesolithic) sites like Amekni ca 8300 B.P. (Camps, 1969) and Delibo Cave ca. 7300 B.P. (Bailloud, 1969) nullified Khartoum Neolithic evolving from Khartoum Mesolithic as suggested by Arkell (1949, 1953). In the same way, some of the Khartoum Neolithic sites were older than the Esh-Shaheinab the modal site just as Kansyore Island does not have the oldest dates for the Kansyore tradition. This implies that cultural affinity could not be explained by evolution as suggested by Arkell (1949, 1953).

Kansyore pottery open shapes and profuse indented decoration is a derivation of the early Holocene pottery of the Nile valley aqualithic or Khartoum horizon (Dale and Ashley, 2010). Migration, exchange networks, and frontier situations are possible factors for identity of Kansyore pottery makers (Dale, 2007: 257). However, "microlithic industries began earlier than assumed and not necessarily as a result of cultural diffusion since they are common in LSA assemblages all over East Africa (Posnansky, 1968a:69).

Though foreign material was not sufficient to ascertain that trade led to cultural affinity, from the historical records the trade with Punt could be one level to support trade as a means of cultural interaction. Chami (2006) suggested trade was one of the possibilities that explained similarity in culture. Examination of the historical records especially Egyptian contacts with Punt can be used to affirm that cultural affinity can be attributed to trade. Davidson (1959) suggested that the trade with Punt provided evidence of contacts between Egypt to as far as the shores of Lake Chad, forests of Congo and uplands of Uganda. And in the view of Davidson (1959:45), there is no reason why Egypt shouldn't have pushed its powers much further south. Arkell (1949) had earlier on suggested that some of the artefacts must have travelled the Nile by way of trade to Khartoum like the glazed steatite beads and blue faience beads at Shaheinab (Haaland, 2009). Besides Chami (2006) and Kitchen (2004) located Punt as far as East Africa at the time of the Khartoum/Kansyore Neolithic traditions.

Another factor was ecological conditions and the adoption of similar strategies in face of environmental challenges leading to independent inventions. This is because sustained research has now produced enough material to assess diffusion and migration models (Zangato and Holl, 2010:9). The early Holocene global warming, convergence in evolutionary pathways made societies to offer comparable solutions to more or less similar problems that accounted for cultural similarities (Holl, 2005;182). Julian Steward noticed that similar types of cultures developed under similar environmental conditions but in geographically separate places hence cultural similarity could be due to correspondences in their culture core using the cultural ecological theory. "Shifting ecological determinants forced man to reorganize his life if he was to survive" (Haury (1958). Thus the rhythm of climatic evolution determines that of human behaviour: hence, adapt or perish'. Therefore, similar cultural traits at times show a period in time of increased contact and communication (Chami, 2006:117).

To examine the mode of cultural interaction the issue of origin is paramount. However this has received diverse explanations. These included the Hamitic explanations that attributed the Kansyore tradition to southern Cushites and the absence of domesticates to tsetse-fly in the Lake Victoria region (David, 1981). These were challenged by other views such as Ehret (2002) who used a linguistic approach and suggested that the Kansyore belong to the southern Rub linguistic group that is part of the Eastern Sahelian language but no archaeological evidence so far can substantiate this argument. Lejju et al (2006) using phytoliths for Munsa cores suggested that banana was used prior to 5170 BP and therefore the Kansyore tradition may be the cultural context in which banana cultivation took place. However, there is need for more research to examine the origin of Kansyore basing on the banana-Kansyore connection (Dale, 2007) among others. Therefore, there is need for archaeologists to frame discussions of prehistoric interactions between communities using multiple criteria and lines of data or explore regional interactions from a multi-disciplinary perspective that would allow archaeological data to be viewed from a wide-ranging vantage point.

The issue of the deserters was another level of evidence on the form of cultural interactions. The deserters could neither be taken as intentional migrants or diffusionists. This is where a possibility of cultural transmission is attributed to military expeditions in the past.

It is clear that frequencies of exchanged artefacts usually decrease with distance from their source (Renfrew, 1977) but the probability of contact related to distance between the groups may not be a sufficient explanation. Therefore some forms of social environment, frequencies, and or similarities in material culture do not fall off with distance in any simple way (Hodder, 1979). This shows that although the down-the-line model (DTLM) trade theory could not account for cultural interaction, evidence of trade could be obtained from the historical records in relation to Punt.

In conclusion therefore, cultural affinity existed in terms of material culture, absence of domesticates and hence diffusion meant affinity. Though no direct evidence was obtained to support trade it was derived from the historical records as one way in which cultures were transmitted. The aqualithic demonstrated diffusion from the south contrary to earlier studies that emphasize north-to-south diffusion hence diffusion was not unilinear but multi-directional. The historical records further confirm that the Nile was not a cul-de sac as it did not hinder interactions in the past. The study for the first time identified roulette in the Neolithic levels and wavy-line pottery in the LSA of East Africa. However the dates of the north and Upper Nile catchment areas are not compatible.

Conclusion

The research answered the research questions it set out to investigate and the research objectives. Therefore cultural and economic interactions existed as shown from the similarities from the ceramics, lithics, faunal remains, and historical connections. Despite that some differences were identified like in the lithic toolkit and execution of the pottery decoration. The nature of interaction was further highlighted by evidence from the survey of historical records that showed that there was total awareness of the south by the people in the north and the attempts to locate the source of the Nile were evidence of north-south interactions. The theoretical considerations like the historical connections suggested that the Nile was not a cul-de-sac but contributed to the spread of the Khartoum Neolithic culture in such a wide area.

The occupants of the Khartoum Neolithic sites and the Kansyore sites were part of the same cultural complex from the affinities in material culture. It should be noted that while similarity in pottery decoration is not affected by function like stone tool production, pottery similarities reflect group values and aesthetics than variability and such similarities can be delimited in time and space implying that the Khartoum Neolithic and Kansyore sites were culturally related. There are key issues that necessitate further excavation especially at Kansyore Island one of them being the issue of chronology and hence dating.

Having made the first attempt to compare Sudan Neolithic and the East African Neolithic it was demonstrated that affinity existed using pottery, lithics, faunal remains but the two areas are not yet comparable in terms of dates. The work's major results were identifying the existence of rouletting in the Neolithic contexts, wavy line in East Africa's LSA and the aqualithic at Kansyore Island.

REFERENCES

Adamson, D., Clark, J. D. and Williams, M. A. J. (1974), "Barbed bone points from central Sudan and the age of the 'Early Khartoum' tradition", Nature 249: 120-123.

Aldred, C. (1961), *Ancient Peoples and Places: The Egyptians*, London: Thames and Hudson.

Amadou-Mohktar, M. (1990), "Preface", in Mokhatar (ed.), *General History of Africa* 11, UNESCO: East African, xvii-xxv.

Ambrose, S. (1990), "Hunter-gatherer/herder interactions in the highlands of East Africa", Paper presented at the Society for African Archaeologists meeting, Center for African Studies, University of Florida: Gainesville.

Andrefsky, W. ([1998]2005), *Lithics: Macroscopic approaches to analysis*, United Kingdom: Cambridge University Press.

Arkell, A. J. (1961), "The Valley of the Nile" in R. Oliver, (ed.), *The Dawn of African History*, London: Oxford University Press, 7-12.

Arkell, A.J. (1972), "Dotted wavy-line pottery in African prehistory", *Antiquity* 46: 221-222.

Arkell, A. J. (1949a), Early *Khartoum*, Oxford: Oxford University Press.

Arkell, A. J. (1949b), "The excavation of the Neolithic site at Esh-Shaheinab", *Sudan notes and records* xxx (1): 212-221.

Arkell, A. J. (1950), "An introduction to African pre-history", *African Affairs* 49 (194):56-67.

Arkell, A. J. (1953), *Esh Shaheinab*, Oxford: Oxford University Press.

Ashey, C. Z. (2010), "Towards a socialised archaeology of ceramics in the Great Lakes of Africa". *African Archaeological Review* 27: 135-163.

Ashmore, W and J. R Sharer (2000), *"Discovering our past; a brief introduction to Archaeology"*, New York: McGraw-Hill.

Ashmore, W and J. R Sharer (2003), *Archaeology: Discovering our past*, New York: McGraw Hill.

Bailloud, G. (1966), "Le Neolithique", in Boutruches, R and Le mere, P (eds.), *La nouvelle cleio la prehistoire*, Paris: Presses Universitaires de France.

Baker, S. J. K. (1958), "The geographical background of Western Uganda", *Uganda Journal* 22 (1): 1-10.

Barthelme, J. (1977), "Holocene sites North-East of Lake Turkana: A preliminary report", *Azania X*II, 33-42.

Bathily, A and C. Meillasoux (1988), "Relations between the different regions of Africa", in M. Elfasi (ed.), *UNESCO General History of Africa 111 from the 7th to the 11th Century*, California: Heinemann, 734-749.

Bernal, M. (1987), *Black Athena: The Afro-Asiatic roots of classical civilisation.* Cambridge: Cambridge University press.

Binford, S. R and L. Binford (1968), *New perspectives in Archaeology*, Chicago: Aldrine.

Bishop, W.W, and M. Posnansky (1960), "Pleistocene environments and early man in Uganda", *Uganda Journal* 24 (1): 44-61.

Bordes, F. (1968), *The Old Stone Age*, New York: McGraw-Hill.

Bower, J. R. F and C. Nelson (1978), "Early pottery and pastoral cultures of the central Rift Valley; Kenya", *Man* 13: 554-566.

Bower, J. R. F *et al* (1977), "Later Stone Age /Pastoral Neolithic: A comparative study in central Kenya; an overview", *Azania* 12: 119-146.

Bower, J. R. F. (1973), "Seronera: excavations at a stone bowl site in the Serengeti National Park; Tanzania", *Azania* VIII: 71-104.

Bower, J. R. F. (1991), "The Pastoral Neolithic of East Africa", *Journal of World Prehistory* 5 (1): 49-82.

Brachi, R. M. (1960), "Excavations of a rock-shelter at Hippo Bay Entebbe", *Uganda Journal* 24 (1):62-70.

Brewer, D. J and E. Teeter (2007), *Egypt and the Egyptians*, New York: Cambridge University Press.

Brown (1968), "Diffusion processes and location: a conceptual framework and bibliography", *Bibliographic series 4*, USA: Regional science institute.

Bushozi, P. G. M. (2011), Lithic technology and hunting behaviour during the Middle Stone Age in Tanzania, Un-published PhD. Thesis, Edmonton: University of Alberta.

Camps, G. (1982), "Beginning of pastoralism and cultivation in north-west Africa and the Sahara: origins of the Berbers", in J.D Clark (ed.), *Cambridge History of Africa 1*, Cambridge: Cambridge University press, 548-623.

Camps-Fabrer, H. (1966), "Matiere et Art mobilier dans la prehistorie Nord-Africaine et Sahrienne". *Memoires du CRAPES* 5: Alger.

Caneva, I. (1983) (ed.), "Pottery using gatherers and hunters at Saggai (Sudan): preconditions for food production", *Origini* 12: Rome.

Caneva, I. (1987), "Pottery decoration in prehistoric Sahara and Upper Nile: A new perspective", in B. E. Barich (ed.), *Archaeology and environment in the Libyan Sahara*, Cambridge Monographs in African archaeology 23 B.A.R International Series 363: Oxford.

Caneva, I. (1988), "El Geili: The history of a Middle Nile Environment 7000 B.C 1500", *BAR International Series* 424, Oxford.

Cary, M. and E. Warmington (1963), *The ancient explorers*, Middlesex: Penguin Books.

Casson, L. (1960), *Ancient Egypt*, Neanderland: Time-life international.

Chami, F. A and A. Kwekason (2003), "Neolithic pottery traditions from the Island, the coast, and the interior of East Africa", *African Archaeological Review* 20(2): 65- 80.

Chami, F. A. (1994), *The Tanzania Coast in the First Millennium AD; Studies in African Archaeology*, Uppsala: Societies Archaeological Uppsaliensis.

Chami, F. A. (1996), "The excavation of Kiwangwa Late Stone Age site", in Pwiti, G. and R. Soper (eds.), *Aspects of African archaeology*, Harare: University of Zimbabwe, 307-316.

Chami, F. A. (1999), "The early Iron Age on Mafia and its relationship with the mainland", *Azania* 34: 1-10.

Chami, F. A. (2001), "A Response to Christopher Ehret's 'Bantu expansions", *The International Journal of African Historical Studies 34* (3): 647- 651.

Chami, F. A. (2004), "The Archaeological evidence of the Mafia Archipelago, Tanzania; new evidence for Neolithic trade links", *Studies in the African Past* 4:73-101.

Chami, F. A. (2004a), "The Egypto-Graeco-Romans and Panchea/Azania sailing in the Erythraean Sea", in P. Lunde and A. Porter (eds.), *Red Sea: Trade and Travel. British Archaeological Reports*, International Series 1269, London: British Museum, 93-103.

Chami, F. A. (2006), *The unity of African ancient history: 3000 BC to AD 500*. Mauritius: E &D.

Chami, F. A. (2007), "Diffusion in the studies of the African past: reflections from new archaeological findings", *African Archaeological Review* 24 (1): 1- 14.

Chami, F.A. (2008), "The Great Lakes: a complexity of cultural wellsprings", in M. Arnold (ed.), *Art in Eastern Africa*, Dar es Salaam: Mkuki Na Nyota, 47-68.

Chami, F.A. (2009), "The long Duree of Zanzibar and Western Indian Ocean Sea Board", in F.A Chami (ed.), *Zanzibar, and the Swahili Coast from c. 30, 000 Years Ago, Dar es Salaam*: E&D, 194-222.

Chaplin, T. (1974), "The prehistoric rock art of the Lake Victoria region", *Azania* 9:1-50.

Chapman, S (1967), "Kansyore Island", *Azania* 2: 554-66.

Chirikure, S; Pikirayi, I and G. Pwiti (2002), "A comparative study of Khami pottery, Zimbabwe", *Studies in African Past* 2:107-128.

Chittick, N. (1980), "Pre-Islamic trade and ports of the horn", in *Proceedings of the 8th Pan-African congress Nairobi 1977*, Leakey, R.E and B.A Ogot (eds.), Nairobi: The International Louis Leakey Memorial Institute for African prehistory: 364-366.

Choldrinicki, M. (1984), "Pottery from the Neolithic settlement at Kadero (central Sudan)", in Krzyzaniak and M. Kobusiewicz (ed.), *Origin, and early development of food producing cultures in North East Africa*, Poznan: Polish Academy of Sciences: 337-341.

Claassen, C. (1998), *Shells:Cambridge manuals in archaeology*, Cambridge: Cambridge University Press.

Clark, J. D. (1965), "Comments on Nile pre-dynastic development". *Current Anthropology* 6: 158-159.

Clark, J. D. (1967), "The problem of Neolithic cultures in culture in sub-Saharan Africa", in W. W. Bishop and J. D. Clark (1967), *The problem of Neolithic culture in sub-Saharan Africa*, Chicago: Chicago: 601-628.

Clark J. D, and M. R Kleindienst (1974), "The Stone Age cultural sequence: terminology, typology and raw material", in J. D Clark (ed.), *Kalambo Falls Prehistoric site; the later prehistoric Cultures*, Cambridge: Cambridge University Press, 71-106.

Clark, J. D. (1980), "Human populations and cultural adaptations in the Sahara and the Nile during the prehistoric times", in M. A. J. Williams and H. Faure (eds.), *The Sahara and the Nile*, Rotterdam: Balkema, 527-582.

Clark, J. D *et al* (1984), "A Middle Stone Age occupation site at Porc Epic Cave, Dire Dawa 9 East –Central Ethiopia", *The African Archaeological Review* 2:37-71.

Clark, J. D. (1989), "Shabona: an early Khartoum settlement on the White Nile", in Krzyzaniak and M. KObusiewicz (eds.), *The late prehistory of the Nile Basin and the Sahara*, Poznan: Poznan Archaeological Museum, 387-410.

Close, A. E. (1995), "Few and far between: Early ceramics in North Africa", W. K Bamett and J. W. Hoopes (eds.), *The emergence of pottery technology and innovation in ancient societies*, Washington D C: Smithsonian.

Cohen, M. (1970), "A reassessment of the stone bowl cultures of the Rift valley, Kenya", *Azania* 5: 27-38.

Cole, S (1954), *The prehistory of East Africa*, Penguin Books, Harmondsworth.

Cole, S. M. (1964), *The Pre-history of East Africa,* Great Britain: George Weidenfeld & Nicolson.

Collet and Robertshaw, P. (1983), "Pottery traditions of early pastoral communities in Kenya", Azania 18: 107-125.

Collet, D. (1982), "Models for the Spread of the Early Iron Age", in Ehret, C and M. Posnansky (eds.), *The Archaeological and Linguistic Reconstruction of African History*, Berkley: University of California Press, 182-198.

Collet, D. P and Robertshaw P. T. (1980), "Early Iron Age and Kansyore pottery: finds from Gogo Falls, South Nyanza". *Azania* XV: 133-145.

Collet, D. P and Robertshaw, P. T. (1983), "Pottery traditions of early pastoral communities in Kenya", *Azania* 18: 107-125.

Connah, G. (1996). "A Chronological sequence for the Ugandan shores of Lake Albert", in Pwiti, G and R. Soper (eds.), *Aspects of African archaeology; papers from the 10th Congress of the Pan African Association for prehistory and related studies*, Harare: University of Zimbabwe, 533-542.

Connah, G. (1997), "The cultural and chronological context of Kibiro-Uganda", *African Archaeological Review* 14 (1): 25-67.

Coon, C. (1965), *The Living Races of Man*, London: Jonathan Cape.

Crabtree, D. E. (1973b), "The Obtuse angle as a functional edge", *Tebiwa* 16 (1): 10-45.

Crawford, O. G. S (1949), "Some medieval ideas about the Nile". *Geographical Journal* 114:6-29.

Dale D. D (2007), "An archaeological investigation of the Kansyore Later Stone Age Hunter- Gatherers in East Africa", PhD. dissertation, Missouri: University of Washington.

Dale, D. D, and C. Z Ashley (2010), "Holocene hunter-fisher-gatherer communities: new perspectives on Kansyore using communities of Western Kenya", *Azania* 5(1): 24-48.

Darvill, T. (2008[2002]), *The Concise Oxford Dictionary of Archaeology*, Oxford: Oxford University Press.

David, N., Harvey, P.and C. J. Goudie, (1981), "Excavations in the southern Sudan," *Azania* XV1, 7-38.

David, N (1982), "The B.I.E.A southern Sudan expedition of 1979, interpretation of archaeological data", In Marks and P. T. Robertshaw (eds.), *Culture history in southern Sudan, Memoir 8*, Nairobi: B.I.E.A, 49-57.

Davidson, B. (1959), *Old Africa rediscovered*, London. Victor Gollancz.

De Paepe, P. (1991), "Appendix A: ceramics from Shaqadud studies by physical methods", in Marks, A. E and Mohammed, A.S (eds.),*The late prehistory of the Sahel*, Dallas: Southern Methodist University press, 261-266.

Diop, C. A (1981a), "Origin of the Ancient Egyptians", in G. Mokhtar (ed.), *General History of Africa*, Cambridge: UNESCO, 27-57.

Diop, C. A. (1981b), *Civilisation, or barbarism: an authentic anthropology*, Paris: Lawrence Hill Books.

Diop, C. A. (1997), "The Meaning of our work", in Grinker, R and C. Steiner (eds.) *perspectives on Africa*, Cambridge: Blackwell, 724-727.

Dixon, J. L. (1971), "Survey: The Nile and its Basin", *Uganda Journal* 35 (2): 123- 138.

Ehret, C. (1998), *An African classical age Eastern and Southern Africa in world history, 1000BC to AD 400*, Oxford: James Carrey.

Ehret, C. (2002), *The Civilisation of Africa; a History to 1800*, Charlottesville: University Press of Virginia.

Ehret, C. (2002). "Language family expansions: broadening our understandings of cause from an African perspective," in *Examining the farming/ language dispersal hypothesis*, P. Bellwood and C. Renfrew (eds.), Cambridge: McDonald Institute Monographs, 163-176.

El-Nadoury, R (1981), "The Legacy of Pharaonic Egypt", in Mokhtar G. (ed.), *UNESCO General History of Africa 11: Ancient Civilisations in Africa*, California: Heinemann, 155-183.

Fagan, B. M and L. Lofgren (1966), "Archaeological sites in the Nile Chobi confluence", *Uganda Journal* XXX: 203.

Fekri, A. H. (1986), "Chronology of Khartoum Mesolithic and Neolithic and related sites in the Sudan: statistical analysis and comparisons with Egypt", African *Archaeological Review* 4: 83-102.

Gabel, C. (1969), "Six rock shelters on the Northern Kavirondo shore of Lake Victoria", *African History studies* II (2): 205-254.

Gifford-Gonzales, D (2003), "The fauna from Ele-Bor; evidence for the persistence of foragers into the later Holocene of arid North Kenya", *African Archaeological Review* 20(2): 81-119.

Gosselain, A.O et al (2010). "Introduction", in A. Haour et al (eds.), *African pottery roulettes past and present: techniques, identification, and distribution*, Oxford: Oxbow books, 1-34.

Gramly, R. M (1975), "Pastoralists and Hunters: recent prehistory in Southern Kenya and Northern Tanzania", PhD Thesis, Cambridge: Harvard University.

Grove, A. T. (1989), *The Changing Geography of Africa* 2nd edition, New York: Oxford University Press.

Haaland, R. (1981), *Migratory herdsmen and cultivating women*, Bergen.

Haaland, R. (1992), "Fish, Pots, and Grain: Early and Mid-Holocene adaptations in the central Sudan", *The African Archaeological Review* 10: 43-64.

Haaland, R. (1995), "Sedentism, cultivation, and plant domestication in the Holocene Middle Nile region", *Journal of Field Archaeology* 22: 157-174.

Haaland, R. (2009), "Aquatic resource utilisation and the emergence of pottery during the Palaeolithic and Mesolithic: a global perspective from the Nile to China", in J. Oestigaard (ed.), *comparing the past and present traditions in the Nile basin region*, Bergen: BRIC, 213-236.

Hall, M. (2002), "Timeless time: Africa and the world", in B. Cunliffe *et al* (eds.), *Archaeology: The widening debate*, Oxford: Oxford University Press.

Hamilton, A. C. (1982), *Environmental history of East Africa: A study of the Quaternary*, London: Academic.

Haour, A. *et al*, (2010), *African pottery roulettes, past and present; techniques, identification and distribution*, Oxford: Oxbow books, glossary.

Haour, A. (2010), "Putting pots and people in the Sahelian empires". *Azania* 46 (1):36-48.

Harris, J. R. (1971), *The legacy of Egypt*, Oxford: Clarendon.

Harris, M. (1968), *The Rise of anthropological theory*, New York: Cromwell.

Harvey, C. P. D, and A. T. Grove (1982) "A pre-historic source of the Nile", *The Geographical Journal* 148 (3): 327-336.

Hays, T. R. (1971), The Sudanese Neolithic: a critical analysis, PhD dissertation, Dallas: Southern Method University.

Hays, T. R. (1974), "Wavy line pottery an element of Nilotic diffusion", *South African Archaeological Bulletin* 29:27-32.

Hays, T. R. (1975), "An examination of the Sudanese Neolithic", *Antiquity*: 85-92.

Hays, T.R and Hassan, F. A. (1974), "Mineralogical analysis of Sudanese Neolithic ceramics", *Archaeometry* 16 (1): 17-79.

Heizer, F. R. and Graham, J. A. (1967), *A guide to field methods in archaeology: approaches to anthropology of the dead*, California: The National Press.

Hiernaux, J and Maquet, E. (1960), "Cultures pre□histoririques de l□age des metaux aux Ruanda-Urundi et au Kivu (Congo Belge)", *2m'e Partie, Mem.de l'Acade. Roy. Des Sc. d'Outre-Mer* 10 (2): 1-88.

Hinkel, F. W. (1977), *The Archaeological map of the Sudan: a guide to its use and explanation of its principles*, Berlin.

Hirsh, C. (1991), "White water rafting potential on the Victoria Nile in Murchison Falls National Park", *Uganda National Parks*, technical assistance to the Uganda Institute of ecology.

Hodder, I. (1977), "The distribution of material culture items in the Baringo district; western Kenya", *Man* 12: 239-269.

Hodder, I. (1979), "Economic and social stress and material culture", *American Antiquity* 44(3):446-454.

Holl, A. F. C. (2005), "Holocene 'Aquatic' civilisations in North Tropical Africa", in A. B. Stahl (ed.), *African Archaeology, A critical Introduction*, U.S.A: Blackwell, 174-186.

Honegger, M. (2006), "Lunate microliths in the Holocene industries of Nubia: multifunctional tools, sickle blades, or weapons?", Proceedings of the World Congress, session 83XVth on *Projectile weapons elements from the upper Palaeolithic to the Neolithic*, 162-174.

Howell F. C and F. Bourliere (1964), "Transcript of discussions", in Howell F. Clark and F. Bourliere (eds.), *African Ecology and Human Evolution*, USA: Methuen, 547-654.

Howell F. C, and J.D Clark (1964), "Acheulian Hunter Gatherers of Sub-Saharan Africa", in Howell F.C amd F. Bourliere (eds.), *African Ecology, and Human Evolution*, USA: Methuen, 459-533.

Huffman, T. H. (1989), *Iron Age Migrations*, Johannesburg: Witwatersrand University Press.

Hugot, H. J (1963), *Recherches prehistoriques dans l'Ahaggar Nord-occidental 1950-1957 centre de Recherches Anthropologiques prehistoriques et. ethnographiques* 1: Paris.

Hugot, H. J. (1968). "The origins of agriculture; Sahara", *Current Anthropology* 9: 483-489.

Hurst, H. E. (1952), *The Nile; a general account of the River and the utilisation of its waters*, London: Constable.

Iliana A. Casini, (2010), "The meaning of "Kombewa" method in Middle Palaeolithic: techno-economic analysis of lithic assemblages from Riparo Tagliente (VR), Carapia (RA), Podere Camponi (BO) and Fossato Conca d'Oro", in, *Museologia Scientifica e Naturalistica* 6:123-130.

Ingrams H. (1960), *Uganda a Crisis of Nationhood*, London: Her Majesty's office.

Johnson, H. (Sir) (1903), *The Nile quest a period of exploration of the Nile and its basin*, London: Lawrence and Bullen.

Johnson, H. (sir) (1902), *The Uganda protectorate, an attempt to give some description of the physical geography, botany, anthropology, languages and history of the territories under British protection in East central Africa between the Congo Free State and the Rift valley and between the first degree of south latitude and the 5th degree of north latitude*, London: Hutchinson.

Johnson, M. (2010), *Archaeological Theory; An introduction*, United Kingdom: Blackwell.

Joukowsky, M. (1980), *A complete manual of field archaeology; tools and techniques of field work for archaeologists,* London: Prentice-Hall.

Karega-Munene (1996), "The East African Neolithic: An alternative view", *The African Archaeology Review* 13 (4): 247-254.

Karega-Munene (2002), *Holocene Foragers, Fishers and Herders of western Kenya*, Cambridge Monographs in African archaeology, 54 BAR International series, and 1037, Oxford: Archeopress.

Karega-Munene (2003), "The East African Neolithic: a historical perspective", in C.M Kusimba, and S.B. Kusimba (eds.), *East African Archaeology; Foragers, Potters, Smiths, and Traders,* Philadelphia: University of Pennsylvania Museum of Archaeology and Anthropology, 17-32.

Keeley, L. H. (1980), *Experimental determination of stone tool uses: A microwear analysis*, Chicago: University of Chicago Press.

Kendall, T. (1997), "Kings of the sacred mountains: Napata and Kushite Twenty-Fifth Dynasty of Egypt", in W. Dietrich (ed.), *Zimbabwe culture: ruins and reactions*, Oxford: Clarendon Press, 260 -74.

Kessy, E. T. (2005), "The relationship between the Later Stone Age and Iron Age cultures of central Tanzania", Phd dissertation, Simon Fraser University.

Kessy, E. T; R. Tibesasa and H. Muwonge (2011), "Excavation of Lwala site, Ssi Mukono district", *Sudies in the African Past* 9: 116-138.

Khabir, A. M. (1987), "New radio carbon dates for Sorourab 2 and the age of the Early Khartoum tradition", *Current Anthropology* 28 (3): 377-380.

Kitchen, K. (1993), "The land of Punt", in S. T. Sinclair *et al* (eds.), *The archaeology of Africa*, London: Routledge, 587-608.

Kitchen, K. (2004), "The Elusive Land of Punt revisited", in P. Lunde and A. Porter (eds.), *Trade and travel in the Red Sea region*, Oxford: BAR International Series, 25-31.

Kiyaga-Mulindwa, D. (1982), "Social and demographic changes in the Birim valley, southern Ghana c.1450 to c.1800", *Journal of African History* 23:63-82.

Kiyaga-Mulindwa, D. (2004), "The archaeology of riverine environments of the Upper Nile Valley in Uganda", *Studies in the African Past* 4: 38-58.

Kiyaga-Mulindwa, D. (2006), "The Archaeology and ethnography of Mutunda, a Nilotic-Lwo/ Bantu Nexus in Northern Uganda", *Studies in the African Past* 5: 224- 242.

Klerruu, W. A. (1962), "The Nile waters question: political aspects of the utilisation of the Nile waters", PhD dissertation (Political science), Los Angeles:University of California.

Kothari, C. R. (2004), *Research Methodology*, New Delhi: Sage Publication.

Krober, A. L (1983), Cultural and natural areas of native North American, Berkeley: University of California publications in American archaeology and ethnology 38.

Krzyzaniak, L. (1978), "New light on early food production in the central Sudan", *The African Archaeological Review* 19 (2): 159-172.

Kusimba, C. 1999, "Hunter-gatherer land use patterns in Later Stone Age East Africa", *Journal of Anthropology*, 18(2):165-200.

Kwekason, A. P. (2010), *Holocene archaeology of southern Coast Tanzania*, PhD Thesis, University of Dar es Salaam.

Kwekason, A. P. (2011), *Holocene archaeology of the southern coast of Tanzania*, Dar es Salaam: E&D.

Lacroix, W. F. (1998), *Africa in Antiquity: a liguistic and taponymic analysis of Ptolemys's map of Africa*. Saarbruken: Verl Fur Entwicklungspolitic.

Lane, E. W. (1963), *Manners and customs of modern Egyptians*, Great Britain, Aldrine

Lane, P. C. (2004), "The 'moving frontier' and the transition to food production in Kenya," *Azania* 34: 243-264.

Lane, P. C. *et'al* (2007), "The transition to farming in East Africa: New faunal and dating evidence from Wadh Lang'o and Usenge, Kenya", *Antiquity*, 61-81.

Langlands, B. W. (1962), "Concepts of the Nile", *Uganda Journal* 26 (1): 1-22.

Langlands, B. W. (1993), "Uganda; physical and social geography", in Africa South of the Sahara 1993, Australia: Europa, 895-915.

Lanning, E. C. (1960), "The Earth Works at Kibengo, Mubende District", *Uganda Journal* 65:1-8.

Lanning, E.C. (1966), "Excavations at Mubende Hill", *Uganda Journal* 30: 160.

Law, M. D. (1959), *Chambers Encyclopaedia* 1, London: George Newness.

Layton, R. (1997), *An introduction to theory in anthropology*, United Kingdom: Cambridge University Press.

Leakey, L. S. B. (1931), *The Stone Age cultures of Kenya colony*, London: Cambridge University Press.

Leakey, L. S. B. (1936), *Stone Age Africa*, London: Oxford University Press.

Leakey, M. D. (1945), "Reports on the excavations at Hyrax Hill, Nakuru, Kenya Colony", *T.R.S.S.A* XXX: 4.

Leakey, M. D and L. Leakey (1950), *Excavations at Njoro River cave*, London: Oxford University Press.

Leclant, J. (1981), "The Empire of Kush: Napata and Meroe", in G. Mokhtar (ed.), *General History of Africa 11: Ancient Civilisations of Africa*, 278-297, California: UNESCO.

Lejju, B. J et al (2006), "Africa's earliest bananas", *Journal of Archaeological science* 33:102-113.

Lombard, M. and L. Phillipson (2010), "Indicators of bow and stone-tipped arrow use 64,000 years ago in Kwa zulu Natal, South Africa", *Antiquity* 84: 1-14.

Lombard, M. (2007), "Finding resolution for the Howiesons Poort through the microscope: micro-residue analysis of segments from Sibudu cave, South Africa", *Journal of Archaeological sciences* 35 (1): 26-41.

Lowe, C. V. R. (1952), "The Pleistocene Geology and Pre-history of Uganda Part II: Prehistory", *Geological Survey of Uganda*, Memoir 6.

Lucas, O. J. (1942), Religion *of the Yoruba: being an account of the religious beliefs and practices of the Yoruba of Southern Nigeria especially in relation to the religion of Ancient Egypt*. Doctor of Divinity University Durham, England: Brown and sons.

Lwanga-Lunyiigo, S. (1976), "The Bantu Problem Reconsidered", *Current Anthropology* 17: 282-286.

Lwanga-Lunyiigo, S. and J. Vansina (1988), "The Bantu- speaking peoples and their expansion", in MelFasi (ed.), *General History of Africa from the Seventh to the Eleventh century*, California: Heinemann, 140-162.

Mabulla, A. Z. P. (1996), "Middle and Later Stone Age land-use and lithic technology in the Eyasi basin, Tanzania", PhD Thesis: University of Florida.

Macks, J and P. T Robertshaw (1982), "Introduction", in Mack, J and P. T. Robertshaw (eds.), *Culture history in the southern Sudan; archaeology, linguistics and ethno-history*, Memoir No.8. Nairobi: British Institute in Eastern Africa, 1-3.

MacNeish, R. S. Et al (1970), *The prehistory of the Tehuacan Valley; Ceramics,* Austin: University of Texas Press.

Makhan, J. (1983), *An introduction to anthropological thought*, India: Vikas.

Malte, S and D. Williamson, (1995), "Murchison Falls National Park Rehabilitation Project, Aerial survey of the Murchison Falls National Park and the Karuma Game Reserve", Kampala.

Manning, P. (2006), *Migration in World History*, London: Routledge.

Mapunda, B. B. B. (1995), *An Archaeological View of the History and Variation of Iron-working in south-western Tanzania*, PhD Dissertation University of Florida: Gainesville.

Marks, A. E. and Mohammed-Ali, A (1991a), *The late prehistory of the eastern Sahel, the Mesolithic and Neolithic of Shaqadud; Sudan*, Dallas: Sudan Southern Methodist University Press, 65-91.

Marks, A. E and Mohammed-Ali, A (1991b), "The place of Shaqadud in the late prehistory of the central Nile valley", in A. E Marks and A, Mohammed-Ali (eds.), *The late prehistory of the eastern Sahel, the Mesolithic and Neolithic of Shaqadud; Sudan*, Dallas: Sudan Southern Methodist University Press, 237-259.

Marks, A. E (1991), "The stone artefacts from Shaqadud cave", in Marks, A. E and A. Mohamed-Ali (eds.), *The Late Pre-history of Eastern Sahel; The Mesolithic and Neolithic of Shaqadud*, Dallas: Southern Methodist University Press, 173-191.

Marks, A. E, Shiner, J. L and Hays, T. R. (1968), "Survey and excavations in the Dongola Reach, Sudan". *Current Anthropology* 9: 319-323.

Marks, A. E. et al (1985), "The prehistory of central Nile as seen from its hinterland: excavations at Shaqadud, Sudan", *Journal of field archaeology* 12(3): 261- 278.

Masao, F. T. (1979), *The Later Stone Age archaeology and the rock paintings of central Tanzania*, Franz S. Verlag: Wiesbaden.

McBrearty, S. (1988), "The Sangoan-Lupemban and MSA sequences at Muguruka site, Western Kenya", *World archaeology* 19 (3): 388-420.

McGaffey, W. (1970), "Concepts of Race in the historiography of North East Africa", in J. Fage and R. Oliver (eds.), *Papers in African Pre-history*, Cambridge: Cambridge University Press, 99-115.

Mcmaster, M. (2005), "Language shift and its reflection in African Archaeology: cord roulette in the Uele and interlacustrine regions", *Azania* XL, 43-72.

Mehlman, M. (1977), "Excavations at Nasera rock, Tanzania", *Azania* 12: 111-118.

Mehlman, M. (1979), "Mumba-Höle revisited; the relevance of a forgotten excavation to some current issues in East African Prehistory", *World Archaeology* II (I): 80-94.

Mehlman, M. 1989. Later Quaternary archaeological sequences in Northern Tanzania, PhD Thesis: Urbana-Champaign University of Illinois.

Mercader, J. (2002), "Forest people: the role of the African rainforest in human evolution and dispersal, *Evolutionary Anthropology* II (3): 117-124.

Meyerowitz, E. L. R. (1960), *The divine kingship in Ghana and Ancient Egypt*, London: Faber and Faber, Chapter 4

Miller, J. (1969), *The Spice trade of the Roman Empire*, Oxford: Clarendon Press.

Mitchell, P. (2005), *Africa Connections; Archaeological Perspectives of Africa and the Wider World*, United Kingdom: Altamira.

Mohammed-Ali, A, S and Khabir, A. M (2003), "The wavy-line and dotted-line pottery in the pre-history of the central Nile and the Sahara-Sahel belt", *African Archaeology Review* 20 (1): 25-58.

Mohammed-Ali, A.S (1982). "The Neolithic Period in Sudan c.6000-2500 B.C", *Cambridge: BAR International Series*, 139.

Mohammed-Ali, A, S. (1984), "Sorourab 1: a Neolithic site in Khartoum province, Sudan", *Current Anthropology* 25 (1): 117-119.

Mohammed-Ali, A. S. (1991), "The Mesolithic and Neolithic ceramics from Shaqadud midden", In A. E. Marks and A. S. Mohammed-Ali, *The late prehistory of the Eastern Sahel, the Mesolithic and Neolithic of Shaqadud*, Dallas, Sudan southern Methodist University press, 65-91.

Monod, T (1964), "The Late Tertiary and Pleistocene in the Sahara and adjacent Southern regions", in F. C. Howell and F Bourliere (eds.), *African ecology and human evolution*, U S A: Methuen, 213-229.

Morgan, W. T. W. (1973), *East Africa: Geographies for advanced study*, New York: Longman.

Munsell colour (1990), Munsell soil colour charts Revised edition, Baltimore, Maryland: Macbeth Division of Kollmorgen instruments.

Muwonge, H (2009), An archaeological investigation of LSA occurrences from open-air contexts in central Uganda: the case of southern Kyaggwe, Un-published M.A dissertation: University of Dar es Salaam.

Nakaweesa, E. (2011), Cultural transition from Later Stone Age to Iron Age cultures: a case study of Nyero rock shelter, Kumi district, eastern Uganda, Unpublished MA Archaeology dissertation, University of Dar es Salaam.

Nassor, H. M. (2010), A stratigraphic analysis of artefacts mainly pottery from a mound site in Southern Unguja Island, Zanzibar, Unpublished M.A dissertation, University of Dar es Salaam.

Nelson, C. M. (1973), "The Late Stone Age in East Africa", Unpublished PhD Thesis, University of California: Barkley.

Nelson, M. C and M. Posnansky (1970), "The Stone tools from the re-excavation of Nsongezi Rock shelter Uganda", *Azania* V: 119-172.

Nicoll, K. (2004), "Recent environmental change and prehistoric human activity in Egypt and Northern Sudan", *Quaternary science reviews* 23: 561-580.

Nordstrom, H. A. (1972), *Neolithic and A-Group sites, the Scandinavian joint expedition to Sudanese Nubia* Volume 3 (1), Stockholm: Scandinavian University Books.

Noten, V. (1979), "The Early Iron Age in the interlacustrine region", *Azania* XIV: 61-80.

O'Brien, T. P. (1939), *The Pre-history of Uganda Protectorate*, Cambridge: Cambridge University Press.

O'Brien, T. P and J. D. Solomon (1939), *The prehistory of the Uganda protectorate.* Cambridge: The Cambridge University press.

O'Brien, T. P. (1966), "The Levalloisian Industry of Nsongezi", *Uganda Journal* 30 (2): 207.

O'Connor, D. and D. A. M Reid (2003a), "Introduction - Locating Ancient Egypt in Africa: modern theories, past realities", in D. O'Connor and D. A. M. Reid, (eds.), *Ancient Egypt in Africa*, Great Britain: UCL.

O'Connor, D and D. A. M. Reid (2003b), *Ancient Egypt in Africa, encounters with ancient Africa* 11, Oxford: Clarendon.

O'Connor, D and D. A. M Reid (eds.) (2003c), *Ancient Egypt in Africa*, London: UCL.

Odell, G. H. (2003), *Lithic analysis; manuals in archaeological method, theory and technique*, United States of America: Springer.

Ojany, F. F. (1968), "The geography of East Africa", in B.A Ogot (ed.), *Zamani: A survey of East African History*, Kenya: Longman, 20-51.

Oliver, R. (1982), "The Nilotic contribution to Bantu Africa". *Journal of African History* 23:433-442.

Onyango-Abuje, J. C. (1977), "Crescent Island", *Azania* 12: 147-160.

Pearce, S and M. Posnansky (1963), 'The re-excavation of Nsongezi rock-shelter, Ankole', *Uganda Journal* 27(1): 85-94.

Peters, J. (1986), A revision of faunal remains from two central Sudanese sites Khartoum Hospital and Esh-Shaheinab, *Archaeozoologica (Mellanges)*: 11-32.

Peters, J. et al (1993), "Mesolithic fishing at the confluence of the Nile and the Atbara, central Sudan", in A. Clason *et al* (eds.), *Skeltons in her cupboard*, Oxford: Oxbow books, 75-83.

Peters, J. (1991), "Mesolithic fishing along the central Sudanese Nile and the lower Atbara", *Sahara; prehistory and history of the Sahara* 4: 33-40.

Phillips, J. E. (1983), "African smoking and pipes", *Journal of African History*, 24 (3): 303-319.

Phillipson, D. W. (1976a), "The Early Iron Age in eastern and southern Africa: critical re-appraisal", *Azania* 7 (11): 1-23.

Phillipson, D. W. (1976b), "The Pre-history of eastern Zambia", *Memoir* No.6, Nairobi: British Institute in Eastern Africa.

Phillipson, D. W. (1977), "Lowasera", *Azania* XII, 1-32.

Phillipson, D. W. (1981), "A preliminary archaeological reconnaissance of the Southern Sudan", 1977-1978, *Azania* XV1: 1-6.

Phillipson, D. W. (2005[1993]), *African Archaeology* 3rd edition, Cambridge: Cambridge University Press.

Pikirayi, I. (1993), *The Archaeological identity of the Mutapa State: towards a historical archaeology of Northern Zimbabwe*, Upssala: Societas Archaeologica Upsaliensis.

Polanyi, K. (1968), *Primitive, archaic and modern economies*, Garden City, New York: Doubleday.

Polanyi, K. (1975), "Traders and Trade", in J. Sabloff and C.C Lamberg (eds.), *Ancient Civilisation and Trade*, USA: Columbia University Press, 133-153.

Posnansky, M. (1961), "Dimple-based pottery from Uganda", *Man* 168:141-42.

Posnansky, M (1967), "The Iron Age in East Africa", in W.W. Bishop and J. D. Clark (eds.), *Background to evolution in Africa*, University of Chicago Press.

Posnansky, M. (1968a), "The Prehistory of East Africa", in B.A Ogot (ed.), *Zamani: A Survey of East Africa History*, Kenya: Longman, 52-69.

Posnansky, M. (1968), "The excavation of an Ankole capital site at Bweyorere", *Uganda Journal* 32 (2):165-182.

Posnansky, M. (1973), "Aspects of early West African trade", *World Archaeology* 5:149-162.

Posnansky, M. (1975), "Connections between the lacustrine peoples and the coast", in H. N. Chittick and R. I. Rotberg (eds.), *East Africa and the Orient Cultural Syntheses in pre-colonial times,* New York: Africana, 216-225.

Posnansky, M. (1982), *Archaeological and linguistic reconstruction in Ghana*, in C. Ehret and M. Posnansky (eds.), *The archaeological and linguistic reconstruction of African History*: Berkley: University of California Press, 256-266.

Posnansky, M., Reid, D. A. M and C. Z Ashley (2005), "Archaeology on Lolui Island, Uganda 1964-5", *Azania* 40: 73-100.

Prendergast, M. E (2008), Forager variability and transition to food production in secondary settings: Kansyore and Pastoral Neolithic economies in East Africa, PhD dissertation, Harvard University.

Prendergast, M. E. (2010), "Diversity in East African foraging and food producing communities", *Azania* 45(1):1-5.

Pwiti, G. (1996), Continuity and change: an archaeological study of farming communities in Zimbabwe: AD 500-1700, *Studies in African archaeology* 13, Upssala: Societas Archaeologica Upsaliensis.

Rawlinson, G. (trans) (1964), *The histories of Herodotus*, London: J. M. Dent.

Reid, A. (1994-95), "Early settlement and social organisation in the interlacustrine region", *Azania* XXIX-XXX: 303-314.

Reid, D. A. M. (1996), "Ntusi and the development of social complexity in southern Uganda", in G. Pwiti and R. Soper (eds.), *Aspects of African archaeology*, Harare: University of Zimbabwe press, 621-628.

Reid, D.A.M and R. Young (2000), "Pottery abrasion and the preparation of African grains", *Antiquity* 74(283): 101-111.

Reid, D. A. M. (2002), Recent archaeological discoveries in Buganda, their implications for heritage management policies, *Uganda Journal* 48: 87-103.

Reid, D. A. M. (2003a), "Ancient Egypt and the source of the Nile", in D. O'Connor and A. Reid (eds.), *Ancient Egypt in Africa,* London: UCL, 55-76.

Reid, D.A.M. (2003b), "Recent research on the archaeology of Buganda", in P. Mitchell., A. Haour and J. Hobart (eds.), *Researching Africa's past*, Oxford University School of Archaeology Monograph 57, Oxford: Oxbow.

Reid, D.A.M. (2005), "Interaction, marginalisation and the archaeology of the Kalahari", in B Stahl (ed.), *African Archaeology a Critical Introduction,* USA, Blackwell, 353-419.

Reid, D. A. M and Ashley, C. Z. (2007), "A context for the Luzira Head", *Antiquity* 82: 99-112.

Renfrew, C. (1975), "Trade as an action at a distance; questions of integration and communication", in J. A. Sabloff and C. C. Lamberg (eds.), *Ancient civilisation and trade,* Albuquerque: University of Mexico, 3-79.

Renfrew, C. (1977), "Alternative models for exchange and spatial distribution" in T. K. Earle (ed.), *Exchange systems in pre-history*, New York: Academic, 71- 90.

Renfrew, C and P. Bahn ([1998]2008), *Archaeology: Theories, Methods and Practices* 5th edition. London: Thames and Hudson.

Rifkin, R. F. (2011), "Assessing the efficacy of red ochre as a pre-historic hide tanning ingredient", *Journal of African Archaeology* 9 (2):133.

Robbins, L. H *et.al* (1977), "Rangi; A Late Stone Age site in Karamoja", *Azania* XII: 209-233.

Roberts[2], A (ed.) (2003), "Protected areas in Uganda, benefits beyond boundaries", published to mark Uganda's participation in the World Parks Congress; Durban, South Africa, Acha Graphics[3]: Uganda Wild Life Authority.

Robertshaw, P. T. and A. Mawson (1981), "Excavations of Eastern Equatoria, Southern Sudan 1980", *Azania* XVI: 55-94.

Robertshaw, P. T. (1982), "Eastern Equatoria in the context of later Eastern African prehistory", in J. Mark and P.T. Robertshaw (eds.), *Culture history in the southern Sudan, archaeology, linguistics, and ethnohistory*, Memoir 8, British Institute in Eastern Africa, 90-100.

Robertshaw, P. T. (1990),"Early pastoralists of south-western Kenya", B.I.E.A: Nairobi.

Robertshaw, P. T. (1991), "Gogo Falls: a complex site east of Lake Victoria", *Azania* 26: 63- 196.

Robertshaw, P. T. (1994), "Archaeological survey, ceramic analysis and state formation in western Uganda", *African archaeological review* 12: 105-131.

Robertshaw, P. T. (1997), "Munsa earthworks: A preliminary report", *Azania* 32: 1 -20.

Robertshaw, P. T. (2003), "The origins of the state in East Africa", in C. M Kusimba and S. B Kusimba (eds.), *East African archaeology: foragers, potters, smiths and traders*, Philadelphia: University of Penslyvannia Museum of archaeology and anthropology.

Safia, A. (1997), "The impact of tourism activities on the local communities the case of Murchison Falls National Park", Unpublished thesis B.A. Tourism, Makerere University.

Sahlins, M. D. (1972), *Stone Age Economics*, Chicago IL: Aldine de Gruyter.

Sanders, E. (1969), "The Hamitic Hypothesis: Its origin and functions in the time perspective", *Journal of African History* 10 (4): 521-532.

Sassoon, H. (1980), "Excavations at the site of Early Mombasa", *Azania* XV: 1-42.

Schimdt, P. R. (1996), *The culture and technology of African iron technology,* U.S.A: University of Florida.

Schimdt, P. R. (1997), *Iron technology in East Africa; symbolism, science and archaeology,* Oxford: James Currey.

Schmidt, P. R. (1975), "A new look at interpretations of the Early Iron Age in East Africa", *History in Africa, a journal of method* 2: 127-136.

Schmidt, P. R. (2006), *Historical archaeology in Africa: Representation, social memory and oral traditions*, New York: Altamira.

Seitsonen, O. (2004), Lithics after Stone Age in East Africa, Unpublished M.A Thesis, University of Helsinki.

Seitsonen, O.(2010), "Lithics use at Kansyore sites in East Africa: technological organisation at four recently excavated sites in Nyanza province, Kenya", *Azania* 45(1): 49-82.

Shepard, A. O. (1963), *Ceramics for the Archaeologist*, Washington D.C: Carnegie Institution of Washington.

Shinnie J. L. (1968), "The Khartoum variant industry", in F, Wendorf (ed.), *The Pre- History of Nubia* Vol. 2, Dallas: Southern Methodist University Press, 768-790.

Shinnie, P L. (1971a), *The African Iron Age*, Oxford: Clarendon.

Shiner, P. L (1971b), 'The Legacy to Africa', in J. R. Harris (ed.), *The Legacy of Egypt*, Great Britain: Oxford University Press.

Shiner, P. L. (1950), "Review of 'Early Khartoum' by Arkell 1949", *Man* 50:10.

Shiner, P. L. (1960), "Excavations at Bigo; 1957", *Uganda Journal* 24(1): 16-28.

Shinnie, P. L. (1967), *Ancient Peoples and Places; Meroe*, London: Thames and Hudson.

Sinclair, P. N *et al*. (1993), "Introduction", in, Sinclair, P.N *et al* (eds.), *The archaeology of Africa; food, metals and towns*, London: Routledge, 1-12.

Skeates, R. (2009), "Trade and interaction", in B. Cunliffe; C. Gosden and R. A. Joyce (eds.), *The Oxford handbook of archaeology*, New York: Oxford University Press, 555-578.

Smith, E.G. (1971), *The Diffusion of culture*, London: Kennikat.

Smith, G. E. (1923), *In the Beginning; the Origin of Civilisation*, London: Gerald Howe.

Smith, G. E. (1928), *In the Beginning; the Origin of Civilisation*, London: Gerald Howe.

Smith, G. E. (1971), *The Diffusion of Culture*, London: Kennikat.

Soper, R. C. (1967), "The Iron Age in East Africa", in W. Bishop, and J. D. Clark (eds.), *Background to Evolution in Africa*, Chicago: Chicago University Press, 629- 649.

Soper, R. C and B. Golden (1969), "An archaeological survey of Mwanza region Tanzania", *Azania* III: 167-74.

Soper, R. C. (1971a), "Early Iron Age pottery types from East Africa: Comparative analysis", *Azania* VI: 39-52.

Soper R. C. (1971b), "Iron Age Archaeological sites in the Chobi sector of Murchison Falls National Park, Uganda", *Azania* VI (1): 53-87.

Soper, R. C. (1985), "Roulette decoration on African Pottery: technical considerations, dating, and distribution, *African Archaeological Review* 3: 29-51.

Staeck J. P. (2002), *Back to the earth; an Introduction to Archaeology*, USA: Mayfield.

Stahl, A. B. (1984), "A history and critique of investigations in early African agriculture", in J. D. Clark and S. A. Brandt (eds.), *From hunters to farmers: the causes and consequences of food-production in Africa.* Berkeley: University of California Press, 9-21.

Sutton, J. E. G. (1966), "The archaeology and early peoples of the highlands of Kenya and northern Tanzania", *Azania* 1:37-57.

Sutton, J. E. G. (1971), "The Interior of East Africa", in Shinnie P. L (ed.), *The African Iron Age*, Oxford: Clarendon, 142-182.

Sutton, J. E. G. (1972), "Ilila: Excavations of Late Iron Age 'brick' sites in Southern Highlands of Tanzania", *Azania* VII: 141-150.

Sutton, J. E. G. (1974), "The Aquatic Civilisation of Middle Africa". *Journal of African History* 15: 527-546.

Sutton, J. E. G. (1977), "The African aqualithic", *Antiquity* 51: 25-34.

Sutton, J. E. G. (1980), "Aquatic reflections", in R. E Leakey and B.A. Ogot (eds.), *Proceedings on the 8th Pan African Congress of Prehistory and quaternary studies Nairobi 1977*, Nairobi: The International Louis Leakey Memorial Institute for African Prehistory, 321-322.

Sutton, J. E. G. (1981), "The prehistory of East Africa", in *General History of Africa I: Methodology and African Prehistory* in Ki-Zerbo (ed.), California: Heinemann.

Tibesasa R. (2008), The Cultural Sequence on Bussi Island Lake Victoria, M. A. Archaeology Dissertation: University of Dar es Salaam.

Trigger, B .G. (1969), "The myth of Meroe and the African Iron Age", *African Historical studies* 2: 23-50.

Uganda geological department, (1936), *Uganda geological survey annual report*, Entebbe: Uganda Government Printer.

Uganda Lands and Survey Department, (1962), *Atlas of Uganda* First Edition, Uganda: Department of Lands and Survey.

Uganda Parks, (1994), "Murchison Falls National Park Rehabilitation Project; Report of baseline survey of communities around the Murchison Falls National Park and Karuma and Bugungu Game Reserve".

Uganda Wildlife Authority (2001), "Assessment report of the short-term potential for tourism development in Murchison Falls conservation Area", Funded by GTZ (Uganda).

UNESCO (1949), "Uganda Colonial Reports, London: His Majesty's Stationery Office.

Uganda Wildlife Authority (2001), Murchison Falls National Park, Bugungu Wildlife Reserve, Karuma Wildlife Reserve (Murchison Falls Protected Area), General Management Plan July 2001- June 2011.

Usai, D. (2005), "The Mesolithic and Neolithic periods in the Nile Valley; problems and perspectives in Africa", *Rivista trimestrale di studi e documentazione deli' Instituto Italiano per L'Africa el'Oriente Anno* 60(3/4): 544-554.

Vansina, J. (1994-95), "A slow revolution: farming in sub-equatorial Africa" *Azania* 29-30: 15-26.

Wachsmann, K. P. (1965), *Some speculations concerning a drum chime in Buganda, wider world*, United Kingdom: Altamira Press.

Wandibba, S. (1990), "Ancient and modern ceramic traditions in the Lake Victoria Basin of Kenya", *Azania* 25: 69-78.

Waterfield, G. (1967), *Egypt*, London: Thames and Hudson.

Waweru, V. J. (2007), Middle Stone Age technology at Cartwright's site, Kenya, PhD Dissertation, University of Connecticut.

Wayland, E. J. (1934), "*Rifts, rivers, rains, and early man in Uganda*", J. Roy Anthropological Institute, Memoir 47, 64:333-45.

Whicker, B. (1990), *Egypt and the Mountains of the Moon*, Minnesota: FDP.

Whittacker, J. C. (1994), *Flint knapping; making and understanding stone tools*, Austin: University of Texas Press.

Willey, G. R and Sabloff J. A. (1974), *A history of American archaeology*, San Francisco: W.H. Freeman.

Willoughby, P. R. (2007), *The Evolution of Modern Humans in Africa: A Comprehensive Guide*, Lanham: Altamira.

World Book Encyclopaedia 6, (1978), Chicago: World Book Child Craft International Inc.

Wreschner, E. E., (1980), "Red ochre and human evolution: a case for discussion", *Current Anthropology* 21 (5): 631-644.

Yellen, E. J. (1998), "Barbed bone points: tradition and continuity in Saharan and sub-Saharan Africa", *African Archaeological Review* 15(3): 173-198.

Yohe II, R. M. (1996), in M. Sutton and B. S. Arkush, *Analysis of flaked stone artefacts*, Dubuque: Kendall/Hunt Publishing Company, 39-65.

Yosef ben-Jochannan, (1986), *"The Nile Valley Civilization and the Spread of African Culture"*, A lecture delivered for the Minority Ethnic Unit of the Greater London Council, London, England, March 6–8, 1986, addressed mainly to the African community in London consisting of African people from the Caribbean and African people from Africa.

Zangato, E. and A. F. C. Holl (2010), "On the iron front, new evidence from north central Africa", *Journal of African Archaeology* 8(1): 7-23.

Zayed, A. H. (1981), "Egyptian Relations with the rest of Africa," in G. Mokhtar (ed.), *General History of Africa: ancient civilizations of Africa Volume 11*: California: UNESCO, 136-154.

Pottery Attributes Analysed

A: **Pottery Catalogue Number**

B: **Sherd Structure**; (1) Rim- R (2) Body-Bo (3) Base - Ba (4) Shoulder -Sho (5) R/N/Sho (6) Neck – Ne (7)R/NB (8) Sho/Bo (9) R/Bo (10) R/Sho (11) Unidentifiable (12) R/Sho/Bo (13) Sho/Bo (14) Ne/Sho (15) Rim/Neck (16) Body/Base (17) Ne/Sho/Bo

C: (1) Diagnostic sherd (2) Un-diagnostic shard (3) Plain rim

D: **Placement of Decoration**
Rim (2) Neck (3) Shoulder (4) Base (5) Body (6) R/N (7) R/N/S (8) Ne/Bo (9) Ne/Sho (10) R/Bo (11) R/Sho (12) R/Sho/Bo (13) Sho/Bo (14) Lip (15) Un-identifiable

E: **Decoration Technique;**
1. Incision (2) Punctuation (3) Grooving (4) Stabbing (5) Rocker Stamping (6) Comb stamping (7) Impression (8) Excision (9) Alternate pivoting

F: **Decorative Elements:** (Refer to Figures: 47 and 52)

G: **Vessel Form Identifiers**

(1) R/Ne/Sho (2) Sho/Bo (3) R/Ne/Bo (4) R/Sho/Bo (5) R/Bo (6) R/Sho (7) Base (8) Rim /Neck (9) Rim(R) (10) Sho (11) Ne/Sho (12) Ne/Sho/Bo

H: **Vessel Types**

(1) Open Bowl (2) Restricted independent vessel/ Necked pot (3) Slightly constricted Bowl (4) Hemispherical bowl (5) Un-identifiable

I: Rim Profiles

1. In-turn rim
2. Up-turn rim
3. Out-turn rim
4. Everted rim
5. Tapered rim
6. Squared rim
7. Flayered rim
8. In-sloping rims
9. Slightly out-turn
10. Plain roundish rim
11. In-sloping squared
13. Slightly sloping upturn
14. Indented rim
15. Round flat topped
16. Vertical out-turning
17. Unidentifiable
18. Out-turn tapered
19. Bulged rim

J: Rim Thickness in Millimeters

K: Base Profile
1. Dimple base
2. Round base
3. Flat base
4. Conical base
5. Ring base

L: Neck Profile
1. Elongated
2. Short
3. Medium
4. Unidentifiable

M: Surface Finishing
1. Burnishing
2. Slipping
3. Painting
4. Glazing
5. Smooth
6. Rough-smooth
7. Slip- burnish
8. Slip-smooth
9. Rough

N: Tempering Material
   (1) Sand; (2) Quartz; (3) Shell; (4) Grog ; (5) Vegetal material (6) Mica

O: Surface Colour of Potsherd
(1)   HUE 7.5 YR 5/8 Strong brown
(2)   6/8 Reddish yellow
(3)   4/6 Dark brown
(4)   3/3 Dark brown
(5)   2.5/1 Black
(6)   HUE 5YR 5/2 Reddish gray
(7)   4/3 Reddish brown
(8)   3/1 very dark gray
(9)   7/1 Light gray
(10) 4/1 Dark gray
(11) 5/3 reddish gray
(12) 4/2 Dark brown
(13) 5/4 Reddish brown
(14) 5/8 yellowish red
(15) 6/3 Light brown
(16) 5/4 Brown
(17) 5/1 Gray
(18) 2.5/1 Dark reddish brown
(19) Tainted with soot

(20) 8/2 Pinkish white

(21) ??/6 Red (HUE 10R)

(22) Light yellowish brown 6/3 and 6/4

(23) 4/2 weak Red (HUE 2.5 YR).

P: Firing Conditions:
(1) Well-fired   (2) Average   (3) Poorly fired   (4) Smudged

Q: Type of Paste/ Texture:
(1) Coarse   (2) Coarse/fine   (3) Fine.

R: Evidence of Entire Vessel Decoration
1. Yes
2. No

S: Forming Methods
(1) Hand-made   (2) Wheel-made

T: Weight in Grams

U: Length (Maximum Length)

V: Decorating Instruments:
1- multi-toothed comb, 2- banana stalk; 4- cord or mat; 5- comb; 6- shell; 7- roller of carved wood; 8-plaited flexible material; 10-stamp; 11- roulette;12- unknown plant; 13- finger tips; 14- shell; 15- bold pointer;16- woven mat; 17-cord wrapped stick (19) cord rolled

W: Number of Bevels
(1)1   (2)2   (3)3   (4)4   (5)5   (6)6   (7)7   (8)8   (9)9

X: Number of Flutes
(1) 1   (2) 2   (3) 3   (4) 4   (5) 5   (6) 6   (7) 7   (8) 8   (9) 9

Y: Fluted and Beveled
1-Yes;   2- No

Z: Number of Bevels (B) and Flutes (F)
(1)1B/ 2F;   (2)1B/1F;   (3) 2B/3F;   (4) 2B/1F

Zz: Surface Placement of Decoration
Exterior (2) Interior

Aa: Thickened Rim
(1) Yes   (2) No

Bb: Shape of Bevel or Flute
Flat (2) Concave

Cc: Direction of Roulette
Horizontal (2) Vertical (3) Oblique (4) Oblique hatched (5) Interlocked/ herring bone- like (6) Un-diagnostic (7) Alternating.

Dd: Direction of Roulette Twist
(1) Left   (2) Right   (3) Undiagnostic   (4) both sides

Ee: Body Thickness (centimeters)

Ff: Decorated lip
(1) Yes   (2) No

Gg: Trench   Hh: Level   Ii: Depth   Jj: Rim
Kk: Neck   Ll: Shoulder   Mm: Body   Nn: Base   Oo: Date

Pp: Pottery Tradition
(1) Kansyore;   (2) Early Iron Working (EIW);
(3) Roulette (LIA);   (4) Transitional (grooved lines/channels;
(5) Bourdine   (6) Unidentifiable

www.ingramcontent.com/pod-product-compliance
Lightning Source LLC
Chambersburg PA
CBHW080532170426
43195CB00016B/2533